THE
NEW BELIEVERS
HYMNBOOK

JOHN RITCHIE LTD
KILMARNOCK, SCOTLAND

Published by John Ritchie Ltd
40 Beansburn, Kilmarnock, Scotland.

Printed 2019

Owners of copyright are gratefully thanked for the permission given to use the hymns which are owned by them and the family of the late Mr Edmund Ewan are thanked for granting permission to use hymns from *Remembrance Hymns*.

Where required, copyright has been sought and given and if in any case copyright has been broken, we apologise and will endeavour to put it right in any subsequent editions.

ISBN - 13: 978-1-912522-38-5

Typeset by John Ritchie Ltd., Kilmarnock.
Printed by Bell & Bain Ltd., Glasgow.

PREFACE

The Believers Hymn Book was first published in 1884. In the first pages of the new hymn book, there was a Preface, entitled 'Praise', which commenced with these words: "It is truly wonderful that God should not only delight Himself in saving us, but also take pleasure in the praise of His reconciled children, telling us that in praising Him we are glorifying Him". It continued by observing that praise is "also full of blessing and edification to the saints". Hymns could be "a vehicle of mutual exhortation of great value", able to comfort in sorrow or to confirm a spiritual truth. The powerful point was then made: "If praise occupies so important a place in the Church, how very important it must be that the selection of hymns be varied and scriptural".

With three hundred and sixty-one "varied and scriptural" hymns", *The Believers Hymn Book* soon became widely used - and in 1959, a *Supplement* added more than a hundred hymns, thus enhancing its appeal.

The *Believers Hymn Book* remains much loved, but the Publishers recognise that there is scope for further improvement.

We are therefore delighted to introduce *The New Believers Hymn Book*. Seventy-five hymns have been removed and more than three hundred have been added, bringing the total to seven hundred. Almost ninety of these come from *Remembrance Hymns*. These and others from other sources are particularly suitable for the Lord's Supper.

The introduction to the original edition of *The Believers Hymn Book* concluded with these words: "No doubt there will be defects, and criticism may find much to lay hold of, but we offer it to the Lord's people as our endeavour to meet a felt need, and we pray and ask all who sympathise with us in this effort, to unite with us in prayer, that God may be pleased to use it for the glory of His name, and for the edification of His saints."

These are our sentiments too as we recall the summons to praise in the last five Psalms of Israel's Psalter, "Praise ye the Lord".

The Publishers,
John Ritchie Ltd,
40 Beansburn,
Kilmarnock

1
8.8.8.8.D.

A DEBTOR to mercy alone,
    Of covenant mercy I sing,
Nor fear, with God's righteousness on,
    My person and offerings to bring.
The terrors of law and of God
    With me can have nothing to do;
My Saviour's obedience and blood
    Hide all my transgressions from view.

2 The work which His goodness began
    The arm of His strength will complete;
His promise is Yea and Amen,
    And never was forfeited yet.
Things future, nor things that are now,
    Not all things below or above,
Can make Him His purpose forego,
    Or sever my soul from His love.

3 My name from the palms of His hands
    Eternity will not erase;
Imprest on His heart, it remains
    In marks of indelible grace.
Yes! I to the end shall endure,
    As sure as the earnest is given;
More happy, but not more secure,
    The souls of the blessèd in heaven.

2
11.10.11.10.

A LITTLE while" of mingled joy and
    sorrow;
    "A little while" to love and serve below,
        To wait the dawning of that blissful
        morrow,
    When morn shall break upon this
    night of woe.

2 A little longer in this vale of weeping,
        Of yearning for the sinless home
        above;
    "A little while" of watching, and of
    keeping
    Our garments, by the power of Him
    we love.

3 "A little while" for winning souls to
    Jesus,
    Ere yet we see His beauty face to face;
        "A little while" for healing soul -
        diseases,
    By telling others of a Saviour's grace.

4 "A little while" to tell the joyful story
        Of Him who made our guilt and
        curse His own;
    "A little while", ere we behold the glory,
        To gather jewels for His heavenly
        crown.

5 "A little while!" and we shall dwell
    for ever
    Within our bright, our everlasting home;
        Where Jesus and His Bride no
        time shall sever,
    Nor blight of sin, nor curse of death
    shall come.

3
8.8.8.8.8.8.

A LITTLE while!" our Lord shall
    come,
    And we shall wander here no more;
        He'll take us to our Father's home,
    Where He for us has gone before,
        To dwell with Him, to see His face,
    And sing the glories of His grace.

2 "A little while!" He'll come again:
        Let us the precious hours redeem;
    Our only grief to give Him pain,
        Our joy to serve and follow Him:
    Watching and ready may we be,
        As those who long their Lord to see.

3 "A little while!" 'twill soon be past:
        Why should we shun the shame
        and Cross?
    O let us in His footsteps haste,
        Counting for Him all else but loss;
    Oh, how will recompense His smile
        The suffering of this little while!

4 "A little while!" Come, Saviour, come!
        For Thee Thy Bride has waited long:
    Oh, take Thy wearied pilgrims home,
        To sing the new, eternal song,
    To see Thy glory, and to be
        In everything conformed to Thee!

4
8.7.8.7.6.6.6.6.7.

A MIGHTY Fortress is our God,
    A Bulwark never failing;
Our Helper He amid the flood
    Of mortal ills prevailing:
For still our ancient foe
    Doth seek to work us woe;
His craft and power are great,
    And, armed with cruel hate,
On earth is not his equal.

2 Did we in our own strength confide,
    Our striving would be losing;
Were not the right Man on our side,
    The Man of God's own choosing:
Dost ask who that may be?
    Christ Jesus, it is He;
Lord Sabaoth His Name,
    From age to age the same,
And He must win the battle.

3 And though this world, with devils filled,
Should threaten to undo us,
    We will not fear, for God hath willed
His truth to triumph through us:
    The Prince of Darkness grim,
We tremble not for him;
    His rage we can endure,
For lo! his doom is sure,
    One little word shall fell him.

4 That word above all earthly powers,
    No thanks to them, abideth;
The Spirit and the gifts are ours
    Through Him who with us sideth:
Let goods and kindred go,
    This mortal life also;
The body they may kill:
    God's truth abideth still,
His Kingdom is forever.

5 C.M.
A MIND at perfect peace with God,
    Oh! what a word is this!
A sinner reconciled through blood;
    This, this indeed is peace.

2 By nature and by practice far,
    How very far from God!
Yet now by grace brought nigh to Him,
    Through faith in Jesus' blood.

3 So near, so very near to God
    I cannot nearer be;
For in the person of His Son
    I am as near as He.

4 So dear, so very dear to God,
    More dear I cannot be;
The love wherewith He loves the Son,
    Such is His love to me.

5 Why should I ever careful be
    Since such a God is mine?
He watches o'er me night and day,
    And tells me "Mine is thine".

6 C.M.
A PERFECT path of purest grace,
    Unblemished and complete,
Was Thine, Thou spotless Nazarite,
    Pure, even to the feet!

2 Thy stainless life, Thy lovely walk,
    In every aspect true,
From the defilement all around,
    No taint of evil drew.

3 No broken service, Lord, was Thine,
    No change was in Thy way;
Unsullied in Thy holiness,
    Thy strength knew no decay.

4 The vow was on Thee - Thou didst come,
    To yield Thyself to death;
And consecration marked Thy path,
    And spoke in every breath.

5 Morning by morning Thou didst wake,
    Amidst this poisoned air;
Yet no contagion touched Thy soul,
    No sin disturbed Thy prayer.

6 Thus, Lord, we love to trace Thy course,
    To mark where Thou hast trod,
And follow Thee with loving eye,
    Up to the throne of God.

7 C.M.
A PILGRIM through this lonely world
    The blessèd Saviour passed;
A mourner all His life was He,
    A dying Lamb at last.

2 That tender heart that felt for all,
    For all its life-blood gave;
It found on earth no resting-place,
    Save only in the grave.

3 Such was our Lord, and shall we fear
    The Cross with all its scorn?
Or love a faithless, evil world,
    That wreathed *His* brow with thorn?

4 No, facing all its frowns and smiles,
    Like Him, obedient still,
We homeward press, through storm
    or calm,
To yon celestial hill.

5 In tents we dwell amid the waste,
    Nor turn aside to roam
In folly's paths, nor seek our rest,
    Where *Jesus* had no home.

6 Dead to the world, with Him who died
    To win our hearts, our love;
We, risen with our risen Head,
    In spirit dwell above.

7 By faith His boundless glories there,
    Our wond'ring eyes behold;
The glories which eternal years
    Shall never all unfold.

8 This fills our hearts with deep desire
    To lose ourselves in love!
Bears all our hopes from earth away,
    And fixes them above.

8   7.6.7.6.D.

A ROCK that stands for ever
    Is Christ my righteousness!
And there I stand unfearing
    In everlasting bliss!
No earthly thing is needful
    To this my life from heaven,
And nought of love is worthy
    Save that which Christ has given.

2 There is no condemnation,
    There is no hell for me!
The torment and the fire
    Mine eyes shall never see!
For me there is no sentence,
    For me death has no sting,
Because the Lord who loves me
    Shall shield me with His wing!

3 No hunger, Lord, nor thirsting,
    No danger, fear, nor fight,
No foe, no tribulation,
    No throne, nor pow'r, nor might,
No height, no depth, no creature
    That has been, or can be,
Can pluck me from Thy bosom -
    Can sever me from Thee!

4 My heart in joy upleapeth -
    Grief cannot linger there!
O Jesus, Lord in glory,
    Thou art my sunshine fair!
The Source of all my singing
    Is Jesus there above;
The Sun that shines upon me
    Is Jesus and His love!

9   8.8.6.8.8.6.

A WEALTH of grace and truth replete,
    Enriched the path those holy feet
With steadfast purpose trod.
    Each faultless step, with fragrance
    fraught,
Fresh grace revealed and pleasure
    brought
To Thee, His Father, God.

2 The wilderness, the mountain-side,
    The wayside well, the stormy tide,
Served to reveal the worth
    Of Him Who had not where to lay
His head on earth, as day by day,
    He told His Father forth.

3 All Satan's wiles, all human power,
    United in that dreadful hour
Of shame, which He foreknew,
    Could not impede Him as He passed
In grace to reach the Cross at last
    His Father's will to do.

4 Well may our souls in worship bow
    To Thee, His God and Father, now,
And offer Thee our praise
    While musing on Thine Only Son,
The altogether lovely One,
    In all His matchless ways.

10   P.M.

A WONDERFUL Saviour is Jesus
    my Lord,
A wonderful Saviour to me;
    He hideth my soul in the cleft of
    the rock,
Where rivers of pleasure I see.

He hideth my soul in the cleft of
the rock
That shadows a dry, thirsty land;
He hideth my life in the depths of
His love,
And covers me there with His hand,
And covers me there with His hand.

2 A wonderful Saviour is Jesus my Lord,
He taketh my burden away;
He holdeth me up and I shall not be
moved,
He giveth me strength as my day.

3 With numberless blessings each
moment He crowns,
And, filled with His fulness divine,
I sing in my rapture, Oh, glory to God,
For such a Redeemer as mine!

4 When clothed in His brightness,
transported I rise
To meet Him in clouds of the sky,
His perfect salvation, His wonderful
love,
I'll shout with the millions on high.

11   8.7.8.7.D.
ABBA, Father! we adore Thee,
    Humbly now our homage pay:
'Tis Thy children's bliss to know
    Thee,
Welcomed through the living way:
    This high honour we inherit,
Thy free gift through Jesus' blood;
    God the Spirit, with our spirit,
Witnesseth we're sons of God.

2 Thine own purpose gave us being,
    When, in Christ, in that vast plan
Thou in Christ didst choose Thy
    people
E'en before the world began:
    O what love the Father bore us!
O how precious in Thy sight!
    When Thou gav'st Thy Church to
    Jesus,
Jesus, Son of Thy delight.

3 Though our nature's fall in Adam
    Shut us wholly out from God,
Thine eternal counsel brought us
    Nearer still, through Jesus' blood;

For in Him we found redemption,
    Grace and glory in Thy Son;
Oh, the height and depth of mercy!
    Christ and His redeemed are one.

4 Hence, through all the changing
    seasons,
Trouble, sickness, sorrow, woe,
    Nothing changeth God's affections,
Love divine shall bring us through;
    Soon shall all Thy blood-bought
    children
Round the throne their anthems
    raise,
And, in songs of rich salvation,
    Shout to God's eternal praise.

12   8.7.8.7.D.
ABBA, Father! we approach Thee
    In our Saviour's precious name;
We, Thy children, here assembling,
    Access to Thy presence claim;
From our sin His blood hath washed us;
    'Tis through Him our souls draw near,
And Thy Spirit, too, hath taught us,
    Abba, Father! name so dear.

2 Once as prodigals we wandered
    In our folly, far from Thee;
But Thy grace, o'er sin abounding,
    Rescued us from misery:
Thou Thy prodigals hast pardoned,
    Loved us with a Father's love;
Welcomed us with joy o'erflowing,
    E'en to dwell with Thee above.

3 Clothed in garments of salvation,
    At Thy table is our place;
We rejoice, and Thou rejoicest,
    In the riches of Thy grace:
It is meet, we hear Thee saying,
    We should merry be and glad;
I have found My once lost children,
    Now they live who once were dead.

4 Abba, Father! all adore Thee,
    All rejoice in heaven above;
While in us they learn the wonders
    Of Thy wisdom, power and love;
Soon, before Thy throne assembled,
    All Thy children shall proclaim,
Glory, everlasting glory,
    Be to God and to the Lamb.

13   7.6.7.6.D.

ABIDE in me, my Saviour,
And let me in Thee live;
Into Thy holy keeping
    My soul, my life I give:
Without Thy grace to keep me
    I know my steps will slide,
So daily, hourly, alway,
    Do Thou in me abide.

2 I long, my Lord and Master,
    To love and serve Thee more,
To live more near to Thee, Lord,
    Than e'er I have before:
To keep more sure and steadfast
    Within the narrow way,
In love's obedience growing
    More perfect day by day.

3 Then let my life and labours
    Henceforth and ever be,
In fervent love abounding,
    Acceptable to Thee;
Upon Thy strength relying
    In weakness and when tried,
And seeking that in all things
    Thy name be glorified.

14   C.M.

ACCORDING to Thy gracious Word,
In meek humility,
This would I do, O Christ my Lord,
    I would remember Thee.

2 Thy body, broken for my sake,
    My bread from heaven shall be;
The cup of blessing I will take,
    And thus remember Thee.

3 Gethsemane can I forget?
    Or there Thy conflict see,
Thine agony and blood-like sweat,
    And not remember Thee?

4 When to the Cross I turn mine eyes
    And rest on Calvary,
O Lamb of God, my sacrifice,
    I must remember Thee.

5 Remember Thee, and all Thy pains,
    And all Thy love to me;
Yea, while a breath, a pulse remains,
    Would I remember Thee.

6 And when, O Lord, Thou com'st again
    And I Thy glory see,
For ever, as the Lamb once slain,
    I will remember Thee.

15   C.M.

ALAS! and did my Saviour bleed?
And did my Sovereign die?
Would He devote that sacred head
    For such a worm as I?

2 Was it for crimes that I have done
    He groaned upon the tree?
Amazing pity! grace unknown!
    And love beyond degree.

3 Well might the sun in darkness hide
    And shut his glories in,
When the incarnate Maker died
    For man, His creature's sin.

4 Thus might I hide my blushing face,
    While His dear Cross appears;
Dissolve my heart in thankfulness,
    And melt my eyes to tears.

5 But drops of grief can ne'er repay,
    The debt of love I owe;
Here, Lord, I give myself away;
    'Tis all that I can do.

16   C.M.

ALL hail the power of Jesus' name!
Let angels prostrate fall;
Bring forth the royal diadem
    And crown Him Lord of all!

2 Crown Him ye martyrs of your God
    Who from His altar call;
Extol the stem of Jesse's rod
    And crown Him Lord of all!

3 Ye seed of Israel's chosen race,
    A remnant weak and small,
Hail Him who saves you by His grace,
    And crown Him Lord of all!

4 Sinners, whose love can ne'er forget
    The wormwood and the gall,
Go, spread your trophies at His feet,
    And crown Him Lord of all!

5 Let every kindred, every tribe,
  On this terrestrial ball,
To Him all majesty ascribe,
  And crown Him Lord of all!

6 O that, with yonder sacred throng,
  We at His feet may fall;
Join in the everlasting song,
  And crown Him Lord of all!

17   L.M.

A LL people that on earth do dwell,
  Sing to the Lord with cheerful
voice;
  Him serve with fear, His praise
    forth tell;
Come ye before Him and rejoice.

2 Know that the Lord is God indeed;
  Without our aid He did us make;
We are His folk, He doth us feed,
  And for His sheep He doth us take.

3 O enter then His gates with praise,
  Approach with joy His courts unto;
Praise, laud, and bless His name
    always,
For it is seemly so to do.

4 For why? the Lord our God is good,
  His mercy is for ever sure;
His truth at all times firmly stood,
  And shall from age to age endure.

5 Praise God, from whom all
    blessings flow;
Praise Him, all creatures here below;
  Praise Him above, ye heav'nly host;
Praise Father, Son, and Holy Ghost!

18   C.M.

A LL that I *was*, my sin, my guilt,
  My death, was all my own;
All that I *am*, I owe to Thee,
  My gracious God alone.

2 The evil of my former state,
  Was mine, and only mine;
The good in which I now rejoice,
  Is Thine, and only Thine.

3 The darkness of my former state,
  The bondage, all was mine;
The light of life in which I walk,
  The liberty is Thine.

4 Thy grace first made me feel my sin,
  It taught me to believe;
Then, in believing, peace I found,
  And now I live, I live!

5 All that I am, e'en here on earth,
  All that I hope to be,
When Jesus comes and glory dawns,
  I owe it, Lord, to Thee.

19   8.7.8.7.D.

A LL the way my Saviour leads me;
  What have I to ask beside?
Can I doubt His tender mercy
  Who through life has been my guide?
Heavenly peace, divinest comfort,
  Here by faith in Him to dwell;
For I know, whate'er befall me,
  Jesus doeth all things well.

2 All the way my Saviour leads me;
  Cheers each winding path I tread;
Gives me grace for every trial,
  Feeds me with the living bread:
Though my weary steps may falter,
  And my soul athirst may be,
Gushing from the rock before me,
  Lo! a spring of joy I see.

3 All the way my Saviour leads me;
  O the fulness of His love!
Perfect rest to me is promised
  In my Father's house above:
When my spirit, clothed immortal,
  Wings its flight to realms of day,
This my song through endless ages,
  Jesus led me all the way.

20   6.5.6.5.D.

A LTOGETHER lovely,
  Jesus Lord art Thou,
Fairest of ten thousand,
  At Thy feet we bow;
As we view Thee coming,
  Saviour from above,
All our hearts are ravished,
  With Thy wondrous love.

2 Precious to the Father,
  All Thy steps below,
Telling out God's glory,
  In this world of woe;

For His will and purpose,
  Was Thy pleasure here,
In devoted service,
  To Thy God so dear.

3 But Thy wondrous beauty,
    And Thy matchless grace,
  Lord, in all their fulness,
    Who can fully trace;
  Yet our hearts enraptured,
    Even here on earth,
  Now would sing Thy praises,
    And proclaim Thy worth.

4 Soon in brightest glory
    We shall see Thy face,
  Praise Thee, and adore Thee,
    Lord for all Thy grace;
  We Thy glory sharing,
    Gazing, Lord, on Thee,
  Altogether lovely,
    Through eternity.

21   C.M. with Chorus
AM I a soldier of the Cross,
  A follower of the Lamb?
And shall I fear to own His cause,
  Or blush to speak His name?

In the name, the precious name,
  Of Him who died for me,
By grace I'll win the promised crown,
  Whate'er my cross shall be.

2 Must I be carried to the skies,
    On flow'ry beds of ease,
  While others fought to win the prize,
    And sailed through raging seas?

3 Are there no foes for me to face?
    Must I not stem the flood?
  Is this vile world a friend to grace,
    To help me on to God?

4 Sure I must fight if I would reign;
    Increase my courage, Lord;
  I'll bear the toil, endure the pain,
    Supported by Thy Word.

5 Thy saints in all this glorious war,
    Shall conquer, though they're
      slain;
  They view the triumph from afar,
    And shall with Jesus reign.

6 When that illustrious day shall rise,
    And all Thy armies shine,
  In robes of vict'ry through the skies,
    The glory shall be Thine.

22   C.M.
AMAZING grace! (How sweet the
  sound!)
That saved a wretch like me!
  I once was lost, but now am found;
Was blind, but now I see.

2 'Twas grace that taught my heart
    to fear,
  And grace my fears relieved;
    How precious did that grace appear
  The hour I first believed.

3 Through many dangers, toils and
    snares,
  I have already come;
    'Tis grace hath brought me safe
      thus far,
  And grace will lead me home.

4 The Lord has promised good to me,
    His Word my hope secures;
  He will my shield and portion be,
    As long as life endures.

5 Yes, when this flesh and heart shall fail,
    And mortal life shall cease,
  I shall possess, within the veil,
    A life of joy and peace.

6 When we've been there ten
    thousand years,
  Bright shining as the sun,
    We've no less days to sing God's
      praise,
  Than when we first begun.

23   L.M.
AMEN! one lasting, long Amen!
  Blest anthem of eternal days,
The fulness of the rapturous song
  To Christ the Saviour's endless praise!

2 Amen! one lasting, long Amen!
    Heaven's blissful cadence,
      deep and loud,
  While every heart before the throne
    In holy, solemn awe is bowed.

3 Amen! Amen! it rolls along,
   Re-echoing from the throne again!
Be ours to mingle with the throng
   In that eternal, loud "Amen!"

24   L.M.

A MIDST us our Belovèd stands,
   And bids us view His piercèd hands,
Points to His wounded feet and side,
   Blest emblems of the Crucified.

2 What food luxurious loads the board
   When at His table sits the Lord!
The wine how rich, the bread how
      sweet,
When Jesus deigns the guests to
      meet.

3 If now, with eyes defiled and dim,
   We see the signs, but see not Him,
Oh, may His love the scales displace
And bid us see Him face to face.

4 Thou glorious Bridegroom of our
      hearts,
   Thy present smile a heaven imparts;
O lift the veil, if veil there be,
Let every saint Thy beauties see.

25   8.8.8.8.8.8.

A ND can it be that I should gain
   An interest in the Saviour's blood?
Died He for me who caused His pain?
   For me who Him to death pursued?
Amazing love! how can it be
   That Thou, my God, shouldst die for
      me?

2 'Tis mystery all! the Immortal dies;
   Who can explore His strange
      design?
In vain the first-born seraph tries
   To sound the depths of love divine;
'Tis mercy all! let earth adore,
   Let angel minds inquire no more.

3 He left His Father's throne above,
   So free, so infinite His grace;
Emptied Himself of all but love,
   And bled for Adam's helpless race;
'Tis mercy all, immense and free;
   For, O my God, it found out me.

4 Long my imprisoned spirit lay
   Fast bound in sin and nature's night;
Thine eye diffused a quickening ray -
   I woke, the dungeon flamed with
      light;
My chains fell off, my heart was free,
   I rose, went forth, and followed Thee.

5 No condemnation now I dread;
   Jesus, and all in Him, is mine,
Alive in Him, my living Head,
   And clothed in righteousness divine,
Bold I approach the eternal throne,
   And claim the crown, through
      Christ, my own.

26   C.M.

A ND did the Holy and the Just,
   The Sovereign of the skies,
Stoop down to wretchedness and dust,
   That guilty worms might rise?

2 Yes, the Redeemer left His throne -
   His radiant throne on high -
(Surprising mercy! love unknown!)
   To suffer, bleed, and die.

3 He took the ruined sinner's place,
   And suffered in his stead:
For man, (O, miracle of grace!)
   For man the Saviour bled.

4 Dear Lord, what heavenly wonders
      dwell
   In Thine atoning blood!
By this are sinners saved from hell,
And rebels brought to God.

5 Jesus, my soul, adoring, bends,
   To love so full, so free;
And may I hope that love extends,
   Its sacred power to me?

6 What glad return can I impart,
   For favours so divine?
O take my all - this worthless heart,
   And make it only Thine.

27   10.10.10.10.

AND is it so! we shall be like Thy
Son,
Is this the grace which He for us has
won?
Father of glory! (thought beyond all
thought)
In glory to His own blest likeness
brought.

2 O Jesus, Lord, who loved us like
to Thee?
Fruit of Thy work, with Thee, too,
there to see
Thy glory, Lord, while endless ages
roll;
Thy saints the prize and travail of
Thy soul.

3 Yet it must be, Thy love had not its rest
Were Thy redeemed not with
Thee fully blest;
That love that gives not as the
world, but shares
All it possesses with its loved co-heirs.

4 Not we alone, Thy loved ones all,
complete,
In glory round Thee there with joy
shall meet,
All like Thee, for Thy glory like Thee,
Lord,
Object supreme of all, by all adored.

5 The heart is satisfied, can ask no
more;
All thought of self is now for ever o'er;
Christ, its unmingled object, fills
the heart
In blest adoring love - its endless part.

28   S.M.

AND shall we see Thy face,
And hear Thy heavenly voice,
Well known to us in present grace?
Well may our hearts rejoice!

2 With Thee in garments white,
Lord Jesus, we shall walk;
And, spotless in that heavenly light,
Of all Thy sufferings talk.

3 Close to Thy trusted side,
In fellowship divine;
No cloud, no distance, e'er shall hide
Glories that then shall shine.

4 Fruit of Thy boundless love,
That gave Thyself for us;
For ever we shall with Thee prove
That Thou still lov'st thus.

5 And we love Thee, blest Lord,
E'en now, though feeble here,
Thy sorrow and Thy Cross record
What makes us know Thee near.

6 We wait to see Thee, Lord,
Yet now within our hearts
Thou dwell'st in love that doth afford
The joy that love imparts.

7 Yet still we wait for Thee,
To see Thee as Thou art;
Be with Thee, like Thee, Lord, and
free
To love with all our heart.

29   6.6.6.6.8.8.

ARISE, my soul, arise!
Shake off thy guilty fears;
The bleeding sacrifice
In my behalf appears:
Before the throne my Surety stands,
My name is written on His hands.

2 He ever lives above,
For me to intercede;
His all-redeeming love,
His precious blood to plead:
His blood atoned for all our race,
And sprinkles now the throne
of grace.

3 Five bleeding wounds He bears;
Received on Calvary;
They pour effectual prayers;
They strongly plead for me:
"Forgive him, Oh, forgive", they cry,
"Nor let that ransomed sinner die!"

4 The Father hears Him pray,
His dear anointed One;
He cannot turn away,

The presence of His Son;
His Spirit answers to the blood,
    And tells me I am born of God.

5 My God is reconciled;
    His pardoning voice I hear;
He owns me for His child;
    I can no longer fear:
With confidence I now draw nigh,
    And "Father, Abba, Father!" cry.

30   7.6.7.6.D.
A ROUND Thy grave, Lord Jesus,
      In spirit here we stand,
With hearts all full of praises,
    To keep Thy blest command;
Our souls by faith rejoicing,
    To trace Thy path of love,
Down through death's angry billows,
    Up to the throne above.

2 Lord Jesus, we remember
    The travail of Thy soul,
When, in Thy love's deep pity,
    The waves did o'er Thee roll;
Baptized in death's cold waters,
    For us Thy blood was shed:
For us Thou, Lord of Glory,
    Wast numbered with the dead.

3 Oh, Lord, Thou now art risen,
    Thy travail all is o'er!
For sin Thou once hast suffered,
    Thou liv'st to die no more;
Sin, death, and hell are vanquished
    By Thee, the Church's Head;
And lo! we share Thy triumphs,
    Thou First-born from the dead.

4 Into Thy death baptizèd,
    We own with Thee we died;
With Thee, our life, we're risen,
    And in Thee glorified:
From sin, the world, and Satan,
    We're ransomed by Thy blood,
And now would walk as strangers,
    Alive with Thee to God.

31   C.M.
A ROUND Thy table, Holy Lord,
      In fellowship we meet,
Obedient to Thy gracious Word;
    This feast of love to eat.

2 Here every one that loves Thy name
    Our willing hearts embrace;
Our source of life and hope the same,
    All debtors to Thy grace.

3 By faith we take the bread of life,
    With which our souls are fed;
And cup, in token of Thy blood,
    That was for sinners shed.

4 Under Thy banner thus we sing,
    The wonders of Thy love,
While we anticipate by faith,
    The heavenly feast above.

5 However poor, despis'd or few,
    We know Thy changeless love,
Dear Lord, is just as warm, as true,
    Now on the throne above.

6 Commune with each at this blest hour,
    And, when we hence depart,
May deeds of love and words of power,
    Engage each faithful heart.

32   C.M.
A S gathered to Thy precious name,
      Thy table we surround,
Thy death, Lord Jesus, to proclaim,
    Oh, may our praise abound!

2 We give what from Thee we receive,
    For all we have is Thine -
Oh, may each heart with joy believe,
    And echo "Thine is mine!"

2 Grace, grace it was that brought
        Thee down;
    Love shone in all Thy ways;
        Through death Thine is the
            Victor's crown,
    And Thine the endless praise.

4 We, or in silence, or in song,
    Together worship Thee;
Before our God we shall ere long
    Give praise eternally.

5 Lord Jesus Christ, Thou comest soon -
   Today Thy death we show;
In light, eclipsing sun at noon,
   Its mystery we shall know.

33
8.5.8.3.

A S in holy contemplation,
   We review His ways,
Lowly manhood in perfection
   Fills our gaze.

2 From His lips in fulness flowing
   Words with wisdom fraught,
With God's will so wholly blended
   Every thought!

3 Ever "altogether lovely",
   Ever, all, "most sweet",
Richest fragrance ever rising
   Round His feet!

4 Contemplating every aspect,
   Every feature fair,
Find we precious, peerless beauty
   Everywhere.

5 Gathered from those holy footsteps,
   Incense fresh we bring,
And, to Thee, His Father, offer
   As we sing.

34
7.7.7.7.8.8.

A S prophets past foretold Him,
   Anointed eyes behold Him.
Together gathered to Him,
   His God we worship through Him,
Remembering, remembering,
   Our Blessèd Lord remembering.

2 His going forth, obeying,
   From that dark place of praying,
The cup of sorrow taking,
   To taste that dread forsaking!
Remembering, remembering;
   Our Blessèd Lord remembering!

3 His meek, majestic bearing
   The mocking purple wearing,
In lowliness submitting
   His face to shame and spitting!
Remembering, remembering;
   Our Blessèd Lord remembering!

4 His patience, unopposing,
   'Mid darkness o'er Him closing,
Those unknown pangs enduring,
   Eternal peace procuring!
Remembering, remembering,
   Our Blessèd Lord remembering!

35
L.M.

A S sinners saved we gladly praise
   The Author of redeeming grace;
Father, 'tis Thine almighty power
   Secures us when the tempests lower.

2 Thy love's a refuge ever nigh,
   Thy watchfulness a mountain high,
Thy name a rock, which winds above
   And waves below can never move.

3 Thy faithfulness, for ever sure,
   Through endless ages shall endure;
Thy perfect work shall ever prove
   The depth of Thine unceasing love.

4 While all things change, Thou
      changest not,
   Forgetting ne'er, though oft forgot;
Thy love, immutably the same,
   Displays the glory of Thy Name.

5 Lord, we would then rejoice and praise
   The source of all this wondrous grace;
Father, Thine everlasting power
   Will keep us safe in danger's hour.

36
C.M.

A SSEMBLED, Lord, at Thy behest,
   We wait Thy voice to hear;
O come and bless this hallowed feast -
   In spirit now draw near.

2 Draw near, yea, linger in our midst;
   Thy waiting saints inspire
With thoughts of Thine unfailing love;
   Grant this our soul's desire.

3 Such love! surpassing human thought,
   That Thou, blest Lamb of God,
Should'st bear sin's curse, and
      interpose
Thine own atoning blood.

4 With hearts adoring thus we view
 Thy table fitly spread;
Love's sweet memorial feast to Thee,
 Our risen, glorious Head.

5 O help us, Lord, while gathered here,
 That we none else may see;
Keep Thou our thoughts graced with
 Thy love,
And wholly stayed on Thee.

37   S.M.

AT rest through Jesus' blood,
 At rest from self and sin,
Saved and at peace with Thee, O God,
 We boldly enter in.

2 At rest and unafraid,
 Yet in befitting fear,
Calm in the perfect peace He made,
 We rev'rently draw near.

3 Our thoughts are backward cast
 O'er all the path He trod,
The blest imperishable past
 That filled Thy heart, O God.

4 The silent loaf and cup
 Speak volumes to the soul,
And heart and voice are lifted up
 And praises heavenward roll.

5 For Thou of Him to us
 Hast spoken wondrously,
And in responding worship thus
 We speak of Him to Thee.

38   6.5.6.5.D.

AT the name of Jesus
 Every knee shall bow,
Every tongue confess Him
 King of glory now.
'Tis the Father's pleasure
 We should call Him Lord,
Who from the beginning
 Was the mighty Word.

2 Mighty and mysterious,
 In the highest height,
God from everlasting,
 Very Light of light:
In the Father's bosom,
 With the Spirit blest,
Love, in love eternal,
 Rest, in perfect rest.

3 At His voice creation
 Sprang at once to sight,
All the angel faces,
 All the hosts of light,
Thrones and dominations,
 Stars upon their way,
All the heavenly orders
 In their great array.

4 Humbled for a season,
 To receive a name
From the lips of sinners
 Unto whom He came,
Faithfully He bore it
 Spotless to the last,
Brought it back victorious,
 When from death He passed.

5 Bore it up triumphant,
 With its human light,
Through all ranks of creatures,
 To the central height:
To the throne of Godhead,
 To the Father's breast,
Filled it with the glory
 Of that perfect rest.

6 In your hearts enthrone Him;
 There let Him subdue
All that is not holy,
 All that is not true;
Crown Him as your Captain
 In temptation's hour;
Let His will enfold you
 In its light and power.

7 Brethren, this Lord Jesus
 Shall return again,
With His Father's glory,
 With His angel train;
For all wreaths of empire
 Meet upon His brow,
And our hearts confess Him
 King of glory now.

39   L.M.

AWAKE, my soul, in joyful lays,
 And sing thy great
Redeemer's praise;
 He justly claims a song from thee;
His loving-kindness - Oh, how free!

2 He saw me ruined in the fall,
 Yet loved me, notwithstanding all;
He saved me from my lost estate;
 His loving-kindness - Oh, how great!

3 When I was Satan's easy prey
    And deep in debt and bondage lay,
  He paid His life for my discharge -
    His loving-kindness - Oh, how large!

4 Though numerous hosts of mighty foes
    Though earth and hell my way
      oppose,
  He safely leads my soul along -
    His loving-kindness - Oh, how strong!

5 When trouble, like a gloomy cloud,
    Has gathered thick and thundered
      loud,
  He near my soul has ever stood;
    His loving-kindness - Oh, how good!

6 Soon shall we mount and soar away
    To the bright realms of endless day,
  And sing, with rapture and surprise,
    His loving-kindness, in the skies.

40
                                      P.M.
B E not dismayed whate'er betide,
  God will take care of you!
Beneath His wings of love abide,
  God will take care of you!

God will take care of you,
  Through ev'ry day, o'er all the way;
He will take care of you;
  God will take care of you!

2 Through days of toil when heart
    doth fail,
  God will take care of you!
    When dangers fierce your path
      assail,
  God will take care of you!

3 All you may need He will provide,
    God will take care of you!
  Trust Him, and you will be satisfied,
    God will take care of you!

4 Lonely and sad, from friends apart,
    God will take care of you!
  He will give peace to your aching heart,
    God will take care of you!

4 No matter what may be the test,
    God will take care of you!
  Lean, weary one, upon His breast,
    God will take care of you!

41
                    10.10.10.10.10.10.
B E still, my soul: the Lord is on thy side;
  Bear patiently the cross of grief
  or pain;
    Leave to thy God to order and
      provide;
In every change, He faithful will remain.
  Be still, my soul: thy best, thy
    heavenly Friend
Through thorny ways leads to a
  joyful end.

2 Be still, my soul: thy God doth undertake
    To guide the future, as He has
      the past.
  Thy hope, thy confidence let
    nothing shake;
  All now mysterious shall be
    bright at last.
  Be still, my soul: the waves and
    winds still know
  His voice who ruled them while
    He dwelt below.

3 Be still, my soul: when dearest
    friends depart,
  And all is darkened in the veil of tears,
    Then shalt thou better know His
    love, His heart,
  Who comes to soothe thy sorrow
    and thy fears.
  Be still, my soul: thy Jesus can repay
    From His own fulness all He
    takes away.

4 Be still, my soul: the hour is
    hast'ning on
  When we shall be forever with the
    Lord,
  When disappointment, grief and
    fear are gone,
  Sorrow forgot, love's purest joys
    restored.
  Be still, my soul: when change and
    tears are past,
  All safe and blessèd we shall meet
    at last.

5 Be still, my soul: begin the song of
    praise
  On earth, believing, to Thy Lord on
    high;
  Acknowledge Him in all thy words
    and ways,
  So shall He view thee with a
    well-pleased eye.
  Be still, my soul: the Sun of life divine
    Through passing clouds shall but
    more brightly shine.

42   10.10.9.10.

BE Thou my vision, O Lord of my
  heart;
Naught be all else to me, save that
  Thou art;
Thou my best thought, by day or by
  night;
Waking or sleeping, Thy presence my
  light.

2 Be Thou my wisdom, and Thou my
    true Word;
  I ever with Thee and Thou with me,
    Lord;
  Thou my great Father and I, Thy
    true son;
  Thou in me dwelling, and I with
    Thee one.

3 Riches I heed not, nor man's empty
    praise;
  Thou mine inheritance, now and
    always;
  Thou and Thou only, first in my heart;
    O King of glory, my treasure Thou
    art.

4 O King of glory, my victory won;
    Rule and reign in me 'til Thy will
    be done;
  Heart of my own heart, whatever befall;
    Still be my vision, O Ruler of all.

43   8.8.8.8.D.

BEFORE the throne of God above
  I have a strong, a perfect plea,
A great High Priest, whose name
  is Love,
Who ever lives and pleads for me.
  My name is graven on His hands,
My name is written on His heart;
  I know that while in heav'n He stands
No tongue can bid me thence depart.

2 When Satan tempts me to despair,
    Telling of evil yet within,
  Upward I look, and see Him there
    Who made an end of all my sin.
  Because the sinless Saviour died,
    My sinful soul is counted free;
  For God, the Just, is satisfied
    To look on Him and pardon me.

3 Behold Him there! the once slain Lamb!
    My perfect, spotless Righteousness,
  The great unchangeable I AM,
    The King of glory and of grace!
  One with Himself, I cannot die;
    My soul is purchased by His blood;
  My life is hid with Christ on high,
    With Christ, my Saviour and my God.

44   S.M.

BEFORE Thine open ear,
  Beneath Thy watching eye,
All clean and full we would appear,
  And thus, O God, draw nigh.

2 With willing heart and mind
    Without the camp we come,
  With eyes for Him no longer blind,
    And lips no longer dumb.

3 Here saints may meet their Lord,
    Amid reproach and shame,
  Gathered according to His Word -
    Into His holy Name.

4 For where are two or three
    Simply assembled so,
  He in the midst is sure to be,
    As they may surely know.

5 Before Thine open ear
    We, in His Name, draw nigh
  To lift our hearts in worship here,
    Beneath Thy watching eye.

45   C.M.

BEHOLD! a spotless Victim dies,
  My surety on the tree;
The Lamb of God, the Sacrifice,
  He gave Himself for me!

2 Whatever curse was mine, He bore;
    The wormwood and the gall,
  There, in that lone mysterious hour,
    My cup - He drained it all!

3 Lord Jesus! Thou, and none beside,
    Its bitterness could know,
  Nor other tell Thy joy's full tide
    That from that cup shall flow.

4 Thine is the joy, but yet 'tis mine.
　　'Tis ours as one with Thee;
　My joy flows from that grief of Thine;
　　Thy death brings life to me!

5 And while the ages roll along,
　　This shall my glory be;
　And this the new and endless song,
　Thy love to us - to me.

46
8.3.8.3.8.8.8.3.

B EHOLD! behold the Lamb of God
　　On the Cross!
For us He shed His precious blood
　　On the Cross!
O hear His all-important cry,
　　"Eli, lama sabachthani?"
Draw near and see the Saviour die
　　On the Cross!

2 Behold His arms extended wide
　　On the Cross!
Behold His bleeding hands and side
　　On the Cross!
The sun withholds its rays of light,
The heav'ns are clothed in shades
　　of night,
While Jesus wins the glorious fight
　　On the Cross!

3 By faith we see Him lifted up
　　On the Cross!
He drinks for us the bitter cup
　　On the Cross!
The rocks do rend, the mountains quake,
　　While Jesus doth atonement make,
While Jesus suffers for our sake
　　On the Cross!

4 And now the mighty deed is done
　　On the Cross!
The battle fought, the vict'ry won
　　On the Cross!
To heav'n He turns His languid eyes,
"'Tis finished" now, the Conqueror cries,
　　Then bows His sacred head and dies
　　On the Cross!

5 Where'er I go I'll tell the story
　　Of the Cross!
Of nothing else my soul shall glory
　　Save the Cross!
Yea, this my constant theme shall be
　　Through time and in eternity,
That Jesus tasted death for me
　　On the Cross!

6 Let every mourner rise and cling,
　　To the Cross!
Let every Christian come and sing,
　　Round the Cross!
There let the preacher take his stand,
　　And, with the Bible in his hand,
Declare the triumphs through the land,
　　Of the Cross!

47
S.M.

B EHOLD the amazing sight,
　　The Saviour lifted high!
The Son of God, His soul's delight,
　　Expires in agony!

2 For whom, for whom, my heart,
　　Were all those sorrows borne?
Why did He feel that piercing smart,
　　And wear that crown of thorn?

3 For us in love He bled,
　　For us in anguish died,
'Twas love that bowed His sacred
　　head,
And pierced His bleeding side.

4 We see, and we adore,
　　Thy deep, Thy dying love,
We feel its strong attractive power
　　To lift our souls above.

5 In Thee our hearts unite,
　　Nor share Thy grief alone
But from Thy Cross pursue our flight
　　To Thy triumphant throne.

48
C.M.

B EHOLD the Lamb with glory
　　crowned!
To Him all power is given;
　　No place too high for Him is found,
No place too high in heaven.

2 He fills the throne - the throne above,
　　Its rights to Him belong;
The object of His Father's love,
　　The theme of angels' song.

3 Though high, yet He accepts the
　　praise
His people offer here;
　　The faintest, feeblest lay they raise
Will reach the Saviour's ear.

4 This song be ours, and this alone,
  That celebrates the Name
Of Him who sits upon the throne,
  And that exalts the Lamb.

5 To Him whom men despise and slight,
  To Him be glory given;
The crown is His, and His by right
  The highest place in heaven.

49   L.M.

B EHOLD the Man by God approved
   As with a steadfast face He moved
Toward Jerusalem to die,
  His Father God to glorify.

2 His perfect love expressed we see,
  To those who, in their enmity,
His kindness and His grace ignored,
  And in return their rage outpoured.

3 O wondrous sight that meets our gaze -
  The Son of God, in sore amaze,
Lies prostrate in Gethsemane
  And weeps and prays in agony!

4 Submissive to His Father's will,
  He shows His deep devotion still
In yonder judgment hall displayed,
  Thorn crowned and purple robe
    arrayed.

5 God's Holy One upon the tree
  Laid down His life triumphantly;
The depth of sorrow there entailed
  His full perfection has unveiled.

6 And thus with hearts that overflow,
  Although we cannot fully know
His preciousness, for Him we raise
  To Thee, O God, our hymn of praise.

50   S.M.

B EHOLD the throne of grace!
   The promise calls us near,
To seek our God and Father's face
  Who loves to answer prayer.

2 That rich, atoning blood,
  Which sprinkled round we see,
Provides for those who come to God
  An all-prevailing plea.

3 My soul, ask what thou wilt,
  Thou canst not be too bold;
Since His own blood for Thee was spilt,
  What else can He withhold?

4 Beyond our utmost wants
  His love and power can bless;
To praying souls He always grants
  More than they can express.

5 Since 'tis the Lord's command,
  Our mouth we'll open wide:
Lord, open Thou Thy bounteous hand,
  That we may be supplied.

6 Thine image, Lord, bestow,
  Thy presence and Thy love;
We seek to serve Thee here below,
  And reign with Thee above.

51   P.M.

B EHOLD, what love, what
   boundless love,
The Father hath bestowed
  On sinners lost, that we should be
Now called the sons of God.

  Behold … what manner of love …
    What manner of love the Father hath
      bestowed upon us,
  that we … that we should be called
  … should be called the sons of God.

2 No longer far from Him, but now
  By precious blood made nigh;
Accepted in the Well-beloved,
  Near to God's heart we lie.

3 What we in glory soon shall be,
  It doth not yet appear;
But when our precious Lord we see,
  We shall His image bear.

4 With such a blessèd hope in view,
  We would more holy be,
More like our risen, glorious Lord,
  Whose face we soon shall see.

52   6.6.6.4.

B ENEATH an eastern sky,
   Amid a rabble's cry,
A Man went forth to die,
  For me! for me!

2 Thorn-crowned His blessèd head,
  Blood-stained His every tread;
Cross-laden He was led,
  For me! for me!

3 Piercèd His hands and feet,
  Three hours o'er Him beat
Fierce rays of noon-tide heat,
  For me! for me!

4 Thus wast Thou made all mine;
  Lord, make me wholly Thine;
Grant grace and strength divine
  To me! to me!

5 In thought and word and deed,
  Thy will to do, O lead
My soul, e'en though it bleed,
  To Thee, to Thee.

53   P.M.

B ENEATH the Cross of Jesus
  I fain would take my stand,
The shadow of a mighty Rock
  Within a weary land;
A home within the wilderness,
  A rest upon the way,
From the burning of the noontide heat
  And the burden of the day.

2 O safe and happy shelter!
  O refuge tried and sweet!
O trysting-place, where heaven's love
And heaven's justice meet!
  As to the pilgrim patriarch
That wondrous dream was given,
  So seems my Saviour's Cross to me
A ladder up to heaven.

3 There lies beneath its shadow,
  But on the farther side,
The darkness of an awful grave
  That gapes both deep and wide;
And there between us stands the
  Cross,
Two arms outstretched to save,
  Like a watchman set to guard
    the way
From that eternal grave.

4 Upon the Cross of Jesus,
  Mine eye at times can see
The very dying form of One
  Who suffered there for me;
And from my smitten heart with tears,
  Two wonders I confess,

The wonder of His glorious love,
  And my own worthlessness.

5 I take the Cross of Jesus
  For my abiding place;
I ask no other sunshine than
  The sunshine of His face;
Content to let the world go by,
  To know no gain nor loss:
My sinful self my only shame,
  My glory all the Cross.

54   8.6.8.8.6.

B EYOND the scenes of darkest night,
  Of death and agony,
We now, in resurrection light,
  Behold the Conqu'ror in the fight
Ascend triumphantly.

2 In conflict knew He no retreat
  From sorrow, shame and woe.
In victory o'er death complete,
  He bruised the serpent 'neath
    His feet
And laid the tyrant low.

3 And now He sits upon the throne
  At God's right hand above,
In grace to care for all His own,
  And thus to them make fully known
His changeless, boundless love.

4 But O, what rapture will it be
  When we no more shall roam,
When, from all sin and sorrow free,
  We dwell with Him eternally,
For evermore at home!

55   P.M.

B LESSÈD assurance, Jesus is mine!
  Oh, what a foretaste of glory divine!
Heir of salvation, purchase of God,
  Born of His Spirit, washed in His
    blood.

  This is my story, this is my song,
    Praising my Saviour all the day long;
  This is my story, this is my song,
    Praising my Saviour all the day long.

2 Perfect submission, perfect delight,
  Visions of rapture now burst on
    my sight;
Angels descending, bring from above
  Echoes of mercy, whispers of love.

3 Perfect submission, all is at rest,
I in my Saviour am happy and blest;
Watching and waiting, looking above,
Filled with His goodness, lost in
His love.

56   6.10.10.6.

B LESSÈD be God, our God!
Who gave for us His well -
belovèd Son,
His Gift of gifts, all other gifts in one;
Blessèd be God, our God!

2 What will He not bestow?
Who freely gave this mighty Gift
unbought,
Unmerited, unheeded, and unsought;
What will He not bestow?

3 He sparèd not His Son!
'Tis this that silences each rising fear,
'Tis this that bids the hard thought
disappear;
He sparèd not His Son!

4 Who shall condemn us now?
Since Christ has died, and
risen, and gone above,
For us to plead at the right hand of
Love,
Who shall condemn us now?

5 'Tis God that justifies!
Who shall recall His pardon or
His grace?
Or who the broken chain of guilt replace?
'Tis God that justifies!

6 The victory is ours!
For us in might came forth the
Mighty One;
For us He fought the fight, the
triumph won;
The victory is ours!

57   6.5.6.5.D.

B LESSÈD God of Glory,
Here our hearts would bow;
Grateful, we adore Thee,
Thankful, praise Thee now
For Thy Son eternal,
Who, revealed in time,
Showed Thy Love supernal,
In His grace sublime.

2 Here, that holy Stranger
We would contemplate,
Who, in yonder manger,
Lay in low estate.
Earthly pomp and splendour
From Him far removed:
What He did surrender
Mightiest Love has proved.

3 Living for Thy pleasure,
Telling out Thy grace,
Love, in boundless measure,
Reached the lowest place.
That, with Him victorious,
We should thus be found
In this service glorious
Where our joys abound.

4 Hearts and voices blending,
Joyfully we raise
Through Thy Son ascending
Sacrifice of praise.
He Thy heart's chief treasure,
Theme of themes so sweet;
Here Thou findest pleasure,
Perfect and complete.

58   8.5.8.3.

B LESSÈD God, our hearts are bringing
Unto Thee, as one,
Sacrifice of praise with singing
Of Thy Son.

2 Thou hast told us all the story
How in grace He came
Manifesting all the glory
Of Thy Name.

3 And, by faith upon Him gazing,
We to Thee draw near,
Thus His holy Person praising
In Thine ear.

4 Of Thy heart's most precious treasure
Praise we raise on high -
Him, Whose path brought perfect
pleasure
To Thine eye.

5 Who, in holy manhood living,
Set Himself apart,
Perfect satisfaction giving
To Thy heart.

6 Who, at last, in holy suff'ring,
   Dying willingly,
Gave Himself, a whole burnt off'ring
   All for Thee.

59
8.7.8.7.7.7.

BLESSÈD God, we come before Thee,
   And with holy rev'rence bow,
While in worship we adore Thee
   As His God and Father now;
Musing on Thy Son today
   In Thine Own appointed way.

2 We remember Him as being
   Found on earth in manhood true,
How He said, His path fore-seeing,
   "Lo, I come, Thy will to do".
Man of single purpose, He
   This accomplished perfectly.

3 In that holy body dwelling,
   Which for Him Thou didst prepare,
Unto men Thy heart forth-telling,
   For Thine interests He would care,
Drawing, binding to Him still,
   Those who do the Father's will!

4 Such a steadfast path reviewing,
   Filled throughout with nought
      but good,
Finding ever in the doing
   Of Thy will and work His food!
We His preciousness proclaim,
   Making mention of His Name.

60
7.7.7.7.

BLESSÈD God, we meditate
   On Thy Son in low estate,
Glory seeking not, nor fame,
   Moving to a Cross of shame.

2 Perfect Man to Thee, His God,
   Beautiful the path He trod!
His delight to do Thy will,
   And the Scriptures to fulfil!

3 Pleasing not Himself on earth,
   Manifesting rarest worth,
Ever doing nought but good,
   All Thy will His pleasant food!

4 Clothed with meekness and with might,
   Turning not to left or right.
Thus the One Whom Thou did'st send
   Journeyed onward to the end.

5 Thee, O Blessèd God, we praise,
   Meditating on His ways
In the perfect path He trod,
   Glorifying Thee, His God.

61
8.7.8.7.4.7.

BLESSÈD Lord, our souls are longing
   Thee, our risen Head, to see;
And the cloudless morning's dawning,
   When Thy saints shall gathered be:
      Grace and glory,
All our well-springs are in Thee.

2 All the sorrow we are tasting
   Is but as the dream of night:
To the day of God we're hasting,
   Looking for it with delight;
      Thou art coming,
This will satisfy our sight.

3 True, the silent grave is keeping
   Many a seed in weakness sown:
But the saints, in Thee now sleeping,
   Raised in power, shall share Thy
      throne,
         Resurrection!
Lord of Glory! 'tis Thine own.

4 As we sing, our hearts grow lighter;
   We are children of the day;
Sorrow makes our hope the brighter;
   Faith regards not the delay;
      Sure the promise!
We shall meet Thee on the way.

62
6.5.6.5.D.

BLESSÈD retrospection,
   Thus His steps to trace!
Tasting His rejection
   In the outside place,
Raptured hearts are raising
   Unto Thee, His God,
Praise beyond all praising
   For the path He trod.

2 In a world without Him,
   Gathered thus apart,
As we think about Him,
   In each musing heart,
Thoughts arise demanding
   Songs of praise anew
With the understanding
   And the spirit too.

3 Thus we contemplate Him,
    Moving on and through:
Sorrows that await Him
    Ever all in view!
Though in full foreknowing
    What He'd reach at length
Comely in His going,
    Steadfast in His strength!

4 Touched with heavenly wonder,
    We, with one accord,
Reverently ponder
    Our Belovèd Lord:
And to Thee, His Father,
    Here in praise express
All our hearts can gather
    Of His preciousness.

63   C.M.

BLEST morning, whose first
    dawning rays
Beheld the Son of God
    Arise triumphant from the grave,
And leave His dark abode.

2 Wrapt in the silence of the tomb
    The great Redeemer lay,
Till the revolving skies had brought
    The third, the appointed day.

3 Hell and the grave combined their force
    To hold our Lord, in vain;
Sudden the Conqueror arose
    And burst their feeble chain.

4 To Thy great name, almighty Lord,
    We sacred honours pay,
And loud hosannahs shall proclaim
    The triumphs of the day.

5 Salvation and immortal praise
    To our victorious King!
Let heaven and earth, and rocks
    and seas,
With glad hosannas ring.

64   S.M.D.

BREAK every barrier down,
    Thou Lamb of Calvary;
Show me the awfulness of sin,
    The thing which grieveth Thee:
Purge Thou my soul from dross,
    Cleanse me from every sin,
Wash me in Thine atoning blood,
    And make me pure within.

2 Break every barrier down
    Till Christ be formed in me;
Till of the travail of Thy soul
    Thou, satisfied, shalt see:
May earth's success seem nought,
    May self be lost to sight,
Reproach for Thee be counted joy
    And weakness turn to might.

3 Break every barrier down,
    Thou risen Son of God;
Take Thou possession of my heart,
    I crown Thee now as Lord!
O for a closer walk,
    A greater love for Thee,
A fuller knowledge of Thyself,
    A life of victory.

4 Break every barrier down
    And reign triumphant, Lord;
May every breathing of my heart
    With Thine be in accord:
Grant me to enter in
    The secret place with Thee,
To walk with Thee, as Enoch walked,
    Into eternity.

65   6.4.6.4.D.

BREAK Thou the bread of life,
    Dear Lord, to me,
As Thou didst break the loaves
    Beside the sea;
Beyond the sacred page
    I seek Thee, Lord;
My spirit pants for Thee,
    O living Word.

2 Break Thou the bread of life,
    O Lord, to me,
That hid within my heart
    Thy word may be:
Mould Thou each inward thought,
    From self set free,
And let my steps be all
    Controlled by Thee.

3 Open Thy word of truth
    That I may see
Thy message written clear
    And plain for me;
Then, in sweet fellowship,
    Walking with Thee,
Thine image on my life
    Engraved will be.

4 Bless Thou the truth, dear Lord,
    To me, to me,
As Thou didst bless the bread
    By Galilee;
Then shall all bondage cease,
    All fetters fall;
And I shall find my peace,
    My all in all.

66   7.7.7.7.

B RETHREN, let us join to bless
   Jesus Christ, our joy and peace;
Him, who bowed His head so low
    Underneath our load of woe.

2 His the curse, the wounds, the gall,
    His the stripes - He bore them all;
His the dying cry of pain
    When our sins He did sustain.

3 He, the accepted Sacrifice,
    From the vanquished grave did rise;
Free Himself, He set us free
    In His perfect liberty.

4 Ransomed now, accepted, free,
    Safe from judgment, Lord, in Thee,
We rejoice that God can bless
    All who do Thy name confess.

5 Praise our God who willed it thus;
    Praise the Lamb who died for us;
Praise the Father, through the Son,
    Who so vast a work hath done.

6 Thee, our Saviour, we adore,
    And would serve Thee more and
      more,
Till with joy Thy face we see,
    And for ever dwell with Thee.

67   C.M.

B RIDE of the Lamb, there is for thee
   One only safe retreat;
Where Jesus is thy heart should be,
    Thy home at His dear feet.

2 When Satan tracks thy lonely way,
    There his temptations meet;
In Jesus' presence watch and pray,
    Yea, conquer at His feet.

3 Since thou hast much to learn, e'en
    though
Thou art in Christ complete,
    In grace and knowledge seek to
     grow
By sitting at His feet.

4 Through tribulation hasten on,
    With Christ the cross is sweet;
The little while will soon be gone,
    Keep only at His feet.

5 Bride of the Lamb, forget the past,
    Prepare the Lord to greet;
'Tis thine to share His throne, and
    cast
Thy wreath before His feet.

68   8.7.8.7.4.7.

B RIGHT with all His crowns of glory,
   See the Royal Victor's brow;
Once for sinners marr'd and gory,
    See the Lamb exalted now,
      While before Him
All His ransomed brethren bow.

2 Blessèd morning! long expected,
    Lo! they fill the peopled air,
Mourners once, by man rejected,
    They, with Him, exalted there,
      Sing His praises,
And His throne of glory share.

3 King of kings! let earth adore Him,
    High on His exalted throne;
Fall, ye nations, fall before Him,
    And His righteous sceptre own;
      All the glory
Be to Him, and Him alone.

69   7.7.7.8.

B RIGHTNESS of God's glory He,
   Full essential deity,
Heir enthroned in majesty,
    Hallelujah, what a Saviour!

2 Willing lower to become
    Learned obedience though a Son,
Perfected, He fills the throne,
    Hallelujah, what a Saviour!

3 Holy, harmless, undefiled,
    Yet by wicked men reviled,
Us to God He reconciled,
    Hallelujah, what a Saviour!

4 Offered once to bear our sin,
    Through His blood He entered in,
Seated there we honour Him,
    Hallelujah, what a Saviour!

5 Sin remembered now no more,
    Bold to enter, near we draw,
Him we worship, Him adore,
    Hallelujah, what a Saviour!

70　　　　　　　　　　8.7.8.7.
B RIGHTNESS of the eternal glory
    Shall Thy praise unuttered lie?
Who would hush the heaven-sent
    story
Of the Lamb who came to die?

2 Came from Godhead's fullest glory
    Down to Calvary's depth of woe;
Now on high, we bow before Thee;
    Streams of praises ceaseless flow!

3 Sing His blest triumphant rising;
    Sing Him on the Father's throne;
Sing - till heaven and earth surprising,
    Reigns the Nazarene alone.

71　　　　　　　　　　8.8.8.4.
B Y Christ redeemed, in Christ
    restored,
We keep the memory adored,
    And show the death of our dear Lord
        Until He come.

2 His body, broken in our stead,
    Is seen in this memorial bread,
And so our feeble love is fed
        Until He come.

3 The drops of His dread agony,
    His life-blood shed for us, we see;
The wine shall tell the mystery
        Until He come.

4 Until the trump of God be heard,
    Until the ancient graves be stirred,
And with the great commanding word
        The Lord shall come.

5 O blessèd hope! with this elate,
    Let not our hearts be desolate,
But, strong in faith, in patience wait
        Until He come.

72　　　　8.7.8.7.D. with Chorus
C AME He to Bethlehem's manger
    Infant, yet glorious Lord?
Stood He in Temple and uttered
    Wondrous and mystical word?
Toiled He in workshop, and lowly
    Bore He the burden of life?
Calmly, and sweetly, and purely
    Mixed He in anger or strife?

Love brought Him down from the
    glory,
Love made Him come from the sky,
    Love in His heart for the sinner
Led Him to suffer and die.

2 Passed He the fiery temptation?
    Was He the homeless and lone?
Was He despised and rejected?
    Claimed He dark sorrow His own?
Came He to Olivet's garden?
    Drank He the dregs of the cup?
Say, was that holy cheek sullied?
    Gave He His precious life up?

3 Went He to Pilate and Herod?
    Bore He the scourge and the thorn?
Prayed He His Father to pardon?
    Died He midst mocking and scorn?
Lay He in grave of the rich man?
    Rose He in majesty grand?
Went He to claim as a victor
    Trophies as countless as sand?

73　　　　　　　　　　7.7.7.7.
C HRIST the Lord is risen on high!
    Sing, ye heavens, and earth reply;
He endured the Cross, the grave,
    Sinners to redeem and save.

2 Love's redeeming work is done,
    Fought the fight, the battle won!
He Himself our ransom paid,
    Peace with God for ever made.

3 Vain the stone, the watch, the seal,
    Christ has burst the gates of hell;
Vain their efforts to enthral,
    He has triumphed over all.

4 Christ our Lord is risen indeed,
  Christ is now the Church's Head;
Loud the song of triumph raise,
  Celebrate the Victor's praise.

74
P.M.

CHRISTIANS, go and tell of Jesus,
  How He died to save our souls;
How that He, from sin might free us,
  Suffered agonies untold.

Yes, we'll go and tell of Jesus,
  The pure and holy, meek and
  lowly Jesus;
Yes, we'll go and tell of Jesus,
  Who died our souls to save.

2 Tell the guilty of their danger
  While they wander far from God;
While they live to Christ a stranger,
  And reject His precious Word.

3 Tell them of the joys of heaven,
  Purchased by the Saviour's blood,
How, that they might be forgiven,
  Jesus left His home above.

4 Tell them how He hath ascended
  To prepare a home on high,
Where all sorrows shall be ended,
  Where the saved shall never die.

75
S.M.

CHRIST'S grave is vacant now,
  Left for the throne above;
His Cross asserts God's right to bless
  In His own boundless love.

2 'Twas there His blood was shed;
  'Twas there His life was poured;
There Mercy gained her diadem,
  While Justice sheathed her sword.

3 And thence the child of faith
  Sees judgment all gone by,
Perceives the sentence fully met:
  "The soul that sins shall die!"

4 Learns how that God in love
  Gave Christ the sins to bear
Of all who own His Lordship now,
  That they His place might share;

5 And cries with wondering joy,
  "As He is so am I,
Pure, holy, loved as Christ Himself;
  Who shall my peace destroy?"

6 Reach my blest Saviour first;
  Take Him from God's esteem;
Prove Jesus bears one spot of sin;
  Then tell me I'm unclean!

7 Nay! for He purged my guilt
  By His own precious blood,
And such its virtue not a stain
  E'er meets the eye of God.

76
6.6.4.6.6.6.4.

COME, all ye saints of God!
  Publish through earth abroad
  Jesus' great fame:
Tell what His love has done;
Trust in His name alone;
  Shout to His lofty throne,
  Worthy the Lamb!

2 Hence! gloomy doubts and fears;
  Dry up your mournful tears;
  Swell the glad throng:
To Christ, the heavenly King,
Strike each melodious string,
  From heart and voice to sing,
  Worthy the Lamb!

3 Hark, how the choirs above,
  Filled with the Saviour's love,
  Dwell on His name!
There, too, shall we be found,
With light and glory crowned,
  While all the heavens resound
  Worthy the Lamb!

77
6.6.6.6.8.8.

COME, every joyful heart
  That loves the Saviour's name,
Your noblest powers exert
  To celebrate His fame;
Tell all above and all below
  The debt of love to Him you owe.

2 He left His starry crown,
  And laid His robes aside;
On wings of love came down,
  And wept, and bled, and died:
What He endured no tongue can tell,
  To save our souls from death and
  hell.

3 From the dark grave He rose -
    The mansion of the dead;
  And thence His mighty foes
    In glorious triumph led:
  Up through the sky the Conqueror rode,
    And reigns on high, the Saviour God.

4 From thence He'll quickly come,
    His chariot will not stay,
    And bear His people home
  To realms of endless day:
    There shall we see His lovely
      face,
  And ever be in His embrace.

5 Jesus, we ne'er can pay
    The debt of love we owe;
  Yet grant us day by day
    Our gratitude to show;
  Our life, our all, to Thee we give,
    To Thee, by whom alone we live.

78   8.3.8.3.8.8.8.3.

C OME, let us all unite to sing,
        God is love.
  Let heaven and earth their praises
    bring;
        God is love.
  Let every soul from sin awake,
    Each in his heart sweet music make,
  And sing with us, for Jesus' sake,
        God is love.

2 O tell to earth's remotest bound,
        God is love.
  In Christ we have redemption found:
        God is love.
  His blood has purged our sins away,
    His Spirit turned our night to day;
  And now we can rejoice to say,
        God is love.

3 How happy is our portion here!
        God is love.
  His promises our spirits cheer;
        God is love.
  He is our sun and shield by day,
    Our help, our hope, our strength,
      and stay,
  He will be with us all the way:
        God is love.

4 In glory we shall sing again,
        God is love.
  Yes, this shall be our lofty strain,
        God is love.
  Whilst endless ages roll along,
    In concert with the heavenly throng,
  This shall be still our sweetest song,
        God is love.

79   C.M.

C OME, let us join our cheerful songs
    With all around the throne;
  Ten thousand thousand are their
    tongues,
  But all their joys are one.

2 "Worthy the Lamb that died", they cry,
    "To be exalted thus";
  "Worthy the Lamb", our lips reply,
    "For He was slain for us".

3 Jesus is worthy to receive
    Honour and power divine;
  And blessings, more than we can give,
    Be, Lord, for ever Thine!

4 Let all that dwell above the sky,
    And air, and earth, and seas,
  Conspire to raise Thy glories high,
    And speak Thine endless praise.

5 Let all creation join in one,
    To bless the sacred name
  Of Him who sits upon the throne,
    And to adore the Lamb.

80   8.8.6.8.8.6.

C OME, let us sing the matchless
    worth,
  And sweetly sound the glories forth
    Which in the Saviour shine:
  To God and Christ our praises bring;
    The song, with which the heavens
      ring,
  We sing by grace divine.

2 How rich the precious blood He spilt,
    Our ransom from the dreadful guilt
  Of sin against our God.
    How perfect is His righteousness,
  In which unspotted beauteous dress
    His saints have ever stood.

3 How rich the character He bears,
    And all the forms of love He wears,
Exalted on the throne;
    In songs of sweet untiring praise,
We would to everlasting days,
    Make all His glories known.

4 And soon the happy day shall come,
    When we shall reach our destined
        home,
And see Him face to face;
    Then with our Saviour, Master, Friend,
The glad eternity we'll spend,
    And celebrate His grace.

81   L.M.

COME, let us sing the song of songs,
    And yield in joyful heavenly strain
The homage which to Christ belongs:
    "Worthy the Lamb, for He was slain!"

2 Slain to redeem us by His blood,
    To cleanse from every sinful stain,
And make us kings and priests to God:
    "Worthy the Lamb, for He was slain!"

3 To Him who suffered on the tree,
    Our souls, at His soul's price, to gain,
Blessing, and praise, and glory be:
    "Worthy the Lamb, for He was slain!"

4 To Him, enthroned by filial right,
    All power in heaven and earth pertain,
Honour, and majesty, and might:
    "Worthy the Lamb, for He was slain!"

5 Long as we live, and should we die,
    And while in heaven with Him we
        reign,
This song our song of songs shall be:
    "Worthy the Lamb, for He was slain!"

82   C.M.

COME, let us to the Lord our God,
    With contrite hearts return;
Our God is gracious, nor will leave,
    The desolate to mourn.

2 His voice commands the tempest
        forth,
    And stills the stormy wave;
    And, though His arm be strong
        to smite,
    'Tis also strong to save.

3 Long hath the night of sorrow reigned;
    The dawn shall bring us light:
God shall appear, and we shall rise
    With gladness in His sight.

4 Our hearts, if God we seek to know,
    Shall know Him, and rejoice;
His coming like the morn shall be,
    Like morning songs His voice.

5 As dew upon the tender herb,
    Diffusing fragrance round,
As showers that usher in the spring,
    And cheer the thirsty ground;

6 So shall His presence bless our souls,
    And shed a joyful light;
That hallowed morn shall chase away
    The sorrows of the night.

83   7.7.7.7.

COME, my soul, thy suit prepare,
    Jesus loves to answer prayer;
He Himself has bid thee pray,
    Therefore will not say thee nay.

2 Thou art coming to a King;
    Large petitions with thee bring;
For His grace and power are such,
    None can ever ask too much.

3 Lord, I come to Thee for rest;
    Take possession of my breast;
There Thy blood-bought right
        maintain,
And without a rival reign.

4 As the image in the glass
    Answers the beholder's face,
Thus unto my heart appear;
    Print Thine own resemblance
        there.

5 While I am a pilgrim here,
    Let Thy love my spirit cheer;
As my Guide, my Guard, my Friend,
    Lead me to my journey's end.

6 Show me what I have to do;
    Every hour my strength renew.
Let me live a life of faith;
    Let me die Thy people's death.

84　　　　　　　　　　　L.M.D.

COME sing, my soul, and praise
　　the Lord,
Who hath redeemed thee by His blood,
　　Delivered thee from chains that
　　　　bound,
And brought thee to redemption ground.

Redemption ground, the ground of
　　peace!
Redemption ground, O wondrous
　　grace!
Here let our praise to God abound,
　　Who saves us on redemption
　　　　ground!

2 Once from my God I wandered far,
　　And with His holy will made war;
　But now my songs to God abound:
　　I'm standing on redemption ground.

3 O joyous hour when God to me
　　A vision gave of Calvary!
　My bonds were loosed, my soul
　　　unbound:
　I sang upon redemption ground.

4 No works of merit now I plead,
　　But Jesus take for all my need;
　No righteousness in me is found,
　　Except upon redemption ground.

85　　　　　　　　　　　8.7.8.7.

COME, Thou Fount of every blessing,
　　Tune my heart to sing Thy grace;
Streams of mercy, never ceasing,
　　Call for songs of loudest praise.

2 Teach me, Lord, some rapturous
　　　measure,
　Meet for blood-bought hosts above;
　　Let me sing the countless treasure,
　Of my God's unchanging love.

3 Jesus sought me when a stranger,
　　Wandering from the fold of God;
　He, to rescue me from danger,
　　Interposed His precious blood.

4 Oh, to grace how great a debtor,
　　Daily I'm constrained to be!
　Let that grace, Lord, like a fetter,
　　Bind my wandering heart to Thee.

5 Prone to wander, Lord, I feel it,
　　Prone to leave the God I love;
　Keep my heart from wandering,
　　　keep it;
　Till I'm perfected above.

6 Here I'll raise my Ebenezer,
　　Hither by Thy help I've come;
　And I hope, by Thy good pleasure,
　　Safely to arrive at home.

86　　　　　　　　　　　C.M.

COME, ye that know the Saviour's
　　name,
And raise your thoughts above;
　　Let every heart and voice unite
To sing - that God is love!

2 His Word this precious truth reveals,
　　And all His mercies prove;
　Creation and redemption join
　　To show - that God is love!

3 His patience, bearing much and long
　　With those who from Him rove,
　His kindness, while He leads them
　　　home,
　Attest - that God is love!

4 The work begun is carried on
　　By power from heaven above;
　And every step, from first to last,
　　Declares - that God is love!

5 O may we all, while here below,
　　His perfect will approve,
　Till nobler songs, in brighter worlds
　　Proclaim - that God is love!

87　　　　　　　　　　　S.M.D.

CROWN Him with many crowns,
　　The Lamb upon His throne;
Hark! how the heavenly anthem
　　drowns
All music but its own;
　　Awake, my soul, and sing
Of Him who died for thee,
　　And hail Him as thy matchless King
Through all eternity.

2 Crown Him the Lord of life
　　Who triumphed o'er the grave,
　And rose victorious in the strife
　　For those He came to save:

His glories now we sing,
  Who died and rose on high,
Who died eternal life to bring,
  And lives that death may die.

3 Crown Him the Lord of heaven,
  Enthroned in worlds above,
The King of kings to whom is given
  The wondrous name of Love:
His reign shall know no end,
  And round His piercèd feet
Fair flowers of Paradise extend
  Their fragrance ever sweet.

4 Crown Him the Lord of lords,
  Who over all doth reign,
Who once on earth, the incarnate
  Word,
For ransomed sinners slain,
  Now lives in realms of light,
Where saints with angels sing
  Their songs before Him day and
    night,
Their God, Redeemer, King.

5 Crown Him the Lord of years,
  The Potentate of time,
Creator of the rolling spheres,
  Ineffably sublime.
All hail, Redeemer, hail!
  For Thou has died for me:
Thy praise and glory shall not fail
  Throughout eternity.

88   7.7.7.7.

C ROWNED with thorns upon the tree,
  Silent in Thine agony;
Dying, crushed beneath the load
  Of the wrath and curse of God.

2 On Thy pale and suff'ring brow,
  Mystery of love and woe;
On Thy grief and sore amaze,
  Saviour, I would fix my gaze!

3 On Thy pierced and bleeding breast
  Thou dost bid the weary rest;
Rest there from the world's false ways,
  Rest there from its vanities.

4 Rest in pardon and relief
  From the load of guilt and grief;
Rest in Thy redeeming blood,
  Rest in perfect peace with God.

5 Sin-atoning Sacrifice,
  Thou art precious in mine eyes;
Thou alone my rest shall be,
  Now and through eternity.

89   7.7.7.7.D.

C ROWNS of glory ever bright
  Rest upon the Victor's head;
Crowns of glory are His right,
  His, who liveth, and was dead.
Jesus fought and won the day,
  Such a day was never fought;
Well His people now may say,
  See what God, our God, has
    wrought.

2 He subdued the powers of hell;
  In the fight He stood alone;
All His foes before Him fell,
  By His single arm o'erthrown.
They have fall'n to rise no more;
  Final is the foe's defeat;
Jesus triumphed by His power,
  And His triumph is complete.

3 His the fight, the arduous toil,
  His the honours of the day,
His the glory and the spoil,
  Jesus bears them all away.
Now proclaim His deeds afar,
  Fill the world with His renown;
His alone the Victor's car,
  His the everlasting crown.

90   7.7.7.7.7.7.

D ARKNESS veiled Gethsemane
  While He prayed in agony;
Sore amazed, His sweat like blood,
  Cries and tears poured forth in
    flood!
His th' exceeding sorrow there,
  His the cup that none might share.

2 Undesired, betrayed and bound,
  Wicked men beset Him round;
Spat on, scourged, and mocked
  in scorn,
Robed in purple, wreathed with thorn!
  'Mid such base indignity,
Matchless His tranquillity.

3 There, upon the tree, He passed
   Into sorrow's depths at last,
He alone, so spotless pure,
   Could such anguish sore endure,
Would in love devoted, free,
   Unto death obedient be.

4 Fadeless scenes thus pond'ring o'er,
   Our adoring thanks we pour
Unto Thee, O God, today,
   For Thy Son in this Thy way;
All His life and death review,
   And His praises sing anew.

91   P.M.

DAY by day, and with each passing
   moment,
Strength I find to meet my trials here;
   Trusting in my Father's wise
      bestowment,
I've no cause for worry or for fear.
   He, whose heart is kind beyond
      all measure,
Gives unto each day what He
   deems best,
Lovingly, its part of pain and pleasure,
   Mingling toil with peace and rest.

2 Every day the Lord Himself is near
   me,
With a special mercy for each hour;
   All my cares He fain would bear
      and cheer me,
He whose name is Counsellor and
   Pow'r.
The protection of His child and
   treasure
Is a charge that on Himself He laid;
"As thy days, thy strength shall be
   in measure",
This the pledge to me He made.

3 Help me then, in every tribulation,
   So to trust Thy promises, O Lord,
That I lose not faith's sweet
   consolation,
Offered me within Thy holy Word.
   Help me, Lord, when toil and
      trouble meeting,
E'er to take, as from a father's hand,
One by one, the days, the moments
   fleeting,
Till I reach the promised land.

92   P.M.

DAYS are filled with sorrow
   and care,
Hearts are lonely and drear;
   Burdens are lifted at Calvary,
Jesus is very near.

Burdens are lifted at Calvary,
   Calvary, Calvary,
Burdens are lifted at Calvary,
   Jesus is very near.

2 Cast your care on Jesus today,
   Leave your worry and fear;
Burdens are lifted at Calvary,
   Jesus is very near.

3 Troubled soul, the Saviour can see,
   Every heartache and tear;
Burdens are lifted at Calvary
   Jesus is very near.

93   P.M.

DEAR Saviour, Thou art mine,
   How sweet the thought to me!
Let me repeat Thy name,
   And lift my heart to Thee.

   Mine! mine! mine!
      I know Thou art mine;
   Saviour, dear Saviour,
      I know Thou art mine.

2 Thou art the sinner's Friend,
   So I Thy friendship claim,
A sinner saved by grace,
   When Thy sweet message came.

3 My hardened heart was touched;
   Thy pardoning voice I heard;
And joy and peace came in,
   While listening to Thy Word.

4 So let me sing Thy praise,
   So let me call Thee mine;
I cannot doubt Thy word,
   I know that I am Thine.

94   P.M.

DOES Jesus care when my
   heart is pained,
Too deeply for mirth or song;
   As the burdens press,
   And the cares distress,
      And the way grows weary and long?

Oh, yes, He cares; I know He cares;
His heart is touched with my grief;
When the days are weary,
The long nights dreary,
I know my Saviour cares.

2 Does Jesus care when my way
    is dark
  With a nameless dread and fear?
    As the daylight fades
  Into deep night shades,
    Does He care enough to be near?

3 Does Jesus care when I've tried
    and failed,
  To resist some temptation strong;
    When in my deep grief
  I find no relief,
    Though my tears flow all the
        night long?

4 Does Jesus care when I've said
    "Goodbye"
  To the dearest on earth to me,
    And my sad heart aches
  Till it nearly breaks -
    Is this aught to Him? Does He see?

95
6.6.6.6.8.8.

D ONE is the work that saves,
    Once and for ever done;
Finished the righteousness
    That clothes the unrighteous one.
The love that blesses us below
    Is flowing freely to us now.

2 The sacrifice is o'er,
    The veil is rent in twain,
The mercy-seat is red
    With blood of Victim slain.
Why stand we then without, in fear?
    The blood of Christ invites us near.

3 The gate is open wide;
    The new and living way
Is clear, and free, and bright
    With love, and peace, and day.
Into the holiest now we come,
    Our present and our endless home.

4 Enthroned in majesty
    The High Priest sits within;
His precious blood, once shed,
    Has made and keeps us clean;
With boldness let us now draw near;
    That blood has banished every fear.

5 Then to the Lamb once slain
    Be glory, praise, and power,
Who died, and lives again,
    Who liveth evermore;
Who loved us, cleansed us by His
    blood,
And made us kings and priests to God.

96
8.5.8.5.D.

D RAWING near in full assurance
    We would seek Thy face,
Praise and worship and adore Thee
    God of matchless grace;
Coming, Lord, with holy boldness
    To the mercy seat,
For the sprinkled blood has made us
    For Thy presence meet.

2 See the sacrifice appointed
    On the altar laid,
Christ, the sinless, spotless offering
    Sin for us was made;
Yet it pleased the Lord to bruise Him
    Blessèd be Thy name
For the wondrous fragrance rising
    From that death of shame.

3 In the evening hour they laid Him
    In a rich man's tomb.
Sad indeed, their hearts and heavy,
    Filled with deepest gloom;
But the resurrection morning
    Chased away their fears;
'He is risen', 'He is risen',
    Wiped away their tears.

4 In the morning we shall see Him,
    Gaze upon His face;
Fall in worship and adore Him
    For His wondrous grace;
With what bliss our hearts shall
    greet Him
    In that morning fair.
There to be for ever with Him,
    And His joy to share.

5 Hark that Hallelujah chorus
    Ringing through the sky,
'Praise the Saviour, praise the
    Saviour!'
    Countless hosts reply:
'He is worthy, He is worthy',
    Join the glad refrain,
Giving everlasting glory
    To the Lamb once slain.

97   8.7.8.7.4.7.

DREAD Golgotha! place of blended
    Love and sorrow all unknown;
On a Cross of shame suspended,
    See the One Whom men disown!
        Comprehended.
By His Father - God alone!

2 Taunting cries and wicked railing
    Rise, His holy ears to greet;
Anguish sore, and thirst assailing,
    Piercèd hands and piercèd feet!
        Love prevailing,
Where such love and sorrow meet!

3 "It is finished!" consummation
    Vast indeed is in that cry;
And a wondrous revelation
    Of His worth, Who came to die!
        His vocation -
God alone to glorify.

4 Thorns around His brow entwining,
    Low His head is laid at last,
On His lifeless breast declining,
    All His shame and suff'ring past.
        Love outshining,
Love unfailing, full, and vast!

5 On Himself thus meditating,
    Unto Thee, His God, we pour
Thanks and praise, appreciating
    Thy Belovèd Son the more.
        Praise creating,
Is the theme for evermore!

98   8.6.8.8.6.

ETERNAL Light! Eternal Light!
    How pure the soul must be
When, placed within Thy searching
        sight,
It shrinks not, but with calm delight
    Can live, and look on Thee.

2 The spirits that surround Thy throne
    May bear the burning bliss;
But that is surely theirs alone,
    Since they have never, never known
A fallen world like this.

3 O how shall I, whose native sphere
    Is dark, whose mind is dim,
Before the Ineffable appear,
    And on my naked spirit bear
The uncreated beam?

4 There is a way for man to rise
    To that sublime abode;
An offering and a sacrifice,
    A Holy Spirit's energies,
An advocate with God.

5 These, these prepare us for the sight
    Of holiness above;
The sons of ignorance and night
    May dwell in the eternal Light,
Through the eternal Love.

99   8.6.8.6.8.8.

ETERNAL Word, eternal Son!
    The Father's constant joy,
What Thou hast done and what
        Thou art
Shall all our tongues employ;
    Our Life, our Lord, we Thee adore;
Worthy art Thou for evermore!

2 The eternal glory's living light,
    Of God the image Thou,
Creator of the universe,
    Upholding all things now;
Our Peace, our Strength, we Thee
        adore;
Worthy art Thou for evermore!

3 The Son, in whom all fulness dwells,
    Through whom all glories flow,
Thou didst the human form assume
    That we our God might know;
Our Life, our Head, we Thee adore,
Worthy art Thou for evermore!

4 Declarer of the Father's name,
    Expression of His grace,
The Word of life, the Light of men,
    The Lord with unveiled face;
Our Joy, our Hope, we Thee adore;
Worthy art Thou for evermore!

100   8.7.8.7.D.

FACE to face with Christ, my Saviour,
    Face to face - what will it be?
When with rapture I behold Him,
    Jesus Christ, who died for me.

Face to face shall I behold Him,
Far beyond the starry sky;
Face to face in all His glory,
I shall see Him by and by!

2 Only faintly now I see Him,
　　With the darkling veil between,
But a blessèd day is coming,
　　When His glory shall be seen.

3 What rejoicing in His presence,
　　When are banished grief and pain;
When the crooked ways are
　　straightened,
And the dark things shall be plain.

4 Face to face! O blissful moment!
　　Face to face - to see and know;
Face to face with my Redeemer,
　　Jesus Christ, who loves me so.

101　　　　　　　　7.6.7.6.D

FACING a task unfinished,
　　That drives us to our knees;
A need that, undiminished,
　　Rebukes our slothful ease;
We, who rejoice to know Thee,
　　Renew before Thy throne,
The solemn pledge we owe Thee
　　To go and make Thee known.

2 Where other lords beside Thee,
　　Hold their unhindered sway,
Where forces that defied Thee,
　　Defy Thee still today;
With none to heed their crying,
　　For life, and love, and light,
Unnumbered souls are dying
　　And pass into the night

3 We bear the torch that flaming,
　　Fell from the hands of those,
Who gave their lives proclaiming,
　　That Jesus died and rose.
Ours is the same commission,
　　The same glad message ours;
Fired by the same ambition,
　　To Thee we yield our powers

4 O Father who sustained them,
　　O Spirit who inspired,
Saviour, whose love constrained them
　　To toil with zeal untired;
From cowardice defend us,
　　From lethargy awake!
Forth on Thine errands send us
　　To labour for Thy sake.

102　　　　　　　　7.7.7.7.

FAINT not, Christian! though the road
　　Leading to Thy blest abode
Darksome be, and dang'rous too,
　　Christ, thy Guide, will bring thee
　　through.

2 Faint not, Christian! though in rage
　　Satan doth thy soul engage;
Take thee faith's anointed shield,
　　Bear it to the battle-field.

3 Faint not, Christian! though the world
　　Hath its hostile flag unfurled;
Hold the Cross of Jesus fast,
　　Thou shalt overcome at last.

4 Faint not, Christian! though within
　　There's a heart so prone to sin;
Christ, thy Lord, is over all,
　　He'll not suffer thee to fall.

5 Faint not, Christian! though thy God
　　Smite thee with the chast'ning rod;
Smite He must with Father's care,
　　That He may His love declare.

6 Faint not, Christian! Christ is near;
　　Soon in glory He'll appear;
Then shall end thy toil and strife,
　　Death be swallowed up of life.

103　　　　　　　　6.5.6.5.D.

FAIRER than the fairest
　　'Mong the sons of men,
Moral glories proved Him
　　Great beyond our ken,
In His perfect pathway
　　As on earth He trod,
Giving perfect pleasure
　　Unto Thee, His God.

2 Majesty surpassing
　　Everything below
Crowned Him with a glory
　　More than men could know;
Yet a lowly meekness,
　　Deep, and sweet, and true,
Marked Him in His movements
　　All His pathway through.

3 Comeliness excelling
   In our Lord we see,
Purest heavenly fragrance
   Flowing full and free.
He our occupation,
   We His praises sing,
And to Thee, His Father,
Raise our offering.

104 C.M.

FATHER of mercies! in Thy Word
   What endless glory shines!
For ever be Thy Name adored
   For these celestial lines.

2 Here may the wretched sons of want
   Exhaustless riches find;
Riches above what earth can grant
   And lasting as the mind.

3 Here may the blind and hungry come,
   And light and food receive;
Here shall the meanest guest have
   room,
And taste, and see, and live.

4 Here the Redeemer's welcome voice
   Spreads heavenly peace around;
And life and everlasting joys
   Attend the blissful sound.

5 Oh, may these holy pages be
   Our ever new delight!
And still new beauties may we see,
   And still increasing light.

6 Divine Instructor! gracious Lord!
   Thou art for ever near;
Teach us to love Thy sacred Word,
   And view a Saviour there.

105 C.M.

FATHER, Thy name our souls
   would bless,
As children taught by grace,
   Lift up our hearts in righteousness
And joy before Thy face.

2 Sweet is the confidence Thou giv'st,
   Though high above our praise,
Our hearts resort to where Thou liv'st
   In heaven's unclouded rays.

3 There in the purpose of Thy love
   Our place is now prepared,
As sons with Him who is above,
   Who all our sorrows shared.

4 Eternal ages shall declare
   The riches of Thy grace,
To those who with Thy Son shall share
   A son's eternal place.

5 Absent as yet, we rest in hope,
   Treading the desert path,
Waiting for Him who takes us up
   Beyond the power of death.

6 We joy in Thee, Thy holy love
   Our endless portion is,
Like Thine own Son, with Him above,
   In brightest heavenly bliss.

7 O holy Father, keep us here
   In that blest name of love,
Walking before Thee without fear
   Till all be joy above.

106 6.6.6.6.8.8.

FATHER, to seek Thy face,
   Thy children now draw near;
Before the throne of grace
   With boldness we appear;
We plead His name, His precious blood
   Who loved, and made us priests
      to God.

2 No more we shun the light,
   No more Thy presence fear;
In robes of spotless white
   Before Thee we appear;
Our great High Priest for us is there,
   And He presents our praise and
      prayer.

3 No power have we to praise
   Thy name, O God of Love;
Unless Thy Spirit raise
   Our thoughts and hearts above;
His grace avails in all our need -
   May He our priestly worship lead!

4 Lord, give us faith to plead
   Thy true and faithful Word -
Grace for each time of need,
   And help to us afford:
Thy promises in Christ are yea,
   In Him, Amen! to endless day.

107

8.7.8.7.D.

FATHER! we, Thy children, bless Thee
  For Thy love on us bestowed:
As our Father we address Thee,
  Called to be the sons of God.
Wondrous was Thy love in giving
  Jesus for our sins to die!
Wondrous was His grace in leaving,
  For our sakes, His home on high.

2 Now the sprinkled blood has freed us,
    Onward go we to our rest;
  Through the desert Thou dost lead us,
    With Thy constant favour blest -
  By Thy truth and Spirit guiding,
    Earnest He of joys to come,
  And with daily food providing,
    Thou dost lead Thy children home.

3 Though our pilgrimage be dreary,
    This is not our resting-place;
  Shall we of the way be weary -
    When we see our Master's face?
  Now, by faith anticipating,
    In this hope our souls rejoice;
  We, His promised advent waiting,
    Soon shall hear His welcome voice.

4 Father, Oh, how vast the blessing,
    When Thy Son returns again!
  Then Thy saints, their rest possessing,
    O'er the earth with Him shall reign.
  For their fathers' sakes belovèd,
    Israel, in Thy grace restored,
  Shall on earth, the curse removèd,
    Be the people of the Lord.

5 Then shall countless myriads wearing
    Robes made white in Jesus' blood,
  Palms (like rested pilgrims) bearing,
    Stand around the throne of God.
  These, redeemed from every nation,
    Shall in triumph bless Thy name;
  Every voice shall cry, "Salvation
    To our God, and to the Lamb!"

108

L.M.

FIGHT the good fight with all thy
  might;
Christ is thy strength, and Christ thy
  right;
Lay hold on life, and it shall be
  Thy joy and crown eternally.

2 Run the straight race through God's
    good grace,
  Lift up thine eyes, and seek His face;
    Life with its way before thee lies;
  Christ is the path, and Christ the prize.

3 Cast care aside; lean on thy Guide,
    His boundless mercy will provide;
  Lean, and the trusting soul shall prove
    Christ is its life, and Christ its love.

4 Faint not, nor fear; His arm is near;
    He changeth not, and thou art dear;
  Only believe, and thou shalt see
    That Christ is all in all to thee.

109

C.M.D.

FILL Thou my life, O Lord my God,
  In every part with praise,
That my whole being may proclaim
  Thy Being and Thy ways;
Not for the lip of praise alone,
  Nor e'en the praising heart,
I ask, but for a life made up
  Of praise in every part.

2 Enduring wrong, reproach, or loss,
    With sweet and steadfast will;
  Loving and blessing those who hate,
    Returning good for ill;
  Surrendering my fondest will
    In all things, great or small;
  Seeking the good of others still,
    Nor pleasing self at all.

3 So shall Thou, Lord, from me - e'en me,
    Receive the glory due;
  And so shall I begin on earth,
    The song for ever new:
  So shall no part of day or night
    From sacredness be free,
  But all my life, in every step,
    Be fellowship with Thee.

110

S.M.D.

FOR ever with the Lord!
  Amen! so let it be;
Life from the dead is in that word,
  'Tis immortality.
Here in the body pent,
  Absent from Him I roam,
Yet nightly pitch my moving tent
  A day's march nearer home.

2 My Father's house on high,
　　Home of my soul, how near
　At times to faith's foreseeing eye
　　Thy golden gates appear!
　My thirsty spirit faints
　　To reach the land I love,
　The bright inheritance of saints,
　　Jerusalem above.

3 And though there intervene,
　　Rough seas and stormy skies.
　Faith will not suffer aught to screen,
　　Thy glory from mine eyes:
　There shall all clouds depart,
　　The wilderness shall cease
　And sweetly shall each gladdened heart
　Enjoy eternal peace.

4 For ever with the Lord!
　　Father, if 'tis Thy will,
　The promise of that faithful word,
　　E'en here to me fulfil.
　Be Thou at my right hand,
　　Then can I never fail;
　Uphold Thou me, and I shall stand,
　　Fight, and I must prevail.

111
6.5.11.6.5.11.

FOR ever with Thee, Lord,
　　And like Thee to be,
For ever with Thee, at Thy coming again;
　We'll live in Thy grace, Lord,
　We'll gaze on Thy face,
　　When finished our race, at Thy
　　coming again.

2 The traits of that face, Lord,
　　Once marred through Thy grace,
　With joy we shall trace at Thy coming
　　again;
　With Thee evermore, Lord,
　　Our hearts will adore,
　Our sorrow be o'er at Thy coming
　　again.

3 We'll sit on Thy throne, Lord,
　　Confessed as Thine own,
　Of all to be known at Thy coming
　　again.
　But glory on high, Lord,
　　Is not like being nigh,
　When all is gone by, at Thy coming
　　again.

112
7.7.7.6.

FOR the bread and for the wine,
　　For the pledge that seals
Him mine,
　For the words of love divine,
　We give Thee thanks, O Lord.

2 Only bread and only wine,
　　Yet to faith the solemn sign
Of the heavenly and divine!
　　We give Thee thanks, O Lord.

3 For the words that turn our eye
　　To the Cross of Calvary,
Bidding us in faith draw nigh,
　　We give Thee thanks, O Lord.

4 For the words that fragrance breathe,
　　These plain symbols underneath,
Words that His own peace bequeath,
　　We give Thee thanks, O Lord.

5 For the words that tell of home,
　　Pointing us beyond the tomb,
"Do ye this, until I come!"
　　We give Thee thanks, O Lord.

6 Till He come we take the bread,
　　Type of Him on whom we feed,
Him who liveth and was dead!
　　We give Thee thanks, O Lord.

7 Till He come we take the cup;
　　As we at His table sup
Eye and heart are lifted up!
　　We give Thee thanks, O Lord.

8 For that coming, here foreshown,
　　For that day to man unknown,
For the glory and the throne,
　　We give Thee thanks, O Lord.

113
8.8.8.6.

FORTH from Gabbatha see Him led,
　　Foes all around and friends all fled,
Wearing the thorns upon His head,
　　Holy and righteous One!

2 Knowing the sorrow of the way,
　　Facing it all unflinchingly,
Moving through all obediently,
　　Patient, submissive One!

3 On to Golgotha and the tree,
　　Uplifted in the midst to be,
Love there to show beyond degree,
　　God's well-belovèd One!

4 Men all their enmity there show,
　　Railing and insult fiercer grow;
　Tempest and flood uprise and flow
　　Against the sinless One!

5 Pressure intense reveals anew
　　Inner perfections gleaming through;
　As in His path, for God so true,
　　Still the devoted One!

6 Issues momentous now fulfilled,
　　Stripped every foe, the tumult stilled,
　Thus would He die, as God had willed,
　　Ever triumphant One!

114
6.6.6.6.8.8.

FORTH in His Name we go,
　　A royal priesthood now,
His excellence to show,
　　To Whom as Lord we bow;
From darkness called to
　　wondrous light,
The sons of day amidst the night.

2 Bearing the torch on high,
　　We go not forth in vain,
For men in darkness die,
　　In darkness to remain.
They know not Him Who is the light,
　　Their sun goes down in endless
　　night.

3 Praying for grace to live
　　As fits a royal race,
We seek to men to give
　　The light of truth and grace:
His Name to bear, His will obey,
　　His steps to follow day by day.

4 Forth in His Name we go,
　　In royal dignity,
His excellence to show
　　In what we do and say :
To tread by faith the path He trod,
　　A royal priesthood unto God.

115
S.M. with Chorus

FROM Egypt lately come,
　　Where death and darkness reign,
We seek our new, our better home,
　　Where we our rest shall gain:

　　Hallelujah!
　　We are on our way to God!

2 There sin and sorrow cease,
　　And every conflict's o'er;
There shall we dwell in endless
　　peace,
And never hunger more -

3 There, in celestial strains,
　　Enraptured myriads sing;
There love in every bosom reigns,
　　For God Himself is King -

4 We soon shall join the throng,
　　Their pleasures we shall share,
And sing the everlasting song,
　　With all the ransomed there -

5 How sweet the prospect is!
　　It cheers the pilgrim's breast;
We're journeying through the
　　wilderness,
But soon shall gain our rest -

116
L.M.

FROM every stormy wind that blows,
　　From every swelling tide of woes,
There is a calm, a safe retreat;
　　'Tis found beneath the Mercy-seat.

2 There is a place where Jesus sheds
　　The oil of gladness on our heads,
A place than all beside more sweet;
　　It is the blood-stained Mercy-seat.

3 There is a spot where spirits blend,
　　Where friend holds fellowship
　　with friend;
Though sundered far, by faith we meet
　　Around one common Mercy-seat.

4 Ah! whither could we flee for aid,
　　When tempted, desolate, dismayed,
Or how the hosts of hell defeat,
　　Had suff'ring saints no Mercy-seat?

5 There, there on eagle-wing we soar,
　　And time and sense appear no more;
There heav'nly joys our spirits greet,
　　And glory crowns the Mercy-seat.

6 Oh, let my hand forget her skill,
    My tongue be silent, cold and still,
This bounding heart forget to beat,
    If I forget the Mercy-seat.

117   4.6.8.8.4.

FROM heaven He came
    Into this scene of shame,
Thy will to do, Thy claims to own,
    Thy law fulfil, Thyself make known;
From heaven He came.

2 To heaven He's gone;
    The throne He sits upon.
Death He annulled. His vict'ry won,
    His work complete - Triumphant One!
To heaven He's gone.

3 In heaven He dwells;
    He all our fear dispels;
As Great High Priest appearing there,
    As Lord and Christ for us to care
In heaven He dwells.

4 From heaven He'll come
    To take His people home.
He came; He's gone; He dwells above;
    And soon for us in wondrous love
From heaven He'll come.

118   C.M.

FROM Salem's gates advancing slow,
    What object meets my eyes,
What means that majesty of woe,
    What mean those mingled cries?

2 Who is the man that groans beneath
    The pond'rous Cross of wood,
Whose soul's oppressed with pangs
    of death,
And body bathed in blood?

3 Is this the man! Can this be He
    The prophets have foretold,
Should with transgressors
    number'd be,
And for my crimes be sold?

4 Yes, now I know, 'tis He, 'tis He,
    E'en Jesus, God's dear Son,
Wrapt in mortality to die,
    For crimes that I have done.

5 Ah, lovely sight! A heavenly form
    For sinful souls to see,
I'll creep beside Him as a worm,
    And see Him die for me.

119   8.8.6.8.8.6.

FROM whence this fear and unbelief,
    If God, my Father, put to grief
His spotless Son for me?
    Can He, the righteous Judge of men,
Condemn me for that debt of sin
    Which, Lord, was charged to Thee?

2 Complete atonement Thou hast made,
    And to the utmost farthing paid
Whate'er Thy people owed;
    How, then, can wrath *on me* take
        place,
    If sheltered in God's righteousness,
And sprinkled by Thy blood?

3 If Thou hast my discharge procured,
    And freely in my place endured
The whole of wrath divine;
    Payment God will not twice demand,
First at my bleeding Surety's hand,
    And then again at mine.

4 Turn then, my soul, unto thy rest;
    The merits of thy great High Priest
Speak peace and liberty;
    Trust in His efficacious blood,
Nor fear thy banishment from God,
    Since Jesus died for thee.

120   7.6.7.6.D.

GARDEN of gloom appalling,
    Where, in His sore amaze,
Earthward in anguish falling,
    Prostrate, the Saviour prays;
Prays in exceeding sorrow,
    Prays, on the ground bowed low
Facing the dark tomorrow
    Full of unfathomed woe!

2 Garden of grief amazing,
    Where, in His agony,
He, His petition raising,
    Prays yet more earnestly,
Prays till His sweat is falling,
    Falling like drops of blood!
Deep unto deep is calling,
    Calling in flood to flood.

3 Garden of tears that never
    Mortal could ever weep!
Not of the common river;
    Drawn from a deeper deep!
Drawn from a depth unsounded,
    Coursing toward the sod,
Telling of love unbounded,
    Sourced in the heart of God!

4 Garden of myrrh unfading,
    Breathing submissive prayer,
Sweet-flowing myrrh, pervading
    Heaven with its fragrance rare!
Myrrh that perfumes our praises,
    Fresh from the tear-wet clod,
Softly the heart upraises
    To Thee, His Father, God.

121   C.M.

GATHERED again to break the bread
    This first day of the week,
We, by the Holy Spirit led,
    Thy face, O God, would seek.

2 No earth-born sentiment inspires,
    No fleshly zeal imparts
The touch that stirs the sacred fires
    In musing, priestly hearts.

3 Here, in the pow'r that ever lives,
    The light that never dies,
The estimate the Spirit gives
    Moves priestly exercise.

4 Thus, in the Holies, we, O God,
    Would unto Thee draw near
To give Thee thanks for Him Who trod
    That perfect path while here.

5 Thus, while our hearts within us burn,
    Rememb'ring rev'rently,
We, in His holy Name, return
    Thanksgivings unto Thee.

122   8.5.8.3.

GATHERED, Lord, around Thy table,
    Now we seek Thy face;
Let us know Thy presence with us,
    Lord of grace.

2 Love divine first drew us to Thee
    In our sin and need;
For our sin, in deep compassion,
    Thou didst bleed.

3 Risen Lord, in glory seated,
    We are one with Thee;
Thou hast snapt the chains that
    bound us:
        We are free.

4 Gratefully we Thee remember
    As we break the bread,
Symbol of Thy body broken
    In our stead.

5 Drink we too the cup of blessing
    Which Thy love has filled;
Through Thy blood we have
    redemption:
        Fears are stilled.

6 Backward look we, drawn to Calvary,
    Musing while we sing;
Forward haste we to Thy coming,
    Lord and King.

123   8.7.8.7.

GATHERED to Thy name, Lord
    Jesus,
Losing sight of all but Thee,
    O what joy Thy presence gives us,
Calling up our hearts to Thee.

2 Loved with love which knows no
    measure
Save the Father's love to Thee,
    Blessèd Lord, our hearts would
    treasure
All the Father's thoughts of Thee.

3 All His joy, His rest, His pleasure,
    All His deep delight in Thee;
Lord, Thy heart alone can measure
    What Thy Father found in Thee.

4 How He set His love upon Thee,
    Called Thee His belovèd Son;
Yet for us He did not spare Thee,
    By Thy death our life was won.

5 O the joy, the wondrous singing
    When we see Thee as Thou art;
Thy blest name, Lord Jesus,
    bringing
Sweetest music to God's heart.

6 Notes of gladness, songs unceasing,
    Hymns of everlasting praise,
Psalms of glory, joy increasing
    Through God's endless day of days.

124   8.7.8.7.

G AZING on Thee, Lord, in glory,
    While our hearts in worship bow,
There we read the wondrous story
    Of the Cross, its shame and woe.

2 Every mark of dark dishonour
    Heaped upon Thy thorn-crowned
        brow,
All the depths of Thy heart's sorrow
    Told in answering glory now.

3 On that Cross, alone, forsaken,
    Where no pitying eye was found;
Now to God's right hand exalted,
    With Thy praise the heavens
        resound.

4 Did Thy God e'en then forsake Thee,
    Hide His face from Thy deep need?
In Thy face, once marred and smitten,
    All His glory now we read.

5 Gazing on it we adore Thee,
    Blessèd, precious, holy Lord;
Thou, the Lamb, art ever worthy;
    This be earth's and heaven's accord.

6 Rise our hearts, and bless the Father,
    Ceaseless song e'en here begun,
Endless praise and adoration
    To the Father and the Son.

125   S.M.

G ENTLY they took Him down;
    Unfixed His hands and feet;
Took from His head the thorny
    crown;
Brought forth a winding sheet.

2 Fine linen, fitly made,
    Wrapped they around His face;
Where never man before was laid
    Made they His resting-place.

3 Spices most sweet they chose;
    Aloes they brought, and myrrh;
Wound Him with these in linen clothes;
    Gave Him a sepulchre;

4 Laid Him in hewn rock;
    Rolled to the door the stone;
Watched the world add its waxen lock,
    And left Him there alone.

5 Dead in a garden gay!
    Dead, with the wanton bloom
Giving, in incongruity,
    Last touches to His tomb!

126   P.M.

G IVE me a sight, O Saviour,
    Of Thy wondrous love to me,
Of the love that brought Thee
    down to earth
To die on Calvary.

    Oh, make me understand it!
      Help me to take it in,
    What it meant to Thee, the Holy One,
      To bear away my sin.

2 Was it the nails, O Saviour,
    That bound Thee to the tree?
Nay, 'twas Thine everlasting love,
    Thy love for me, for me.

3 Oh, wonder of all wonders,
    That through Thy death for me,
My open sins, my secret sins,
    Can all forgiven be.

4 Then melt my heart, O Saviour,
    Bend me, yea, break me down,
Until I own Thee Conqueror,
    And Lord and Sovereign crown.

127   8.7.8.7.4.7.

G LORY, glory everlasting,
    Be to Him who bore the Cross,
Who redeemed our souls by tasting
    Death, the death deserved by us!
        Spread His glory,
Who redeemed His people thus.

2 His is love, 'tis love unbounded,
  Without measure, without end;
Human thought is here confounded,
  'Tis too vast to comprehend!
      Praise the Saviour!
Magnify the sinner's Friend.

3 Dwelling on the wondrous story
    Of the Saviour's Cross and shame,
Sing we, "Everlasting glory
    Be to God and to the Lamb!"
        Saints and angels,
    Give ye glory to His name!

128   8.7.8.7.D.

G LORY, Lord, is Thine for ever,
    Ever Thine - Thou art the Son!
Great the glory Thou art given,
    Great the glory Thou hast won;
Great the glory and the splendour
    Of the holy heavenly place;
Greater far the Godhead glory
    Shining, Saviour, in Thy face!

2 Lord of glory, Thou didst enter
    This dark world of sin and woe;
Veiled Thy glory, yet 'twas witnessed
    By Thine own while here below.
Thou didst die, and now we
    praise Thee
In Thy glory, Lord, above;
    For in death Thou hast declarèd
All the fulness of God's love.

3 Yes, we see Thee crowned with glory,
    Highest honour to Thee given;
But the glory of Thy Person
    Is the light that shines in heaven.
Thou art greater, glorious Saviour,
    Than the glory Thou hast won;
This the greatness of Thy glory -
    Ever blest - Thou art the Son!

129   6.6.4.6.6.6.4.

G LORY to God on high!
    Peace upon earth and joy!
Good will to man!
    We who God's blessings prove,
Join with the hosts above
    To praise the Saviour's love,
        Too vast to scan.

2 Mercy and truth unite;
    Oh, 'tis a wondrous sight,
All sights above!
    Jesus the curse sustains!
Bitter the cup He drains!
    Nothing for us remains,
        Nothing but love.

3 Love that no tongue can teach,
    Love that no thought can reach,
No love like His!
    God is its blessèd source,
Death ne'er can stop its course,
    Nothing can stay its force,
        Matchless it is.

4 Blest in this love we sing,
    To God our praises bring,
All sins forgiven!
    Jesus, our Lord, to Thee
Honour and majesty
    Now and for ever be
        Here, and in heaven.

130   10.4.10.4.10.10.

G LORY to Thee; Thou Son of God
    most High,
        All praise to Thee!
Glory to Thee, enthroned above the
    sky,
        Who died for me;
High on Thy throne, Thine ear, Lord
    Jesus, bend
As grateful hearts now to Thyself
    ascend.

2 Deep were Thy sorrows, Lord,
    when heaven frowned -
        Gethsemane!
    Bloodlike Thy sweat, Lord, falling
        to the ground
            So heavily;
    Dark was the night, but heaven
        was darker still,
O Christ my God! - is this the
    Father's will?

3 Thorns wreathed Thy brow when
    hanging on the tree,
        Man's cruelty!
    Why lavish love like this, O Lord,
        on me?
            Thou lovest me!

Would that my soul could understand
　　its length,
Its breadth, depth, height, and
　　everlasting strength!

4 Thy precious blood was freely shed
　　for me
　　　　On Calvary
To save me from a lost eternity;
　　　　Glory to Thee!
Nor death, nor hell, nor things
　　below - above
Can sever me from Thy eternal love.

5 Like shoreless seas, Thy love can
　　know no bound;
　　　　Thou lovest me!
Deep, vast, immense, unfathomed,
　　Lord - profound,
　　　　Lord, I love Thee!
And when above, my crown is at
　　Thy feet,
I'll praise Thee still for Calvary's
　　mercy seat.

131   7.7.7.7.

G LORY unto Jesus be!
　　From the curse He set us free;
All our guilt on Him was laid,
　　He the ransom fully paid.

2 All the blessèd work is done;
　　God's well pleasèd in His Son;
He has raised Him from the dead,
　　Set Him over all as Head.

3 All should sing His work and worth,
　　All above, and all on earth;
As they sing around the throne,
　　"Thou art worthy, Thou alone".

4 Ye who love Him, cease to mourn,
　　He will certainly return;
All His saints with Him shall reign -
　　"Come, Lord Jesus, come! Amen."

132   L.M.

G O, labour on; spend, and be spent,
　　Thy joy to do the Father's will;
It is the way the Master went,
　　Should not the servant tread it still?

2 Go, labour on; 'tis not for naught;
　　Thy earthly loss is heavenly gain;
Men heed thee, love thee, praise
　　thee, not;
The Master praises - what are men?

3 Go, labour on; enough, while here,
　　If He shall praise thee, if He deign
The willing heart to mark and cheer;
　　No toil for Him shall be in vain.

4 Go, labour on; your hands are weak,
　　Your knees are faint, your soul
　　cast down;
Yet falter not; the prize you seek
　　Is near - a kingdom and a crown!

5 Go, labour on, while it is day,
　　The world's dark night is
　　　hastening on;
Speed, speed thy work, cast sloth
　　away;
It is not thus that souls are won.

6 Men die in darkness at your side,
　　Without a hope to cheer the tomb;
Take up the torch and wave it wide,
　　The torch that lights time's
　　　thickest gloom.

7 Toil on, faint not, keep watch and
　　pray;
Be wise the erring soul to win;
　　Go forth into the world's highway,
Compel the wanderer to come in.

8 Toil on, and in thy toil rejoice;
　　For toil comes rest, for exile home;
Soon shalt thou hear the
　　Bridegroom's voice,
The midnight peal, Behold, I come!

133   P.M.

G OD hath not promised skies
　　always blue,
Flower-strewn pathways all our
　　lives through;
God hath not promised sun
　　without rain,
Joy without sorrow, peace without
　　pain.

But God hath promised strength
for the day,
Rest for the labour, light for the way;
Grace for the trials, help from
above,
Unfailing sympathy, undying love.

2 God hath not promised we shall
not know
Toil and temptation, trouble and woe;
He hath not told us we shall not
bear
Many a burden, many a care.

3 God hath not promised smooth
roads and wide,
Swift, easy travel, needing no guide;
Never a mountain, rocky and steep,
Never a river, turbid and deep.

134
8.4.8.8.4.

G OD holds the key of all unknown,
And I am glad;
If other hands should hold the key,
Or if He trusted it to me,
I might be sad, I might be sad.

2 What if tomorrow's cares were here
Without its rest!
I'd rather He unlocked the day;
And, as the hours swing open, say,
My will is best, My will is best.

3 The very dimness of my sight
Makes me secure;
For, groping in my misty way,
I feel His hand; I hear Him say,
My help is sure, My help is sure.

4 I cannot read His future plans;
But this I know;
I have the smiling of His face,
And all the refuge of His grace,
While here below, while here below.

5 Enough! this covers all my wants,
And so I rest!
For what I cannot, He can see,
And in His care I saved shall be,
Forever blest, forever blest.

135
C.M.

G OD moves in a mysterious way,
His wonders to perform;
He plants His footsteps in the sea,
And rides upon the storm.

2 Deep in unfathomable mines,
Of never-failing skill,
He treasures up His bright designs,
And works His sovereign will.

3 Ye fearful saints, fresh courage take;
The clouds ye so much dread,
Are big with mercy, and shall break,
In blessings on your head.

4 Judge not the Lord by feeble sense,
But trust Him for His grace;
Behind a frowning providence,
He hides a smiling face.

5 His purposes will ripen fast,
Unfolding every hour;
The bud may have a bitter taste,
But sweet will be the flower.

6 Blind unbelief is sure to err,
And scan His work in vain;
God is His own interpreter,
And He will make it plain.

136
P.M.

G OD sent His Son, they called
Him Jesus;
He came to love, heal and forgive;
He lived and died to buy my pardon,
An empty grave is there to prove
my Saviour lives!

Because He lives,
I can face tomorrow,
Because He lives,
All fear is gone;
Because I know,
He holds the future
And life is worth the living,
Just because He lives!

2 How sweet to hold a newborn baby
And feel the pride and joy he
brings;
But greater still the calm assurance:
This child can face uncertain
days because He lives.

3 And then one day, I'll cross the river
I'll fight life's final war with pain
And then, as death gives way
to victory,
I'll see the lights of glory and I'll
know He lives.

137
8.4.8.4.8.8.8.4.

GOD'S almighty arms are round me,
  Peace, peace is mine!
Judgment scenes need not
  confound me,
Peace, peace is mine!
  Jesus came Himself and sought me;
Slave of sin, He found and bought me;
  Then my blessèd freedom taught
    me,
Peace, peace is mine!

2 While I hear life's surging billows,
    Peace, peace is mine!
Why suspend my harp on willows?
    Peace, peace is mine!
I may sing with Christ beside me,
    Though a thousand ills betide me:
Safely He hath sworn to guide me,
    Peace, peace is mine!

3 Every trial draws Him nearer,
    Peace, peace is mine!
All His strokes but make Him dearer,
    Peace, peace is mine!
Bless I then the hand that smiteth
    And in grace to heal delighteth;
'Tis against my sins He fighteth,
    Peace, peace is mine!

4 Welcome! ev'ry morning sunlight,
    Peace, peace is mine!
Nearer home each passing
  midnight,
    Peace, peace is mine!
Death and hell cannot appal me,
    Safe in Christ whate'er befall me,
Calmly wait I, till He call me,
    Peace, peace is mine!

138
7.6.7.6.D.

GOLGOTHA'S scene recalling,
  With reverence we view
His sorrow so appalling,
  His love devoted, true.
Impressions freshly gleaning
  Of matchless worth and grace,
Some glimpses of its meaning
  We, by the Spirit, trace.

2 His friends have fled in trembling;
  His foes in rage abound,
Tumultuously assembling,
  The evil hosts surround;
What grace He shows in bearing
  Derision, shame, and scorn!
What meekness His, in wearing
  The crown of piercing thorn!

3 His heavenly wisdom ever
  In fulness shineth clear;
His holy zeal was never
  More manifest than here.
The grace within Him dwelling,
  Revealed at such a time,
With emphasis most telling,
  His character sublime.

4 Unblemished life's fruition,
  Unique and fitting crown
He, of His own volition,
  That precious life lays down.
Death of a Cross the measure
  Of His obedience still -
To give the Father pleasure
  And do the Father's will!

139
S.M.

GRACE! 'tis a charming sound,
  Harmonious to the ear;
Heaven with the echo shall resound,
  And all the earth shall hear.

2 Grace first contrived the way
  To save rebellious man;
And all the steps that grace display,
  Which drew the wondrous plan.

3 'Twas grace that wrote my name
  In life's eternal book;
'Twas grace that gave me to the Lamb,
  Who all my sorrows took.

4 Grace taught my wandering feet
  To tread the heavenly road;
And new supplies each hour I meet,
  While pressing on to God.

5 Grace saved us from the foe
  Grace taught us how to pray
And God will ne'er His grace forego
  Till we have won the day.

6 Grace taught my soul to pray,
  And made my eyes o'erflow;
'Tis grace has kept me to this day,
  And will not let me go.

7 O let Thy grace inspire
  My soul with strength divine;
May all my powers to Thee aspire,
  And all my days be Thine.

8 Grace all the work shall crown
  Through everlasting days;
It lays in heaven the topmost stone,
  And well deserves the praise.

140

7.7.7.6.

GRACIOUS God, we worship Thee,
  Reverently we bow the knee;
Jesus Christ our only plea;
  Father, we adore Thee.

2 Vast Thy love, how deep, how wide,
  In the gift of Him who died;
Righteous claims all satisfied;
  Father, we adore Thee.

3 Low we bow before Thy face,
  Sons of God, O wondrous place!
Great the riches of Thy grace;
  Father, we adore Thee.

4 By Thy Spirit grant that we
  Worshippers in truth may be;
Praise, as incense sweet to Thee;
  Father, we adore Thee.

5 Yet again our song we raise,
  Note of deep adoring praise;
Now, and soon through endless days;
  Father, we adore Thee.

141

8.8.8.8.8.8.

GREAT God of wonders! all Thy ways
  Display Thine attributes divine;
But the bright glories of Thy grace
  Above Thine other wonders shine:
Who is a pardoning God like Thee?
  Or who has grace so rich and free?

2 Such deep transgressions to forgive!
  Such guilty, daring worms to spare!
This is Thy grand prerogative,
  And in this honour none shall share:
Who is a pardoning God like Thee?
  Or who has grace so rich and free?

3 Pardon, from an offended God!
  Pardon, for sins of deepest dye!
Pardon, bestowed through Jesus' blood!
  Pardon, that brings the rebel nigh!
Who is a pardoning God like Thee?
  Or who has grace so rich and free?

142

C.M.

GREAT God, with wonder and
  with praise
On all Thy works I look;
  But still Thy wisdom, power, and
    grace
Shine brighter in Thy Book.

2 The stars, which in their courses roll,
  Have much instruction given;
But Thy good Word informs my soul
  How I may rise to heaven.

3 The fields provide me food, and show
  The goodness of the Lord;
But fruits of life and glory grow
  In Thy most holy Word.

4 Here are my choicest treasures hid,
  Here my best comfort lies,
Here my desires are satisfied,
  And hence my hopes arise.

5 Lord, make me understand Thy law:
  Show what my faults have been;
And from the Gospel let me draw
  Pardon for all my sin.

6 Here would I learn how Christ has died,
  To save my soul from hell;
Not all the books on earth beside
  Such heavenly wonders tell.

7 Then let me love my Bible more;
  And take a fresh delight
By day to read these wonders o'er,
  And meditate by night.

143

P.M.

"GREAT is Thy faithfulness",
  O God my Father,
There is no shadow of turning
  with Thee;
Thou changest not,
  Thy compassions, they fail not:
As Thou hast been,
  Thou forever wilt be.

"Great is Thy faithfulness!"
"Great is Thy faithfulness!"
  Morning by morning new
    mercies I see;
All I have needed Thy hand hath
  provided -
"Great is Thy faithfulness", Lord,
  unto me!

2 Summer and winter, and
  springtime and harvest,
Sun, moon and stars in their
  courses above,
Join with all nature in manifold witness
  To Thy great faithfulness, mercy
    and love.

3 Pardon for sin and a peace that
    endureth,
Thine own dear presence to
    cheer and to guide;
Strength for today and bright
    hope for tomorrow,
Blessings all mine, with ten
    thousand beside!

144   6.6.6.6.8.8.

GREAT Shepherd of the sheep!
  Brought forth from death's domain,
He all His flock shall keep,
    Their every cause maintain.
This hope imbues their hearts with
    cheer -
Soon the Chief Shepherd will appear!

2 On high, within the veil,
    Hath Jesus entered in;
His priesthood cannot fail,
    'Tis He preserves from sin.
Forerunner there - a proof that we
    With Him in glory soon shall be!

3 "The Lord Himself" - blest word! -
    From heaven shall descend;
The dead in Christ bestirred
    With living ones ascend.
Soon shall the quick'ning shout
    resound,
Gath'ring His own from utmost bound!

4 Blest moment, when we rise
    From sinful scenes below!
Blest hope that purifies,
    That sets our hearts aglow!
"Like Him", through all-surpassing
    grace,
"With Him", before the Father's face!

145   L.M.

GREAT Shepherd of Thy chosen
  flock,
Thy people's shield, their shadowing
    rock,
Once more we meet to hear Thy voice,
    Once more before Thee to rejoice.

2 Now may Thy Spirit, by the Word,
    Refresh each wearied heart, O Lord,
Wearied of earth's vain strife and
    woe,
And longing more Thyself to know.

3 Thine is the heart our griefs to feel,
    And Thine the love each wound
    to heal;
Home Thou art gone for us to care,
    Returning soon to take us there.

146   8.7.8.7.4.7.

GUIDE us, O Thou great Jehovah,
  Pilgrims through this barren land;
We are weak, but Thou art mighty;
    Hold us by Thy powerful hand:
        Bread of heaven!
Feed us now and evermore.

2 Open wide the living fountain
    Whence the healing waters flow;
Be Thyself our cloudy pillar
    All the dreary desert through:
        Strong Deliverer!
Be Thou still our strength and shield.

3 While we tread this vale of sorrow
    May we in Thy love abide;
Keep us, O our gracious Saviour!
    Cleaving closely to Thy side:
        Still relying
On our Father's changeless love.

4 Saviour, come! we long to see Thee,
    Long to dwell with Thee above;
And to know, in full communion,
    All the sweetness of Thy love:
        Come, Lord Jesus!
Take Thy waiting people home.

147   L.M.

HAIL, sovereign love, that first began
  The scheme to rescue fallen man;
Hail, matchless, free, eternal grace,
    That gave my soul a hiding place.

2 Against the God who rules the sky,
    I fought with hands uplifted high;
Despised the mention of His grace,
    Too proud to seek a hiding place.

3 Enwrapped in thick Egyptian night,
    And fond of darkness more that light,
Madly I ran the sinful race,
    Secure without a hiding place.

4 But lo! the eternal counsel rang,
    "Almighty love, arrest that man!"

I felt the arrows of distress,
  And found I had no hiding place!

5 Indignant justice stood in view,
    To Sinai's fiery mount I flew;
  But justice cried with frowning face,
    "This mountain is no hiding place!"

6 But lo! a heavenly voice I heard,
    And mercy's angel soon appeared:
  Who led me on a pleasing pace,
    To Jesus Christ, my hiding place!

7 Should storms of sevenfold
      vengeance roll,
  And shake this globe from pole to pole:
    No thunder-bolt shall daunt my face,
  While Jesus is my hiding place!

8 On Him almighty vengeance fell,
    Which must have sunk a world
      to hell
  He bore it for a sinful race,
    And thus became their hiding place.

9 A few more rolling suns at most
    Shall land me safe on heaven's
      coast,
  There I shall sing the song of grace
    To Jesus Christ, my hiding place!

3 Saviour, hail! amid the glory,
    Where for us Thou dost abide;
  We, by faith, do now adore Thee,
    Seated at Thy Father's side.
  There, for us, Thou now art pleading
    While Thou dost our place prepare;
  For Thy saints still interceding,
    Till in glory we appear.

4 Worship, honour, praise and
      blessing,
  Thou shalt then from all receive;
    Loudest praises, without ceasing,
  All that earth or heaven can give:
    In that day Thy saints will meet
      Thee,
  Welcome Thee with grateful song;
    Joyful hearts will ever greet Thee,
  Source of joy to all the throng.

5 Soon we shall, with those in glory,
    His transcendent grace relate;
  Gladly sing th' amazing story
    Of His dying love so great:
  In that blessèd contemplation,
    We for evermore shall dwell,
  Crown'd with bliss and consolation,
    Such as none below can tell.

148   8.7.8.7.D.
HAIL, Thou once despisèd Jesus!
    Hail, Thou still rejected King!
Thou didst suffer to release us,
    Thou didst free salvation bring;
Through Thy death and resurrection,
    Bearer of our sin and shame!
We enjoy divine protection,
    Life and glory through Thy name.

2 Paschal Lamb, by God appointed,
    All our sins on Thee were laid;
By our Father's love anointed,
    Thou hast full atonement made:
All who trust Thee are forgiven
    Through the virtue of Thy blood;
Rent in Thee the veil of heaven,
    Grace shines forth to man from
      God.

149   7.6.7.6.D
HAIL to the Lord's Anointed,
    Great David's greater Son!
Hail, in the time appointed,
    His reign on earth begun;
He comes to break oppression,
    To set the captive free;
To take away transgression
    And rule in equity.

2 He shall come down like showers
    Upon the fruitful earth:
And love, joy, hope, like flowers,
    Spring in His path to birth;
Before Him on the mountains
    Shall peace, the herald, go;
And righteousness in fountains
    From hill to valley flow.

3 Kings shall fall down before Him,
 And gold and incense bring;
All nations shall adore Him,
 His praise all people sing:
For He shall have dominion
 O'er river, sea, and shore,
Far as the eagle's pinion
 Or dove's light wing can soar.

4 For Him shall prayer unceasing,
 And daily vows ascend;
His kingdom still increasing,
 A kingdom without end:
The mountain-dews shall nourish
 A seed in weakness sown,
Whose fruit shall spread and flourish,
 And shake like Lebanon.

5 O'er every foe victorious
 He on His throne shall rest;
From age to age more glorious,
 All-blessing and all-blest:
The tide of time shall never
 His covenant remove;
His Name shall stand for ever,
 That Name to us is - Love.

150   8.7.8.7.8.8.8.6.
HALLELUJAH! Hallelujah!
 Let the heavens declare His Name;
Let the highest heights of Glory
 All His majesty proclaim.
Let His angels all adore Him;
 Ye His hosts fall down before Him;
Hallelujah! Hallelujah!
 Praise His Name! Praise His Name!

2 Sun and moon repeat the story,
 Tell His praise, ye stars of light;
Let the heavens in all their splendour
 Evermore extol His might.
He hath 'stablished them for ever;
 His decree it faileth never.
Hallelujah! Hallelujah!
 Praise His Name! Praise His Name!

3 Let the earth and teeming ocean
 Join their voice the strain to swell;
Let the elements that serve Him
 His supremacy forthtell.
Lofty peaks of rugged feature;
 Fruitful fields, yea, every creature:
Hallelujah! Hallelujah!
 Praise His Name ! Praise His Name!

4 Kings and peoples, bend before Him;
 Rulers, hail the only Lord;
Young and old, the youth, the maiden,
 To His Name the praise accord.
Name sublime! Alone excelling
 All in earth or heaven dwelling!
Hallelujah! Hallelujah!
 Praise His Name! Praise His Name!

5 Mighty chorus, mingling, blending,
 Hear its cadence rise and fall!
Ye His saints, can ye be silent,
 Ye who owe Him most of all?
Ye, of all His creatures nighest,
 Well may raise your notes the
 highest.
Hallelujah! Hallelujah!
 Praise His Name! Praise His Name!

151   8.7.8.7.4.7.
HAPPY they who trust in Jesus!
 Sweet their portion is, and sure;
When the foe on others seizes,
 He will keep His own secure:
 Happy people!
Happy, though despised and poor.

2 Since His love and mercy found us
 We are precious in His sight;
Thousands now may fall around us,
 Thousands more be put to flight;
 But His presence
 Keeps us safe by day and night.

3 Lo! our Saviour never slumbers;
 Ever watchful is His care:
Though we cannot boast of numbers,
 In His strength secure we are:
 Sweet their portion
Who the Saviour's kindness share.

4 As the bird, beneath her feathers,
 Guards the objects of her care,
So the Lord His children gathers,
 Spreads His wings and hides
 them there:
 Thus protected
All their foes they boldly dare.

152   7.7.7.7.
HARK! my soul, it is the Lord;
 'Tis thy Saviour! hear His word;
Jesus speaks, and speaks to thee:
 "Say, poor sinner, lov'st thou Me?"

2 "I delivered thee when bound,
    And when wounded, healed thy
        wound;
  Sought thee wand'ring, set thee right,
    Turned thy darkness into light."

3 "Can a woman's tender care
    Cease towards the child she bare?
  Yes, she may forgetful be,
    Yet will I remember thee."

4 "Mine is an unchanging love,
    Higher than the heights above,
  Deeper than the depths beneath,
    Free and faithful, strong as death."

5 "Thou shalt see My glory soon
    When the work of grace is done;
  Partner of My throne shalt be:
    Say, poor sinner, lov'st thou Me?"

6 Lord, it is my chief complaint
    That my love is cold and faint;
  Yet I love Thee, and adore;
    O for grace to love Thee more.

153   8.7.8.7.

HARK! ten thousand voices crying,
    "Lamb of God!" with one accord;
Thousand, thousand saints replying,
    Wake at once the echoing chord.

2 "Praise the Lamb", the chorus waking,
    All in heaven together throng,
  Loud and far, each tongue partaking,
    Rolls along the endless song.

3 Grateful incense this, ascending
    Ever to the Father's throne;
  Every knee to Jesus bending,
    All the mind in heaven is one.

4 All the Father's counsels claiming
    Equal honours to the Son;
  All the Son's effulgence beaming
    Makes the Father's glory known.

5 By the Spirit all pervading,
    Hosts unnumbered round the Lamb,
  Crowned with light and joy unfading,
    Hail Him as the great I AM.

6 Joyful now the new creation
    Rests in undisturbed repose;
  Blest in Jesus' full salvation,
    Sorrow now, nor thraldom knows.

7 Hark! still louder swells the singing,
    As the notes are heard again;
  Through creation's vault is ringing
    Joy's response, "Amen! Amen!"

154   7.7.7.7.D. with Chorus

HARK! the herald angels sing,
    "Glory to the newborn King,
Peace on earth, and mercy mild,
    God and sinners reconciled!"
Joyful, all ye nations, rise,
    Join the triumph of the skies;
With the angelic host proclaim,
    "Christ is born in Bethlehem!"

Hark! the herald angels sing,
    "Glory to the newborn King!"

2 Christ, by highest heaven adored,
    Christ, the everlasting Lord,
  Late in time behold Him come,
    Offspring of a virgin's womb;
  Veiled in flesh the Godhead see;
    Hail, the Incarnate Deity,
  Pleased as Man with man to dwell,
    Jesus our Immanuel.

3 Hail, the heavenly Prince of Peace!
    Hail, the Sun of Righteousness!
  Light and life to all He brings,
    Risen with healing in His wings;
  Mild, He lays His glory by,
    Born that man no more may die,
  Born to raise the sons of earth,
    Born to give them second birth.

155   6.4.6.4.6.7.6.4.

HARK! 'tis the watchman's cry,
    Wake, brethren, wake!
Jesus, our Lord, is nigh;
    Wake, brethren, wake!
Sleep is for sons of night;
    Ye are children of the light,
Yours is the glory bright;
    Wake, brethren, wake!

2 Call to each waking band,
   Watch, brethren, watch!
   Clear is our Lord's command;
   Watch, brethren, watch!
   Be ye as men that wait
     Always at their Master's gate,
     E'en though the hour seem late;
   Watch, brethren, watch!

3 Heed we the steward's call,
   Work, brethren, work!
   There's room enough for all;
   Work, brethren, work!
   This vineyard of the Lord
     Constant labour will afford;
   Yours is a sure reward;
   Work, brethren, work!

4 Hear we the Shepherd's voice,
   Pray, brethren, pray!
   Would ye His heart rejoice?
   Pray, brethren, pray!
   Sin calls for constant fear,
     Weakness needs the strong
       One near,
     Long as ye struggle here;
   Pray, brethren, pray!

5 Now sound the final chord,
   Praise, brethren, praise!
   Thrice holy is our Lord;
   Praise, brethren, praise!
   What more befits the tongues
     Soon to lead the eternal songs,
   While heaven the note prolongs?
   Praise, brethren, praise!

156   8.7.8.7.D.

H AST thou heard Him, seen
  Him, known Him?
Is not thine a captured heart?
   Chief among ten thousand own
     Him;
Joyful choose the better part.

Captivated by His beauty,
   Worthy tribute haste to bring;
Let His peerless worth constrain
   thee,
Crown Him now unrivalled King.

2 Idols oft they won thee, charmed
   thee,
   Lovely things of time and sense;
     Gilded, thus does sin disarm thee,
   Honeyed lest thou turn thee hence.

3 What has stripped the seeming
   beauty,
   From the idols of the earth?
     Not a sense of right or duty,
   But the sight of peerless worth.

4 Not the crushing of those idols,
     With its bitter void and smart,
   But the beaming of His beauty,
     The unveiling of His heart.

5 Who extinguishes their taper,
     Till they hail the rising sun?
   Who discards the garb of winter,
     Till the summer hath begun?

6 'Tis the look that melted Peter,
     'Tis the face that Stephen saw,
   'Tis the heart that wept with Mary,
     Can alone from idols draw.

7 Draw and win and fill completely,
     Till the cup o'erflow the brim;
   What have we to do with idols
     Who have companied with Him?

157   8.8.8.8.8.8.

H AVE I an object, Lord, below,
  Which would divide my heart
from Thee;
   Which would divert its even flow
In answer to Thy constancy?
   Oh, may this wandering heart return,
   Filled with Thy love afresh to burn!

2 Have I a hope, however dear,
     Which would defer Thy coming, Lord,
   Which would detain my spirit here,
     Where nought can lasting joy
       afford?
   From it, my Saviour, set me free,
     To look, and long, and wait for Thee.

3 Be Thou the object, bright and fair,
     To fill and satisfy my heart;
   My hope to meet Thee in the air,
     And nevermore from Thee to part;
   That I may undistracted be
     To follow, serve, and wait for Thee.

158 5.4.5.4.D.

HAVE Thine own way, Lord!
Have Thine own way!
Thou art the Potter;
    I am the clay.
Mould me and make me
    After Thy will,
While I am waiting
    Yielded and still.

2 Have Thine own way, Lord!
    Have Thine own way!
Wounded and weary,
    Help me, I pray!
Power - all power -
    Surely is Thine!
Touch me and heal me,
    Saviour divine!

3 Have Thine own way, Lord!
    Have Thine own way!
Hold o'er my being
    Absolute sway!
Fill with Thy Spirit
    Till all shall see
Christ only, always,
    Living in me!

159 8.6.8.6.8.6.

HE bears the cruel scourge from men
    In meek and lowly grace,
The platted crown of thorns which then
    Upon His head they place:
Submissive when in hate again
    They spit upon His face.

2 God's chosen One men disallow;
    The Lord they crucify,
While He completes His service now
    Upon a Cross raised high,
Revealing how He thus would bow
    Obediently to die.

3 And sitting down they watch Him there,
    And mock His holy Name;
And gaze with rude and vulgar stare
    Upon that Cross of shame;
All this they dare, nor know, nor care,
    To suffer thus He came.

4 O God, our praise we offer Thee
    For Thy Belovèd Son,
Whose precious death upon the tree
    Declares Thy will is done,
In love so free, and perfectly,
    With endless glory won.

160 C.M.

HE comes! He comes! with
    hearts aglow,
We fill our lips with song;
    He comes! He comes! and this
        we know -
He will not now be long.

2 He comes! why should the saints
        be sad?
    Why should they weep and wail?
    He comes! He comes! O tidings
        glad!
    The promise cannot fail.

3 He comes! no longer shall we roam
    Unwanted and unknown;
    He comes! He comes to take us home
    To share His glorious throne.

4 He comes! let all the saints prepare,
    With hearts tuned to the chord -
    He comes! He comes! with joyful care
    Make ready for the Lord.

5 He comes ! let every heart and voice
    Take up the glad refrain -
    He comes! He comes! rejoice! rejoice!
    Again and yet again.

161 P.M.

HE dies! He dies! the lowly
    Man of sorrows,
On whom were laid our many
    griefs and woes;
Our sins He bore beneath God's
    awful billows,
And He hath triumphed over all
    our foes.

I am He that liveth, that liveth,
    and was dead;
I am He that liveth, that liveth,
    and was dead;
And behold, ... I am alive ... for
    evermore ...
Behold ... I am alive ... for
    evermore ...
I am He that liveth, that liveth,
    and was dead;
And behold, ... I am alive ... for
    evermore.

2 He lives! He lives! what glorious
   consolation!
  Exalted at His Father's own right
   hand;
  He pleads for us, and, by His
   intercession,
  Enables all His saints by grace
   to stand.

3 He comes! He comes! O blest
   anticipation!
  In keeping with His true and
   faithful word;
  To call us to our heavenly
   consummation -
  Caught up, to be for ever with the
   Lord.

4 He comes! He comes! full soon,
   to break oppression,
  And set the wretched captive
   prisoners free;
  He comes to hush the groaning of
   creation,
  And reign in righteousness and
   equity.

162   12.11.12.11.

H E giveth more grace when
  the burdens grow greater,
He sendeth more strength when
  the labours increase,
  To added afflictions He addeth
   His mercy,
  To multiplied trials, His multiplied
   peace.

2 When we have exhausted our
   store of endurance,
  When our strength has failed ere
   the day is half-done,
  When we reach the end of our
   hoarded resources
  Our Father's full giving is only
   begun.

3 Fear not that thy need shall
   exceed His provision,
  Our God ever yearns His
   resources to share;
  Lean hard on the arm everlasting,
   availing;
  The Father both thee and thy load
   will upbear.

4 His love has no limit, His grace
   has no measure,
  His power no boundary known
   unto men;
  For out of His infinite riches in
   Jesus
  He giveth and giveth and
   giveth again.

163   8.7.8.7.D. with Chorus

H E is coming, coming for us;
  Soon we'll see His light afar,
On the dark horizon rising,
  As the Bright and Morning Star,
Cheering many a waiting watcher,
  As the star whose kindly ray
Heralds the approaching morning
  Just before the break of day.

Oh, what joy, as night hangs round us,
  'Tis to think of morning's ray!
Sweet to know He's coming for us,
  Just before the break of day.

2 He is coming, coming for us;
  Soon we'll hear His voice on high;
  Dead and living, rising, changing,
   In the twinkling of an eye,
  Shall be caught up all together,
   For the meeting in the air;
  With a shout, the Lord, descending,
   Shall Himself await us there.

Oh, what joy, that great foregathering,
  Trysted meeting in the air!
Sweet to know He's coming for us,
  Calling us to join Him there.

3 He is coming - Oh, how solemn,
  When the Judge's voice is heard,
  And in His own light He shows us,
   Every thought, and act, and word!
  Deeds of merit, as we thought them,
   He will show us were but sin;
  Little acts, we had forgotten,
   He will tell us were for Him.

Oh, what joy, when He imputeth,
  Righteousness instead of sin,
Sweet to take the linen garments,
  All a gift and all from Him.

4 He is coming as the Bridegroom,
    Coming to unfold at last
The great secret of His purpose,
    Mystery of ages past.
And the bride, to her is granted,
    In His beauty then to shine,
As in rapture she exclaimeth,
    "I am His, and He is mine!"

Oh, what joy that marriage union
    Mystery of love divine!
Sweet to sing in all its fullness,
    "I am His, and He is mine".

164
8.7.8.7.

HE is coming! how this gladdens
    Days of darkness in this vale,
With so much that tries and saddens,
    Causing faith and hope to fail.

2 He is coming! word unfailing!
    All the pains and tears will cease;
No more weeping, no more wailing,
    Nought but joy and calm and peace!

3 He is coming! we are hasting
    To our place prepared above,
All His goodness here foretasting,
    All His fulness, all His love.

4 He is coming! long benighted,
    Soon we'll hear the wakening cry,
And, with loved ones reunited,
    Reach, at last, our home on high.

5 He is coming! sweet the keeping
    Of the feast until He come,
When, with those through Jesus
    sleeping,
We shall see Himself, at home.

6 He is coming! O the glory
    To be with Him where He is,
And to tell the wondrous story
    Through the countless years
        of bliss!

165
8.7.8.7.D.

HE is not a disappointment!
    Jesus is far more to me
Than in all my glowing daydreams
    I had fancied He could be;
And the more I get to know Him,
    So the more I find Him true,
And the more I long that others
    Should be led to know Him too.

2 He is not a disappointment!
    He has saved my soul from sin;
All the guilt and all the anguish,
    Which oppressed my heart within,
He has banished by His presence,
    And His blessèd kiss of peace
Has assured my heart for ever
    That His love will never cease.

3 He is not a disappointment!
    He is coming by and by;
In my heart I have the witness
    That His coming draweth nigh.
All the scoffers may despise me,
    And no change around may see,
But He tells me He is coming,
    And that's quite enough for me.

4 He is not a disappointment!
    He is all in all to me -
Blessèd Saviour, Sanctifier,
    The unchanging Christ is He!
He has won my heart's affections,
    And He meets my every need;
He is not a disappointment,
    For He satisfies indeed.

166
L.M.D.

HE leadeth me! O blessèd thought!
    O words with heavenly
comfort fraught!
    Whate'er I do, where'er I be,
Still 'tis God's hand that leadeth me!

He leadeth me! He leadeth me!
    By His own hand He leadeth me!
His faithful follower would I be,
    For by His hand He leadeth me!

2 Sometimes 'mid scenes of deepest
    gloom,
Sometimes where Eden's bowers
    bloom,
By waters still, o'er troubled sea,
    Still 'tis His hand that leadeth me!

3 Lord, I would clasp Thy hand in mine,
    And never murmur nor repine;
Content, whatever lot I see,
    Since 'tis my God that leadeth me!

4 And when my task on earth is done,
    When, by Thy grace, the victory's won,
E'en death's cold wave I will not flee,
    If God through Jordan leadeth me!

167   L.M.

HE lives - the great Redeemer
    lives;
What joy the blest assurance gives!
    And now before His Father, God,
    Pleads the full merits of His blood.

2 Repeated crimes awake our fears,
    And justice arm'd with frowns
        appears;
But in the Saviour's lovely face
    Sweet mercy smiles, and all is
        peace.

3 Hence then, ye black despairing
        thoughts;
Above our fears, above our faults,
    His powerful intercessions rise,
And guilt recedes, and terror dies.

4 In every dark, distressful hour,
    When sin and Satan join their
        power;
Let this blest truth repel each dart,
    That Jesus bears us on His heart.

5 Great Advocate, Almighty Friend!
    On Him our humble hopes depend;
Our cause can never, never fail,
    For Jesus pleads, and must prevail.

168   C.M.

HE sitteth o'er the waterfloods,
    And He is strong to save;
He sitteth o'er the waterfloods,
    And guides each drifting wave.

2 Though loud around the vessel's prow
    The waves may toss and break;
Yet at His word they sink to rest,
    As on a tranquil lake.

3 He sitteth o'er the waterfloods,
    As in the days of old,
When o'er the Saviour's sinless head
The waves and billows rolled.

4 Yea, all the billows passed o'er Him;
    Our sins - they bore Him down;
For us He met th' o'erwhelming storm,
    He met th' Almighty's frown.

5 He sitteth o'er the waterfloods;
    Then doubt and fear no more,
For He who passed through all
        the storms
Has reached the heavenly shore.

6 And every tempest-driven barque,
    With Jesus for its Guide,
Will soon be moored in harbour calm,
    In glory to abide.

169   10.10.10.10

HE took a loaf, gave thanks,
    and brake the bread.
"This is My body which is given for
    you;
This do in memory of Me", He said;
    And we, in memory of Him, "this
        do".

2 He took a loaf. The simple action
        showed
His incarnation and His wondrous
        birth.
He took that body, and therein abode,
    The Lord of Glory as a Man on
        earth.

3 And He gave thanks, such was
        His heart's delight -
To please His Father in the path
        He trod,
To be, as Man, a pleasure in His
        sight,
To glorify His Father and His God.

4 And then He brake - to make the
        broken whole,
To turn to gain irreparable loss.
    That simple act, O ponder it, my
        soul!
Announced the gloom-veiled
    breakings of the Cross.

5 O God, thus, as He did, the loaf
        we take,
And, as He did, return our thanks
        to Thee,
And, as He did, the symbol bread
        we break,
Remembering our Lord adoringly.

170

8.7.8.7.D.

HERE is love, vast as the ocean,
Loving-kindness as the flood,
When the Prince of Life, our Ransom,
Shed for us His precious blood.
Who His love will not remember?
Who can cease to sing His praise?
He can never be forgotten
Throughout heav'n's eternal days.

2 On the Mount of Crucifixion
Fountains opened deep and wide;
Through the floodgates of God's
mercy
Flowed a vast and gracious tide.
Grace and love, like mighty rivers,
Poured incessant from above,
And heav'n's peace and perfect
justice
Kissed a guilty world in love.

3 Let me all Thy love accepting,
Love Thee ever all my days;
Let me seek Thy Kingdom only,
And my life be to Thy praise;
Thou alone shalt be my glory,
Nothing in the world I see,
Thou hast cleansed and
sanctified me,
Thou Thyself hast set me free.

4 In Thy truth Thou dost direct me
By Thy Spirit through Thy Word;
And Thy grace my need is meeting
As I trust in Thee, my Lord.
Of Thy fulness Thou art pouring
Thy great love and power on me,
Without measure, full and boundless,
Drawing out my heart to Thee.

171

10.10.10.10.

HERE, O my Lord, I see Thee
face to face;
Here faith can touch and handle
things unseen;
Here would I grasp with firmer hand
Thy grace,
And all my weariness upon Thee lean.

2 Here would I feed upon the bread
of God;
Here drink with Thee the royal wine
of heaven;
Here would I lay aside each earthly
load;
Here taste afresh the calm of sin
forgiven.

3 Mine, mine the sin, but Thine the
righteousness;
Mine, mine the guilt, but Thine
the cleansing blood;
Here is my robe, my refuge, and
my peace -
Thy blood, Thy righteousness, O
Lord my God!

4 I have no help but Thine; nor do
I need
Another arm save Thine to lean upon;
It is enough, my Lord, enough
indeed;
My strength is in Thy might, Thy
might alone.

5 Too soon we rise; the symbols
disappear;
The feast, though not the love, is
past and gone;
The bread and wine remove, but
Thou art here -
Nearer than ever - still my Shield
and Sun.

6 But see, the Pillar-cloud is rising now,
And moving onward through the
desert night;
It beckons, and I follow, for I know
It leads me to the heritage of light.

7 Feast after feast thus comes and
passes by;
Yet, passing, points to the glad
feast above,
And gives sweet foretastes of the
festal joy,
The Lamb's great bridal feast of
bliss and love.

172

P.M.

HERE o'er the earth as a
stranger I roam,
Here is no rest - is no rest;
Here as a pilgrim I wander alone,
Yet I am blest - I am blest;
For I look forward to that glorious
day
When sin and sorrow shall vanish
away;
My heart doth leap while I hear
Jesus say,
"There, there is rest - there is rest".

2 Here are afflictions and trials severe,
  Here is no rest - is no rest;
  Here I must part with the friends I
    hold dear,
  Yet I am blest - I am blest;
    Sweet is the promise I read in
      Thy Word;
  Blessèd are they who have
    died in the Lord;
  They have been called to receive
    their reward;
  "There, there is rest - there is rest".

3 This world of care is a wilderness
    state,
  Here is no rest - is no rest;
    But I must bear from the world
      all its hate,
  Yet I am blest - I am blest.
    Soon shall I be from the wicked
      released;
  Soon shall the weary for ever be
    blest;
  Soon shall I lean upon Jesus' breast;
    "There, there is rest - there is rest".

173   6.10.10.6.
HERE we remember Him,
  His walk, and works, and ways
afresh review,
  Reflect upon His words of grace
    anew;
Here we remember Him.

2 Himself the vision fills
    As all His perfect path again we
      trace,
  Appreciate the glory and the grace;
    Himself the vision fills.

3 Fairer than all is He.
    The sons of men in moral gloom
      obscure,
  He, like the sun, in glory clear and
    pure!
  Fairer than all is He.

4 Precious and peerless One!
    Beyond compare in thought
      and word and deed,
  Unique recipient of heaven's meed,
    Precious and peerless One!

5 Our praise ascends to Thee
    For Him, the "altogether lovely" One,
  Thy Perfect Servant, Thy Belovèd
    Son;
  Our praise ascends to Thee.

174   C.M.
HIGH on a cruel Cross of shame,
  'Mid mockery and scorn,
Nailed with His superscribèd Name,
  Wearing a crown of thorn!

2 Friend of the friendless and the sad,
    Who wept o'er others' woes,
  Left by the failing friends He had,
    Friendless among His foes!

3 Giver to all of life, and breath,
    And riches that endure,
  Ranked with the robbers in His death,
    Poorest among the poor!

4 Mocked by the mob that round
    Him stands
  To view their work complete -
    Nails through His holy, healing
      hands,
  And through His holy feet!

5 Patient in suffering and shame,
    To do His Father's will
  Perfect in life, in death the same,
    Pleasing His Father still!

6 Pouring appreciative praise
    From hearts His worth has won,
  To Thee, His God, our hymn we
    raise,
  Remembering Thy Son.

175   6.6.6.6.8.8.
HIMSELF He could not save!
  He on the Cross must die,
Or mercy could not come
  To ruined sinners nigh;
Yes, Christ, the Son of God, must
  bleed
That sinners might from sin be freed.

2 Himself He could not save!
    For justice must be done;
  And sin's full weight must fall

Upon the sinless One;
For nothing less could God accept
In payment of our fearful debt.

3 Himself He could not save!
    For He as Surety stood
For all who now rely
    Upon His precious blood;
He bore the penalty for thee
    When dying on the accursèd tree.

4 Himself He could not save!
    Yet, now a Saviour, He
Bids sinners to Him come,
    And live eternally,
Believing in Him, now, we prove,
    His saving power, His
        changeless love.

176 L.M.
"HIS exodus" - the wondrous theme
    Upon the holy mountain high -
Revealeth all His grace supreme
    Whose precious Name we magnify.

2 Deep sorrows at the Cross enclose
    Him round, and men revile and
        stare,
While He would thus, beset by foes,
    "His exodus" accomplish there!

3 With all God's will done perfectly,
    "'Tis finished" is the Victor's shout;
With calmness then His spirit He
    Dismisses at "His going out".

4 Our thoughts around Himself are
        twined;
On such a life and death we dwell;
    Our privilege in this, we find -
Such thoughts to Thee, O God,
        to tell.

177 8.6.8.8.6.
HIS fame we sing, His victory,
    Rejoicing, we proclaim,
Who, on the third, th' appointed day,
    Swept all the power of death away
And forth in triumph came.

2 He ne'er by death could holden be;
    His God hath loosed its bands,
And raised Him up that all may see
    In resurrection victory
The Lord of Glory stands.

3 Death He annulled effectively,
    And life hath brought to light,
    And incorruptibility,
With glory for eternity
    As spoil from that dread fight.

4 Dead He became; alive is He
    Whom all our souls adore,
The First, the Last, eternally
    The Living One, triumphantly,
Alive for evermore.

5 Together truth and mercy meet,
    And righteousness and peace,
With holy kiss, each other greet
    To bear abiding fruit most sweet
In union ne'er to cease.

178 11.10.11.10.
HOLD Thou my hand! so weak
    I am, and helpless,
I dare not take one step without
    Thy aid;
Hold Thou my hand! for then, O
    loving Saviour,
No dread of ill shall make my soul
    afraid.

2 Hold Thou my hand! and closer,
        closer draw me
To Thy dear self - my hope, my
        joy, my all:
Hold Thou my hand, lest haply I
        should wander;
And, missing Thee, my trembling
        feet should fall.

3 Hold Thou my hand! the way is
        dark before me
Without the sunlight of Thy face
        divine;
But when by faith I catch its
        radiant glory,
What heights of joy, what
        rapturous songs are mine!

4 Hold Thou my hand! that when I
        reach the margin
Of that lone river Thou didst cross
        for me,
A heav'nly light may flash along
        its waters,
And every wave like crystal bright
        shall be.

179   8.7.8.7.7.7.

HOLY Father, we address Thee,
    Loved in Thy belovèd Son:
Holy Son of God, we bless Thee,
    Boundless grace hath made us one;
May the Spirit aid our songs -
    This glad work to Him belongs.

2 Wondrous was Thy love, O Father!
    Wondrous Thine, O Son of God!
Vast the love that bruised and
    wounded!
Vast the love that bore the rod!
    May the Spirit still reveal
How those stripes alone could heal.

3 Gracious Father, Thy good pleasure
    Is to love us as Thy Son,
Meting out the self-same measure,
    Since Thou seest us as one:
By Thee, Saviour, loved are we,
    As the Father loveth Thee!

4 Hallelujah! we are hasting
    To our Father's house above;
By the way our souls are tasting
    Rich and everlasting love:
In Jehovah is our boast -
    Father, Son and Holy Ghost!

180   11.12.12.10.

HOLY, holy, holy! Lord God
    Almighty!
Early in the morning our song
    shall rise to Thee;
Holy, holy, holy! merciful and mighty,
    God in Three Persons, blessèd
    Trinity!

2 Holy, holy, holy! All the saints
    adore Thee,
Casting down their golden crowns
    around the glassy sea;
Cherubim and seraphim falling
    down before Thee,
Who wert, and art, and evermore
    shalt be.

3 Holy, holy, holy! though the
    darkness hide Thee,
Though the eye of sinful man Thy
    glory may not see;
Only Thou art holy, there is none
    beside Thee,
Perfect in power, in love, and purity.

4 Holy, holy, holy! Lord God Almighty!
    All Thy works shall praise Thy
name, in earth, and sky, and sea;
    Holy, holy, holy! merciful and
    mighty,
God in Three Persons, blessèd
    Trinity.

181   8.7.8.7.4.7.

HOLY Saviour! we adore Thee
    Seated on the throne of God;
While the heavenly hosts before
    Thee
Gladly sing Thy praise aloud.
    Thou art worthy!
We are ransomed by Thy blood.

2 Saviour! though the world
    despised Thee,
Though Thou here wast crucified,
    Yet the Father's glory raised Thee,
Lord of all creation wide;
    Thou art worthy!
We shall live, for Thou hast died.

3 And though here on earth rejected,
    'Tis but fellowship with Thee;
Should we not with joy expect it
    Here like Thee, our Lord, to be?
Thou art worthy,
    Thou from earth hast set us free.

4 Haste the day of Thy returning
    With Thy ransomed church to
    reign;
Then shall end our days of mourning,
    We shall sing with rapture then:
Thou art worthy!
    Come, Lord Jesus, come, Amen.

182   C.M.

HOPE of our hearts, O Lord, appear!
    Thou glorious Star of day,
Shine forth, and chase the dreary night,
    With all our tears, away.

2 No resting-place we seek on earth,
    No loveliness we see;
Our eye is on the royal crown,
    Prepared for us and Thee.

3 But, dearest Lord! however bright
    That crown of joy above,

What is it to the brighter hope
    Of dwelling in Thy love?

4 What to the joy, the deeper joy,
    Unmingled, pure, and free,
Of union with our living Head,
    Of fellowship with Thee?

5 This joy e'en now on earth is ours;
    But only, Lord, above,
Our hearts, without a pang, shall know
    The fulness of Thy love.

6 There, near Thy heart, upon the throne,
    Thy ransomed Church shall see
What grace was in the bleeding Lamb,
    Who died to make her free.

183
6.4.6.4.6.6.6.4.

HOW bright that blessèd hope!
    Jesus will come!
Let us our heads lift up,
    Jesus will come!
Morning so bright and clear,
    Mansions of God appear,
Sin shall not enter there,
    Jesus will come.

2 Him every eye shall see
    When He appears;
Bright will the glory be
    When He appears;
Soon shall the trumpet speak,
    Each sleeping saint awake,
And the glad morning break
    When He appears.

3 Raised unto glory then
    At His return;
Joyous our song shall be
    At His return;
Gathered around to Him
    All learn the heav'nly hymn;
Jesus our joyful theme
    At His return.

4 Full of this blessèd hope
    Till He shall come;
Let us the cross take up
    Till He shall come;
Happy reproach to bear,
    Shame, for His sake, to share,
Since we the crown shall wear
    When He shall come.

184
8.7.8.7.D.

HOW deep the Father's love
    for us,
How vast beyond all measure,
    That He should give His only Son
To make a wretch His treasure.
    How great the pain of searing loss -
The Father turns His face away,
    As wounds which mar the Chosen
      One
Bring many sons to glory.

2 Behold the man upon a Cross,
    My sin upon His shoulders;
Ashamed, I hear my mocking voice
    Call out among the scoffers.
It was my sin that held Him there
    Until it was accomplished;
His dying breath has brought me
    life -
I know that it is finished.

3 I will not boast in anything,
    No gifts, no power, no wisdom;
But I will boast in Jesus Christ,
    His death and resurrection.
Why should I gain from His reward?
    I cannot give an answer;
But this I know with all my heart -
    His wounds have paid my ransom.

185
11.11.11.11.

HOW firm a foundation, ye
    saints of the Lord,
Is laid for your faith in His
    excellent Word!
What more can He say, than to
    you He hath said,
To you who for refuge to Jesus
    have fled?

2 "Fear not, I am with thee; Oh, be
    not dismay'd!
For I am thy God, I will still
    give thee aid;
I'll strengthen thee, help thee, and
    cause thee to stand,
Upheld by My gracious
    omnipotent hand."

3 "When through the deep waters I
    call thee to go,
The rivers of sorrow shall not overflow;

For I will be with thee, thy trials
    to bless,
And sanctify to thee, thy deepest
    distress."

4 "When through fiery trials thy
    pathway shall lie,
My grace, all-sufficient, shall be
    thy supply:
The flame shall not hurt thee: I
    only design
Thy dross to consume, and thy
    gold to refine."

5 "The soul that on Jesus hath
    leaned for repose,
I will not, I cannot desert to its
    foes;
That soul, though all hell should
    endeavour to shake,
I'll never - no never - no never
    forsake!"

186   8.8.8.8.

H OW good is the God we adore,
  Our faithful, unchangeable
Friend,
    Whose love is as great as His
      power,
And knows neither measure nor end.

2 'Tis Jesus, the First and the Last,
    Whose Spirit shall guide us
    safe home;
We'll praise Him for all that is past,
    And trust Him for all that's to
    come.

187   C.M.

H OW great, our Father, was
  Thy love,
How wonderful Thy grace,
    In sending forth Thy Well-beloved,
To save our ruined race!

2 As being in the form of God,
    Eternally the same,
With Thee, the Father, He, the Son,
    Equality could claim.

3 But, Thy blest counsels to fulfil,
    He left His glorious throne;

And made Himself of no repute,
    A servant's form to own.

4 Thus found in fashion as a man,
    All blameless, spotless, pure,
He was obedient unto death,
    Sin's judgment to endure.

5 To Him, above all heavens, dost
    Thou
His rightful place accord,
    That every knee to Him should
    bow,
Each tongue confess Him Lord.

6 Soon, thro' those opened
    heavens again,
The Saviour will appear;
    With Him in highest glory then,
Our praises Thou wilt hear.

188   8.7.8.7.D.

H OW I praise Thee, precious
  Saviour!
That Thy love laid hold of me;
    Thou hast saved and cleansed
    and filled me,
That I might Thy channel be.

Channels only, blessèd Master,
    But with all Thy wondrous power
Flowing through us, Thou canst
    use us
Every day and every hour.

2 Just a channel, full of blessing,
    To the thirsty hearts around;
To tell out Thy full salvation,
    All Thy loving message sound.

3 Emptied that Thou shouldest fill me,
    A clean vessel in Thy hand;
With no power but as Thou givest
    Graciously with each command.

4 Witnessing Thy power to save me,
    Setting free from self and sin;
Thou hast bought me to possess me,
    In Thy fulness, Lord, come in.

5 Jesus, fill now with Thy Spirit
    Hearts that full surrender know;
That the streams of living water
    From our inner man may flow.

189
11.11.11.11. with Chorus

HOW sweet is the story of
God's boundless love,
That brought His own Son from
the glory above,
Who died in our stead upon
Calvary's tree,
Obtaining redemption that we
might be free!

Sound His praise! Sound His praise!
All the work has been done;
Praise His name! Praise His name!
God's own blessèd Son.
We give Him the glory, our Saviour
and Friend;
Our song is of Jesus and never will
end.

2 How wondrous the story! The
claims of God's throne
Were met by that blood which for
guilt did atone;
The judgment of sin has been
borne by the Son,
Who glorified God in the work He
has done -

3 How brilliant the glory where Christ
is enthroned!
How rightly His name above all
names is owned!
Yes, Jesus, the Saviour, the glory -
crowned Lord,
Is worthy by all to be ever adored -

4 How blessèd the hope of all those
who believe,
That Jesus is coming, "His own" to
receive!
What rapture, what glory, for ever
will be,
When "caught up" to meet Him,
their Saviour they see!

190
C.M.

HOW sweet the Name of Jesus
sounds
In a believer's ear!
It soothes his sorrows, heals
his wounds,
And drives away his fear.

2 It makes the wounded spirit whole,
And calms the troubled breast;
'Tis Manna to the hungry soul,
And to the weary rest.

3 Dear Name! the Rock on which
we build,
Our Shield and Hiding-place,
Our never-failing Treasury, filled
With boundless stores of grace.

4 Jesus, our Saviour, Shepherd, Friend,
Prophet, and Priest, and King;
Our Lord, our Life, our Way, our End,
Accept the praise we bring.

5 Weak is the effort of our heart,
And cold our warmest thought;
But when we see Thee as Thou art,
We'll praise Thee as we ought!

6 Till then we would Thy love proclaim
With every fleeting breath;
And may the music of Thy Name
Refresh my soul in death.

191
11.10.11.10.D.

HOW wonderful! that Thou the
Son hast come,
And here for us as Son of man
hast died;
Our sins were laid on Thee, Thou
didst become
Salvation's Rock, when Thou
wast crucified;
And faith perceives Thy finished
work - the rest
Where love well-known, yet
passing human thought,
Has set our feet; as those in
Jesus blest,
We praise and worship by Thy
Spirit taught.

2 To Thee, O Lord, we bring our
note of praise,
To Thee who bore for us the Cross
of shame!
What grief Thou knewest on that
day of days,
When curse and death on Thee,
the Victim, came!

How great Thy grace! no mind of
    man can grasp
The love told out in suffering on
    the tree;
Love that has gathered now
    within its clasp
Those once far off, but now
    brought home to Thee.

3 How wonderful that love made
    manifest
  In Thee - its fulness told! so that
    the heart,
  Touched by Thy kindness, finds in
    Thee its rest,
  And lost in Thee, adoring, knows
    its part;
  There to our hearts Thy rich
    unmeasured grace,
  And love's full fountain more and
    more revealed,
  Call forth from every mouth Thine
    endless praise,
  And willing lips their heart-felt
    homage yield.

192 C.M.D

I AM redeemed, oh, praise the Lord;
    My soul from bondage free,
Has found at last a resting place
  In Him who died for me.

I am redeemed, I am redeemed,
* I'll sing it o'er and o'er;*
I am redeemed, oh, praise the Lord;
* Redeemed forevermore.*

2 I looked, and lo! from Calvary's Cross
    A healing fountain streamed;
  It cleansed my heart, and now I sing,
    Praise God, I am redeemed.

3 The debt is paid, my soul is free,
    And by His mighty power,
  The blood that washed my sins away
    Still cleanseth every hour.

4 All glory be to Jesus' name;
    I know that He is mine,
  For on my heart the Spirit seals
    His pledge of love divine.

193 11.10.11.10.

I AM the Lord's! O joy beyond
    expression,
O sweet response to voice of love
    divine;
Faith's joyous 'Yes!' to the
    assuring whisper,
Fear not, I have redeemed thee,
    thou art Mine.

2 I am the Lord's! it hushes every
    murmur,
  It soothes the fevered spirit to its
    rest;
  I am the Lord's! it is the child's
    rejoinder,
  Who knows and feels the Father's
    will is best.

3 I am the Lord's! O eagerly and
    gladly,
  Triumphantly and gratefully we sing;
    I am the Lord's! It is the rock
    unfailing
  To which our storm-tossed souls
    in danger cling.

4 I am the Lord's! yet teach me all it
    meaneth,
  All it involves of love and loyalty,
    Of holy service, full and glad
    surrender,
  And unreserved obedience unto
    Thee.

5 I am the Lord's! yes; body, soul
    and spirit;
  They're sealed, and irrecoverably
    Thine;
  As Thou, Belovèd, in Thy grace
    and fulness
  For ever and for evermore art mine.

6 I am the Lord's! It is the glad
    confession
  Wherewith the Bride recalls the
    happy day,
  When love's "I will" accepted
    Him forever,
  "The Lord's", to love, to honour
    and obey.

194 P.M.

I AM Thine, O Lord,
   I have heard Thy voice,
And it told Thy love to me;
   But I long to rise in the arms of faith,
And be closer drawn to Thee.

Draw me nearer, nearer, blessèd Lord,
   To the Cross where Thou hast died;
Draw me nearer, nearer, nearer,
   blessèd Lord,
To Thy precious, wounded side.

2 Consecrate me now to Thy
      service, Lord,
   By the power of grace divine;
   Let my soul look up with a
      steadfast hope,
   And my will be lost in Thine.

3 O the pure delight of a single hour
      That before Thy throne I spend,
   When I kneel in prayer, and with
      Thee, my God,
   I commune as friend with friend.

4 There are depths of love that I
      cannot know
   Till I cross the narrow sea;
      There are heights of joy that I
         may not reach
   Till I rest in peace with Thee.

195 8.7.8.7.D.

I AM waiting for the dawning
   Of that bright and blessèd day
When the darksome night of sorrow
   Shall have vanished far away;
When for ever with the Saviour,
   Far beyond this vale of tears,
I shall swell the song of worship
   Through the everlasting years.

2 I am looking at the brightness,
   See, it shineth from afar,
Of the clear and joyous beaming
   Of the "Bright and Morning Star";
Through the dark grey mist of morning
   Do I see its glorious light;
Then away with every shadow
   Of this sad and weary night.

3 I am waiting for the coming
   Of the Lord who died for me;
Oh, His words have thrilled my spirit,
   "I will come again for thee".
Faith can almost hear His footfall
   On the threshold of the door,
And my heart, my heart is longing
   To be with Him evermore.

196 C.M.

I BOW me to Thy will, O God,
   And all Thy ways adore,
And every day I live I'd seek
   To please Thee more and more.

2 Why should I care, O blessèd Lord?
   Since all my cares are Thine;
Why not in triumph live, since Thou
   Hast made Thy triumphs mine?

3 Lead on, lead on triumphantly,
   O blessèd Lord! lead on;
Faith's pilgrim sons behind Thee seek
   The road that Thou hast gone.

4 He always wins who sides with God,
   To him no chance is lost;
God's will is sweetest to him when
   It triumphs at his cost.

5 Ill that God blesses is our good,
   And unblest good is ill;
And all is right that seems most wrong,
   If it be His sweet will.

197 8.6.8.8.6.

I CANNOT breathe enough of Thee,
   O gentle breeze of love;
More fragrant than the myrtle tree
   The Rose of Sharon is to me,
The Balm of heaven above.

2 I cannot gaze enough on Thee,
   Thou Fairest of the Fair;
My heart is filled with ecstasy,
   As in Thy face of radiancy
I see such beauty there.

3 I cannot work enough for Thee,
   My Saviour, Master, Friend;
I do not wish to go out free,
   But ever, always, willingly,
To serve Thee to the end.

4 I cannot sing enough of Thee,
   The sweetest name on earth;
A note so full of melody
   Comes from my heart so joyously,
And fills my soul with mirth.

5 I cannot speak enough of Thee,
   I have so much to tell;
Thy heart it beats so tenderly
   As Thou dost draw me close to Thee,
And whisper, "All is well".

198   11.10.11.10.11.10.11.12.

I CANNOT tell why He, whom
   angels worship,
Should set His love upon the
   sons of men,
Or why, as Shepherd, He should
   seek the wanderers,
To bring them back, they know
   not how or when.
But this I know, that He was born
   of Mary
When Bethl'em's manger was His
   only home,
And that He lived at Nazareth and
   laboured,
And so the Saviour, Saviour of
   the world, is come.

2 I cannot tell how silently He
   suffered,
   As with His peace He graced this
   place of tears,
   Or how His heart upon the Cross
   was broken,
   The crown of pain to three and
   thirty years.
   But this I know, He heals the
   broken-hearted
   And stays our sin and calms our
   lurking fear
   And lifts the burden from the
   heavy-laden;
   For still the Saviour, Saviour of
   the world, is here.

3 I cannot tell how all the lands
   shall worship,
   When at His bidding every storm
   is stilled,
   Or who can say how great the
   jubilation

When every heart with love and
   joy is filled.
But this I know, the skies will thrill
   with rapture,
And myriad, myriad human voices
   sing,
And earth to heav'n, and heav'n to
   earth, will answer,
"At last the Saviour, Saviour of the
   world, is King!"

199   C.M.

I CANNOT work my soul to save,
   For that my Lord has done;
But I would work like any slave,
   From love to God's dear Son.

2 He gave Himself upon the Cross,
   A sacrifice for me;
And God accepts what He has done,
   To save and pardon me.

3 His precious blood has cleansed
   my soul,
My sins are all forgiven;
   And now I long to see His face,
And serve Him more in heaven.

200   P.M.

I DO not know what lies ahead,
   The way I cannot see,
But One stands near to be my guide,
   He'll show the way to me.

I know who holds the future
   And He'll guide me with His hand;
With God things don't just happen,
   Everything by Him is planned.
So as I face tomorrow,
   With its problems large and small,
I'll trust the God of miracles,
   Give to Him my all.

2 I do not know how many days
   Of life are mine to spend,
But One who knows and cares for me
   Will keep me to the end.

3 I do not know the course ahead,
   What joys and griefs are there,
But One stands near who fully knows,
   I'll trust His loving care.

201

I HAVE a Friend whose faithful love
  Is more than all the world to me,
'Tis higher than the heights above,
And deeper than the soundless sea:
    So old, so new,
    So strong, so true;
Before the earth received its frame,
    He loved me -
Blessèd be His Name!

2 He held the highest place above,
    Adored by all the sons of flame,
Yet, such His self-denying love,
He laid aside His crown and came
    To seek the lost,
    And, at the cost
Of heav'nly rank and earthly fame,
    He sought me -
Blessèd be His Name!

3 It was a lonely path He trod,
    From every human soul apart,
Known only to Himself and God
Was all the grief that filled His heart:
    Yet from the track,
    He turned not back,
Till where I lay in want and shame,
    He found me -
Blessèd be His Name!

4 Then dawned at last that day of dread
    When, desolate but undismayed,
With wearied frame and thorn -
    crowned head
He, now forsaken and betrayed,
    Went up for me
    To Calvary,
And dying there in grief and shame,
    He saved me -
Blessèd be His Name!

5 Long as I live my song shall tell
    The wonders of His matchless love:
And when at last I rise to dwell
In the bright home prepared above,
    My joy shall be
    His face to see,
And bowing then with loud acclaim,
    I'll praise Him -
Blessèd be His Name!

202

I HAVE a home above
  From sin and sorrow free;
A mansion which eternal love
  Designed and formed for me.

2 My Father's gracious hand
    Has built this blest abode;
From everlasting it was planned
    My dwelling-place with God.

3 My Saviour's precious blood
    Has made my title sure:
He passed through death's dark
    raging flood
To make my rest secure.

4 The Comforter is come,
    The earnest has been given;
He leads me onward to the home
    Reserved for me in heaven.

5 Loved ones are gone before
    Whose pilgrim days are done;
I soon shall greet them on that shore
    Where partings are unknown.

6 But more than all, I long
    His glories to behold,
Whose smile fills all the radiant throng
    With ecstasy untold.

7 That bright, yet tender smile,
    My sweetest welcome there,
Shall cheer me through the "little while"
    I tarry for Him here.

8 Thy love, most gracious Lord,
    My joy and strength shall be,
Till Thou shalt speak the gladd'ning
    word
That bids me rise to Thee.

9 And then, through endless days
    Where all Thy glories shine,
In happier, holier strains I'll praise
    The grace that made me Thine.

203

I HAVE a Shepherd, One I love
   so well;
How He has blessed me tongue
   can never tell;
On the Cross He suffered, shed
   His blood and died,
That I might ever in His love
   confide.

Following Jesus, ever day by day,
   Nothing can harm me when He
   leads the way;
Darkness or sunshine, whate'er befall,
   Jesus, the Shepherd, is my All in All.

2 Pastures abundant doth His hand
   provide,
Still waters flowing ever at my side,
   Goodness and mercy follow on
   my track,
With such a Shepherd nothing
   can I lack.

3 When I would wander from the
   path astray,
Then He will draw me back into the
   way;
In the darkest valley I need fear no ill,
   For He, my Shepherd, will be with
   me still.

4 When labour's ended and the
   journey done,
Then He will lead me safely to my
   home;
There I shall dwell in rapture sure
   and sweet,
With all the loved ones gathered
   round His feet.

204

I HAVE been at the altar and
   witnessed the Lamb
Burnt wholly to ashes for me;
   And watched its sweet savour
   ascending on high,
Accepted, O Father, by Thee.

2 And lo, while I gazed at the
   glorious sight,
A voice from above reached mine
   ears:

"By this thine iniquity's taken away,
   And no trace of it on thee appears".

3 "An end of thy sin has been made
   for thee here
By Him who its penalty bore;
   With blood it is blotted eternally
   out,
And I will not remember it more."

4 O Lord, I believe it with wonder
   and joy;
Confirm, Thou, this precious belief;
   While daily I learn that I am in
   myself
Of sinners the vilest and chief.

205

I HAVE only one life on this earth
   And as vapour it's passing away.
I must labour for treasures of worth,
   Ere toil ends at the close of
   the day.

Only one life to give!
   I must never withhold it from God.
Only one life to live!
   I must not miss the "Well
   done!" of God.

2 Only one life, and white are the
   fields,
With compassion this great need
   I view;
This one life that I have, I will yield;
   And the little I can, let me do.

3 This one life that I have, I may lose,
   And, in losing, a hundred-fold
   gain!
Then to fall on the Rock, I will choose,
   And be broken, God's best to
   obtain.

4 One poor life, small the offering
   at best,
Yet the world and the flesh often call;
   This my answer must be to each
   test:
"I'll not serve God with less than
   my all!"

206
S.M.

I HEAR the accuser roar
Of ills that I have done;
I know them well, and thousands more;
Jehovah findeth none.

2 Sin, Satan, Death, press near
To harass and appal;
Let but my risen Lord appear,
Backward they go and fall.

3 Before, behind, around,
They set their fierce array
To fight and force me from my ground
Along Immanuel's way.

4 I meet them face to face
Through Jesus' conquest blest;
March in the triumph of His grace
Right onward to my rest.

5 There, in His book I bear
A more than conq'ror's name,
A soldier, son, and fellow-heir,
Who fought and overcame.

6 His be the Victor's name
Who fought our fight alone:
Triumphant saints no honour claim,
Their conquest was His own.

7 By weakness and defeat
He won the meed and crown;
Trod all our foes beneath His feet
By being trodden down.

8 He hell in hell laid low;
Made sin, He sin o'erthrew;
Bowed to the grave, destroyed it so,
And death, by dying, slew.

9 Bless, bless the Conq'ror slain!
Slain in His victory!
Who lived, who died, who lives again,
For thee, His Church, for thee.

207
S.M.

I HEAR the words of love,
I gaze upon the blood,
I see the mighty sacrifice,
And I have peace with God.

2 'Tis everlasting peace!
Sure as Jehovah's Name,
'Tis stable as His steadfast throne,
For evermore the same.

3 The clouds may go and come,
And storms may sweep my sky;
This blood-sealed friendship changes not,
The Cross is ever nigh.

4 My love is ofttimes low,
My joy still ebbs and flows,
But peace with Him remains the same,
No change Jehovah knows.

5 I change, He changes not;
The Christ can never die:
His love, not mine, the resting-place,
His truth, not mine, the tie.

6 That which can shake the Cross
May shake the peace it gave,
Which tells me Christ has never died,
Or never left the grave!

7 Till then my peace is sure,
It will not, cannot yield,
Jesus, I know, has died and lives,
On this firm rock I build.

8 I know He liveth now
At God's right hand above;
I know the throne on which He sits,
I know His truth and love.

208
C.M.

I HEARD the voice of Jesus say,
"Come unto Me and rest;
Lay down, thou weary one, lay down
Thy head upon My breast".

2 I came to Jesus as I was,
Weary, and worn, and sad;
I found in Him a resting-place,
And He has made me glad.

3 I heard the voice of Jesus say,
"Behold, I freely give
The living water: Thirsty one
Stoop down, and drink, and live".

4 I came to Jesus, and I drank
    Of that life-giving stream;
My thirst was quenched, my soul
    revived,
And now I live in Him.

5 I heard the voice of Jesus say,
    "I am this dark world's Light;
Look unto Me, thy morn shall rise,
    And all thy day be bright".

6 I looked to Jesus, and I found
    In Him my Star, my Sun;
And in that light of life I'll walk
    Till trav'lling days are done.

209   10.10.10.10.

I JOURNEY through a desert
    drear and wild,
Yet is my heart by such sweet
    thoughts beguiled
Of Him on whom I lean, my
    Strength, my Stay,
I can forget the sorrows of the way.

2 Thoughts of His love - the root of
    ev'ry grace
Which finds in this poor heart a
    dwelling-place;
The sunshine of my soul, than
    day more bright,
And my calm pillow of repose by
    night.

3 Thoughts of His sojourn in this
    vale of tears;
The tale of love unfolded in those
    years
Of sinless suffering and patient
    grace,
I love again and yet again to trace.

4 Thoughts of His glory - on the
    Cross I gaze,
And there behold its sad yet
    healing rays;
Beacon of hope which, lifted up
    on high,
Illumes with heavenly light the
    tear-dimmed eye.

5 Thoughts of His coming; for that
    joyful day
In patient hope I watch, and wait,
    and pray;
The dawn draws nigh, the
    midnight shadows flee,
O what a sunrise will that advent be!

210   P.M.

I KNOW not the hour of His coming,
    Nor how He will speak to my heart;
Or whether at morning or mid-day,
    My spirit to Him will depart.

But I know ... I shall wake in the
    likeness
Of Him ... I am longing to see;
    I know ... that mine eyes shall
        behold Him,
Who died ... for a sinner like me.

2 I know not the bliss that awaits me,
    At rest with my Saviour above;
I know not how soon I shall enter,
    And bathe in the ocean of love.

3 Perhaps in the midst of my labour,
    A voice from my Lord I shall hear;
Perhaps in the slumber of midnight,
    Its message may fall on my ear.

4 I know not, but oh I am watching,
    My lamp ever burning and bright!
I know not if Jesus will call me
    At morning, at noon, or at night.

211   8.6.8.8.6.

I KNOW not when, but this I know,
    That I shall see His face:
I may be called by death to go,
    Or wait His coming here below,
But I shall see His face.

2 That face once spit upon for me,
    That holy, blessèd face!
And stared at in His agony,
    While hanging on the cursèd tree,
Yes, I shall see that face.

3 But not a cloud of sorrow now
    Can shade His glorious face,

Eternal gladness crowns His brow,
    Where heavenly hosts before
    Him bow,
There I shall see His face.

4 E'en now by faith my soul can say,
    I see my Saviour's face,
Though mine be here a darkened
    way,
This cheers me on from day to day,
    Until I see His face.

212
7.6.7.6.D.

I LAY my sins on Jesus
    The spotless Lamb of God;
He bears them all, and frees us,
    From the accursèd load.
I bring my guilt to Jesus;
    To wash my crimson stains
White in His blood most precious,
    Till not a spot remains.

2 I lay my wants to Jesus,
    All fulness dwells in Him;
Ho healeth my diseases,
    He doth my soul redeem.
I lay my griefs on Jesus,
    My burdens and my cares;
He from them all releases,
    He all my sorrows shares.

3 I rest my soul on Jesus,
    This weary soul of mine;
His right hand me embraces,
    I on His breast recline.
I love the Name of Jesus,
    Immanuel, Christ, the Lord!
Like fragrance on the breezes
    His Name abroad is poured.

4 I long to be like Jesus,
    Meek, loving, lowly, mild;
I long to be like Jesus,
    The Father's holy Child.
I long to be with Jesus
    Amid the heavenly throng,
To sing with saints His praises,
    To learn the angels' song .

213
P.M.

I LEFT it all with Jesus long ago;
    All my sins I brought Him, and
my woe:
    When by faith I saw Him on the tree,
Heard His still, small whisper,
    "'Tis for thee",
From my heart the burden rolled away:
    Happy day!

2 I leave it all with Jesus, for He knows
    How to steal the bitter from life's
    woes;
How to gild the tear-drop with His
    smile,
Make the desert garden bloom awhile:
    When my weakness leaneth on
    His might,
        All seems light.

3 I leave it all with Jesus day by day;
    Faith can firmly trust Him, come
    what may:
Hope has dropped her anchor,
    found her rest
In the calm, sure haven of His breast;
    Love esteems it heaven to abide
        At His side.

4 Oh, leave it all with Jesus,
    drooping soul!
Tell not *half* thy story, but the whole.
    Worlds on worlds are hanging
    on His hand,
Life and death are waiting His
    command;
Yet His tender bosom makes *thee*
    room -
        Oh, come home!

214
7.6.7.6.D.

I NEED Thee, precious Saviour!
    O Thou art all to me;
Before the throne for ever
    I stand complete in Thee.
Though Satan loud accuses,
    Yet I can ever see
The blood of Christ most precious,
    The sinner's perfect plea.

2 I need Thee, precious Saviour!
    For I am very poor;
A stranger and a pilgrim,
    I have no earthly store.
I need Thy love, Lord Jesus!
    To cheer me on my way,
To guide my doubting footsteps,
    To be my strength and stay.

3 I need Thee, precious Saviour!
    I need a friend like Thee;
A friend to soothe and comfort,
    A friend to care for me.
I need Thy heart, Lord Jesus!
    To feel each anxious care,
To bear my ev'ry burden,
    And all my sorrow share.

4 I need Thee, precious Saviour!
    For I am very blind,
A weak and foolish wand'rer,
    With dark and evil mind.
I need Thy light, Lord Jesus!
    To tread the thorny road,
To guide me safe to glory
    Where I shall see my God.

5 I need Thee, precious Saviour!
    I need Thee day by day
To fill me with Thy fulness,
    To lead me on my way.
I need Thy Holy Spirit
    To teach me what I am,
To show me more of Jesus,
    To point me to the Lamb.

6 I need Thee, precious Saviour!
    And hope to see Thee soon,
Encircled with the rainbow
    And seated on Thy throne;
There, with Thy blood-bought
    people,
My joy shall ever be
    To sing Thy praise, Lord Jesus,
And ever gaze on Thee.

215   11.11.11.11.
I ONCE was a stranger to grace
    and to God;
I knew not my danger, I felt not
    my load;
Though friends spoke in rapture
    of Christ on the tree,
Jehovah Tsidkenu was nothing
    to me.

2 Like tears from the daughters of
    Zion that roll,
I wept when the waters went over
    His soul;
Yet thought not that my sins had
    nailed to the tree
Jehovah Tsidkenu - 'twas nothing
    to me.

3 When free grace awoke me by
    light from on high,
Then legal fears shook me, I
    trembled to die;
No refuge, no safety in self could
    I see,
Jehovah Tsidkenu my Saviour
    must be.

4 My terrors all vanished before the
    sweet Name;
My guilty fears banished, with
    boldness I came
To drink at the fountain, life-giving
    and free;
Jehovah Tsidkenu is all things to me.

5 E'en treading the valley, the
    shadow of death,
This watchword shall rally my
    faltering breath;
For when from life's fever my God
    sets me free,
Jehovah Tsidkenu, my death song
    shall be.

216   C.M. with Chorus
I SAW One hanging on a tree,
    In agony and blood;
He fixed His languid eyes on me,
    As near His Cross I stood.

Oh, can it be, upon a tree
    The Saviour died for me?
My soul is thrilled,
    My heart is filled,
To think He died for me!

2 Sure, never, till my latest breath,
    Can I forget that look:
It seemed to charge me with His
    death,
Tho' not a word He spoke.

3 My conscience felt and owned the guilt,
    And plunged me in despair;
  I saw my sins His blood had spilt
    And helped to nail Him there.

4 Alas! I knew not what I did,
    But now my tears are vain:
  Where shall my trembling soul be hid?
    For I the Lord have slain.

5 A second look He gave, which said,
    "I freely all forgive;
  This blood is for thy ransom paid,
    I die that thou may'st live".

6 Thus while His death my sin displays
    In all its blackest hue,
  Such is the mystery of grace,
    It seals my pardon too.

217   7.6.7.6.D.

I SAW the Cross of Jesus
    When burdened with my sin,
  I sought the Cross of Jesus
    To give me peace within;
  I brought my soul to Jesus,
    He cleansed it in His blood;
  And in the Cross of Jesus
    I found my peace with God.

2 I love the Cross of Jesus;
    It tells me what I am:
  A vile and guilty creature,
    Saved only through the Lamb.
  No righteousness, no merit,
    No beauty can I plead;
  Yet in the Cross I glory,
    My title there I read.

3 I trust the Cross of Jesus,
    In every trying hour,
  My sure and certain refuge,
    My never-failing tower;
  In every fear and conflict,
    I more than conqueror am;
  Living, I'm safe, or dying,
    Through Christ, the risen Lamb.

4 Safe at the Cross of Jesus;
    There let my weary heart
  Still rest in peace unshaken
    Till with Him - ne'er to part;
  And then in strains of glory
    I'll sing His wondrous power,
  Where sin can never enter,
    And death is known no more.

218   P.M.

I SERVE a risen Saviour,
    He's in the world today;
  I know that He is living,
    Whatever men may say;
  I see His hand of mercy;
    I hear His voice of cheer;
  And just the time I need Him
    He's always near.

*He lives, He lives, Christ Jesus
    lives today!*
*He walks with me and talks with
    me along life's narrow way.*
*He lives, He lives, salvation to
    impart!*
*You ask me how I know He lives?
    He lives within my heart.*

2 In all the world around me
    I see His loving care,
  And though my heart grows weary,
    I never will despair;
  I know that He is leading,
    Through all the stormy blast;
  The day of His appearing
    Will come at last.

3 Rejoice, rejoice, O Christian,
    Lift up your voice and sing
  Eternal hallelujahs
    To Jesus Christ the King!
  The Hope of all who seek Him,
    The Help of all who find,
  None other is so loving,
    So good and kind.

219   P.M.

I STAND all amazed at the love
    Jesus offers me,
  Confused at the grace that so
    fully He proffers me;
  I tremble to know that for me He
    was crucified,
  That for me, a sinner, He
    suffered, He bled, and died.

*Oh! it is wonderful that He should
    care for me,*
Enough to die for me!
Oh, it is wonderful, wonderful to me!

2 I marvel that He would descend
    from His throne divine,
  To rescue a soul so rebellious and
    proud as mine;
  That He should extend His great
    love unto such as I,
  Sufficient to own, to redeem, and
    to justify.

3 I think of His hands, pierced and
    bleeding to pay the debt!
  Such mercy, such love and
    devotion can I forget?
  No, no! I will praise and adore at
    the mercy seat,
  Until at the glorified throne I kneel
    at His feet.

220   P.M.

I STAND amazed in the presence
  Of Jesus the Nazarene,
And wonder how He could love me,
  A sinner, condemned, unclean.

How marvellous! How wonderful!
  And my song shall ever be:
How marvellous! How wonderful!
  Is my Saviour's love for me!

2 For me it was in the garden
    He prayed, "Not My will, but Thine";
  He had no tears for His own griefs,
    But sweat drops of blood for mine.

3 In wonder angels beheld Him,
    And came from the world of light
  To comfort Him in the sorrows
    He bore for my soul that night.

4 He took my sins and my sorrows,
    He made them His very own;
  He bore the burden to Calvary,
    And suffered and died alone.

5 When with the ransomed in glory
    His face I at last shall see,
  'Twill be my joy thro' the ages
    To sing of His love for me.

221   L.M.

I THIRST, but not as once I did,
  The vain delights of earth to share:
Thy wounds, Emmanuel, all forbid
  That I should seek my pleasure
    there.

2 It was the sight of Thy dear Cross
    First weaned my soul from
      earthly things;
  And taught me to esteem as dross
    The mirth of fools and pomp of
      kings.

3 I want that grace that springs
    from Thee,
  That quickens all things where it
    flows,
  And makes a wretched thorn, like me,
    Bloom as the myrtle, or the rose.

4 Great fountain of delight unknown!
    No longer sink below the brim;
  But overflow, and pour me down
    A living, and life-giving stream!

5 For sure, of all the plants that share
    The notice of Thy Father's eye,
  None proves less grateful to His
    care,
  Or yields Him meaner fruit than I.

222   C.M.

I TO the hills will lift mine eyes,
  From whence doth come mine aid.
My safety cometh from the Lord,
  Who heav'n and earth hath made.

2 Thy foot He'll not let slide, nor will
    He slumber that thee keeps.
  Behold, He that keeps Israel,
    He slumbers not, nor sleeps.

3 The Lord thee keeps, the Lord
    thy shade
  On thy right hand doth stay:
    The moon by night thee shall
      not smite,
  Nor yet the sun by day.

4 The Lord shall keep thy soul; He shall
    Preserve thee from all ill.
  Henceforth thy going out and in
    God keep for ever will.

223

S.M.D.

I WAS a wand'ring sheep,
  I did not love the fold;
I did not love my Shepherd's voice,
  I would not be controlled.
I was a wayward child,
  I did not love my home;
I did not love my Father's voice,
  I loved afar to roam.

2 The Shepherd sought His sheep,
    The Father sought His child,
  And followed me o'er vale and hill,
    O'er desert waste and wild.
  Yea, found me nigh to death,
    Famished, and faint, and lone,
  And bound me with the bands of love,
    And saved the wand'ring one.

3 Jesus my Shepherd is,
    'Twas He that loved my soul,
  'Twas He that cleansed me by His
    blood,
  'Twas He that made me whole.
    'Twas He that sought the lost,
  That found the wand'ring sheep;
    'Twas He that brought me to the fold,
  'Tis He that still doth keep.

4 No more a wand'ring sheep
    I love to be controlled.
  I love my tender Shepherd's voice,
    I love the peaceful fold.
  No more a wayward child
    I seek no more to roam;
  I love my heavenly Father's voice,
    I love, I love His home.

224

P.M.

I WAS sinking deep in sin,
  Sinking to rise no more;
Overwhelmed by guilt within,
  Mercy I did implore.
Then the Master of the sea,
  Heard my despairing cry,
Christ my Saviour lifted me,
  Now safe am I.

Love lifted me!
Love lifted me!
When no-one but Christ could help,
Love lifted me!
Love lifted me!
Love lifted me!
When no-one but Christ could help,
Love lifted me!

2 All my heart to Him I give,
    Ever to Him I'll cling;
  In His blessèd presence live,
    Ever His praises sing.
  Love so mighty and so true
    Merits my soul's best songs;
  Faithful, loving service, too,
    To Him belongs.

3 When the waves of sorrow roll,
    When I am in distress,
  Jesus takes my hand in His,
    Ever He loves to bless.
  He will every fear dispel,
    Satisfy every need;
  All who heed His loving call,
    Find rest indeed.

225

8.7.8.7.D.

I WILL never, never leave thee,
  I will never thee forsake!
I will guard, and save, and keep thee,
  For My Name and mercy's sake!
Fear no evil, fear no evil,
  Only all My counsel take,
For I'll never, never leave thee,
  I will never thee forsake.

2 When the storm is raging round thee,
    Call on Me in humble prayer,
  I will fold my arms about thee,
    Guard thee with the tend'rest care;
  In the trial, in the trial
    I will make thy pathway clear.
  For I'll never, never leave thee,
    I will never thee forsake.

3 When the sky above is glowing,
    And around thee all is bright,
  Pleasure like a river flowing,
    All things tending to delight,
  I'll be with thee, I'll be with thee,
    I will guide thy steps aright,
  For I'll never, never leave thee,
    I will never thee forsake.

4 When thy soul is dark and clouded,
   Filled with doubt, and grief, and
      care,
   Through the mist by which 'tis
      shrouded,
   I will make a light appear;
      And the banner, and the banner
   Of my love I will uprear.
      For I'll never, never leave thee,
   I will never thee forsake.

226   8.7.8.7.D.

I WILL sing of my Redeemer
   And His wondrous love to me;
On the cruel Cross He suffered,
   From the curse to set me free.

Sing, O sing of my Redeemer!
   With His blood He purchased me;
On the Cross He sealed my pardon,
   Paid the debt and made me free.

2 I will tell the wondrous story,
   How my lost estate to save,
In His boundless love and mercy,
   He the ransom freely gave.

3 I will praise my dear Redeemer,
   His triumphant power I'll tell;
How the victory He giveth
   Over sin, and death, and hell.

4 I will sing of my Redeemer,
   And His heav'nly love to me;
He from death to life hath brought me,
   Son of God, with Him to be.

227   P.M.

I WOULD love to tell you what I
   think of Jesus,
Since I found in Him a friend so
   strong and true;
I would tell you how He changed
   my life completely,
He did something that no other
   friend could do.

No one ever cared for me like Jesus,
   There's no other friend so kind
      as He;
No one else could take the sin and
   darkness from me,
O how much He cared for me!

2 All my life was full of sin when
   Jesus found me,
All my heart was full of misery
   and woe;
Jesus placed His strong and
   loving arms around me,
And He led me in the way I ought
   to go.

3 Every day He comes to me with
   new assurance,
More and more I understand His
   words of love;
But I'll never know just why He
   came to save me,
Till some day I see His blessèd
   face above.

228   P.M.

I'D rather have Jesus than silver
   or gold;
I'd rather be His than have riches
   untold;
I'd rather have Jesus than houses
   or land,
I'd rather be led by His nail-pierced
   hand

Than to be the king of a vast domain
   And be held in sin's dread sway;
I'd rather have Jesus than anything
   This world affords today.

2 I'd rather have Jesus than men's
   applause;
I'd rather be faithful to His dear cause;
   I'd rather have Jesus than world-
      wide fame,
I'd rather be true to His holy name.

3 He's fairer than lilies of rarest bloom;
   He's sweeter than honey from
      out the comb;
He's all that my hungering spirit needs,
   I'd rather have Jesus and let Him
      lead.

229 P.M.

I'M a pilgrim and a stranger,
　Rough and thorny is the road,
Often in the midst of danger,
　But it leads to God.
Clouds and darkness oft distress me,
　Great and many are my foes;
Anxious cares and thoughts
　oppress me:
　　But my Father knows.

2 O how sweet is this assurance
　'Midst the conflict and the strife!
Although sorrows past endurance
　Follow me through life.
Home in prospect still can cheer me;
　Yes, and give me sweet repose,
While I feel His presence near me:
　　For my Father knows.

3 Yes, He sees and knows me daily;
　Watches over me in love;
Sends me help when foes assail me,
　Bids me look above.
Soon my journey will be ended,
　Life is drawing to a close;
I shall then be well attended:
　　This my Father knows.

4 I shall then with joy behold Him,
　Face to face my Saviour see;
Fall with rapture and adore Him
　For His love to me.
Nothing more shall then distress me
　In the land of sweet repose;
Jesus stands engaged to bless me:
　　This my Father knows.

230 C.M. with Chorus

I'M not ashamed to own my Lord,
　Or to defend His cause;
Maintain the honour of His Word,
　The glory of His Cross.

*At the Cross, at the Cross, where
　I first saw the light,
And the burden of my heart roll'd
　away;
It was there by faith I received
　my sight,
And now I am happy all the day.*

2 Jesus, my Lord! I know His name -
　His name is all my trust;
Nor will He put my soul to shame,
　Nor let my hope be lost.

3 Firm as His throne His promise
　stands,
And He can well secure
　What I've committed to His hands
Till the decisive hour.

4 Then will He own my worthless name
　Before His Father's face;
And in the new Jerusalem
　Appoint my soul a place.

231 P.M.

I'M waiting for Thee, Lord,
　Thy beauty to see, Lord,
I'm waiting for Thee, for Thy
　coming again.
Thou'rt gone over there, Lord,
　A place to prepare, Lord,
Thy home I shall share at Thy
　coming again.

2 'Mid danger and fear, Lord,
　I'm oft weary here, Lord;
The day must be near of Thy
　coming again.
'Tis all sunshine there, Lord,
　No sighing or care, Lord,
But glory so fair at Thy coming
　again.

3 Whilst Thou art away, Lord,
　I stumble and stray, Lord;
O hasten the day of Thy coming
　again!
This is not my rest, Lord;
　A pilgrim confest, Lord,
I wait to be blest at Thy coming
　again.

4 Our loved ones before, Lord,
　Their troubles are o'er, Lord,
I'll meet them once more at Thy
　coming again.
The blood was the sign, Lord,
　That marked them as Thine, Lord,
And brightly they'll shine at Thy
　coming again.

5 E'en now let my ways, Lord,
    Be bright with Thy praise, Lord,
For brief are the days ere Thy
    coming again.
I'm waiting for Thee, Lord,
    Thy beauty to see, Lord;
No triumph for me like Thy
    coming again.

232
8.7.8.7.D.

I'VE found a Friend; oh such a Friend!
    He loved me ere I knew Him;
He drew me with the cords of love,
    And thus He bound me to Him.
And round my heart still closely twine
    Those ties which nought can sever,
For I am Christ's, and He is mine,
    For ever and for ever.

2 I've found a Friend; oh such a Friend!
    He bled, He died to save me;
And not alone the gift of life,
    But His own self He gave me.
Nought that I have, mine own I'll call,
    I'll hold it for the Giver:
My heart, my strength, my life, my all,
    Are His, and His for ever.

3 I've found a Friend; oh such a Friend!
    All power to Him is given
To guard me on my onward course
    And bring me safe to heaven.
Eternal glories gleam afar
    To nerve my faint endeavour;
So now to watch! to work! to war!
    And then to rest for ever.

4 I've found a Friend; oh such a Friend!
    So kind, and true, and tender,
So wise a Counsellor and Guide,
    So mighty a Defender.
From Him, who loves me now so well,
    What power my soul can sever?
Shall life? or death? shall earth?
    or hell?
No! I am His for ever.

233
7.6.7.6.D

I'VE found a joy in sorrow,
    A secret balm for pain,
A beautiful tomorrow
    Of sunshine after rain.
I've found a branch of healing
    Near ev'ry bitter spring,
A whispered promise stealing
    O'er ev'ry broken string.

2 I've found a glad hosanna
    For every woe and wail;
A handful of sweet manna
    When grapes of Eshcol fail;
I've found the Rock of Ages
    When desert wells are dry;
And, after weary stages,
    I've found an Elim nigh.

3 An Elim with its coolness,
    Its fountains, and its shade;
A blessing in its fulness,
    When buds of promise fade.
O'er tears of soft contrition
    I've seen a rainbow light,
A glory and fruition,
    So near! yet out of sight.

4 My Saviour, Thee possessing,
    I have the joy, the balm,
The healing and the blessing,
    The sunshine and the psalm;
The promise for the fearful,
    The Elim for the faint,
The rainbow for the tearful,
    The glory for the saint.

234
C.M.

I'VE found the precious Christ of God,
    My heart doth sing for joy;
And sing I must, for Christ I have,
    A precious Christ have I.

2 Christ Jesus is the Lord of lords,
    He is the King of kings;
He is the Sun of Righteousness
    With healing in His wings.

3 Christ is my meat, Christ is my drink,
    My med'cine and my health;
My peace, my strength, my joy,
    my crown,
My glory and my wealth.

4 Christ is my Shepherd and my Friend,
    My Saviour whom I love,
  My Head, my Hope, my Counsellor,
    My Advocate above.

5 Christ Jesus is the heaven of heaven;
    My Christ what shall I call?
  Christ is the First, Christ is the Last,
    And Christ is all in all.

235   11.11.11.11.

IMMORTAL, invisible, God only wise,
  In light inaccessible hid from
our eyes,
  Most blessèd, most gracious, the
    Ancient of Days,
  Almighty, victorious, Thy great
    name we praise.

2 Unresting, unhasting, and silent
    as light,
  Nor wanting, nor wasting, Thou
    rulest in might;
  Thy justice like mountains high
    soaring above
  Thy clouds which are fountains of
    goodness and love.

3 To all, life Thou givest - to both
    great and small;
  In all life Thou livest, the true life of all;
    We blossom and flourish as
      leaves on the tree,
  And wither and perish - but nought
    changeth Thee.

4 Great Father of glory, pure Father
    of light,
  Thine angels adore Thee, all
    veiling their sight;
  All laud we would render: O help us
    to see
  'Tis only the splendour of light
    hideth Thee.

236   8.8.8.8.D.

IN Christ alone my hope is found;
  He is my light, my strength, my song;
This cornerstone, this solid ground,
  Firm through the fiercest drought
    and storm.

What heights of love, what depths
  of peace,
When fears are stilled, when
  strivings cease!
My Comforter, my all in all -
  Here in the love of Christ I stand.

2 In Christ alone, who took on flesh,
    Fulness of God in helpless babe!
  This gift of love and righteousness,
    Scorned by the ones He came
      to save.
  Till on that Cross as Jesus died,
    The wrath of God was satisfied;
  For every sin on Him was laid -
    Here in the death of Christ I live.

3 There in the ground His body lay,
    Light of the world by darkness
      slain;
  Then bursting forth in glorious day
    Up from the grave He rose again!
  And as He stands in victory
    Sin's curse has lost its grip on me,
  For I am His and He is mine -
    Bought with the precious blood
      of Christ.

4 No guilt in life, no fear in death -
    This is the power of Christ in me;
  From life's first cry to final breath,
    Jesus commands my destiny.
  No power of hell, no scheme of man,
    Can ever pluck me from His hand;
  Till He returns or calls me home -
    Here in the power of Christ I'll
      stand.

237   7.6.7.6.D.

IN heavenly love abiding,
  No change my heart shall fear;
And safe is such confiding,
  For nothing changes here:
The storm may roar without me,
  My heart may low be laid,
But God is round about me,
  And can I be dismayed?

2 Wherever He may guide me,
    No want shall turn me back;
  My Shepherd is beside me,
    And nothing can I lack:

His wisdom ever waketh,
　His sight is never dim;
He knows the way He taketh,
　And I will walk with Him.

3 Green pastures are before me,
　Which yet I have not seen;
Bright skies will soon be o'er me,
　Where dark the clouds have been:
My hope I cannot measure,
　My path to life is free;
My Saviour is my treasure
　And He will walk with me.

238
C.M.

IN holy majesty He moved
　Towards a Cross of shame;
And every step the fuller proved
　The glory of His Name.

2 Not even Messianic birth
　His honour could enhance;
The bogus dignity of earth
　Was withered in His glance.

3 Before the earth on which He trod
　Its circuit had begun,
Forever was He Son of God,
　Forever God the Son.

4 Unqualified perfection sealed
　The witness of His Word;
And every touch afresh revealed
　None other than the Lord.

5 And yet, O lowliness most high!
　For this to earth He came,
As Man for guilty men to die
　Upon a Cross of shame.

239
10.10.10.10.

IN hope we lift our wishful, longing
　eyes,
Waiting to see the Morning Star arise;
　How bright, how gladsome will
　　His advent be,
Before the Sun shines forth in majesty!

2 How will our eyes to see His face
　delight,
Whose love has cheered us
　through the darksome night!

How will our ears drink in His well-
　known voice,
Whose faintest whisper makes
　our soul rejoice!

3 No stain within, no foes or snares
　around;
No jarring notes shall there
　discordant sound;
All pure without, all pure within the
　breast;
No thorns to wound, no toil to mar
　our rest.

4 If here on earth the thoughts of
　Jesus' love
Lift our poor hearts this weary
　world above,
If even here the taste of heavenly
　springs
So cheers the spirit that the
　pilgrim sings: -

5 What will the sunshine of His glory
　prove?
What the unmingled fulness of His
　love?
What hallelujahs will His presence
　raise?
What, but one loud eternal burst
　of praise!

240
P.M.

IN loving kindness Jesus came
　My soul in mercy to reclaim,
And from the depths of sin and
　shame
Through grace He lifted me.

From sinking sand He lifted me,
　With tender hand He lifted me,
From shades of night to plains
　of light,
Oh, praise His name, He lifted me!

2 He called me long before I heard,
　Before my sinful heart was stirred,
But when I took Him at His word,
　Forgiven, He lifted me.

3 His brow was pierced with many
　a thorn,
His hands by cruel nails were torn,
　When from my guilt and grief, forlorn,
In love He lifted me.

4 Now on a higher plane I dwell,
    And with my soul I know 'tis well;
Yet how or why, I cannot tell,
    He should have lifted me.

241   P.M.

IN seasons of grief to my God
    I'll repair,
When my heart is o'erwhelmed
    with sorrow and care;
From the ends of the earth to
    Thee will I cry,
Lead me to the Rock that is
    higher than I.

*Higher than I, higher than I,
    Lead me to the Rock that is
        higher than I.*

2 When Satan, my foe, shall come
    in like a flood,
To drive my poor soul from the
    Fountain of good,
I'll pray to the Saviour who
    meekly did die;
Lead me to the Rock that is
    higher than I.

3 And while as a stranger I sojourn
    below,
Thy covenant blessings, Lord,
    freely bestow;
In affliction's dark night to Thy
    throne let me fly,
Lead me to the Rock that is
    higher than I.

4 And when I have ended my
    pilgrimage here,
In Jesus' pure righteousness let
    me appear:
From the swellings of Jordan to
    Thee will I cry:
Lead me to the Rock that is
    higher than I.

5 And when the last trumpet shall
    sound through the skies,
And the dead from the dust of the
    earth shall arise,
With the millions I'll join, far above
    yonder sky,
To praise the Great Rock that is
    higher than I.

242   7.6.7.6.D.

IN smooth and silken whiteness,
    Without a rough'ning grain,
In clear, unbroken brightness,
    Without a speck or stain,
The fine flour in its beauty
    The perfect man portrays
In all His path of duty,
    In all His heavenly ways.

2 In softness unresisting
    The rough and ruthless touch,
In purity consisting
    As not another such,
In every feature flawless,
    In every aspect fair,
The search of sinners lawless
    Could find no blemish there.

3 A wealth of heavenly glory
    Unfolds before our gaze:
Remembering the story
    Of all His wondrous ways,
We muse in conscious weakness
    On gentleness and power,
On lowliness and meekness -
    Frankincense and fine flour.

4 O God, His God and Father,
    What shall we say to Thee?
Our hearts would incense gather
    And raise it rev'rently.
In worship thus ascending,
    To Thee our hymn we sing,
The theme our thoughts
    transcending,
Thy Son remembering.

243   C.M.D.

IN songs of praise, our God, to Thee,
    We lift our voices high,
For each unfolded mystery,
    Of grace us brought nigh:
Wondrous the love that first began,
    In counsel deep to lay
Foundation sure for ruined man,
    Thy glory to display.

2 We praise Thee for that gift divine -
    The Son, from off Thy throne,
Whose ways of truth and mercy shine
    In perfectness Thine own:
We praise Thee for the Holy Ghost,
    Sent forth to win a Bride
From out the lost - a ransomed host -
    For Jesus glorifed.

3 Father of mercies, Thee we praise!
    The glory Thine alone!
Thy Son, Thy Spirit, sent to raise
    Lost sinners to a throne!
And this throughout the hosts above,
    The joy and song shall be -
The Father's wondrous work of love,
    Redemption's mystery!

244   L.M.

IS it Thy will that I should be
    Buried, in symbol, Lord, with Thee?
Owning Thee by this solemn sign,
    Telling the world that I am Thine.

2 Gladly I yield obedience now;
    In all things to Thy will I'd bow;
I'll follow where my Saviour led,
    And humbly in His footsteps tread.

3 This emblematic, watery grave
    Shows forth His love, who
        came to save;
And as I enter it, I see
    The price my Saviour paid for me.

4 Forth from Thy burial, Lord, I come,
    For Thou hast triumphed o'er
        the tomb;
Thy resurrection life I share,
    My portion is no longer here.

5 O may I count myself to be
    Dead to the sins that wounded Thee,
Dead to the pleasures of this earth
    Unworthy of my heavenly birth.

4 Lord Jesus, when I gaze on Thee
    And all Thy radiant glory see,
That joy will far exceed the shame
    I bear on earth for Thy loved name.

245   L.M.

IT is a thing most wonderful,
    Almost too wonderful to be,
That God's own Son should come
    from heaven,
And die to save a child like me.

2 And yet I know that it is true:
    He chose a poor and humble lot,
And wept and toiled, and
        mourned and died,
For love of those who loved Him not.

3 I cannot tell how He could love
    A child so weak and full of sin;
His love must be most wonderful,
    If He could die my love to win.

4 I sometimes think about His Cross,
    And shut my eyes, and try to see
The cruel nails, and crown of thorns,
    And Jesus crucified for me.

5 But even could I see Him die,
    I could but see a little part
Of that great love, which, like a fire,
    Is always burning in His heart.

6 It is most wonderful to know
    His love for me so free and sure;
But 'tis more wonderful to see
    My love for Him so faint and poor.

7 And yet I want to love Thee, Lord:
    O light the flame within my heart,
And I will love Thee more and more
    Until I see Thee as Thou art!

246   P.M.

IT may be at morn,
    When the day is awaking,
When sunlight through darkness
    And shadow is breaking,
That Jesus will come
    In the fulness of glory
To receive from the world His own.

    O Lord Jesus, how long?
    How long - ere we shout the glad
        song?
    Christ returneth! Hallelujah!
        Hallelujah! Amen!
        Hallelujah! Amen!

2 It may be at midday,
   It may be at twilight,
It may be, perchance,
   That the blackness of midnight
Will burst into light
   In the blaze of His glory
When Jesus receives His own.

3 While hosts cry Hosanna,
   From heaven descending,
With glorified saints
   And the angels attending,
With grace on His brow,
   Like a halo of glory
Will Jesus receive His own.

4 O joy! O delight!
   Should we go without dying;
No sickness, no sadness,
   No dread, and no crying;
Caught up through the clouds
   With our Lord into glory
When Jesus receives His own.

247   10.10.10.10.4.
IT passeth knowledge, that dear
   love of Thine,
Lord Jesus, Saviour; yet this soul
   of mine
Would of Thy love, in all its
   breadth and length,
Its height and depth, its
   everlasting strength
Know more and more.

2 It passeth telling, that dear love
   of Thine,
Lord Jesus, Saviour; yet these
   lips of mine
Would fain proclaim to sinners, far
   and near,
A love which can remove all guilt
   and fear,
And love beget.

3 It passeth praises, that dear love
   of Thine,
Lord Jesus, Saviour; yet this heart
   of mine
Would sing that love, so full, so
   rich, so free,
Which brings a rebel sinner, even me,
   Nigh unto God.

4 But though I cannot sing, or tell, or
   know
The fulness of Thy love while here
   below,

My empty vessel I may freely bring;
   O Thou, who art of love the living
   spring,
My vessel fill.

5 I am an empty vessel - not one
   thought,
Or look of love, I ever to Thee brought;
   Yet I may come, and come again
   to Thee,
With this, the empty sinner's only
   plea -
Thou lovest me.

6 Then fill me, O my Saviour, with
   Thy love!
Lead, lead me to the living fount above;
   Thither may I in simple faith draw
   nigh,
And never to another fountain fly,
   But unto Thee.

7 And when, Lord Jesus, Thine own
   face I see,
When at Thy lofty throne I bow the
   knee,
Then of Thy love, in all its breadth
   and length,
Its height and depth, its
   everlasting strength,
My soul shall sing.

248   C.M. with Chorus
IT was alone the Saviour prayed
   In dark Gethsemane;
Alone He drained the bitter cup
   And suffered there for me.

Alone, alone, He bore it all alone;
   He gave Himself to save His own,
He suffered, bled and died alone,
   alone.

2 It was alone the Saviour stood
   In Pilate's judgment hall;
Alone the crown of thorns He wore
   Forsaken thus by all.

3 Alone upon the Cross He hung
   That others He might save;
Forsaken then by God and man
   Alone, His life He gave.

249
6.6.6.6.8.8.

JEHOVAH is our strength,
  And He shall be our song;
We shall o'ercome at length,
  Although our foes be strong:
In vain then Satan doth oppose,
The Lord is stronger than His foes.

2 The Lord our refuge is,
    And ever will remain;
  Since He hath made us His
    He will our cause maintain:
  In vain our enemies oppose,
  For God is stronger than His foes.

3 The Lord our portion is;
    What can we wish for more?
  As long as we are His
    We never can be poor:
  In vain do earth and hell oppose,
  For God is stronger than His foes.

4 The Lord our Shepherd is;
    He knows our ev'ry need;
  And since we now are His,
    His care our souls will feed:
  In vain do sin and death oppose
  For God is stronger than His foes.

250
8.7.8.7.

JESUS calls us! o'er the tumult
  Of our life's wild restless sea,
Day by day His sweet voice soundeth,
  Saying, "Christian, follow Me".

2 As of old, apostles heard it
    By the Galilean lake,
  Turned from home and toil and kindred,
    Leaving all for His dear sake.

3 Jesus calls us from the worship
    Of the vain world's golden store,
  From each idol that would keep us
    Saying, "Christian, love Me more".

4 In our joys and in our sorrows,
    Days of toil and hours of ease,
  Still He calls, in cares and pleasures,
    "Christian, love Me more than these".

5 Jesus calls us! by Thy mercies,
    Saviour, may we hear Thy call,
  Give our hearts to Thine obedience,
    Serve and love Thee best of all.

251
8.7.8.4.8.4.

JESUS CHRIST, Thou King of Glory,
  Born a Saviour-Prince to be,
While the angel-hosts adore Thee,
  We joy in Thee,
Singing of Thy grace the story,
  Praise, praise to Thee.

2 Thou the bands of death didst sever,
    Conflict Thine and victory;
  God is for us now and ever;
    We joy in Thee.
  We are Thine, Thine own for ever,
    Praise, praise to Thee.

3 Thou the ransom price hast given,
    Setting thus the captive free;
  Thou art Lord of earth and heaven;
    We joy in Thee.
  Through Thy blood we stand forgiven,
    Praise, praise to Thee.

4 Risen Lord! at Thy returning
    Sweet and full our song shall be;
  Hasting to that blissful morning
    We joy in Thee.
  Thou hast read our spirits' yearning,
    Praise, praise to Thee.

252
8.7.8.7.D.

JESUS, I am resting, resting
  In the joy of what Thou art;
I am finding out the greatness
  Of Thy loving heart:
Thou hast bid me gaze upon Thee,
And Thy beauty fills my soul,
  For, by Thy transforming power,
Thou hast made me whole.

  Jesus, I am resting, resting
    In the joy of what Thou art;
  I am finding out the greatness
    Of Thy loving heart.

2 O how great Thy loving-kindness!
    Vaster, broader than the sea:
  O how marvellous Thy goodness
    Lavished all on me!
  Yes, I rest in Thee, Belovèd,
    Know what wealth of grace is Thine,
  Know Thy certainty of promise,
    And have made it mine.

3 Simply trusting Thee, Lord Jesus,
　　I behold Thee as Thou art,
　And Thy love, so pure, so changeless,
　　Satisfies my heart;
　Satisfies its deepest longings,
　　Meets, supplies its every need,
　Compasseth me round with blessings;
　　Thine is love indeed.

4 Ever lift Thy face upon me
　　As I work and wait for Thee,
　Resting 'neath Thy smile, Lord Jesus,
　　Earth's dark shadows flee;
　Brightness of my Father's glory,
　　Sunshine of my Father's face,
　Keep me ever trusting, resting;
　　Fill me with Thy grace.

253
8.7.8.7.

JESUS in His heav'nly temple,
　Sits with God upon the throne;
Now no more to be forsaken,
　His humiliation gone.

2 Never more shall God, Jehovah,
　　Smite the Shepherd with the sword;
　Ne'er again shall cruel sinners
　　Set at nought our glorious Lord.

3 Dwelling in eternal sunshine
　　Of the countenance of God,
　Jesus fills all heav'n with incense
　　Of His reconciling blood.

4 On His heart our names are graven;
　　On His shoulders we are borne;
　Of our God beloved in Jesus
　　We can love Him in return.

254
C.M.

JESUS! in Thee our eyes behold
　A thousand glories more
Than the rich gems and polished gold
　The sons of Aaron wore.

2 They first their own sin-offering
　　brought,
　To purge themselves from sin;
　Thy life was pure, without a spot,
　And all Thy nature clean.

3 Fresh blood, as constant as the day,
　　Was on their altar spilt;
　But Thy *one* offering takes away
　　For ever all our guilt.

4 Their priesthood ran through
　　several hands,
　For mortal was their race;
　　Thy never-changing office stands,
　Eternal as Thy days.

5 Their range was earth, nor higher
　　soared;
　The heaven of heavens is Thine:
　　Thy majesty and priesthood, Lord,
　Through endless ages shine.

255
L.M.

JESUS! in whom all glories meet,
　Whose praise through earth
and heaven shall ring,
　Thy name, than all beside more
　　sweet,
With hearts adoring would we sing.

2 Thou as our Paschal Lamb wast slain,
　　Thy blood has met the avenger's
　　eye;
　Beneath that shelter we remain,
　　And keep the feast, nor fear, nor
　　die.

3 A Priest for ever, Thou art there
　　For us, the holiest within;
　Our names upon Thy breast to bear,
　　Absolved from every charge of sin.

4 There, in the Father's love we dwell,
　　Called by His grace His sons to be,
　And now in songs adoring tell,
　　We owe it all, O Lord, to Thee!

256
P.M.

JESUS is coming! Sing the glad word!
　Coming for those He redeemed
by His blood,
　Coming to reign as the glorified Lord!
　　Jesus is coming again!

Jesus is coming, is coming again!
　Jesus is coming again!
Shout the glad tidings o'er
　mountain and plain,
　　Jesus is coming again!

2 Jesus is coming! The dead shall arise,
    Loved ones shall meet in a joyful
        surprise,
  Caught up together to Him in the skies:
      Jesus is coming again!

3 Jesus is coming! His saints to release;
    Coming to give to the warring
        earth peace;
  Sinning, and sighing, and sorrow,
    shall cease:
      Jesus is coming again!

4 Jesus is coming! The promise is true;
    Who are the chosen, the faithful,
        the few
  Waiting and watching, prepared for
    review?
      Jesus is coming again!

257   11.11.11.11.
J ESUS is our Shepherd, wiping
    ev'ry tear,
  Folded in His bosom what have we
    to fear?
  Only let us follow whither He doth lead,
    To the thirsty desert, or the dewy
        mead.

2 Jesus is our Shepherd, well we
    know His voice!
  How its gentlest whisper makes our
    hearts rejoice:
  Even when He chideth, tender is
    His tone;
  None but He shall guide us; we are
    His alone.

3 Jesus is our Shepherd; for the
    sheep He bled;
  Ev'ry lamb is sprinkled with the
    blood He shed;
  Then on each He setteth His own
    secret sign,
  "They that have My Spirit, these",
    saith He, "are Mine".

4 Jesus is our Shepherd; guarded by
    His arm,
  Though the wolves may ravin none
    can do us harm;

If we tread death's valley, dark
  with fearful gloom,
We shall fear no evil, victors o'er
  the tomb.

5 Jesus is our Shepherd; with His
    goodness now,
  And His tender mercy, He doth us
    endow.
  Let us sing His praises with a
    gladsome heart
  Till in heaven we meet Him,
    nevermore to part.

258   P.M.
J ESUS, keep me near the Cross,
    There a precious fountain
  Free to all, a healing stream,
    Flows from Calvary's mountain.

  In the Cross, in the Cross
    Be my glory ever;
  Till my ransomed soul shall find
    Rest beyond the river.

2 Near the Cross, a trembling soul,
    Love and mercy found me;
  There the Bright and Morning Star,
    Shed its beams around me.

3 Near the Cross! O Lamb of God,
    Bring its scenes before me;
  Help me walk from day to day,
    With its shadows o'er me.

4 Near the Cross I'll watch and wait,
    Hoping, trusting ever,
  Till I reach the golden strand
    Just beyond the river.

259   8.7.8.7.7.7.
J ESUS, Lord, I need Thy presence
    As I journey on my way,
  For without Thee I am lonely,
    And my feet are apt to stray;
  But if Thou wilt walk with me
    Life will calm and holy be.

2 Jesus, Lord, I need Thy wisdom,
    For perplexing problems press,
  And without Thee I am foolish,

Nor can bear the strain and stress;
But if Thou wilt counsel me
  I shall true and upright be.

3 Jesus, Lord, I need Thy power,
    For temptations come and go,
  And without Thee I am helpless,
    With no strength to meet the foe;
  But if Thou wilt strengthen me
    Life will all-triumphant be.

4 Jesus, Lord, I need Thy guidance,
    Fire by night, and cloud by day,
  For without them I am sightless,
    Groping for the proper way;
  But if Thou dost lead me on
    I will follow Thee alone.

5 Jesus, Lord, Thy love so tender
    Is my greatest need of all,
  For without Thee pride and anger
    From unguarded lips will fall;
  But if Thou Thy love impart
    I shall have a gracious heart.

260   8.7.8.7.4.7.

JESUS, Lord, I'm never weary
  Looking on Thy Cross and shame;
Gazing there I seem so near Thee,
  Dear to me each throb of pain.
    Ever near Thee,
Ling'ring here I would remain.

2 Little cared I for the anguish
    Of Thy bitter, bitter cry;
  Left alone, Lord, there to anguish,
    None to share Thy parting sigh.
      All forsaken!
  Left alone, O Lord, to die.

3 Jesus, Saviour, I have found Thee
    All my utmost need required;
  In Thyself, Lord, Thou hast found me
    All Thy loving heart desired.
      I would praise Thee
  From my soul by love inspired.

4 All my sins were laid upon Thee,
    All my guilt was on Thee laid,
  And the blood of Thine atonement
    All my utmost debt has paid.
      Gracious Saviour,
  I believe, for Thou hast said.

5 Thine almighty arms are round me,
    And my head is on Thy breast,
  For my weary soul has found Thee
    Such a perfect, perfect rest.
      Gracious Saviour,
  Now I know that I am blest.

261   7.7.7.7. with Chorus

JESUS, Lord, Thy love to me,
  Led Thee to the shameful tree,
There to take my bitter cup,
  And its dregs Thou drankest up:

  Keep me, keep me,
  Saviour, keep me near the Cross!
    There is centred all my hope,
  All for Thee I'd count but loss.

2 Judgment threatened like a flood,
    'Neath it, guilty, vile, I stood;
  All its billows beat on Thee,
    Thou didst sink! Now peace
      for me!

3 Sin, in all its crimson hue,
    Marked against me, did pursue;
  Thine own blood, by grace so free,
    Shed for sinners, cleanseth me!

4 Death and judgment left behind,
    Now Thy glory fills the mind;
  Saviour, Thou wilt come for me,
    I shall ever dwell with Thee!

262   8.7.8.7.

JESUS, Lord, we come together
  In the bonds of Thine own love;
Thou hast drawn our footsteps
    hither
Its deep meaning now to prove.

2 Here together we recall Thee,
    In Thy presence break the bread;
  Never more can grief befall Thee,
    Thou art risen from the dead.

3 But Thy love remains, that entered
    Into death to make us Thine;
  In that death all love was centred;
    Thankful now we drink the wine.

4 Thou dost make us taste the blessing,
   Soon to fill a world of bliss;
And we bless Thy name, confessing
   Thine own love our portion is.

5 Sweet it is to sit before Thee,
   Sweet to hear Thy blessèd voice,
Sweet to worship and adore Thee,
   While our hearts in Thee rejoice.

263   8.7.8.7.D.

JESUS, Lord, we know Thee present
   At Thy table freshly spread,
Seated at Thy priceless banquet
   With Thy banner overhead.
Precious moments at Thy table
   From all fear and doubt set free;
Here to rest, so sweetly able,
   Occupied alone with Thee.

2 Here rejoicing in Thy nearness,
   Gladly by Thy Spirit led;
Calmly in the blest remembrance
   Of Thy precious blood once shed.
Lord, we take each simple token
   In fond memory of Thee;
Muse upon Thy body broken,
   And Thy blood shed on the tree.

3 Oh, what joy it is to see Thee,
   In these chosen emblems here!
In the bread and wine of blessing,
   Bread to strengthen, wine to cheer!
Lord, behold us met together,
   One in Thee, our risen Head,
Thus we take the cup of blessing,
   Thus we share the broken bread.

4 Lord, we know how true Thy promise
   To be with us where we meet,
When in Thy loved Name we gather
   To enjoy communion sweet;
Dearer still that looked-for promise,
   To each waiting, yearning heart,
That with Thee we soon shall be, Lord,
   Yea, "for ever" where Thou art.

264   7.7.7.7.D.

JESUS, Lover of my soul,
   Let me to Thy bosom fly,
While the nearer waters roll,
   While the tempest still is high:
Hide me, O my Saviour, hide,
   Till the storm of life is past;
Safe into the haven guide,
   O receive my soul at last!

2 Other refuge have I none;
   Hangs my helpless soul on Thee;
Leave, ah! leave me not alone,
   Still support and comfort me.
All my trust on Thee is stayed,
   All mine help from Thee I bring;
Cover my defenceless head
   With the shadow of Thy wing.

3 Thou, O Christ, art all I want,
   More than all in Thee I find;
Raise the fallen, cheer the faint,
   Heal the sick, and heal the blind.
Just and holy is Thy name,
   I am all unrighteousness!
Vile and full of sin I am,
   Thou art full of truth and grace.

4 Plenteous grace with Thee is found,
   Grace to cover all my sin;
Let the healing streams abound;
   Make and keep me pure within.
Thou of life the fountain art;
   Freely let me take of Thee;
Spring Thou up within my heart
   Now, and to eternity.

265   P.M.

JESUS, my Lord, will love me forever,
   From Him no power of evil can sever,
He gave His life to ransom my soul;
   Now I belong to Him.

Now I belong to Jesus,
   Jesus belongs to me,
Not for the years of time alone,
   But for eternity.

2 Once I was lost in sin's degradation,
   Jesus came down to bring me
   salvation,
Lifted me up from sorrow and shame,
   Now I belong to Him.

3 Joy floods my soul for Jesus has
     saved me,
  Freed me from sin that long had
     enslaved me;
  His precious blood, He gave to redeem,
  Now I belong to Him.

266   10.4.10.4.10.10
JESUS, our Lord, Thy worthiness
     we sing,
Thy peerless fame.
     Our sacrifice of praise to Thee we
        bring,
And bless Thy Name.
     Thy glories fill our vision with delight,
And heart and voice to honour Thee
     unite.

2 Yet wider praise in Zion waits for Thee,
     Her Lord and King;
  Creation too, in rest and liberty,
     Shall tribute bring;
  Both heav'n and earth shall Thy
     dominion own,
  And every tongue confess Thee
     Lord alone.

3 More blessèd still - Thine own
     peculiar joy
  Thy saints shall be,
     Who then shall find their
  constant blest employ
     In praising Thee;
  And with Thee, Lord, Thy glory shall
     behold,
  While love delights its wonders to
     unfold.

267   11.10.11.10.
JESUS, our Lord, with what joy
     we adore Thee,
Chanting our praise to Thyself on
     the throne,
Blest in Thy presence, we
     worship before Thee,
Own Thou art worthy, and worthy
     alone.

2 Verily God, yet become truly human -
     Lower than angels - to die in our
        stead;

How hast Thou, long promised
     Seed of the woman,
Trod on the serpent and bruisèd
     his head!

3 How didst Thou humble Thyself to
     be taken,
  Led by Thy creatures, and nailed
     to the Cross?
  Hated of men, and of God, too,
     forsaken,
  Shunning not darkness, the curse,
     and the loss.

4 How hast Thou triumphed, and
     triumphed with glory,
  Battled death's forces, rolled back
     every wave!
  Can we refrain, then, from telling
     the story,
  How Thou art victor o'er death
     and the grave?

     Lord, Thou art worthy:
     Lord, Thou art worthy;
     Lord, Thou art worthy,
        and worthy alone!
     Blest in Thy presence,
        We worship before Thee,
     Own Thou art worthy,
        and worthy alone!

268   C.M.
JESUS, our Saviour Thou and Lord,
     How precious is Thy Word!
To lowly and believing hearts
     What joy it doth afford!

2 Thy Word of pure, eternal truth
     Shall yet unshaken stay,
  When all that man has thought or
     planned,
  Like chaff has passed away.

3 Thy Word, Lord, speaks to us of
     Thee,
  And Thine exceeding grace;
     In it Thy thoughts and ways of love
  With wondering joy we trace.

4 Thy Word upon our daily path,
     Its light divine doth shed;
  By it our feet through Satan's snares,
     In safety may be led.

5 Oh, may it richly dwell within,
    And mould our every thought;
  And be each heart to Thy blest sway,
    In full subjection brought!

6 Lord, by Thy Spirit teach and lead,
    While seated at Thy feet,
  That we may in Thy holy will,
    Stand perfect and complete.

269   L.M.
JESUS shall reign where'er the sun
  Doth his successive journeys run;
His kingdom stretch from shore to
    shore
  Till moons shall wax and wane no
    more.

2 For Him shall endless prayer be made,
    And praises throng to crown His
      head;
  His name like sweet perfume shall rise
    With every morning sacrifice.

3 People and realms of every tongue
    Dwell on His love with sweetest
      song;
  And infant voices shall proclaim
    Their early blessings on His name.

4 Blessings abound where'er He reigns,
    The prisoner leaps to lose his chains,
    The weary find eternal rest,
      And all the sons of want are blest.

5 Where He displays His healing power,
    Death and the curse are known
      no more;
  In Him the sons of Adam boast
    More blessings than their father
      lost.

6 Let every creature rise and bring
    Peculiar honours to our King,
  Angels descend with songs again,
    And earth repeat the loud Amen.

270   P.M.
JESUS! Source of life eternal,
  Jesus! Author of our breath,
Victor o'er the hosts infernal
  By defeat and shame and death.
Thou through deepest tribulation
  Deigned to pass for our salvation:
Thousand, thousand praises be,
  Lord of Glory unto Thee.

2 Thou, O Son of God, wert bearing
    Cruel mockings, hatred, scorn;
  Thou, the King of Glory, wearing,
    For our sake, the crown of thorn;
  Dying, Thou didst us deliver
    From the chains of sin for ever:
  Thousand, thousand praises be,
    Precious Saviour, unto Thee.

3 All the shame men heaped upon Thee,
    Thou didst patiently endure;
  Not the pains of death too bitter
    Our redemption to procure.
  Wondrous Thy humiliation
    To accomplish our salvation:
  Thousand, thousand praises be,
    Precious Saviour, unto Thee.

4 Heartfelt praise and adoration,
    Saviour, thus to Thee we give;
  For Thy life humiliation,
    For Thy death, whereby we live.
  All the grief Thou wert enduring,
    All the bliss Thou wert securing:
  Evermore the theme shall be
  Of thanksgivings, Lord, to Thee.

271   L.M.
JESUS, the Lord our Righteousness!
  Our beauty Thou, our glorious dress;
Before the throne, when thus arrayed,
  With joy shall we lift up the head.

2 When from the dust of death I rise,
    To claim my mansion in the skies;
  E'en then shall this be all my plea,
    "Jesus has lived and died for me".

3 Bold shall we stand in that great day,
    For who aught to our charge shall lay,
  Since by Thy blood absolved we are
    From sin and guilt, from shame
      and fear?

4 Thus Abraham, the friend of God,
    Thus all the saints redeemed
      by blood,
  Saviour of sinners Thee proclaim,
    And all their boast is in Thy Name.

5 This spotless robe the same appears,
    When ruined nature sinks in years;
  No age can change its glorious hue,
    The robe of Christ is ever new.

6 Till we behold Thee on Thy throne,
    We boast in Thee, in Thee alone;
    Our beauty this, our glorious dress,
    Jesus, the Lord our Righteousness!

272   C.M.

JESUS, the name high over all,
    In hell, or earth, or sky;
Angels and men before it fall,
    And devils fear and fly.

2 Jesus, the name to sinners dear,
    The name to sinners given;
It scatters all their guilty fear;
    It turns their hell to heaven.

3 Jesus the prisoner's fetters breaks,
    And bruises Satan's head;
Power into strengthless souls He
    speaks,
And life into the dead.

4 Oh, that the world might taste
    and see
    The riches of His grace;
    The arms of love that compass
    me,
Would all mankind embrace.

5 Thee I shall constantly proclaim,
    Though earth and hell oppose;
Bold to confess Thy glorious Name
    Before a world of foes.

6 His only righteousness I show,
    His saving truth proclaim:
'Tis all my business here below
    To cry, "Behold the Lamb!"

7 Happy, if with my latest breath
    I may but gasp His name;
Preach Him to all, and cry, in death,
    "Behold, behold the Lamb!"

273   C.M.

JESUS! the very thought of Thee
    With sweetness fills my breast;
But sweeter far Thy face to see,
    And in Thy presence rest.

2 Nor voice can sing, nor heart can frame,
    Nor can the mem'ry find
  A sweeter sound than Thy blest Name,
    O Saviour of mankind.

3 O hope of every contrite heart,
    O joy of all the meek,
To those who fall, how kind Thou art;
    How good to those who seek.

4 But what to those who find? Ah, this
    Nor tongue, nor pen can show;
The love of Jesus! what it is
    None but His loved ones know.

5 Saviour, our only joy be Thou,
    As Thou our crown wilt be;
Be Thou, O Lord, our glory now,
    And through eternity.

274   L.M.

JESUS, Thou Joy of loving hearts!
    Thou Fount of life! Thou Light
of men!
    From the best bliss that earth
    imparts,
We turn unfilled to Thee again.

2 Thy truth unchanged hath ever stood;
    Thou savest those that on Thee call;
To them that seek Thee, Thou art good,
    To them that find Thee, All in all!

3 We taste Thee, O Thou living Bread,
    And long to feast upon Thee still;
We drink of Thee, the Fountain-head,
    And thirst our souls from Thee
    to fill.

4 Our restless spirits yearn for Thee
    Where'er our changeful lot is cast;
Glad, when Thy gracious smile we
    see;
  Blest, when our faith can hold Thee
    fast.

5 Lord Jesus, ever with us stay!
    Make all our moments calm
    and bright!
  Chase the dark night of sin away,
    Shed o'er the world Thy holy light.

275   L.M.

JESUS, Thy dying love I own -
    A love unfathomed and unknown!
All other love can measured be,
    But not Thy dying love to me.

2 Oh, wonder to myself I am,
   Thou loving, bleeding, suffering Lamb,
That I can scan the mystery o'er,
   And not be moved to love Thee
     more!

3 'Tis well, my Lord, that 'twas *Thy* love,
   Not *mine*, that brought Thee from
     above;
And well that 'twas Thy bitter grief,
   Not mine, that gave my soul relief.

4 Loved now, and ever on Thy throne,
   Adored and loved, Thou timeless
     One!
Thou wilt, through one eternal day,
   The height and depth of love
     display!

276   6.4.6.4.6.6.6.4.

JESUS, Thy Name I love!
   Jesus, my Lord!
All other names above
   Jesus, my Lord!
Thou, Lord, my all must be!
Nothing to please I see,
Nothing apart from Thee,
   Jesus, my Lord!

2 Thou blessèd Son of God,
   Jesus, my Lord!
Hast bought me with Thy blood,
   Jesus, my Lord!
Great was indeed Thy love,
All other loves above,
Love Thou didst clearly prove,
   Jesus, my Lord!

3 When unto Thee I flee,
   Jesus, my Lord!
Thou wilt my refuge be,
   Jesus, my Lord!
Whom, then, have I to fear?
What trouble, grief or care?
Since Thou art ever near,
   Jesus, my Lord!

4 Soon Thou wilt come again,
   Jesus, my Lord!
I shall be happy then,
   Jesus, my Lord!
When Thine own face I see;
Then I shall like Thee be;
Then evermore with Thee,
   Jesus, my Lord!

277   6.4.6.4.6.6.6.4.

JESUS was slain for me,
   At Calvary.
Crownèd with thorns was He,
   At Calvary.
There He in anguish died,
   There from His opened side,
Poured forth the crimson tide,
   At Calvary.

2 Pardoned is all my sin,
   At Calvary.
Cleansed is my heart within,
   At Calvary.
Now robes of praise I wear,
   Gone are my grief and care,
Christ bore my burdens there,
   At Calvary.

3 Wondrous His love for me,
   At Calvary.
Glorious His victory,
   At Calvary.
Vanquished are death and hell,
   Oh, let His praises swell,
Ever my tongue shall tell,
   Of Calvary.

278   6.6.6.6.8.8.

JOIN all the glorious names
   Of wisdom, love, and power,
That mortals ever knew,
   That angels ever bore:
All are too mean to speak Thy worth,
   Too mean to set Thee, Saviour,
     forth.

2 Great Prophet of our God!
   Our tongues would bless Thy Name;
By Thee the joyful news
   Of our salvation came -
The joyful news of sins forgiven,
   Of hell subdued, of peace with
     heaven.

3 But O what gentle terms,
   What condescending ways
Doth our Redeemer use
   To teach His heav'nly grace!
Mine eyes with joy and wonder see
   What forms of love He bears
     for me.

4 Be Thou our Counsellor,
    Our Pattern, and our Guide;
And through this desert land
    Still keep us near Thy side.
Oh, let our feet ne'er run astray,
    Nor rove, nor seek the crooked way!

5 We love our Shepherd's voice;
    His watchful eyes shall keep
Our wand'ring souls among
    The thousands of His sheep:
He feeds His flock, He calls their
    names,
His bosom bears the tender lambs.

6 Should all the hosts of death,
    And pow'rs of hell unknown,
Put their most dreadful forms
    Of rage and mischief on;
I shall be safe, for Christ displays
    Superior pow'r, and guardian grace.

279
8.8.8.6.

JUST as I am, Thine own to be,
    Friend of the young, who lovest me,
To consecrate myself to Thee,
    O Jesus Christ, I come.

2 In the glad morning of my day,
    My life to give, my vows to pay,
With no reserve and no delay,
    With all my heart, I come.

3 I would live ever in the light,
    I would work ever for the right,
I would serve Thee with all my might,
    Therefore to Thee, I come.

4 Just as I am, young, strong, and free,
    To be the best that I can be
For truth, and righteousness, and Thee,
    Lord of my life, I come.

5 And for Thy sake to win renown,
    And then to take the victor's crown,
And at Thy feet to lay it down,
    O Master, Lord, I come.

280
4.6.8.8.4.

KEPT, safely kept;
    My fears away are swept;
In weakness to my God I cling,
    Though foes be strong I calmly sing,
    Kept, safely kept.

2 Kept by His power,
    Whatever dangers lower
The strength of God's almighty arm
    Doth shield my soul from every harm,
    Kept by His power.

3 Through simple faith,
    Believing what He saith,
Unshaken on my God I lean,
    And realise His power unseen,
    But known to faith.

4 Kept all the way,
    E'en to salvation's day,
His mighty love ne'er cold shall wax,
    Nor shall His pow'rful grasp relax,
    Through all the way.

281
C.M. with Chorus

KING of my life, I crown Thee now;
    Thine shall the glory be;
Lest I forget Thy thorn-crowned brow,
    Lead me to Calvary.

Lest I forget Gethsemane,
Lest I forget Thine agony,
Lest I forget Thy love for me,
Lead me to Calvary.

2 Show me the tomb where Thou
    wast laid,
Tenderly mourned and wept;
    Angels in robes of light arrayed
Guarded Thee whilst Thou slept.

3 Let me, like Mary, through the gloom,
    Come with a gift to Thee;
Show to me now the empty tomb -
    Lead me to Calvary.

4 May I be willing, Lord, to bear
    Daily my cross for Thee;
Even Thy cup of grief to share -
    Thou hast borne all for me

5 Fill me, O Lord, with Thy desire
    For all that know not Thee;
Then touch my lips with holy fire,
    To speak of Calvary.

282   8.7.8.7.D.

LAMB OF GOD! our souls adore Thee
While upon Thy face we gaze;
  There the Father's love and glory
Shine in all their brightest rays.
  Thine almighty power and wisdom
All creation's works proclaim;
  Heaven and earth alike confess Thee
As the ever great I AM.

2 Lamb of God! Thy Father's bosom
    Ever was Thy dwelling-place;
  His delight, in Him rejoicing,
    One with Him in power and grace:
  Oh what wondrous love and mercy!
    Thou didst lay Thy glory by
  And for us didst come from heaven,
    As the Lamb of God, to die.

3 Lamb of God! when we behold Thee
    Lowly in the manger laid;
  Wand'ring as a homeless stranger
    In the world Thy hands had made;
  When we see Thee in the garden
    In Thine agony of blood;
  At Thy grace we are confounded,
    Holy, spotless Lamb of God.

4 When we see Thee, as the Victim,
    Bound to the accursèd tree,
  For our guilt and folly stricken,
    All our judgment borne by Thee.
  Lord, we own, with hearts adoring,
    Thou hast loved us unto blood;
  Glory, glory everlasting
    Be to Thee, Thou Lamb of God!

5 Lamb of God! Thou now art seated
    High upon Thy Father's throne;
  All Thy gracious work completed,
    All Thy mighty vict'ry won.
  Every knee in heaven is bending
    To the Lamb for sinners slain;
  Every voice and harp is swelling,
    "Worthy is the Lamb to reign".

6 Lord, in all Thy pow'r and glory,
    Still Thy thoughts and eyes are here,
  Watching o'er Thy ransomed people
    To Thy gracious heart so dear.
  Thou for us art interceding,
    Everlasting is Thy love;
  And a blessèd rest preparing
    In the Father's house above.

7 Lamb of God! Thou soon in glory
    Will to this sad earth return;
  All Thy foes shall quake before Thee,
    All that now despise Thee mourn;
  Then Thy saints appearing with Thee
    With Thee in Thy kingdom reign;
  Thine the praise, and Thine the glory
    Lamb of God, for sinners slain!

283   8.7.8.7.7.7.

LET us love and sing and wonder!
  Let us praise the Saviour's Name!
He has hushed the law's loud thunder,
  He has quenched Mount Sinai's
    flame;
He has washed us in His blood,
  He has brought us nigh to God.

2 Let us love the Lord that bought us,
    Pitied us when wand'ring far;
  Called us by His grace, and taught us
    Where our joys and blessings are;
  He has washed us in His blood,
    He presents our souls to God.

3 Let us sing, though fierce temptations
    Threaten hard to bear us down;
  For the Lord, our strong salvation,
    Holds in view the conq'ror's crown;
  He who washed us in His blood,
    Has secured our way to God.

4 Let us wonder; grace and justice
    Join, and point to mercy's store;
  When through grace in Christ our
    trust is,
  Justice smiles, and asks no more;
    He who washed us in His blood
  Soon will bring us home to God.

284   C.M.

LET us rejoice in Christ the Lord
  Who claims us for His own;
The hope that's built upon His Word
  Can ne'er be overthrown.

2 Though many foes beset us round,
    And feeble is our arm,
  Our life is hid with Christ in God
    Beyond the reach of harm.

3 Weak as we are, we shall not faint
    Or fainting, cannot fail;
  Jesus, the strength of every saint,
    Must in the end prevail.

4 Though now He's unperceived by
    sense,
  Faith sees Him always near;
    A guide, a glory, a defence,
  To save from every fear.

5 As surely as He overcame,
    And conquered death and sin,
  So surely those who trust His Name
    Will all His triumph win.

285   C.M.

L IGHT of the world, shine on our
      souls;
  Thy grace to us afford;
    And while we meet to learn Thy truth,
  Be Thou our teacher, Lord.

2 As once Thou didst Thy Word expound,
    To those who walked with Thee,
  So teach us, Lord, to understand,
    And its blest fulness see -

3 May we its riches, power, and depth
    Its holiness discern;
  Its joyful news of saving grace
    By blest experience learn.

4 Help us each other to assist;
    Thy Spirit now impart;
  Keep humble, but with love inspire,
    To Thee and Thine, each heart.

5 Thus may Thy Word be dearer still,
    And studied more each day;
  And as it richly dwells within,
    Thyself in it display.

286   6.5.6.5.D. with Chorus

L IKE a river, glorious
      Is God's perfect peace,
  Over all victorious
    In its bright increase,
  Perfect, yet it floweth
    Fuller every day,
  Perfect, yet it groweth
    Deeper all the way.

Stayed upon Jehovah,
    Hearts are fully blest;
  Finding, as He promised,
    Perfect peace and rest.

2 Hidden in the hollow
    Of His blessèd hand,
  Never foe can follow,
    Never traitor stand;
  Not a surge of worry,
    Not a shade of care,
  Not a blast of hurry
    Touch the spirit there.

3 Every joy or trial
    Falleth from above,
  Traced upon our dial
    By the Sun of love:
  We may trust Him solely
    All for us to do;
  They who trust Him wholly
    Find Him wholly true.

287   8.7.8.7.4.7.

L O, He comes! with clouds
      descending,
  Once for favoured sinners slain;
    Thousand thousand saints
      attending
  Swell the triumph of His train;
    Hallelujah!
  Jesus comes, and comes to reign!

2 Every eye shall now behold Him
    Robed in brightest majesty;
  Those who set at naught and sold
    Him,
  Pierced and nailed Him to the tree,
    Deeply wailing,
  Shall the true Messiah see.

3 Lo, the tokens of His passion
    Still His glorious body bears;
  Cause of endless exultation
    To His ransomed worshippers;
    Hallelujah!
  Now the day of Christ appears.

4 Yea, Amen! let all adore Thee,
    High on Thine eternal throne;
  Saviour, take the power and glory,
    Claim the kingdom for Thine own;
    O come quickly!
  Hallelujah! come Lord, come!

288   8.7.8.7.4.7.

L OOK, ye saints, the sight is
      glorious;
See the Man of Sorrows now;
   From the fight returned victorious,
   Every knee to Him shall bow:
      Crown Him! Crown Him!
Crowns become the Victor's brow.

2 Crown the Saviour, angels crown Him;
   Rich the trophies Jesus brings;
In the seat of power enthrone Him,
   While the vault of heaven rings;
      Crown Him! Crown Him!
   Crown the Saviour, King of kings.

3 Sinners in derision crowned Him;
   Mocking thus the Saviour's claim:
Saints and angels crowd around
   Him,
Own His title, praise His Name:
      Crown Him! Crown Him!
   Spread abroad the Victor's fame.

4 Hark, those bursts of acclamation!
   Hark! those loud triumphant chords!
Jesus takes the highest station;
   O what joy the sight affords!
      Crown Him! Crown Him!
   King of kings, and Lord of lords.

289   6.6.4.6.6.6.4.

L OOSED are the bands of death!
      "Thou art My Son", God saith
      To Jesus raised.
Holden He could not be,
   God's Holy One is free,
Firstfruit of victory;
      Let God be praised!

2 Past are the shades of night,
   Dawn shows in clearest light
      An empty tomb.
Risen, the Lord appears,
   Calms all His people's fears,
Stands in the midst and clears
   Away their gloom.

3 Mighty, stupendous power!
   Unique, triumphant hour!
      Alive is He!

Sure proof of righted wrong,
   Earnest of ransomed throng,
Spoils taken from the strong
      Eternally!

4 His Father's glory too,
   Enhanced with honour due
      That scene of joy.
So would we now acclaim,
   And magnify the Name
Of Him, Whose deathless fame
      Our lips employ.

290   8.5.8.3.

L ORD and Saviour, we remember,
      In Thine hour of shame,
Thou to God *Thyself* didst render -
      Praise Thy name!

2 Blessèd Saviour, we remember
   Thou didst meet our foe,
When the darkness gathered
   round Thee,
      And the woe.

3 Holy Saviour, we remember
   Bitter was Thy cry,
When, for sin by God forsaken,
   Wrath was nigh.

4 Glorious Saviour, we remember
   Thou didst overcome;
Through Thy victory we, once captive,
   Are brought home.

5 Lord and Saviour, we remember
   And would prize Thy love;
All its fulness do Thou teach us
   From above!

291   C.M.

L ORD, e'en to death Thy love
      could go -
A death of shame and loss;
   To vanquish for us every foe,
Thou didst endure the Cross!

2 Oh, what a load was Thine to bear,
   Alone in that dark hour -
Our sins, in all their terror there,
   God's wrath, and Satan's power!

3 The storm that bowed Thy blessèd
   head
  Is hushed for ever now,
    And rest divine is ours instead,
  Whilst glory crowns Thy brow.

4 Within the Father's house on high,
   We soon shall sing Thy praise;
  But here, where Thou didst bleed
   and die,
  We learn that song to raise.

292   C.M.
L ORD, I desire to live as one,
  Who bears a blood-bought name,
As one who fears but grieving Thee,
  And knows no other shame.

2 As one by whom Thy walk below
   Should never be forgot;
  As one who fain would keep apart
   From all Thou lovest not.

3 Grant me to live as one who knows,
   Thy fellowship of love;
  As one whose eyes can pierce beyond
   The pearl-built gates above.

4 As one who daily speaks to Thee,
   And hears Thy voice divine
  With depths of tenderness declare,
   "Belovèd! thou art Mine".

293   L.M.
L ORD, in Thy form and comeliness
  The Father's brightest glories shine,
Displaying perfect holiness,
  Revealing all His love divine.

2 The world despised, rejected Thee;
   We bow in worship, and confess
  That all Thy sufferings on the tree
   Proclaim our sin and guiltiness.

3 Though our transgressions wounded
   Thee,
  Thy precious blood our pardon sealed;
   And, bruised for our iniquity,
  Thy stripes our sinful hearts have
   healed.

4 Ours was the guilt that kept us far
   From heaven, from happiness,
   from Thee;
  Thine was the blood that brought
   us near,
  That cancelled sin, and set us free.

5 Thine was the blood, the precious
   blood,
  That cleansed each stain and made
   us meet,
  To worship in the courts of God,
   Redeemed and made in Thee
   complete.

294   C.M.
L ORD JESUS, are we one with Thee?
  Oh height, Oh depth of love!
Once slain for us upon the tree,
  We're one with Thee above.

2 Such was Thy grace, that for our sake
   Thou didst from heaven come down;
  With us of flesh and blood partake,
   In all our sorrow one.

3 Our sins, our guilt, in love divine,
   Confessed and borne by Thee;
  The gall, the curse, the wrath
   were Thine,
  To set Thy members free.

4 Ascended now, in glory bright,
   Lord, one with us Thou art!
  Nor life, nor death, nor depth, nor
   height,
  Thy saints from Thee can part!

5 Oh, teach us, Lord, to know and own
   This wondrous mystery,
  That Thou with us art truly one,
   And we are one with Thee!

6 Soon, soon shall come that glorious
   day,
  When, seated on Thy throne,
   Thou shalt to wondering worlds
   display,
  That we with Thee are one!

295　　　　　　　　　　　L.M.

L ORD JESUS CHRIST, we seek
　　Thy face,
Within the veil we bow the knee;
　　Oh, let Thy glory fill the place,
　　And bless us while we wait on Thee!

2 We thank Thee for the precious blood
　　That purged our sins and brought
　　　　us nigh,
　　All cleansed and sanctified, to God,
　　Thy holy Name to magnify.

3 Shut in with Thee, far, far above
　　The restless world that wars below,
　　We seek to learn and prove Thy love,
　　Thy wisdom and Thy grace to know.

4 The brow that once with thorns was
　　　　bound,
　　Thy hands, Thy side, we fain would
　　　　see;
　　Draw near, Lord Jesus, glory-crowned,
　　And bless us while we wait on
　　　　Thee!

296　　　　　　　　　4.6.8.8.4.

L ORD JESUS, come!
　　Nor let us longer roam
Afar from Thee, and that bright place
　　Where we shall see Thee face
　　　　to face.
　　　　Lord Jesus, come!

2 Lord Jesus, come!
　　Thine absence here we mourn;
　　No joy we know apart from Thee,
　　　　No sorrow in Thy presence see.
　　　　Come, Saviour, come!

3 Lord Jesus, come!
　　And claim us as Thine own;
　　Our weary feet would wander o'er
　　　　This dark and sinful world no more.
　　　　Come, Saviour, come!

4 Lord Jesus, come!
　　And take Thy people home;
　　That all Thy flock, so scattered here,
　　　　With Thee in glory may appear.
　　　　Lord Jesus, come!

297　　　　　　　　　7.6.7.6.D.

L ORD JESUS, Friend unfailing!
　　How dear Thou art to me!
Are cares or fears assailing?
　　I find my strength in Thee:
Why should my feet grow weary
　　Of this my pilgrim way?
Rough though the path and dreary,
　　It ends in perfect day.

2 Nought, nought I count as pleasure,
　　Compared, O Christ, with Thee;
Thy sorrow without measure
　　Earned peace and joy for me.
I love to own, Lord Jesus,
　　Thy claims o'er me divine;
Bought with Thy blood most precious
　　Whose can I be but Thine?

3 What fills my heart with gladness?
　　'Tis Thy abounding grace!
Where can I look in sadness,
　　But, Saviour, on Thy face?
My all is Thy providing,
　　Thy love can ne'er grow cold;
In Thee, my refuge, hiding,
　　No good wilt Thou withhold.

4 Why should I droop in sorrow?
　　Thou'rt ever by my side!
Why, trembling, dread the morrow?
　　What ill can e'er betide?
If I my cross have taken,
　　'Tis but to follow Thee;
If scorned, despised, forsaken,
　　Nought severs Thee from me.

5 O worldly pomp and glory,
　　Your charms are spread in vain;
I've heard a sweeter story,
　　I've found a truer gain.
Where Christ a place prepareth
　　There is my loved abode,
There shall I gaze on Jesus,
　　There shall I dwell with God.

6 From every tribulation,
　　From every sore distress,
In Christ I've full salvation,
　　Sure help and quiet rest:
No fear of foes prevailing,
　　I triumph, Lord, in Thee!
Lord Jesus, Friend unfailing!
　　How dear Thou art to me.

298 10.10.10.10.

LORD JESUS, gladly do our lips
   express
Our hearts' deep sense of all Thy
   worthiness;
Thou risen One, the Holy and the True,
   We give Thee now the praise so
   justly due.

2 Thou giv'st us, Lord, once more
   to taste down here,
   The joy Thy presence brings, its
   warmth and cheer;
   With great delight we 'neath Thy
   shadow rest;
   Thy fruit is sweet to those Thy
   love has blest.

3 Thou wast alone, till like the
   precious grain,
   In death Thou layest, but did'st rise
   again;
   And in Thy risen life, a countless host
   Are "all of one" with Thee, Thy joy
   and boast.

4 We bless Thee, Lord, Thou lov'st
   to take Thy place,
   Amongst Thine own, who taste
   Thy boundless grace;
   'Tis here we learn Thee, as
   Thou'rt known above,
   In heav'nly glory - home of perfect
   love.

299 11.11.11.11.

LORD JESUS, I love Thee, I
   know Thou art mine,
My rock and my fortress, my
   Surety divine;
My gracious Redeemer, my song
   shall be now,
'Tis Thou who art worthy, Lord
   Jesus, 'tis Thou!

2 I love Thee because Thou hast
   first lovèd me,
   And purchased my pardon on
   Calvary's tree;
   I love Thee for wearing the thorns
   on Thy brow;
   'Tis Thou who art worthy, Lord
   Jesus, 'tis Thou!

3 I would love Thee in life, I would
   love Thee in death,
   And praise Thee as long as Thou
   lendest me breath,
   And sing, should the death-dew
   lie cold on my brow,
   'Tis Thou who art worthy, Lord
   Jesus, 'tis Thou!

4 And when the bright morn of Thy
   glory shall come,
   And the children ascend to the
   Father's glad home,
   I'll shout with Thy likeness
   impressed on my brow,
   'Tis Thou who art worthy, Lord
   Jesus, 'tis Thou!

300 8.8.8.8.8.8

LORD JESUS, in Thy Name alone
   We soon shall meet around the
throne;
With this sole claim, on this sole
   ground,
Thy table here we now surround;
   What can we mention to our God,
Except Thine own most precious
   blood?

2 O Jesus, Lord! there is, indeed,
   Enough in Thee to meet our need,
   Enough in Thee to make us glad!
   Why should Thy ransomed ones
   be sad?
   This hope have we before our God,
   Salvation through Thy precious
   blood.

3 What joy it is to walk with Thee!
   But O what joy Thy face to see!
   And when our bliss is all complete,
   We still shall worship at Thy feet,
   And mention nothing to our God
   But that same ever precious
   blood.

301 7.6.7.6.D.

LORD JESUS, my Saviour!
   How vast Thy love to me!
I'll bathe in its full ocean
   To all eternity;
And wending on to glory
   This all my song shall be,
I am a feeble sinner,
   But Jesus died for me.

2 O Calvary! O Calvary!
 The thorn-crown and the spear,
'Tis here Thy love, Lord Jesus,
 Thy flowing wounds appear.
O depths of grace and mercy!
 To those dear wounds I flee;
I am a feeble sinner,
 But Jesus died for me.

3 Adore Him! Adore Him!
 The glorious work is done;
The Father will not punish me,
 'Twas laid upon His Son.
'Tis finished, cried His suff'ring soul,
 And I my title see;
I am a feeble sinner,
 But Jesus died for me.

4 In glory, in glory,
 For ever with the Lord,
I'll tune my harp, and with the saints
 I'll sing with sweet accord;
And as I strike the golden strings
 This all my song shall be,
I was a feeble sinner,
 But Jesus died for me.

302   4.6.8.8.4.

L ORD JESUS, Thine;
 No more this heart of mine
Shall seek its joy apart from Thee;
 The world is crucified to me,
  And I am Thine.

2 Thine, Thine alone,
 My joy, my hope, my crown;
Now earthly things may fade and die,
 They charm my soul no more, for I
  Am Thine alone.

3 Thine, ever Thine,
 For ever to recline
On love eternal, fixed and sure;
 Yes, I am Thine for evermore,
  Lord Jesus, Thine.

4 Then let me live,
 Continual praise to give
To Thy dear Name, my precious Lord;
 Henceforth alone, beloved, adored,
  To Thee I'd live.

5 Till Thou shalt come
 And bear me to Thy home,
For ever freed from earthly care,
 Eternally Thy love to share:
  Lord Jesus, come!

303   10.10.10.10.

L ORD JESUS, Thou by whom
 the worlds were made,
As holy Babe wast in a manger laid;
 Yet did angelic hosts Thy title own,
And highest glory give to God alone.

2 Thy lowly pathway grace and truth
  displayed,
But wicked hands Thy brow with
  thorns arrayed;
Now glory-crowned, blest answer
  to Thy shame,
Thy saints with joy Thy worthiness
  acclaim.

3 To win Thy bride what depths of woe
  were Thine,
Scorned and betrayed, beset by
  powers malign!
Thy piercèd hands, Thy riven side
  revealed
The strength of love that by Thy
  death was sealed.

4 Most blessèd Lord, fain would we
  learn of Thee
To fill our part, yea, more like
  Thee to be;
With purpose fixed, Thy path our
  happy choice,
Thyself our all, until we hear Thy
  voice.

304   8.8.8.8.8.8.

L ORD JESUS, Thou who only art
 The endless source of purest joy,
Oh, come and fill this longing heart;
 May nought but Thee my
  thoughts employ;
Teach me on Thee to fix my eye,
 For none but Thee can satisfy.

2 The joys of earth can never fill
 The heart that's tasted of Thy love;
No portion would I seek until
 I reign with Thee, my Lord, above,
When I shall gaze upon Thy face,
 And know more fully all Thy grace.

3 When from Thy radiant throne on high
 Thou didst my fall and ruin see,
Thou cam'st on earth for me to die

That I might share that throne
  with Thee.
Loved with an everlasting love,
  My hopes, my joys are all above.

4 Oh, what is all that earth can give?
    I'm called to share in God's own
      joy;
  Dead to the world, in Thee I live,
    In Thee I've bliss without alloy:
  Well may I earthly joys resign;
    All things are mine, and I am Thine!

5 Till Thou shalt come to take me home,
    Be this my one ambition, Lord,
  Self, sin, the world, to overcome,
    Fast clinging to Thy faithful Word;
  More of Thyself each day to know,
    And more into Thine image grow.

305   8.8.8.8.
L ORD JESUS, to tell of Thy love,
   Our souls shall for ever delight,
And join with the blessèd above
  In praises by day and by night.

2 Wherever we follow Thee, Lord,
    Admiring, adoring, we see
  That love which was stronger than
    death
  Flow out without limit, and free.

3 Descending from glory on high,
    With men Thy delight was to dwell;
  Contented, our Surety to die,
    By dying to save us from hell.

4 Enduring the grief and the shame,
    And bearing our sins on the Cross,
  Oh, who would not boast of Thy love,
    And count the world's glory but
      dross!

306   L.M.
L ORD, speak to me, that I may
   speak
In living echoes of Thy tone;
  As Thou hast sought, so let me
    seek,
Thy erring children lost and lone.

2 Oh, lead me, Lord, that I may lead
    The wand'ring and the
      wav'ring feet;
  Oh, feed me, Lord, that I may feed
    Thy hung'ring ones with
      manna sweet.

3 Oh, strengthen me, that while I stand
    Firm on the Rock, and strong in
      Thee,
  I may stretch out a loving hand
    To wrestlers with the troubled sea.

4 Oh, teach me, Lord, that I may
    teach
  The precious things Thou dost impart;
    And wing my words, that they
      may reach
  The hidden depths of many a heart.

5 Oh, give Thine own sweet rest to me,
    That I may speak with soothing
      power
  A word in season, as from Thee,
    To weary ones in needful hour.

6 Oh, fill me with Thy fulness, Lord,
    Until my very heart o'erflow
  In kindling thought and glowing
    word,
  Thy love to tell, Thy praise to show.

7 Oh, use me, Lord, use even me,
    Just as Thou wilt, and when,
      and where;
  Until Thy blessèd face I see,
    Thy rest, Thy joy, Thy glory share.

307   8.7.8.7.D.
L ORD, Thy ransomed Church
   is waking
Out of slumber far and near,
  Knowing that the morn is breaking
When the Bridegroom shall appear;
  Waking up to claim the treasure
With Thy precious life-blood bought,
  And accept in fuller measure
All Thy wondrous death hath wrought.

2 Praise to Thee for this glad shower,
    Precious drops of latter rain;
  Praise, that by Thy Spirit's power
    Thou hast quickened us again,

That Thy gospel's priceless treasure
  Now is borne from land to land,
And that all the Father's pleasure
  Prospers in Thy piercèd hand.

4 Praise to Thee for saved ones yearning
  O'er the lost and wandering throng;
Praise for voices daily learning
  To upraise the glad, new song;
Praise to Thee for sick ones hasting
  Now to touch Thy garment's hem;
Praise for souls believing, tasting
  All Thy love has won for them.

5 Set on fire our hearts' devotion
  With the love of Thy dear name;
Till o'er every land and ocean
  Lips and lives Thy Cross proclaim:
Fix our eyes on Thy returning,
  Keeping watch till Thou shalt come;
Loins well girt, lamps brightly burning:
  Then, Lord, take Thy servants home!

308   6.6.6.6.
L ORD, Thy word abideth,
  And our footsteps guideth;
Who its truth believeth
  Light and joy receiveth.

2 When our foes are near us,
  Then Thy word doth cheer us,
Word of consolation,
  Message of salvation.

3 When the storms are o'er us,
  And dark clouds before us,
Then its light directeth,
  And our way protecteth.

4 Who can tell the pleasure,
  Who recount the treasure,
By Thy word imparted
  To the simple-hearted?

5 Word of mercy, giving
  Succour to the living;
Word of life, supplying
  Comfort to the dying.

6 O that we, discerning
  Its most holy learning,
Lord, may love and fear Thee,
  Evermore be near Thee.

309   8.7.8.7.3.
L ORD! to Thee my heart ascending
  For Thy mercy full and free,
Thankful sings for grace transcending,
  Grace vouchsafed to sinful me,
    Even me.

2 Holy Father! who with yearning
  Of eternal love didst see
Hatred in my bosom burning,
  Thou didst give Thy Son for me,
    Even me.

3 Precious Saviour! Great Redeemer!
  Praise, eternal praise to Thee;
Though so long a wand'ring sinner
  Thou hast kindly welcomed me,
    Even me.

4 But I'm lost in joyful wond'ring,
  And I say, O can it be
That there will be no more sund'ring
  'Twixt my blessèd Lord and me?
    Even me.

5 Can it be that I, an alien,
  Now a child shall ever be?
Can it be that, all forgiven,
  Glory is prepared for me?
    Even me.

6 Yes! for Jesus liveth ever,
  And His blood hath made me free;
From His love no foe can sever,
  For He gave Himself for me,
    Even me.

7 Lord! I thank Thee for salvation,
  Grace so mighty and so free;
Take my all in consecration,
  Glorify Thyself in me,
    Even me.

310   L.M.D.
L ORD, we are *Thine*: our God
  Thou art,
Fashioned and made we are by Thee;
  These curious frames! in every part
Thy wisdom, power, and love we see;
  Each breath we draw, each pulse
    that beats,
Each organ formed by skill divine,
  Each precious sense aloud repeats
Great God, that we are only Thine.

2 Lord, we are *Thine*: in Thee we live,
　　Supported by Thy tender care;
　Thou dost each hourly mercy give;
　　　Thine earth we tread, we breathe
　　　　Thine air;
　Raiment and food Thou dost supply;
　　Thy sun's bright rays around us
　　　shine:
　Guarded by Thine all-seeing eye,
　　We own that we are only Thine.

3 Lord, we are *Thine*: bought by Thy
　　blood:
　Once the poor guilty slaves of sin;
　　Thou didst redeem us to our God,
　And made Thy Spirit dwell within.
　　　Thou hast our sinful wand'rings
　　　borne
　With love and patience all divine:
　　As brands, then, from the burning
　　　torn
　We own that we are wholly Thine.

4 Lord, we are *Thine*: Thy claims we
　　own,
　Ourselves to Thee we humbly give;
　　Reign Thou within our hearts alone,
　And make us to Thy glory live.
　　Here let us each Thy mind display,
　In all Thy brilliant virtues shine;
　　And haste that long-expected day
　When Thou shalt own that we are
　　Thine.

311
8.7.8.7.D.

LORD, we love to trace Thy footprints
　Here amidst the desert sand,
Ponder o'er Thy path of suffering -
　Wondrous heart and healing hand;
See Thy stoop to Bethlehem's manger,
　Hear Thee still the raging wave,
Learn Thy love in all its fulness
　At the Cross and in the grave.

2 Lord, we bow in adoration
　　As we watch that stream of love;
　Find its mighty tide still flowing
　　From Thee now as crowned above.
　'Tis a love no heart can fathom,
　　Which to us Thou dost unfold,
　Inexhaustible and boundless -
　　Wondrous theme that ne'er
　　　grows old.

312
8.7.8.7.

LORD, we treasure with affection
　All Thy path of sorrow here,
And those closing scenes of anguish
　To our hearts Thyself endear.

2 Deep Thy sorrow then, Lord Jesus,
　　Deeper far than thought can reach;
　Grief intense and suff'rings holy,
　　Far beyond all tongues to teach.

3 None could follow there, blest Saviour,
　　When Thou didst for sin atone,
　For those suff'rings, deep, unfathomed,
　　Were, Lord Jesus, Thine alone!

4 Thou didst measure then sin's
　　distance,
　Darkness, wrath and curse were Thine;
　　Man-betrayed, by God forsaken;
　Thus we learn Thy love divine!

313
L.M.

LORD, we would ne'er forget Thy
　love,
Who hast redeemed us by Thy blood;
　And now, as our High Priest above,
Dost intercede for us with God.

2 Lord, we would not forget the pain,
　　The blood-like sweat, the shameful
　　　tree,
　The wrath Thy soul did once sustain
　　From sin and death to set us free.

3 We would remember we are one
　　With every saint that loves Thy Name;
　United to Thee on the throne,
　　Our life, our hope, our Lord the
　　　same.

4 Here, in the broken bread and wine,
　　We hear Thee say, "Remember Me!
　I gave My life to ransom thine,
　　I bore the wrath to set thee free".

5 Lord, we are Thine, we praise Thy
　love,
　One with Thy saints, all one in Thee;
　　We would, until we meet above,
　In all our ways remember Thee.

314 C.M.D.

L ORD, when I think upon the love,
    Which Thou to me hast shown,
To die upon the Cross that Thou,
    Mayest claim me for Thine own,
I cannot tell why Thou didst show,
    Such love to one like me,
Save that it is that I might know
    I owe it all to Thee.

2 There is no goodness in myself,
    To win such precious love;
I loved Thee not - Thou lovest me,
    And called me from above:
I heard Thy voice, it won my heart,
    And bade my doubtings flee;
It gave me rest and peace - O, yes,
    I owe it all to Thee.

3 And still upheld by power divine,
    I urge my way along,
In haste to reach the promised rest,
    The bright, glad home of song,
And then when glory on me bursts,
    And I Thy glory see,
Again I'll raise the happy song,
    "I owe it all to Thee".

315 7.6.7.6.D.

L OVE bound Thee to the altar,
    The Father's love and Thine,
For us, O peerless Victim,
    That we with Thee might shine.
Thy wealth Thou didst surrender,
    Thyself didst freely give,
Thy life in grace unbounded,
    That we with Thee might live.

2 In those long hours of anguish,
    When men passed scoffing by,
When Satan sore assailed Thee,
    When God heard not Thy cry,
Then were our sins Thy burden,
    Our guilt, our grief, Thy bands;
And then our names were graven
    For ever on Thy hands.

3 We praise Thee, Lord most holy,
    Thou First-born from the dead;
Now o'er all powers triumphant,
    O'er all things Lord and Head;

But ever and for ever
    The memory of Thy pain
Shall raise our songs in worship,
    For Thou for us wast slain.

316 8.7.8.7.D

L OVE divine, all loves excelling,
    Joy of heaven, to earth come down;
Making us Thy humble dwelling,
    All Thy faithful mercies crown:
Jesus, Thou art all compassion;
    Pure, unbounded love Thou art,
Visit us with Thine affection,
    Enter every longing heart.

2 Come, Almighty, to deliver!
    Let us all Thy grace receive,
Follow in Thy steps, and never,
    Nevermore the pathway leave:
Then our hearts will yield their
    blessing,
Sweet incense to God above,
    Offer praises without ceasing,
Glory in Thy perfect love.

3 Firstfruits of Thy new creation,
    Faithful, holy, may we be,
Joyful in Thy great salvation,
    Daily more conformed to Thee:
Changed from glory into glory,
    Till in heaven we take our place,
Then to worship and adore Thee,
    Lost in wonder, love, and praise.

317 8.7.8.7. with Chorus

L OVE divine, so great and wondrous,
    Deep and mighty, pure, sublime!
Coming from the heart of Jesus,
    Just the same through tests of time.

He the pearly gates will open,
    So that I may enter in;
For He purchased my redemption,
    And forgave me all my sin.

2 Love divine, so great and wondrous,
    All my sins He then forgave!
I will sing His praise forever,
    For His blood, His pow'r to save.

318   7.7.7.7.D.

L OVED with everlasting love,
  Led by grace that love to know;
Spirit, breathing from above,
  Thou hast taught me it is so!
Oh, this full and perfect peace!
  Oh, this transport all divine!
In a love which cannot cease,
  I am His, and He is mine.

2 Heaven above is softer blue,
  Earth around is sweeter green!
Something lives in every hue
  Christless eyes have never seen:
Birds with gladder songs o'erflow,
  Flowers with deeper beauties shine,
Since I know, as *now* I know,
  I am His, and He is mine.

3 Things that once were wild alarms
  Cannot now disturb my rest;
Closed in everlasting arms,
  Pillowed on the loving breast,
Oh, to lie forever here,
  Doubt, and care, and self resign,
While He whispers in my ear -
  I am His, and He is mine.

4 His for ever, only His;
  Who the Lord and me shall part?
Ah, with what a rest of bliss
  Christ can fill the loving heart!
Heaven and earth may fade and flee,
  First-born light in gloom decline;
But, while God and I shall be,
  I am His, and He is mine.

319   7.6.7.6.7.7.

L OVE'S immensity behold:
  O'er His suff'rings ponder,
Whose perfections deep are told
  At Golgotha yonder.
God's Beloved upon the tree,
  Bruised and wounded there we see.

2 Man of sorrows in this scene,
  And with grief acquainted,
In the midst of men unclean,
  Blameless and untainted.
What He thus in love endures,
  Glory to His God secures.

3 For His Father's pleasure still,
  Freely now He layeth
Down His life of His own will,
  Unto death obeyeth.
Infinite devotion sealed!
  Love's immensity revealed!

320   P.M.

L OW in the grave He lay,
  Jesus, my Saviour!
Waiting the coming day,
  Jesus, my Lord!

Up from the grave He arose
With a mighty triumph o'er His foes;
* He arose a victor from the dark*
*   domain,*
And He lives for ever with His
* saints to reign;*
*   He arose! He arose!*
*   Hallelujah! Christ arose!*

2 Vainly they watch His bed,
  Jesus, my Saviour!
Vainly they seal the dead,
  Jesus, my Lord!

3 Death cannot keep his prey,
  Jesus, my Saviour!
He tore the bars away,
  Jesus, my Lord!

321   10.10.10.10.10.10.

L OW on the ground the Lord of
  Glory lies,
Around Him rolls dark sorrow's
  fearful flood,
Forth from His soul prayer pours
  with tears and cries,
Falls to the sod His sweat, like
  drops of blood.
The awful cup He takes, submissive
  still,
To drink the last dark drop - it is the
  Father's will.

2 Silent He stands amid the mocking
  throng,
The thorny crown upon His holy brow,
In patient grace, content to suffer
  wrong -

It is the Father's pleasure for Him now.
    Meekness majestical! submissive
      still,
In robe, and reed, and thorn, to do
    the Father's will.

3 Meekly He bows His sacred head
      to die;
  The agony, the shame, are almost o'er,
      The parchèd lips have framed
        their last lone cry,
  The tender heart of Christ need bear
      no more.
  But yet He bows the head; submissive
      still,
  E'en in the hour of death, to all the
      Father's will.

322   C.M.

M AJESTIC sweetness sits enthroned
    Upon the Saviour's brow;
His head with radiant glories crowned,
  His lips with grace o'erflow.

2 Behold the beauties of His face,
    And on His glories dwell;
  Think of the wonders of His grace,
    And all His triumphs tell.

3 No mortal can with Him compare
    Among the sons of men;
  Fairer is He than all the fair
    That fill the heavenly train.

4 He saw me plunged in deep distress,
    He came to my relief;
  For me He bore the shameful Cross,
    And carried all my grief.

5 To Him I owe my life and breath,
    And all the joys I have;
  He makes me triumph over death,
    He saves me from the grave.

6 To heaven, the place of His abode,
    He'll bring my weary feet,
  Display the glories of my God,
    And make my joy complete.

7 Since from His bounty I receive
    Such proofs of love divine,
  Had I a thousand hearts to give,
    Lord, they should all be Thine!

323   7.7.7.8.

"M AN of Sorrows!" what a name
    For the Son of God, who came
Ruined sinners to reclaim!
    Hallelujah! what a Saviour!

2 Bearing shame and scoffing rude,
    In my place condemned He stood;
  Sealed my pardon with His blood:
    Hallelujah! what a Saviour!

3 Guilty, vile, and helpless, we;
    Spotless Lamb of God was He:
  "Full atonement", can it be?
    Hallelujah! what a Saviour!

4 "Lifted up" was He to die,
    "It is finished", was His cry;
  Now in heaven exalted high:
    Hallelujah! what a Saviour!

5 When He comes, our glorious King,
    All His ransomed home to bring,
  Then anew this song we'll sing:
    Hallelujah! what a Saviour!

324   7.6.7.6.D.

M AN'S day is fast receding,
    The day of God will come,
And lingering feet are needing
    Oft to be speeded home;
We need to stir affection,
    Dull conscience to awake,
Faith's shield for our protection
    With firmer grasp to take.

2 The world hath many a wonder,
    And many a witching snare;
  But see the glory yonder -
    What can with that compare?
  The Lord a crown is keeping
    For all who faithful stand,
  Who, midst a world that's sleeping,
    Watch for the day at hand.

3 Our labour and our pleasure
    Be this - to do His will;
  To fill our little measure
    With loving service still:
  The cup of water given
    For Him, will find reward,
  Both now and soon in heaven,
    Remembered by the Lord.

4 Lord, may Thy love constrain us
     Through all the "little while",
   Nor fear of man restrain us,
     Nor love of praise beguile;
   Then, at Thy glorious coming,
     Enough, O Lord, if we,
   Shall hear Thy voice approving
     Aught we have done for Thee.

325   8.7.8.7.7.7.

M ASTER, speak! Thy servant
   heareth,
   Waiting for Thy gracious word,
     Longing for Thy voice that cheereth,
   Master, let it now be heard:
     I am listening, Lord, for Thee;
   What hast Thou to say to me?

2 Master, speak! though least and
     lowest,
   Let me not unheard depart;
     Master, speak! for, oh, Thou knowest
   All the yearning of my heart:
     Knowest all its truest need;
   Speak! and make me blest indeed.

3 Master, speak! and make me ready
     When Thy voice is truly heard,
   With obedience glad and steady
     Still to follow every word:
   I am listening, Lord, for Thee:
     Master, speak, O speak to me!

4 Speak to me by name, O Master!
     Let me know it is to me;
   Speak! that I may follow faster
     With a step more firm and free,
   Where the Shepherd leads the flock
     In the shadow of the rock.

326   8.7.8.5.

M AY the mind of Christ my Saviour
   Live in me from day to day,
   By His love and power controlling
     All I do and say.

2 May the word of God dwell richly
     In my heart from hour to hour,
   So that all may see I triumph
     Only through His power.

3 May the peace of God my Father
     Rule my life in everything,
   That I may be calm to comfort
     Sick and sorrowing.

4 May the love of Jesus fill me
     As the waters fill the sea;
   Him exalting, self abasing,
     This is victory.

5 May I run the race before me,
     Strong and brave to face the foe,
   Looking only unto Jesus
     As I onward go.

6 May His beauty rest upon me,
     As I seek the lost to win,
   And may they forget the channel,
     Seeing only Him.

327   7.7.7.7.7.7.

M EETING in the Saviour's Name,
   "Breaking bread" by His
   command,
     To the world we thus proclaim
   On what ground we hope to stand,
     When the Lord shall come with
       clouds,
   Joined by heaven's exulting crowds.

2 From the Cross our hope we draw
     'Tis the sinner's sure resource;
   Jesus magnified the law,
     Jesus bore its awful curse;
   What a joyful truth is this!
     O how full of hope it is!

3 Jesus died, and then arose;
     Yes, He rose, He lives to reign;
   He will vanquish all His foes
     When to earth He comes again;
   His the triumph and the crown,
     His the glory and renown.

4 Sing we, then, of Him who died,
     Sing of Him who rose again;
   By His blood we're justified,
     And with Him we hope to reign:
   Yes, we look to see our Lord,
     And to share His bright reward.

328　　　　　　　　　　6.5.6.5.D.

MEMORABLE morning,
　　First day of the week!
Loved ones to the garden
　　Came their Lord to seek,
Ready to anoint Him,
　　Thinking all was o'er,
Heavy in their mourning,
　　Full of sorrow sore.

2 But the tomb was empty,
　　Th' stone was rolled away;
And as they beheld it
　　In perplexity,
Two in shining garments
　　Stood where He was laid,
Said to them affrighted,
　　"Be ye not afraid".

3 "Why the Living seek ye
　　Thus among the dead?
He indeed is risen
　　Even as He said."
Then they ran rejoicing,
　Wondrous news to tell -
That the Lord was living,
　And that all was well.

4 Glorious resurrection!
　　Past are all His woes.
Hail the mighty Victor
　　Who in triumph rose.
From our hearts responsive
　　Joyful songs of praise
Unto Thee, His Father,
　　Rev'rently we raise.

329　　　　　　　　　　8.7.8.7.4.7.

'MID the splendours of the glory,
　　Which we hope ere long to share,
Christ, our Head, and we, His members,
　　Shall appear divinely fair;
　　　Oh, how glorious!
When we meet Him in the air!

2 From the dateless, timeless, periods,
　　He has loved us without cause;
And for all His blood-bought myriads,
　　His is love that knows no pause;
　　　Matchless Lover!
Changeless as th' eternal laws!

3 Oh, what gifts shall yet be granted,
　　Palms and crowns, and robes of
　　　white,
When the hope for which we panted
　　Bursts upon our gladdened sight,
　　　And our Saviour
Makes us glorious through His
　　might!

4 Bright the prospect soon that greets us
　　Of that longed-for nuptial day,
When our heavenly Bridegroom
　　meets us
On His kingly, conquering way;
　　　In the glory,
Bride and Bridegroom reign for aye!

330　　　　　　　　　　7.7.7.5.D.

MIDNIGHT shadows close around
　　As, in agony profound,
Bowed in grief upon the ground,
　　Prayer he offers up
With strong crying and with tears;
　　Mystery to mortal ears
Is the prayer His Father hears,
　　O'er the awful cup.

2 Dawn upon the dreadful morn,
　　Shows Him bearing hate and scorn,
Lowly in His crown of thorn,
　　Patient in His grace.
To the scourge His back is bare,
　　From His cheeks they pluck the hair,
Rich and poor, united there,
　　Mock His marrèd face.

3 Then, with every sin surpassed,
　　For His vesture lots they cast,
Him they crucify at last,
　　Human guilt complete.
Pity still His heart within,
　　Seeks He pardon for their sin
As the nails they hammer in
　　Through His hands and feet.

4 All creation, draped in gloom,
　　Trembles on the brink of doom
Of an everlasting tomb,
　　Evermore undone:
But, from out the depth arise
　　Lonely and mysterious cries,
And He bows His head and dies,
　　Endless vict'ry won.

331

8.5.8.5.D.

'MIDST the darkness, storm, and
　　sorrow,
One bright gleam I see;
　Well I know the blessèd morrow
Christ will come for me.
　'Midst the light, and peace, and
　　　glory
Of the Father's home,
　Christ for me is waiting, watching,
Waiting till I come.

2 Long the blessèd Guide has led me
　　By the desert road;
　Now I see the golden towers,
　　City of my God.
　There, amidst the love and glory,
　　He is waiting yet;
　On His hand a name is graven
　　He can ne'er forget.

3 There, amidst the songs of heaven,
　　Sweeter to His ear
　Is the footfall through the desert
　　Ever drawing near.
　There, made ready are the mansions,
　　Glorious, bright, and fair;
　But the Bride the Father gave Him
　　Still is wanting there.

4 Who is this who comes to meet me,
　　On the desert way,
　As the Morning Star foretelling
　　God's unclouded day?
　He it is who came to win me
　　On the Cross of shame;
　In His glory well I know Him
　　Evermore the same.

5 Oh, the blessèd joy of meeting,
　　All the desert past!
　Oh, the wondrous words of greeting
　　He shall speak at last!
　He and I together ent'ring
　　Those bright courts above;
　He and I together sharing
　　All the Father's love.

6 Where no shade nor stain can enter,
　　Nor the gold be dim;
　In that holiness unsullied
　　I shall walk with Him.

Meet companion, then, for Jesus,
　From Him, for Him, made;
Glory of God's grace for ever
　There in me displayed.

7 He, who in the hour of sorrow
　　Bore the curse alone;
　I, who through the lonely desert
　　Trod where He had gone.
　He and I in that bright glory
　　One deep joy shall share;
　Mine, to be for ever with Him,
　　His, that I am there.

332

C.M.

MINE eyes are unto Thee, my God,
　My soul on Thee doth wait,
My hope is in Thy faithful word,
　And in Thy love so great.

2 Thy promise true my faith receives
　　And claims it for its own;
　My trusting heart with joy believes
　　The covenant-keeping One.

3 What if Thy love impose a task
　　Too hard for me to scan?
　I will not question it, nor ask
　　The meaning of Thy plan.

4 O Lord, I only ask for grace
　　To work it out with Thee;
　And as in faith each step I take
　　I'll more its beauty see.

5 Its rich unfoldings on my soul
　　Each day shall burst anew,
　Till glory, bright and endless, dawns
　　Upon my ransomed view.

6 Till then, oh keep me safely, Lord,
　　Full trusting only Thee,
　Till that blest, happy moment come,
　　When, Lord, Thy face I'll see.

333

P.M.

MORE about Jesus would I
　know,
More of His grace to others show;
　More of His saving fulness see,
More of His love who died for me.

More, more about Jesus,
More, more about Jesus;
More of His saving fulness see,
More of His love who died for me.

2 More about Jesus let me learn,
    More of His holy will discern;
Spirit of God, my teacher be,
    Showing the things of Christ to me.

3 More about Jesus; in His Word
    Holding communion with my Lord;
Hearing His voice in every line,
    Making each faithful saying mine.

4 More about Jesus; on His throne,
    Riches in glory all His own;
More of His kingdom's sure increase;
    More of His coming - Prince of
        Peace.

334   6.5.6.5.D.
M ORE holiness give me,
    More strivings within;
More patience in suffering,
    More sorrow for sin;
More faith in my Saviour,
    More sense of His care;
More joy in His service,
    More purpose in prayer.

2 More gratitude give me,
    More trust in the Lord;
More zeal for His glory,
    More hope in His Word;
More tears for His sorrows,
    More pain at His grief;
More meekness in trial,
    More praise for relief.

3 More purity give me,
    More strength to o'ercome;
More freedom from earth-stains,
    More longings for home;
More fit for the kingdom,
    More useful I'd be;
More blessèd and holy,
    More, Saviour, like Thee.

335   6.4.6.4.6.6.4.4.
M ORE love to Thee, O Christ,
    More love to Thee!
Hear Thou the prayer I make
    On bended knee;

This is my earnest plea -
    More love, O Christ, to Thee!
      More love to Thee!
      More love to Thee!

2 Once earthly joy I craved,
    Sought peace and rest;
Now, Thee alone I seek,
    Give what is best;
This all my prayer shall be -
    More love, O Christ, to Thee!
      More love to Thee!
      More love to Thee!

3 Let sorrow do its work,
    Send grief or pain;
Sweet are Thy messengers,
    Sweet their refrain,
When they can sing with me -
    More love, O Christ, to Thee!
      More love to Thee!
      More love to Thee!

4 Then shall my latest breath
    Whisper Thy praise;
This be the parting cry
    My heart shall raise;
This still its prayer shall be -
    More love, O Christ, to Thee!
      More love to Thee!
      More love to Thee!

336   11.4.11.4.
M Y chains are snapt, the bonds
    of sin are broken,
    And I am free;
O let the triumphs of His grace be
    spoken,
      Who died for me.

2 O death! O grave! I do not dread
    your power,
      The ransom's paid;
On Jesus, in that dark and dreadful
    hour,
      My guilt was laid.

3 Yes, Jesus bore it, bore, in love
    unbounded,
      What none can know;
He passed through death and
    gloriously confounded
      Our every foe.

4 And now He's risen, proclaim the
    joyful story,
        The Lord's on high;
And we in Him are raised to
    endless glory,
        And ne'er can die.

5 We wait to see the Morning Star
    appearing
        In glory bright;
This blessèd hope illumes, with
    beams most cheering,
        The hours of night.

337   C.M.

M Y Father's way may twist and turn
    My heart may throb and ache,
But in my soul I'm glad to know,
    He maketh no mistake.

2 My cherished plans may go astray,
    My hopes may fade away,
But still I'll trust my Lord to lead,
    For He doth know the way.

3 Tho' night be dark and it may seem
    That day will never break,
I'll pin my faith, my all, in Him,
    He maketh no mistake.

4 There's so much now I cannot see,
    My eyesight's far too dim,
But come what may, I'll simply trust
    And leave it all to Him.

5 For by and by the mist will lift,
    And plain it all He'll make,
Through all the way, tho' dark to me,
    He made not one mistake.

338   L.M.

M Y glorious Victor, Prince divine,
    Clasp these surrendered
hands in Thine;
    At length my will is all Thine own,
Glad vassal of a Saviour's throne.

2 My Master, lead me to Thy door;
    Pierce this now willing ear once
        more:
Thy bonds are freedom; let me stay
    With Thee, to toil, endure, obey.

3 Yes, ear and hand, and thought and
    will,
Use all in Thy dear slavery still!
    Self's weary liberties I cast
Beneath Thy feet; there keep them
    fast.

4 Tread them still down; and then I know
    These hands shall with Thy gifts
        o'erflow;
And piercèd ears shall hear the tone
    Which tells me Thou and I are one.

339   P.M.

M Y GOD, I am Thine;
    What a comfort divine!
What a blessing to know
    That Jesus is mine!

    Hallelujah! Thine the glory.
        Hallelujah! Amen.
    Hallelujah! Thine the glory.
        Revive us again.

2 In the heavenly Lamb
    Thrice happy I am,
And my heart doth rejoice
    At the sound of His Name.

3 My Saviour to know,
    And feel His love flow,
'Tis life everlasting,
    'Tis heaven below.

4 Yet onward I haste
    To the heavenly feast;
That, that is the fulness,
    But this is the taste.

5 And this I shall prove,
    Till with joy I remove
To the heaven of heavens,
    In Jesus' own love.

340   P.M.

M Y GOD, I have found
    The thrice blessèd ground,
Where life, and where joy,
    And true comfort abound.

    Hallelujah! Thine the glory.
        Hallelujah! Amen.
    Hallelujah! Thine the glory.
        Revive us again.

2 'Tis found in the blood
    Of Him who once stood
My refuge and safety,
    My surety with God.

3 He bore on the tree
    The sentence for me,
And now both the surety
    And sinner are free.

4 Accepted I am
    In the once-offered Lamb;
It was God who Himself
    Had devisèd the plan.

5 And though here below,
    'Mid sorrow and woe,
My place is in heaven
    With Jesus, I know.

6 And this I shall find,
    For such is His mind,
"He'll not be in glory
    And leave me behind".

7 For soon He will come,
    And take me safe home,
And make me to sit with
    Himself on His throne.

    Hallelujah! Thine the glory.
    Hallelujah! Amen.
    Hallelujah! soon the glory.
    Come, Saviour, again!

341   8.8.8.4.
M Y GOD, my Father, while I stray
    Far from my home on life's
rough way,
    Oh, teach me from my heart to say -
        "Thy will be done!"

2 If dark my path and hard my lot,
    May I be still and murmur not;
But breathe the prayer divinely
    taught -
        "Thy will be done!"

3 What though in lonely grief I sigh,
    For friends beloved, no longer nigh,
Submissive still would I reply -
        "Thy will be done!"

4 If Thou shouldst call me to resign
    What most I prize - it ne'er was
    mine,
I only yield Thee what is Thine:
        "Thy will be done!"

5 Should pining sickness waste away
    My life in premature decay,
My Father! help me still to say -
        "Thy will be done!"

6 Renew my will from day to day,
    Blend it with Thine, and take away
All that now makes it hard to say -
        "Thy will be done!"

7 And when on earth I breathe no more
    The prayer oft mixed with tears
    before,
I'll sing on heaven's blissful shore -
        "Thy will be done!"

342   C.M.
M Y GOD! what cords of love
    are Thine,
How gentle, yet how strong!
    Thy truth and grace their power
    combine
To draw our souls along.

2 The guilt of twice ten thousand sins
    One moment takes away;
And when the fight of faith begins,
    Our strength is as our day.

3 Comfort, through all this vale of tears,
    In rich profusion flows;
And glory of unnumbered years
    Eternity bestows.

4 Drawn by such cords we'll onward
    move
Till round the throne we meet,
    And, captives in the chain of love,
Embrace our Saviour's feet.

343   P.M.
M Y heart can sing when I pause
    to remember,
A heartache here is but a stepping
    stone,
Along a path that's winding always
    upward.
This troubled world is not my final
    home.

But until then, my heart will go on
singing,
Until then, with joy I'll carry on,
Until the day my eyes behold
that city,
Until the day God calls me home.

2 The things of earth will dim and lose
their value,
If we recall they're borrowed for a while;
And things of earth that cause this
heart to tremble,
Remembered there will only bring
a smile.

344   C.M.

M Y heart is bubbling over, Lord,
I will give thanks and sing,
My gladsome sacrifice of praise,
To Thy great name I bring.

2 How fair and lovely, Lord, art Thou,
How beautiful and sweet,
My grateful heart to Thee would bow,
Before the mercy seat.

3 Thy name is more than tongue can
tell,
Revealed at Calvary,
And ever would my spirit dwell,
On such great love to me.

4 Grace sought me when I wandered
far,
In all my sin and shame,
And living waters brought to me,
All glory to Thy name.

5 Grace comes indeed from that deep
well,
Of God's great heart of love,
Its fullest proof is seen in Him,
Who brought it from above.

6 My soul attracted to Thyself,
Fresh beauties in Thee see,
And treasures all Thy wondrous words,
"None ever spake like Thee".

7 My heart is bubbling over, Lord,
And till Thy face I see,
I fain would praise Thy name for all,
Thy love and grace to me.

345   8.8.8.8.8.8.

M Y heart is full of Christ, and longs
Its glorious matter to declare,
Of Him I make my loftier songs,
And cannot from His praise forbear;
My ready tongue makes haste to sing
The glories of my heavenly King.

2 Fairer than all the earth-born race,
Perfect in comeliness Thou art;
Replenished are Thy lips with grace,
And full of love Thy tender heart;
God ever blest! we bow the knee,
And own all fulness dwells in Thee.

3 Gird on Thy thigh the Spirit's sword,
And take to Thee Thy power divine;
Stir up Thy strength, almighty Lord,
All power and majesty are Thine:
Assert Thy worship and renown;
O all-redeeming God, come down!

4 Come, and maintain Thy righteous
cause
And let Thy glorious toil succeed;
Extend the victory of Thy Cross,
Ride on, and prosper in Thy deed;
Through earth triumphantly ride on,
And reign in every heart alone.

346   8.8.8.8.8.8.

M Y hope is built on nothing less
Than Jesus' blood and
righteousness;
I dare not trust the sweetest frame,
But wholly lean on Jesus' Name.

On Christ, the solid Rock, I stand;
All other ground is sinking sand.

2 When darkness seems to veil His
face,
I rest on His unchanging grace;
In every high and stormy gale
My anchor holds within the veil.

3 His oath, His covenant, and blood,
Support me in the whelming flood;
When all around my soul gives way
He then is all my hope and stay.

4 When He shall come with trumpet
sound,
  Oh, may I then in Him be found;
    Clothed in His righteousness alone,
Faultless to stand before the throne!

347   P.M.

M Y Lord has garments so
  wondrous fine,
And myrrh their texture fills;
    Its fragrance reached to this heart
      of mine,
With joy my being thrills.

Out of the ivory palaces,
  Into a world of woe,
Only His great, eternal love
  Made my Saviour go.

2 His life had also its sorrows sore,
  For aloes had a part;
And when I think of the Cross He bore,
  My eyes with tear-drops start.

3 His garments too were in cassia
  dipped,
  With healing in a touch;
    Each time my feet in some sin
      have slipped,
  He took me from its clutch.

4 In garments glorious He will come,
  To open wide the door;
And I shall enter my heavenly home,
  To dwell for evermore.

348   8.7.8.7.4.7.

M Y Redeemer! Oh what beauties
  In that lovely Name appear;
None but Jesus, in His glories,
  Shall the honoured title wear.
    My Redeemer!
Thou hast my salvation wrought.

2 Sunk in ruin, sin, and misery,
  Bound by Satan's captive chain,
Guided by his artful treachery,
  Hurrying on to endless pain;
    My Redeemer
Plucked me as a brand from hell.

3 Mine by covenant, mine for ever,
  Mine by oath, and mine by blood,
Mine - nor time the bond shall sever,
  Mine as an unchanging God.
    My Redeemer!
Oh how sweet to call Thee mine!

4 When in heaven I see Thy glory,
  When before Thy throne I bow,
Perfected I shall be like Thee,
  Fully Thy redemption know.
    My Redeemer
Then shall hear me shout His praise.

349   11.11.11.11.

M Y rest is in heaven, my rest
  is not here,
Then why should I murmur when
  trials are near?
Be hushed my sad spirit, the
  worst that can come
But shortens the journey and
  hastens me home.

2 It is not for me to be seeking my bliss,
  And building my hopes in a region
    like this;
  I look for a city which hands have
    not piled;
  I pant for a country by sin undefiled.

3 Afflictions may press me, they
    cannot destroy,
  One glimpse of His love turns
    them all into joy;
  And the bitterest tears, if He smile
    but on them,
  Like dew in the sunshine, grow
    diamond and gem.

4 Let trial and danger my progress
    oppose,
  They only make heaven more
    sweet at the close;
  Come joy or come sorrow,
    whate'er may befall,
  A home with my God will make up
    for it all.

5 With Christ in my heart, and His
    Word in my hand,
  I travel in haste through an
    enemy's land;

The road may be rough, but it
    cannot be long,
So I journey on singing the
    conqueror's song.

350   7.6.7.6.D.
MY Saviour, I would own Thee,
    Amid the world's proud scorn -
The world that mocked and
    crowned Thee
With diadem of thorn;
    The world that now rejects Thee,
Makes nothing of Thy love,
    Counts naught the grace and pity
That brought Thee from above.

2 My Lord, my Master, help me
    To walk apart with Thee,
Outside the camp, where only
    Thy beauty I can see;
Far from the world's loud turmoil,
    Far from its busy din,
Far from its praise and honour,
    Its unbelief and sin.

3 Oh, keep my heart at leisure
    From all the world beside;
In close communion ever,
    With Thee, Lord, to abide,
That I Thy whispered breathings
    Of love and truth may hear,
And hail Thee with rejoicing,
    When Thou shalt soon appear.

351   6.6.8.4.D.
MY Shepherd is the Lamb,
    The living Lord who died;
With all things good I ever am
    By Him supplied;
He richly feeds my soul
    With blessings from above;
And leads me where the rivers roll
    Of endless love.

2 My soul He doth restore
    Whene'er I go astray;
He makes my cup of joy run o'er
    From day to day;
His love, so full, so free,
    Anoints my head with oil;
Mercy and goodness follow me,
    Fruit of His toil.

3 When faith and hope shall cease,
    And love abide alone,
Then shall I see Him face to face,
    And know as known;
Still shall I lift my voice,
    His praise my song shall be;
And I will in His love rejoice
    Who died for me.

352   6.6.6.6.6.4.4.4.4.
MY song is love unknown,
    My Saviour's love to me;
Love to the loveless shown,
    That they might lovely be.
O who am I,
    That for my sake,
My Lord should take
    Frail flesh and die?

2 He came from His blest throne
    Salvation to bestow;
But man made strange, and none
    The longed-for Christ would know.
But oh, my Friend,
    My Friend indeed,
Who at my need
    His life did spend!

3 Sometimes they strew His way
    And His sweet praises sing;
Resounding all the day
    Hosannas to their King.
Then "Crucify!"
    Is all their breath,
And for His death
    They thirst and cry.

4 Why, what hath my Lord done?
    What makes this rage and spite?
He made the lame to run,
    He gave the blind their sight.
Sweet injuries!
    Yet they at these
Themselves displease,
    And 'gainst Him rise.

5 They rise, and needs will have
    My dear Lord made away;
A murderer they save,
    The Prince of Life they slay.
Yet cheerful He
    To suffering goes,
That He His foes
    From thence might free.

6 In life, no house, no home
    My Lord on earth might have;
In death, no friendly tomb
    But what a stranger gave.
What may I say?
    Heav'n was His home,
But mine the tomb
    Wherein He lay.

7 Here might I stay and sing,
    No story so divine;
Never was love, dear King,
    Never was grief like Thine.
This is my Friend,
    In whose sweet praise
I all my days
    Could gladly spend.

353   C.M.

M Y soul, amid this stormy world,
    Is like some fluttered dove,
And fain would be as swift of wing
    And flee to Him I love.

2 The cords that bound my heart to
        earth
    Are loosed by Jesus' hand;
    Before His Cross I now am left
A stranger in the land.

3 That visage marred, those sorrows
        deep,
    The thorns, the scourge, the gall,
    These were the golden chains
        of love
His captive to enthral!

4 Fain would I, Saviour, know Thy love,
    Which yet no measure knows,
Would search the depths of all Thy
        wounds,
    The secret of Thy woes.

5 Fain would I strike the golden harp,
    And wear the promised crown;
And at Thy feet, while bending low,
    Would sing what grace has done.

354   S.M.

M Y times are in Thy hand;
    My God, I wish them there;
My life, my soul, my all, I leave
    Entirely to Thy care.

2 My times are in Thy hand,
    Whatever they may be;
Pleasing or painful, dark or bright,
    As best may seem to Thee.

3 My times are in Thy hand;
    Why should I doubt or fear?
My Father's hand will never cause
    His child a needless tear.

4 My times are in Thy hand,
    Jesus, the Crucified!
The hand my many sins have
        pierced
Is now my guard and guide.

5 My times are in Thy hand,
    Jesus, my Advocate!
Nor is that hand outstretched
    in vain,
For me to supplicate.

6 My times are in Thy hand,
    I'll always trust in Thee;
Till I have left this weary land,
    And all Thy glory see.

355   8.8.8.6.

N AILED to a Cross! those holy
    hands
That healed the helpless in their pain,
    That loosed with tender touch their
        bands
And brought them life again!

2 Those holy hands that broke the bread
    When, in His kindness and His care,
The fainting multitude He fed
    In yonder desert bare!

3 Nailed to a Cross! those holy feet
    That trod that lowly, lovely way,
Each step a wealth of fragrance sweet,
    Sweet for eternity!

4 Those holy feet that never strayed
    Nor stumbled in the path, but trod,
Unfaltering and unafraid,
    On in the will of God!

5 Nailed to a Cross! The Prince of Life!
    The Lord of Glory's dying place!
A Cross that leaves a world of strife
    Forever in disgrace!

6 O thorn-crowned head in death
   bowed low!
Obedience to surrendered breath!
   O Love most wonderful in woe!
Most beautiful in death!

356   C.M.

NO act of power could e'er atone,
   No wonder-working word
Could, from the brightness of the throne,
   Make love's sweet voice be heard.

2 If sinners ever were to know
   The depths of love divine,
All Calv'ry's weakness and its woe,
   Blest Saviour, must be Thine.

3 God's righteousness is there proclaimed,
   His mercy's depths are known,
While to the full Thou hast maintained
   The glory of His throne.

4 God now is glorified in Thee,
   In Thee, His only Son;
His hand, His house, His heart are
   free,
Because Thy work is done.

5 For Thou hast brought again to Him
   More than by man He lost;
And in the very place of sin
   We see His glory most.

6 And drawn to Thee in holy love,
   A song of joy we raise;
In concert with the heav'ns above
   We crown Thee with our praise.

357   6.6.8.6.10.12.

NO blood, no altar now,
   The sacrifice is o'er;
No flame, no smoke ascends on high,
   The lamb is slain no more;
But richer blood has flowed from
   nobler veins
To purge the soul from guilt, and
   cleanse the reddest stains.

2 We thank Thee for the *blood*,
   The blood of Christ, Thy Son,
The blood by which our peace is made,

Our victory is won:
Great victory o'er hell and sin and woe,
   That needs no second fight and
   leaves no second foe.

3 We thank Thee for the *grace*
   Descending from above,
That overflows our widest guilt,
   Th' eternal Father's love,
Love of the Father's everlasting Son,
   Love of the Holy Ghost,
   Jehovah, Three in One.

4 We thank Thee for the *hope*,
   So glad, and sure, and clear;
It holds the drooping spirit up
   Till the long dawn appear;
Fair hope! with what a sunshine
   does it cheer
Our roughest path on earth, our
   dreariest desert here!

5 We thank Thee for the *crown*
   Of glory and of life;
'Tis no poor with'ring wreath of
   earth,
Man's prize in mortal strife;
   'Tis incorruptible as is the throne,
The kingdom of our God and His
   incarnate Son.

358   7.6.7.6.D.

NO bone of Thee was broken,
   Thou spotless, paschal Lamb!
Of life and peace a token
   To us who know Thy Name;
The Head, for all the members,
   The curse, the vengeance bore,
And God, our God, remembers
   His people's sins no more.

2 We, Thy redeemed, are reaping
   What Thou didst sow in tears;
This feast which we are keeping
   Thy Name to us endears;
It tells of justice hiding
   The face of God from Thee;
Proud men around deriding
   Thy sorrows on the tree.

3 Thy death of shame and sorrow
   Was like unto Thy birth,
Which would no glory borrow,
   No majesty from earth.

Thy pilgrims, we are hasting
  To our eternal home,
Its joy already tasting
  Of vict'ry o'er the tomb.

4 Thy life and death reviewing,
    We tread the narrow way;
  Our homeward path pursuing,
    We watch the dawn of day.
  We eat and drink with gladness
    The symbol bread and wine,
  And sing with sweetest sadness
    Our song of love divine.

359 C.M.

"NO condemnation!" O my soul
  'Tis God that speaks the word;
Perfect in comeliness art thou
  In Christ thy glorious Lord.

2 In God's own presence now for us
    The Saviour doth appear;
  His saints as jewels on His heart
    Jesus doth ever bear.

3 "No condemnation!" precious word!
    Consider it, my soul;
  Thy sins were all on Jesus laid,
    His stripes have made thee whole.

4 Teach us, O God, to fix our eyes
    On Christ, the spotless Lamb;
  So shall we love Thy gracious will
    And glorify Thy Name.

360 P.M.

NO future but glory, Lord
  Jesus, have we -
How bright is the prospect of
  being with Thee!
O home of all homes, with the
  Father above!
O wonderful dwelling of infinite love!
  Home, home, bright, bright home!
How blessèd the prospect, Lord
  Jesus, of home!

2 A moment's affliction, Lord Jesus,
    is light,
  And works for us glory surpassingly
    bright;
  Whilst viewing not things which
    are but for a time,

But objects far brighter in glory
  sublime;
Home, home, bright, bright home!
  Our future's eternal in Thy
    blessèd home!

3 "One thing" would we do, we
    would press toward the goal,
  Thyself, Lord, in glory, the prize of
    our soul -
  Forget what's behind, for the
    bright things before,
  Since all they who know Thee
    would know Thee still more:
  Home, home, bright, bright home!
    We press on to know Thee and
      reach Thee, at home!

4 In heaven alone is our city and state,
    From thence, Lord, as Saviour,
      Thyself we await;
  Our bodies to change and
    conform them to Thine,
  That we in Thine image and glory
    may shine;
  Home, home, bright, bright home!
    Soon we shall be with Thee
      and like Thee, at home!

361 S.M.

NO gospel like this feast
  Spread for us, Lord, by Thee;
No prophets or evangelists
  Preach the glad news more free.

2 All Thy redemption cost,
    All our redemption won;
  All it has won for us, the lost,
    All it cost Thee, the Son.

3 *Thine* was the bitter price,
    Ours is the free gift given;
  Thine was the blood of sacrifice,
    Ours is the wine of heaven.

4 To Thee, our curse and doom
    Wrapt round Thee with our sin;
  The horror of that midday gloom,
    The deeper night within.

5 Here we would rest midway,
    As on a sacred height;
  That darkest and that brightest day
    Meeting before our sight.

6 From that dark depth of woes
    Thy love for us has trod,
  We soar to heights of blest repose
    Thy love prepares with God.

7 Thus, from self's chains released,
    One sight alone we see,
  Still at the Cross, while at this feast,
    We see Thee, *only Thee!*

362   C.M.

N O lips like Thine, most blessèd
    Lord,
  None ever spake like Thee,
    As sweetest honey or as myrrh,
    Flows fragrant from the tree.

2 Thy lips "like lilies"! What so pure,
    So lovely in their grace,
  With secret power, in hours of grief,
    To kindle thoughts of praise!

3 Forth from those lips rich grace is
    poured,
    To comfort all who mourn;
      No tongue like Thine to cheer the
      faint,
    Thou Friend of the forlorn!

4 As softening showers upon the grass,
    Gentle as early dew,
  Thy speech distils into the soul,
    Its graces to renew.

5 Ages have passed since at Thy voice
    Men marvelled as they heard;
  And still our hearts within us burn
    While listening to Thy word.

363   P.M.

N O room in the inn for the
    Saviour was found,
  Who from childhood was treated
    with scorn;
  No place but the manger where
    cattle were brought,
  When in Bethlehem Jesus was born.

2 But heaven was opened to give
    Him the praise,
  Denied Him by man on the earth;
    And heavenly hosts broke forth
    in their songs,
  Of wonder and joy at His birth.

3 No home but the mountain of Olives
    was His,
  Though the bird of the air had its nest;
    No love but the Father's, whose
    side He had left,
  Could give Him refreshment and rest.

4 No comforters came, when for
    comfort He looked,
  No pity, when pity He sought;
    For sin He was wounded and
    smitten of God,
  And sinners did set Him at nought!

5 And angels, who ministered oft to
    His need,
  Were sent to His help from the throne,
    When, weary and weak in the
    bitterest hour,
  His people had left Him alone!

6 But neither the manger, the Cross,
    nor the shame,
  Are now by this blessèd One known;
    Gethsemane's sorrows for ever
    are past,
  And the fruit of them all is His own.

7 And now that He dwells in the
    mansions of bliss,
  He has room for each trusting one
    there;
  And His sorrows remembered will
    heighten the joy,
  Which all will eternally share.

364   9.9.9.

N O shadows yonder! All light and
    song!
  Each day I ponder and say, "How long
    Shall time me sunder from that
    glad throng?"

2 No weeping yonder! All fled away;
    While here I wander, each weary
    day,
  And sigh as I ponder my long, long
    stay.

3 No partings yonder! No space or time
    Hearts e'er shall sunder in that
    fair clime,
  Dearer and fonder, friendships
    sublime!

4 None wanting yonder bought by the
   Lamb!
   All gathered under the sheltering palm,
   Loud as the thunder swells the
   glad psalm!

365   S.M.

NO unforeseen event
   E'er took Him by surprise;
Toward the Cross with fixed intent
   He moved with open eyes.

2 Men reckless deeds will vaunt
   And count as courage true
The daring of the ignorant
   Who know not what they do.

3 He knew the reason why
   The Father sent the Son;
He knew that He had come to die,
   A Man for men undone.

4 He weighed that weight of woe
   In each particular;
The length and depth to which He'd go
   He measured from afar.

5 The scourging and the scorn,
   The worst that men could do,
The meaning of the crown of thorn
   Lay open to His view.

6 He knew! and love can look
   And see in light most sweet
The glory of the way He took,
   The beauty of His feet.

366   10.10.10.10.

NONE but Thyself, O God,
   could estimate
His riches vast, His
   condescension great,
His stoop from glory's sphere in
   grace sublime,
To move in servant form through
   scenes of time.

2 His path on earth we rev'rently review,
   In every step so faithful and so true,
Misunderstood by friends, despised
   by foes,
Yet marked throughout by inward
   calm repose.

3 How kind His heart! how full of
   fragrance sweet!
How clean His hands! how beautiful
   His feet!
How pure His words! how gracious
   every deed!
And all for Thee, the while He met
   man's need!

4 So we remember Him, in all His ways,
   The Man of Thy good pleasure,
   through those days
Of earthly sojourn, suffering and
   shame
And give Thee thanks for Him in His
   blest Name.

367   S.M.

NONE teacheth, Lord, like Thee,
   None can such truth impart,
Such treasures from Thy Word unfold,
   Nor so impress the heart.

2 How blest Thy servants were,
   When with them on their way
Thou didst commune, and sweetly
   chase
Their sorrows all away!

3 So now to us draw near,
   And speak to every heart;
Our light in darkness, joy in grief,
   Our "All in All", Thou art.

4 Open to us Thy Word,
   Thy precious thoughts reveal,
Thy purposes and ways explain,
   And teach us all Thy will.

5 So shall our doubt and fear,
   Our care and grief subside,
And each enraptured heart exclaim,
   O Lord, with us abide!

368   S.M.

NOT all the blood of beasts,
   On Jewish altars slain,
Could give the guilty conscience
   peace,
Or wash away one stain.

2 But Christ, the heavenly Lamb,
   Took all our sins away,
   A sacrifice of nobler name
   And richer blood than they.

3 By faith we lay our hand
   On that dear head of Thine;
   With broken, contrite hearts we stand,
   And there confess our sin.

4 We now look back to see
   The burden Thou didst bear,
   When hanging on the accursèd tree,
   And know our guilt was there.

5 Believing, we rejoice
   To see the curse remove;
   We bless the Lamb with cheerful voice,
   And sing redeeming love.

369   L.M.D.

NOT now, but in the coming years,
   It may be in the better land,
We'll read the meaning of our tears,
   And there, some time, we'll
      understand.

Then trust in God through all thy days;
   Fear not! for He doth hold thy hand;
Though dark thy way, still sing and
   praise;
Some time, some time we'll
   understand.

2 We'll catch the broken threads again,
   And finish what we here began;
Heaven will the mysteries explain,
   And then, ah then, we'll understand.

3 We'll know why clouds instead of sun
   Were over many a cherished plan;
Why song has ceased when scarce
   begun;
'Tis there, some time, we'll understand.

4 Why what we long for most of all,
   Eludes so oft our eager hand;
Why hopes are crushed and castles
   fall,
Up there, some time, we'll understand.

5 God knows the way, He holds the
   key,
   He guides us with unerring hand;
   Some time with tearless eyes
      we'll see;
Yes, there, up there, we'll understand.

370   10.10.10.10.

NOT what I am, O Lord, but what
   Thou art -
That, that alone can be my soul's
   true rest;
Thy love, not mine, bids fear and
   doubt depart,
And stills the tempest of my tossing
   breast.

2 It is Thy perfect love that casts out
   fear;
   I know the voice that whispers "It
      is I";
   And in Thy well-known words of
      heavenly cheer,
   I find the joy that bids each sorrow
      fly.

3 Thy name is Love! I hear it from
   Thy Cross;
   Thy name is Love! I read it in Thy
      tomb;
   All meaner love is perishable dross,
      But this shall light me through
         time's thickest gloom.

4 'Tis what I know of Thee, my Lord
   and God,
   That fills my soul with peace, my
      lips with song;
   Thou art my health, my joy, my
      staff and rod;
   Leaning on Thee, in weakness I
      am strong.

5 More of Thyself, oh, show me, hour
   by hour,
   More of Thy glory, O my God and
      Lord;
   More of Thyself, in all Thy grace
      and power;
   More of Thy love and truth,
      Incarnate Word!

371

NOT what my hands have done
　Can save this guilty soul;
Not what my toiling flesh has borne
　Can make my spirit whole.
Not what I feel or do
　Can give me peace with God;
Not all my prayers and sighs and
　tears
Can bear my awful load.

2 Thy work alone, O Christ,
　Can ease this weight of sin;
Thy blood alone, O Lamb of God,
　Can give me peace within.
Thy love to me, O God,
　Not mine, O Lord, to Thee,
Can rid me of this dark unrest,
　And set my spirit free.

3 Thy grace alone, O God,
　To me can pardon speak;
Thy power alone, O Son of God,
　Can this sore bondage break.
No other work, save Thine,
　No meaner blood will do;
No strength, save that which is
　divine,
Can bear me safely through.

4 I bless the Christ of God;
　I rest on love divine;
And with unfaltering lip and heart
　I call this Saviour mine.
His Cross dispels each doubt;
　I bury in His tomb
Each thought of unbelief and fear,
　Each lingering shade of gloom.

5 I praise the God of grace;
　I trust His truth and might;
He calls me His, I call Him mine,
　My God, my joy and light.
In Him is only good,
　In me is only ill;
My ill but draws His goodness forth,
　And me He loveth still.

6 'Tis He who saveth me,
　And freely pardon gives;
I love because He loveth me,
　I live because He lives.
My life with Him is hid,
　My death has passed away,
My clouds have melted into light,
　My midnight into day.

372

NOW I have found a Friend,
　Jesus is mine;
His love shall never end,
　Jesus is mine;
Though earthly joys decrease,
Though earthly friendships cease,
Now I have lasting peace,
　Jesus is mine.

2 Though I grow poor and old,
　Jesus is mine;
He will my faith uphold,
　Jesus is mine;
He will my wants supply,
His precious blood is nigh,
Nought can my hope destroy,
　Jesus is mine.

3 Farewell, mortality!
　Jesus is mine;
Welcome, eternity!
　Jesus is mine.
He my redemption is,
Wisdom and righteousness,
Life, light, and holiness,
　Jesus is mine.

4 Father! Thy Name I bless,
　Jesus is mine;
Thine was the sovereign grace,
　Praise shall be Thine;
Spirit of holiness,
Sealing the Father's grace,
He made my soul embrace
　Jesus as mine.

373

NOW, in a song of grateful praise,
　To our blest Lord the voice we
raise;
　With all His saints we join to tell -
*Our Saviour hath done all things
　well!*

2 All worlds His glorious power confess;
　His wisdom all His works express;
But oh, His love, what tongue can
　tell?
*Our Saviour hath done all things
　well!*

3 And since our souls have known
     His love,
  What mercies hath He made us
     prove!
  Mercies which all our praise excel -
  *Our Saviour hath done all things
     well!*

4 Though many a fiery, flaming dart,
     The tempter levels at the heart,
  With this we all his rage repel -
  *Our Saviour hath done all things
     well!*

5 And when on that bright day we rise,
     And join the anthems of the skies,
  Among the rest this note shall swell -
  *Our Saviour hath done all things
     well!*

  *And above the rest this note shall
     swell,*
  *This note shall swell, this note
     shall swell,*
  *And above the rest this note shall
     swell,*
  *Our Saviour hath done all things
     well!*

374   6.6.6.6.8.8.

O BLESSÈD God! how kind
    Are all Thy ways to me,
Whose dark benighted mind
    Was enmity with Thee.
Yet now, subdued by sovereign
    grace,
My spirit longs for Thine embrace.

2 How precious are Thy thoughts
     That o'er my spirit roll!
  They rise beyond my faults,
     And captivate my soul:
  How great their sum, how high they
     rise,
  Can ne'er be known beneath the
     skies.

3 Preserved by Jesus, when
     My feet made haste to hell!
  And there should I have gone,
     But Thou dost all things well:
  Thy love was great, Thy mercy free,
     Which from the pit delivered me.

4 Before Thy hands had made
     The sun to rule the day,
  Or earth's foundation laid,
     Or fashioned Adam's clay,
  What thoughts of peace and
     mercy flowed
  In Thy great heart of love, O God.

5 A monument of grace,
     A sinner saved by blood,
  The streams of love I trace
     Up to the fountain, God,
  And in His sovereign counsels see
     Eternal thoughts of love to me.

375   L.M.

O BLESSÈD God, to Thee we
    raise
The fruit of lips in priestly praise
Of Him Who bows our hearts
    as one -
Thy Holy Son, Thy Holy Son.

2 Thy Holy Son in lowly guise,
     Supremely precious in Thine eyes,
  Most fair to Thee apparelled thus,
     And fair to us, most fair to us.

3 Thy Holy Son in manhood true,
     Thy heart to please, Thy will
        to do,
  Thy Name on earth to glorify,
     For this to live, for this to die.

4 Thy Holy Son descending low
     Thy love to tell, Thy heart to show,
  The full expression of Thy mind,
     In grace so kind, so wondrous
        kind.

5 Thy Holy Son in human form,
     Baring His bosom to the storm
  In patient grace for men undone,
     Thy Holy Son! Thy Holy Son!

6 O Blessèd God, the shame, the
     scorn,
  The cruel Cross, the crown of thorn
     We ever will "remember yet",
  And ne'er forget, no, ne'er forget.

376 C.M.

O BLESSÈD Lord, what hast
Thou done!
How vast a ransom paid!
God's only well-belovèd Son
Upon the altar laid!

2 The Father, in His willing love,
Could spare Thee from His side;
And Thou couldst stoop, to bear above,
At such a cost, Thy Bride.

3 While our full hearts in faith repose
Upon Thy precious blood,
Peace in a steady current flows,
Filled from Thy mercy's flood.

4 What boundless joy will fill each heart,
Our every grief efface,
When we behold Thee as Thou art,
And all Thy love retrace.

5 Unseen we love Thee, dear Thy
Name!
But when our eyes behold,
With joyful wonder we'll proclaim
"The half hath not been told!"

6 For Thou exceedest all the fame
Our ears have ever heard:
Happy are they who know Thy name,
And trust Thy faithful word!

377 10.10.10.10.

O BLESSÈD moment, ever
drawing nigh,
When every shadow shall have
passed away,
When that clear light shall fill the
tear-dimmed eye,
And this dark night give place to
endless day !

2 Then all misunderstanding shall
have passed,
Estrangement shall for evermore
have flown,
And fellowship its fulness reach at
last;
We'll love and know as we are
loved and known.

3 Then everlasting joy we shall
obtain,
Sorrow and sighing then shall flee
away;
There shall be neither grief, nor cry,
nor pain,
To cast a shadow o'er th' eternal day.

4 Then shall we evermore be with the
Lord,
And love shall rest in endless ecstasy,
When adoration strikes the
perfect chord
In full-toned praise of Him eternally.

378 C.M.

O BLESSÈD Saviour! is Thy love
So great, so full, so free?
Fain would we give our hearts, our
minds,
Our lives, our all, to Thee.

2 We love Thee for the glorious worth
Which in Thyself we see;
We love Thee for the shameful Cross
Endured so patiently.

3 No man of greater love can boast
Than for his friend to die;
Thou for Thine enemies wast slain!
What love with Thine can vie?

4 Though in the very form of God,
With heavenly glory crowned,
Thou didst partake of human flesh,
Beset with sorrows round.

5 Thou wouldst like sinful man be made
In everything but sin,
That we as like Thee might become,
As we unlike have been.

6 Like Thee in faith, in meekness, love,
In every heavenly grace,
From glory thus to glory changed,
Till we behold Thy face.

7 O Lord! we treasure in our souls
The memory of Thy love;
And ever may Thy Name to us
A grateful odour prove.

379 P.M.

O CHILD of God, there is for thee
A hope that shines amid the
gloom,
A gladsome hope that thou shalt
see
Thy Lord, for He will surely come.

He'll come, … yes, He'll come
and tarry not;
He'll come, … yes, He'll come
and tarry not;
He'll come, … He'll come, …
He'll come and tarry not.

2 When in this world His hands had
made,
No room was found for Jesus then;
The mountainside was oft His bed;
Now, glorified, He comes again.

3 Exalted now to heaven's throne,
The Saviour there of sinful men;
His loving heart yearns o'er His own,
And for them He will come again.

4 O child of God, thy lot may be
Oft mixed with trial, grief and pain;
Look up, He'll surely come for thee;
He says, "I'll quickly come again".

5 Then joy unmingled will be thine,
Earth's tears and trials all forgot;
So cheer thy heart, no more repine,
His word is sure: He'll tarry not.

380 C.M.D.

O CHRIST, in Thee my soul
hath found,
And found in Thee alone,
The peace, the joy I sought so
long,
The bliss till now unknown.

Now none but Christ can satisfy,
None other Name for me;
There's love, and life, and lasting
joy,
Lord Jesus, found in Thee.

2 I sighed for rest and happiness,
I yearned for them, not Thee;
But while I passed my Saviour by
His love laid hold on me.

3 I tried the broken cisterns, Lord,
But, ah! the waters failed;
E'en as I stooped to drink they fled,
And mocked me as I wailed.

4 The pleasures lost I sadly mourned,
But never wept for Thee,
Till grace the sightless eyes received,
Thy loveliness to see.

381 S.M.

O CHRIST, Thou heavenly Lamb!
Joy of the Father's heart;
Now let Thy love my soul inflame,
Fresh power to me impart.

2 Power to know the loss
Suffered, O Lord, by Thee;
Power to glory in the Cross
Thou didst endure for me.

3 Power to feel Thy love,
And all its depths to know;
Power to fix the heart above,
And die to all below.

4 Power to keep the eye
For ever fixed on Thee;
Power to lift the warning cry
To souls from wrath to flee.

5 Power lost souls to win
From Satan's mighty hold;
Power the wanderers to bring
Back to the heavenly fold.

6 Power to watch and pray,
"Lord Jesus, quickly come!"
Power to hail the happy day
Destined to bear me home.

7 Lord Jesus, then to me
Power divine impart,
To swell redemption's song to Thee,
For worthy, Lord, Thou art.

382 S.M.D.

O CHRIST, Thou Son of God!
Thou glorious Lord of all,
Thou living One who once wast slain,
Before Thy face we fall:
To Thee, O Lord, we look,
To Thee ourselves we yield;
Be Thou throughout our earthly course
Our refuge and our shield.

2 Though all around may change
     No change Thou e'er shalt know;
  The same art Thou upon the throne
     As Thou wast here below;
  The same today Thou art
     As yesterday Thou wast,
  The same e'en to eternal days
     As in the wondrous past.

3 Lord Jesus, take our hearts,
     From self-love set them free;
  Help us, however dark our path,
     To stay our souls on Thee:
  Though evil waxes worse,
     And many hearts grow cold,
  Help us to cleave unto Thy name,
     Thy faithful Word to hold.

4 Help us to look beyond
     The dark and gloomy night,
  To wait for that blest hour when Thou
     Wilt come in glory bright:
  When we Thy voice shall hear,
     Thy glorious face shall see,
  And, like Thee, in Thy presence stand
     And ever worship Thee.

383   6.6.8.6.8.8.

O CHRIST! we rest in Thee,
     In Thee ourselves we hide;
  Laden with guilt and misery,
     Where could we rest beside?
  'Tis on Thy meek and lowly breast
     Our weary souls alone can rest.

2 Thou Holy One of God!
     The Father rests in Thee,
  And in the savour of that blood
     Once shed on Calvary.
  The curse is gone - through Thee
     we're blest;
  God rests in Thee - in Thee we rest.

3 Soon the bright, glorious day,
     The rest of God, shall come;
  Sorrow and sin shall pass away,
     And we shall reach our home;
  Then, of the promised land
     possessed,
  Our souls shall know eternal rest.

384   8.6.8.6.8.6.

O CHRIST, what burdens bowed
     Thy head!
  Our load was laid on Thee;
     Thou stoodest in the sinner's stead,
  Bear'st all my ill for me.
     A victim led, Thy blood was shed;
  Now there's no load for me.

2 Death and the curse were in our cup,
     O Christ, 'twas full for Thee!
  But Thou hast drained the last dark
     drop,
  'Tis empty now for me.
     That bitter cup, love drank it up;
  Now blessings' draught for me.

3 Jehovah lifted up His rod;
     O Christ, it fell on Thee!
  Thou wast sore stricken of Thy God;
     There's not one stroke for me.
  Thy tears, Thy blood, beneath it
     flowed;
  Thy bruising healeth me.

4 The tempest's awful voice was heard;
     O Christ, it broke on Thee!
  Thy open bosom was my ward;
     It braved the storm for me.
  Thy form was scarred, Thy visage
     marred;
  Now cloudless peace for me.

5 Jehovah bade His sword awake;
     O Christ, it woke 'gainst Thee!
  Thy blood the flaming blade must
     slake,
  Thy heart its sheath must be;
     All for my sake my peace to make,
  Now sleeps that sword for me.

6 For me, Lord Jesus, Thou hast died,
     And I have died in Thee;
  Thou'rt risen; my bands are all untied,
     And now Thou liv'st in me.
  The Father's face of radiant grace
     Shines now in light on me.

385   L.M.

O COME, Thou stricken Lamb of
   God!
Who shed'st for us Thine own life-
   blood,
And teach us all Thy love: then pain
   Were light, and life or death were
   gain.

2 Take Thou our hearts, and let them be
      For ever closed to all but Thee;
   Thy willing servants, let us wear
      The seal of love for ever there.

3 How blest are they who still abide
      Close sheltered by Thy watchful side;
   Who life and strength from Thee
      receive,
   And with Thee move, and in Thee live!

4 Ah, Lord! enlarge our scanty thought
      To know the wonders Thou hast
         wrought;
   Unloose our stamm'ring tongues to
      tell
   Thy love, immense, unsearchable.

5 First-born of many brethren, Thou!
      To whom both heaven and earth
         must bow!
   Heirs of Thy shame and of Thy throne,
      We bear the cross, and seek the
         crown.

386   7.6.7.6.

O EVER homeless Stranger,
   Thus, dearest Friend to me;
An outcast in a manger,
   That Thou might'st with us be!

2 Oh, strange yet fit beginning
      Of all that life of woe,
   In which Thy grace was winning
      Poor man his God to know!

3 O Love, all thought surpassing!
      That Thou should'st with us be,
   Nor yet in triumph passing,
      But human infancy!

4 Midst sin and all corruption,
      Where hatred did abound,

Thy path of true perfection
   Was light on all around.

5 Yet with all grief acquainted,
      The Man of Sorrows view,
   Unmoved, by ill untainted,
      The path of grace pursue.

6 No eye was found to pity,
      No heart to bear Thy woe,
   But shame, and scorn, and spitting:
      None cared Thy name to know.

7 O day of greatest sorrow,
      Day of unfathomed grief!
   When Thou didst taste the horror
      Of wrath without relief.

8 In death, obedience yielding
      To God His Father's will,
   Love still its power is wielding
      To meet all human ill.

9 We worship, when we see Thee
      In all Thy sorrowing path;
   We long soon to be with Thee
      Who bore for us the wrath!

387   11.11.11.11.

O EYES that are weary, and
   hearts that are sore,
Look off unto Jesus and sorrow no
   more;
The light of His countenance
   shineth so bright,
That on earth, as in heaven, there
   need be no night.

2 Looking off unto Jesus, my eyes
      cannot see
   The troubles and dangers that
      throng around me;
   They cannot be blinded with
      sorrowful tears,
   They cannot be shadowed with
      unbelief fears.

3 Looking off unto Jesus, my spirit is
      blest;
   In the world I have turmoil, in Him I
      have rest;

The sea of my life all about me may
   roar;
When I look unto Jesus I hear it no
   more.

4 Looking off unto Jesus, I go not
      astray;
   My eyes are on Him, and He shows
      me the way;
   The path may seem dark, as He
      leads me along,
   But following Jesus, I cannot go
      wrong.

5 Looking off unto Jesus, my heart
      cannot fear,
   Its trembling is still, when I see Jesus
      near;
   I know that His power my safeguard
      will be,
   For, "Why are you troubled?" He
      saith unto me.

6 Soon, soon shall I know the full
      beauty and grace
   Of Jesus, my Lord, when I stand
      face to face;
   I shall know how His love went
      before me each day,
   And wonder that ever my eyes
      turned away.

388   C.M.

OH! for a closer walk with God!
   A calm and heavenly frame!
A light to shine upon the road
   That leads me to the Lamb!

2 Where is the blessèdness I knew,
      When first I saw the Lord?
   Where is the soul-refreshing view
      Of Jesus and His word?

3 What peaceful hours I once enjoyed!
      How sweet their memory still!
   But they have left an aching void
      The world can never fill.

4 The dearest idol I have known,
      Whate'er that idol be,
   Help me to tear it from Thy throne,
      And worship only Thee.

5 So shall my walk be close with God,
      Calm and serene my frame;
   So purer light shall mark the road
      That leads me to the Lamb.

389   C.M.

OH for a thousand tongues to sing
   My great Redeemer's praise,
The glories of my God and King,
   The triumphs of His grace!

2 My gracious Master and my God,
      Assist me to proclaim,
   To spread through all the earth abroad,
      The honours of Thy Name.

3 Jesus! the Name that charms our fears,
      That bids our sorrows cease;
   'Tis music in the sinner's ears,
      'Tis life, and health, and peace.

4 He breaks the power of cancelled sin,
      He sets the prisoner free;
   His blood can make the foulest clean,
      His blood availed for me.

5 I felt my Lord's atoning blood
      Close to my soul applied;
   Me, me He loved - the Son of God,
      For me, for me He died!

6 He speaks and, listening to His voice,
      New life the dead receive;
   The mournful, broken hearts rejoice;
      The humble poor believe.

7 Glory to God, and praise and love,
      Be ever, ever given;
   By saints below and saints above,
      The Church in earth and heaven.

390   11.10.11.10.

OH, for the peace that floweth
   as a river!
Making life's desert places bloom
   and smile;
Oh, for the faith to grasp heaven's
   bright "for ever"!
Amid the shadows of earth's "little
   while".

2 "A little while" for patient vigil keeping,
  To face the storm and wrestle with
    the strong;
  "A little while" to sow the seed with
    weeping,
  Then bind the sheaves and sing the
    harvest song.

3 "A little while" the earthen pitcher
    taking
  To wayside brooks, from far-off
    fountains fed;
  Then the parched lip its thirst for
    ever slaking
  Beside the fulness of the Fountain-
    head.

4 "A little while" to keep the oil from
    failing,
  "A little while" faith's flick'ring lamp
    to trim;
  And then the Bridegroom's coming
    footsteps hailing,
  We'll haste to meet Him with the
    bridal hymn.

391
7.6.7.6.D.

OH for the robes of whiteness,
    Oh for the tearless eyes;
Oh for the glorious brightness
    Of the unclouded skies!
Oh for the no more weeping
    Within the land of love;
The endless joy of keeping
    The bridal feast above!

2 Oh for the bliss of rising,
    My risen Lord to meet;
Oh for the rest of lying
    For ever at His feet!
Oh for the hour of seeing
    My Saviour face to face;
The hope of ever being
    In that sweet meeting-place!

3 Jesus, Thou King of Glory,
    We soon shall dwell with Thee!
We soon shall sing the story
    Of love so rich and free;
Meanwhile our thoughts would enter
    E'en now before Thy throne,
That all our love might centre
    On Thee, and Thee alone.

392
10.10.10.10.

O GLORIOUS Lord! what
    thoughts Thy mind did fill,
When from Thy God Thou cam'st to
    do His will!
How deep, indeed, the joy that filled
    Thy heart -
That myriad sons with Thee should
    find their part!

2 Thy brethren, Lord, Thine own and
    one with Thee,
Were in Thy heart when dying
    on the tree;
Thy church complete and in Thy
    beauty dressed -
The day of God, and love divine at
    rest.

3 O blessèd Lord! those treasured
    thoughts unfold
In light divine, as we Thy face behold!
    And on our view unbounded
    glories break,
That speak Thy fame and songs
    eternal wake.

393
C.M.

O GOD, can we Thy Son forget,
    Forget His agony,
Forget His tears and blood-like sweat
    In dark Gethsemane?

2 Can we forget Him seized and led,
    Forsaken by His own,
When all His friends afar had fled
    And left Him all alone?

3 Forget that base indignity
    Within the judgment hall,
Forget Him led, in mockery,
    Without the city wall?

4 Forget those piercèd hands and feet,
    That thorn-crowned head bowed low,
Forget that sacrifice most sweet
    Upon that Cross of woe?

5 Forget Him? Nay! we love to dwell
    In this remembrance meet
Upon the One Who pleased Thee well
    And on His work complete.

394   8.8.8.6.

O GOD His Father, rev'rently
  We offer up our praise today,
Engaged in Thine appointed way
  With Thy Belovèd Son.

2 We look on One supremely great,
  Ponder o'er ways immaculate,
As we together meditate
  On Thy Belovèd Son.

3 That path, with moral glories bright,
  Resplendent in Thy holy sight,
Showed nought to mar Thy heart's
  delight
    In Thy Belovèd Son.

4 Performed in perfect purity,
  A perfect service do we see,
Rendered through every day to Thee
  By Thy Belovèd Son.

5 Boundless in might, and yet so meek!
  In every circumstance unique!
None else we see, and only speak
  Of Thy Belovèd Son.

395   C.M.

O GOD of Bethel! by whose hand
  Thy people still are fed;
Who through this weary pilgrimage
  Hast all our fathers led.

2 Our vows, our prayers, we now present
  Before Thy throne of grace:
God of our fathers! be the God
  Of their succeeding race.

3 Through each perplexing path of life
  Our wandering footsteps guide;
Give us each day our daily bread,
  And raiment fit provide.

4 O spread Thy covering wings around
  Till all our wanderings cease,
And at our Father's loved abode
  Our souls arrive in peace.

5 Such blessings from Thy gracious
  hand
  Our humble prayers implore;
    And Thou shalt be our chosen God,
And portion evermore.

396   C.M.

O GOD of everlasting days,
  Through Jesus Christ our Lord,
In His own Name we gladly raise
  Our praise with one accord.

2 We magnify His Name Who shared
  Thy glory in the past,
And marvel at His grace Who cared
  His lot with man to cast.

3 Through Him were made the
  heavens and earth,
And yet, in lowliness,
  He graced a manger at His birth
Thy glory to express.

4 In meekness and obedience through
  His youth's obscurity,
He in Thy holy favour grew,
  In perfect purity.

5 And when the Adversary sought
  To reach His heart within
That life to mar, in Him was nought
  That could respond to sin.

6 We thank Thee for the path He trod,
  For every kindness shown,
The way He moved for Thee, His God,
  And made Thy glory known.

397   C.M.D.

O GOD of glorious majesty,
  Messiah, King of grace,
Unveil to us Thy loveliness,
  And let us see Thy face!
Obedient to Thy loving voice,
  We've turned aside awhile,
To wait beside Thy guiding feet,
  And rest beneath Thy smile.

2 Oh, nerve us for the conflict, Lord,
  That thickens day by day,
That we, amidst our alien foes,
  Thy banner may display!
We've but a little while to fight,
  To work, to wait for Thee;
Help us to labour in Thy cause
  With holy energy.

3 Help us upon our watch to stand,
    And never quail for fear,
Till in the glowing eastern sky
    The Morning Star appear;
Then with Thy waiting saints above,
    Thine advent, Lord, we'll hail,
And over death, and sin, and woe,
    We'll joyfully prevail.

398　　　　　　　　　6.6.8.6.8.8.
O GOD of matchless grace,
    We sing unto Thy Name!
We stand accepted in the place
    That none but Christ could claim.
Our willing hearts have heard Thy voice,
And in Thy mercy we rejoice.

2 'Tis meet that Thy delight
    Should centre in Thy Son;
That Thou shouldst place us in Thy sight,
    In Him, Thy Holy One.
    Thy perfect love has cast out fear;
    Thy favour shines upon us here.

3 Eternal is our rest,
    O Christ of God, in Thee!
Now of Thy peace, Thy joy possessed,
    We wait Thy face to see.
Now to the Father's heart received,
    We know in whom we have believed.

4 A sacrifice to God
    In life or death are we;
Then keep us ever, blessèd Lord,
    Thus set apart to Thee.
Bought with a price, we're not our own;
We died, we live to God alone!

399　　　　　　　　　10.10.10.10.
O GOD our Father, we would
    come to Thee
In virtue of our Saviour's precious blood;
All distance gone, our souls by grace set free,
We worship Thee, our Father and our God.

2 We would, O God, present before
    Thy face
The fragrant name of Thy belovèd Son;
    By faith we view Him in that holy place,
Which, by His dying, He for us has won.

3 Thy joy in Him who is with Thee we share;
Our hearts delight in Thy delight in Him;
Chiefest of thousands, fairer than the fair;
His glory nought can tarnish, nought can dim.

4 We bow in worship now before Thy throne,
By faith the Object of Thy love would see;
Who, in the midst, His brethren's song doth lead.
To Him, our Saviour, shall the glory be!

400　　　　　　　　　C.M.
O GOD, our help in ages past,
    Our hope for years to come,
Our shelter from the stormy blast,
    And our eternal home.

2 Under the shadow of Thy throne
    Thy saints have dwelt secure;
Sufficient is Thine arm alone,
    And our defence is sure.

3 Before the hills in order stood,
    Or earth received her frame,
From everlasting Thou art God,
    To endless years the same.

4 A thousand ages in Thy sight
    Are like an evening gone;
Short as the watch that ends the night
    Before the rising sun.

5 Time, like an ever-rolling stream,
    Bears all its sons away;
They fly, forgotten, as a dream
    Dies at the op'ning day.

6 O God, our help in ages past,
    Our hope for years to come,
Be Thou our guard while life shall last,
    And our eternal home.

401   8.8.8.8.8.8.

O GOD, Thou now hast glorified
 Thy holy, Thine eternal Son!
The Nazarene, the Crucified,
 Now sits exalted on Thy throne:
To Him, in faith, we cry aloud,
 "Worthy art Thou, O Lamb of God!"

2 Father, Thy holy name we bless,
 And gladly hail Thy just decree,
That every tongue shall yet confess
 Jesus the Lord of all to be;
But Thy rich grace has taught *us* now
 To Him as Lord the knee to bow.

3 Him as *our* Lord we gladly own,
 To Him alone we now would live:
We bow our hearts before Thy throne,
 And in His name our praises give;
Our willing voices cry aloud,
 "Worthy art Thou, O Lamb of God!"

402   P.M.

O HAPPY day, that fixed my choice
 On Thee, my Saviour and my God!
Well may this glowing heart rejoice,
 And tell its raptures all abroad.

Happy day! happy day!
 When Jesus washed my sins away.
He taught me how to watch and pray,
 And live rejoicing every day.
Happy day! happy day!
 When Jesus washed my sins away.

2 'Tis done - the great transaction's done!
 I am my Lord's, and He is mine;
He drew me, and I followed on,
 Charmed to confess the voice divine.

3 Now rest, my long-divided heart,
 Fixed on this blissful centre, rest;
Nor ever from Thy Lord depart,
 With Him of every good possessed.

4 High heaven that heard the solemn vow,
 That vow renewed shall daily hear,
Till in life's latest hour I bow
 And bless in death a bond so dear.

403   L.M.

O HAPPY day! when first we felt
 Our souls with deep contrition melt,
And saw our sins of crimson guilt,
 All cleansed by blood on Calvary
 spilt.

2 O happy day! when first Thy love
 Began our grateful hearts to move;
And gazing on Thy wondrous Cross,
 We saw all else as worthless dross.

3 O happy day! when we no more
 Shall grieve Thee whom our souls
 adore,
When sorrows, conflicts, fears shall
 cease,
And all our trials end in peace.

4 O happy day! when we shall see
 And fix our longing eyes on Thee,
On Thee, our Light, our Life, our Love,
 Our All below, our heaven above.

5 O happy day of cloudless light!
 Eternal day without a night;
Lord, when shall we its dawning see,
 And spend it all in praising Thee?

404   C.M. with Chorus

O HAPPY home! O happy home!
 Prepared by Jesus' hand;
We soon shall be within thy walls,
 With all the ransomed band.

Where sinners saved by grace,
 Redeemed by Jesus' blood,
Shall see Him face to face -
 Their Saviour and their God.

2 O happy home! O happy home!
 Where come no cares nor fears,
Nor death, nor sorrows, for God's
 hand
Shall wipe away all tears -

3 O happy home! O happy home!
 Where we shall sin no more;
Where spotless, sinless, perfect, pure
 We'll dwell for evermore -

4 O happy home! O happy home!
    Where Jesus we shall see;
    When He appears in glory bright,
    Like Him we all shall be -

5 O happy home! O happy home!
    May thy bright, glorious ray
    Pierce through the clouds, and
        cheer our steps,
    Here on our pilgrim way! -

405
7.6.7.6.D.

O HEAD, so full of bruises,
    So full of pain and scorn,
'Midst other sore abuses,
    Mocked with a crown of thorn!
O Head, ere now surrounded
    With brightest majesty,
In death once bowed and wounded
    Accursèd on the tree!

2 Thou Countenance transcendent,
    Thou life-creating Sun
To worlds on Thee dependent,
    Yet bruised and spit upon!
O Lord! what Thee tormented
    Was our sin's heavy load;
We had the debt augmented
    Which Thou didst pay in blood!

3. Thy grief and Thy compassion
    Were all for sinners' gain;
Mine, mine was the transgression,
    But Thine the deadly pain.
Beneath Thy Cross abiding
    Forever would I rest,
In Thy dear love confiding,
    And with Thy presence blest.

4 And oh, what consolation
    Doth in our hearts take place,
When we Thy toil and passion
    Can gratefully retrace!
Ah! should we, while thus musing
    On our Redeemer's Cross,
E'en life itself be losing,
    Great gain would be that loss!

5 We give Thee thanks unfeignèd,
    Lord Jesus, Friend in need!
For what Thy soul sustainèd
    When Thou for us didst bleed;
Grant us to lean unshaken
    Upon Thy faithfulness,
Until, to glory taken,
    We see Thee face to face.

406
P.M.

OH, how happy are they,
    Who the Saviour obey,
And have laid up their treasures above!
    Tongue can never express
The sweet comfort and peace
    Of a soul in its earliest love.

*It is good to be here, it is good to
    be here;*
Thy perfect love drives away fear,
    *And light streaming down makes
        the pathway all clear:*
It is good for us, Lord, to be here.

2 That sweet comfort was mine,
    When the favour divine
I received through the blood of the
    Lamb;
When my heart first believed,
    What a joy I received,
What a heaven in Jesus' name!

3 'Twas a heaven below
    My Redeemer to know;
And the angels could do nothing more
    Than to fall at His feet,
And the story repeat,
    And the Lover of sinners adore.

4 Jesus, all the day long
    Was my joy and my song;
Oh, that all His salvation might see!
    "He hath loved me", I cried;
"He hath suffered and died,
    To redeem a poor rebel as me".

5 Oh! the rapturous height
    Of that holy delight
Which I felt in the life-giving blood!
    Of my Saviour possessed,
I was perfectly blest
    As if filled with the fulness of God.

407
6.4.6.4.6.6.6.4.

OH, it was kind of Him!
    Blest be His Name!
Unto death binding Him,
    Love drawn He came
Bearing our form below,
    Draining our cup of woe,
Deeper than we could know;
    Blest be His Name!

2 Sorrows gat hold of Him,
    Suff'rings untold,
Darkness enfolded Him;
    Over Him rolled
Billows of judgment dread,
    Loosed on His sinless head
Thorn-crownèd in our stead;
    Blest be His Name!

3 Earth wore a sullen frown,
    Heaven hid its light,
When God's own Son went down
    Into the night,
Under the chilling wave,
    Into the silent grave,
Sin-stricken souls to save;
    Blest be His Name!

4 Gone is the captive's chain
    Blest be His Name!
Rent is the veil in twain,
    Blest be His Name!
Deigning for us to die,
    To God He brought us nigh
Over a Jordan dry;
    Blest be His Name!

408   C.M.

O JESUS CHRIST, grow Thou
    in me,
And all things else recede;
    My heart be daily nearer Thee,
From sin be daily freed.

2 Each day let Thy supporting might
    My weakness still embrace;
My darkness vanish in Thy light,
    Thy life my death efface.

3 In Thy bright beams which on me fall,
    Fade every evil thought;
That I am nothing, Thou art all,
    I would be daily taught.

4 More of Thy glory let me see,
    Thou holy, wise and true;
I would Thy living image be,
    In joy and sorrow too.

5 Fill me with gladness from above,
    Hold me by strength divine;
Lord, let the glow of Thy great love
    Through my whole being shine.

6 Make this poor self grow less and less,
    Be Thou my life and aim;
Oh make me daily, through Thy grace,
    More meet to bear Thy name.

409   7.6.7.6.D.

O JESUS, I have promised
    To serve Thee to the end;
Be Thou for ever near me,
    My Master and my Friend!
I shall not fear the battle,
    If Thou art by my side;
Nor wander from the pathway
    If Thou wilt be my Guide.

2 Oh, let me feel Thee near me,
    The world is ever near;
I see the sights that dazzle,
    The tempting sounds I hear;
My foes are ever near me,
    Around me and within;
But, Jesus, draw Thou nearer,
    And shield my soul from sin.

3 Oh, let me hear Thee speaking,
    In accents clear and still,
Above the storms of passion,
    The murmurs of self-will.
Oh speak to re-assure me,
    To hasten or control;
Oh speak, and make me listen,
    Thou Guardian of my soul.

4 O Jesus, Thou hast promised
    To all who follow Thee,
That where Thou art in glory
    There shall Thy servant be!
And, Jesus, I have promised
    To serve Thee to the end;
Oh, give me grace to follow,
    My Master and my Friend!

5 Oh, let me see Thy footmarks,
    And in them plant mine own;
My hope to follow duly
    Is in Thy strength alone;
Oh, guide me, call me, draw me,
    Uphold me to the end;
And then in heaven receive me,
    My Saviour and my Friend!

410 8.8.8.6.

O JESUS, Lord, 'tis Thee alone
    The Holy Spirit would enthrone
In every heart, that we may own
    Thou art our chiefest joy.

2 Feebly Thy value we conceive;
    Yet with our hearts we do believe,
And would confess from morn to eve,
    Thou art our chiefest joy.

3 When unbelief its discord flings
    Across our harps, or stills their strings,
Touched by Thy love our spirit sings,
    Thou art our chiefest joy.

4 Should this world's dazzling,
        transient light
    Turn from eternal things our sight,
    Be Thou than noonday sun more
        bright;
Thou art our chiefest joy.

5 And when our Father's face we see,
    In unveiled brightness shine in Thee,
We'll sing, in glorious liberty,
    Thou art our chiefest joy.

411 P.M.

O JOY of the justified, joy of the free!
    I'm washed in that crimson
tide opened for me;
    In Christ, my Redeemer, rejoicing
        I stand,
And point to the print of the nail in
    His hand.

O sing of His mighty love,
    Sing of His mighty love,
Sing of His mighty love,
    Mighty to save!

2 Lord Jesus, the crucified, now Thou
    art mine;
    Though once a lost sinner, yet now
        I am Thine;
    In conscious salvation I sing of His
        grace
    Who lifts now upon me the smile of
        His face.

3 Oh, bliss of the purified! bliss of the pure!
    No wound hath the soul that His
        blood cannot cure;
No sorrow-bowed head but may
    sweetly find rest,
No tears but may dry them upon
    Jesus' breast.

4 Lord Jesus, my Saviour, I'll still sing
    of Thee,
    Yes, sing of Thy precious blood
        poured out for me;
And when in the mansions of glory
    above,
I'll praise and adore Thine
    unchangeable love.

412 7.6.7.6.D.

O LAMB of God! still keep us
    Near to Thy wounded side;
'Tis only there in safety
    And peace we can abide!
What foes and snares surround us!
    What lusts and fears within!
The grace that sought and found us
    Alone can keep us clean.

2 'Tis only in Thee hiding
    We know our life secure;
Only in Thee abiding
    The conflict can endure.
Thine arm the victory gaineth
    O'er every hurtful foe;
Thy love each heart sustaineth
    In all its cares and woe.

3 Soon shall our eyes behold Thee,
    With rapture, face to face;
The half hath not been told us
    Of all Thy power and grace.
Thy beauty, Lord, and glory,
    The wonders of Thy love,
Shall be the endless story
    Of all Thy saints above!

413 8.8.6.8.8.6.

O LAMB of God! 'tis joy to know
    That path is o'er of shame
and woe,
    For us so meekly trod.
All finished is Thy work of toil;
    Thou reapest now the fruit and spoil,
Exalted by our God.

2 Thy holy head, once bound with
      thorns,
   The crown of glory now adorns;
      Thy seat, the Father's throne.
   Ten thousand thousands sing Thy
      praise,
   Their harps the eternal anthem
      raise,
   Worthy the Lamb alone!

3 And, Lord, for us Thou sittest there;
      Thy members here Thy fulness
         share,
   For us Thou dost receive.
      Thy wisdom, riches, honours,
         powers,
   Thy boundless love has made all ours,
      Who in Thy love believe.

4 We triumph in Thy triumphs, Lord;
      Thy joys our deepest joys afford,
   And make our faces shine.
      While sorrowing, suffering, toiling
         here,
   How does the thought our spirits
      cheer,
   The throne of glory's Thine.

414
C.M.

O LAMB of God, we lift our eyes
      To Thee amidst the throne;
   Shine on us, bid Thy light arise,
      And make Thy glory known.

2 We know Thy work for ever done,
      Ourselves alive and free;
   Graced with the Spirit of the Son,
      Made nigh to God in Thee.

3 Yet would we prove Thine instant
      grace,
   Thy present power would feel;
      Lift on us now Thy glorious face,
   Thyself, O Lord, reveal.

4 From Thy high place of purest light,
      O Lamb, amidst the throne,
   Shine forth upon our waiting sight,
      And make Thy glory known.

415
C.M.

O LORD, how infinite Thy love!
      It spans all time and space,
   Enwraps Thy loved ones to the end
      In its encircling grace.

2 We shew Thy death till Thy return -
      Thou for our sins didst die!
   "Remember Me", Thy parting word;
      "Amen", our hearts reply.

3 In life and glory one with Thee,
      We own no place below,
   Save that which links us with Thy
      death,
   Whence life and glory flow.

4 With Thee, apart from all things here,
      We worship, we adore;
   While pleasures at our God's right
      hand
   Await us evermore.

416
C.M.

O LORD, how much Thy Name
      unfolds
   To every opened ear;
      The pardoned sinner's memory
   holds
      None other half so dear.

2 Jesus! it speaks a life of love,
      And sorrows meekly borne;
   It tells of sympathy above,
      Whatever griefs we mourn.

3 It tells us of Thy sinless walk
      In fellowship with God;
   And to our ears no tale so sweet
      As Thine atoning blood.

4 This Name encircles every grace
      That God, as man, could show;
   There only can the Spirit trace
      A perfect life below.

5 The mention of Thy Name shall bow
      Our hearts to worship Thee;
   The chiefest of ten thousand Thou!
      The chief of sinners we.

417   C.M.

O LORD, I would delight in Thee,
   And on Thy care depend;
To Thee in every trouble flee,
   My sure, my steadfast Friend.

2 When all created streams are dried,
   Thy fulness is the same;
May I with this be satisfied,
   And glory in Thy Name.

3 Why should I thirst for aught below,
   While there's a fountain near -
A fountain which doth ever flow,
   The fainting heart to cheer?

4 Oh that I may by simple faith
   Abide within the veil,
And rest on what my Saviour saith,
   Whose word can never fail!

5 Thou who hast made my heaven
   secure,
   Wilt here all good provide;
   While Christ is rich, can I be poor,
What can I want beside?

6 O Lord, I cast my care on Thee;
   I triumph and adore;
Henceforth my great concern shall be
   To love and praise Thee more.

418   10.10.10.10.

O LORD, it is Thyself; none,
   none but Thee
Could so call forth response from
   every heart;
The love that stood the test of
   Calvary's tree
Doth to our longing souls fresh joy
   impart.

2 Thou speakest, Lord, of Him Thou
   hast revealed,
   Thy Father, whom Thou lov'st - His
   glory, Thine.
Thou, His eternal joy, Thyself didst
   yield
To bring to pass His thought of love
   divine.

3 Thy heart, our God, made known -
   all, all is told!
The glory of Thy love, all time before,
   He to our raptured hearts doth
   now unfold,
And moves our souls to worship and
   adore.

4 O circle of affections all divine,
   The foretaste of eternity's bright
   scene,
Where all the glories of His love
   shall shine
In everlasting joy and peace serene!

419   C.M.D.

O LORD, it is Thyself to meet,
   To this sweet feast we come;
Like Mary, resting at Thy feet,
   We learn of Thee alone:
We well remember Thou hast said,
   This do, remembering Me;
So thus we take the wine, the bread,
   In memory of Thee.

2 O Lord, we come, not for our need,
   Nor with our grief to Thee;
But on the bread and wine to feed,
   And to remember Thee:
Yes, to remember all Thy love,
   Remember all Thy woe,
Remember Thou art now above,
   Yet in our midst below.

3 O Lord, from Thee the bread we take,
   From Thy pierced hand the wine;
In rest - accepted for Thy sake -
   Our meetness, Lord, is Thine:
We praise Thee for this quiet hour
   Spent with Thyself alone,
In which we feel the Spirit's power,
   And all His teachings own.

4 O Lord, we come, for Thou art here;
   Enrich each memory;
Thy faithful promise brings Thee near
   And gathers us to Thee:
O body broken! poured out blood!
   Blest memories ever dear;
Thou Son of man! Thou Lamb of God!
   How good to meet Thee here!

420 P.M.

O LORD my God! when I in
awesome wonder
Consider all the works Thy hands
have made.
I see the stars, I hear the rolling
thunder,
Thy power throughout the universe
displayed.

Then sings my soul,
My Saviour God, to Thee:
How great Thou art!
How great Thou art!
Then sings my soul,
My Saviour God, to Thee:
How great Thou art!
How great Thou art!

2 When through the woods and forest
glades I wander,
And hear the birds sing sweetly in
the trees;
When I look down from lofty
mountain grandeur,
And hear the brook and feel the
gentle breeze:

3 And when I think that God, His Son
not sparing,
Sent Him to die, I scarce can take
it in;
That on the Cross, my burden gladly
bearing,
He bled and died to take away my sin:

4 When burdens press, and seem
beyond endurance,
Bowed down with grief, to Him I lift
my face;
And then in love He brings me
sweet assurance:
"My child! for thee sufficient is My
grace".

5 When Christ shall come with shout
of acclamation,
And take me home, what joy shall fill
my heart!
Then I shall bow in humble adoration,
And there proclaim, "My God, how
great Thou art!"

421 8.8.8.4.

O LORD of heaven, and earth,
and sea!
To Thee all praise and glory be:
How shall we show our love to Thee,
Who givest all?

2 For peaceful homes and healthful days,
For all the blessings earth displays,
Our God, we owe Thee thanks
and praise,
Who givest all.

3 Thou didst not spare Thine only Son,
But gav'st Him for a world undone,
And freely with that Blessèd One
Thou givest all.

4 Thou gav'st the Holy Spirit's dower,
Spirit of life, of love and power,
And dost His sevenfold graces shower
Upon us all.

5 For souls redeemed, for sins forgiven,
For present grace and hopes of
heaven,
Father, what can to Thee be given,
Who givest all?

6 We lose what on ourselves we spend;
We have as treasure without end
Whatever, Lord, to Thee we lend,
Who givest all.

7 As from Thyself we all derive -
Our life, our gifts, our power to give,
Oh, may we ever to Thee live
Who givest all!

422 7.6.7.6.D.

O LORD, Thy love's unbounded!
So sweet, so full, so free!
My soul is all transported
Whene'er I think on Thee.
Yet, Lord, alas! what weakness
Within myself I find;
No infant's changing pleasure
Is like my wandering mind.

2 And yet Thy love's unchanging,
   And doth recall my heart
To enjoy in all its brightness,
   The peace its beams impart!
Yet, sure, if in Thy presence
   My soul still constant were,
Mine eye would, more familiar,
   Its brighter glories bear.

3 And thus Thy deep perfections
   Much better should I know,
And, with adoring fervour
   Should in Thy likeness grow.
Still, sweet 'tis to discover,
   If clouds have dimmed my sight,
When passed, eternal Lover,
   Towards me, as e'er, Thou'rt bright.

4 Oh, keep my soul, Lord Jesus,
   Abiding still with Thee;
And if I wander, teach me
   Soon back to Thee to flee,
That all Thy gracious favour
   May to my soul be known;
And versed in this Thy goodness,
   My hopes Thyself shalt crown.

423   C.M.
O LORD! 'tis joy to look above,
   And see Thee on the throne;
To search the heights and depths
   of love
Which Thou to us hast shown.

2 To look beyond the dark, long night
   And hail the coming day,
When Thou, to all the saints in light,
   Thy glories wilt display.

3 And, Oh, 'tis joy the path to trace
   By Thee so meekly trod;
Learning of Thee to walk in grace
   And fellowship with God.

4 Joy to confess Thy blessèd Name,
   The virtues of Thy blood,
And to the wearied heart proclaim,
   Behold the Lamb of God!

424   C.M.
O LORD, when we the path retrace
   Which Thou on earth hast trod,
To man Thy wondrous love and grace,
   Thy faithfulness to God.

2 Thy love, by man so sorely tried,
   Proved stronger than the grave;
The very spear that pierced Thy side
   Drew forth the blood to save.

3 Faithful amidst unfaithfulness,
   Midst darkness only light,
Thou didst Thy Father's Name confess,
   And in His will delight.

4 Unmoved by Satan's subtle wiles,
   By suffering, shame, and loss;
Thy path, uncheered by earthly smiles,
   Led only to the Cross.

5 O Lord, with sorrow and with shame,
   We meekly would confess,
How little we, who bear Thy Name,
   Thy mind, Thy ways express.

6 Give us Thy meek, Thy lowly mind;
   We would obedient be;
And all our rest and pleasure find
   In fellowship with Thee.

425   L.M.
O LORD, where'er Thy people
      meet,
There they behold Thy mercy-seat:
   Where'er they seek Thee, Thou
   art found,
And every place is hallowed ground.

2 Great Shepherd of Thy chosen few
   Thy former mercies here renew;
Here to our waiting hearts proclaim
   The sweetness of Thy saving Name.

3 Here may we prove the power of
      prayer
To strengthen faith and banish care;
   To teach our faint desires to rise,
And bring all heaven before our eyes.

4 Lord! we are weak, but Thou art near,
   Nor short Thine arm, nor deaf
   Thine ear;
Oh, fill us with Thy grace divine,
   And may our hearts be wholly Thine!

426　　　　　　　　　　　　　　C.M.

O LORD, who art Thy people's
　　light,
When shall Thy face be seen?
　　When wilt Thou meet our longing
　　　sight,
Without a cloud between?

2 We know, Lord Jesus, that Thy heart
　　Still for Thy saints doth care;
But we would see Thee as Thou art,
　　And Thy full image bear.

3 Thy love sustains us on our way,
　　While pilgrims here below;
And grace to help us day by day
　　Thou dost, O Lord, bestow.

4 But oh, the more we learn of Thee,
　　And Thy rich mercy prove,
The more we long Thyself to see,
　　And fully know Thy love.

427　　　　　　　　　　　　7.6.7.6.D.

O LORD, who now art seated
　　Above the heavens on high,
The gracious work completed,
　　For which Thou cam'st to die.
To Thee our hearts are lifted
　　While pilgrims wand'ring here,
For Thou art truly gifted
　　Our every weight to bear.

2 We know that Thou hast bought us,
　　And cleansed us by Thy blood;
We know Thy grace has brought us
　　As kings and priests to God.
We know that soon the morning,
　　Long looked for, hast'neth near,
When we, at Thy returning,
　　In glory shall appear.

3 O Lord, Thy love's unbounded!
　　So full, so vast, so free!
Our thoughts are all confounded
　　Whene'er we think on Thee.
For us Thou cam'st from heaven,
　　For us to bleed and die;
That, purchased and forgiven,
　　We might ascend on high.

4 O let this love constrain us
　　To give our hearts to Thee;
Let nothing henceforth pain us,
　　But that which paineth Thee.
Our joy, our one endeavour,
　　Through suff'ring, conflict, shame,
To serve Thee, gracious Saviour,
　　And magnify Thy Name.

428　　　　　　　　　　8.8.6.8.8.6.

O LOVE divine, how sweet Thou
　　art!
When shall I find my longing heart
　　All taken up by Thee?
Oh, may I pant and thirst to prove
　　The greatness of redeeming love!
The love of Christ to me.

2 God only knows the love of God:
　　Oh that it more were shed abroad
In this poor longing heart!
　　For love I sigh, for love I pine;
This only portion, Lord, be mine,
　　Be mine this better part.

3 Oh that I may for ever sit,
　　Like Mary, at the Master's feet!
Be this my happy choice;
　　My only care, delight, and bliss,
My joy, my heaven on earth, be this -
　　To hear the Bridegroom's voice.

4 Oh that I may, like favoured John,
　　Recline my wearied head upon
My dear Redeemer's breast!
　　From care, and sin, and sorrow free,
Give me, O Lord, to find in Thee
　　My everlasting rest!

429　　　　　　　　　　8.8.8.8.6.

O LOVE that wilt not let me go,
　　I rest my weary soul in Thee;
I give Thee back the life I owe,
　　That in Thine ocean depths its flow
May richer, fuller be.

2 O Light that followest all my way,
　　I yield my flickering torch to Thee;
My heart restores its borrowed ray,
　　That in Thy sunshine's blaze its day
May brighter, fairer be.

3 O Joy that seekest me through pain,
   I cannot close my heart to Thee;
I trace the rainbow through the rain,
   And feel the promise is not vain
That morn shall tearless be.

4 O Cross that liftest up my head,
   I dare not ask to fly from Thee,
I lay in dust life's glory dead,
   And from the ground there
      blossoms red
Life that shall endless be.

430   7.6.7.6.D.

O MASTER! when Thou callest
   No voice may say Thee nay,
For blest are they that follow
   Where Thou dost lead the way:
In freshest prime of morning,
   Or fullest glow of noon,
The note of heavenly warning
   Can never come too soon.

2 O Master! where Thou callest
   No foot may shrink in fear,
For they who trust Thee wholly
   Shall find Thee ever near;
And quiet room and lonely,
   Or busy harvest field,
Where Thou, Lord, rulest only,
   Shall precious produce yield.

3 O Master! whom Thou callest
   No heart may dare refuse:
'Tis honour, highest honour,
   When Thou dost deign to use;
Our brightest and our fairest,
   Our dearest - all are Thine;
Thou who for each one carest,
   We hail Thy love's design.

4 They who go forth to serve Thee,
   We, too, who serve at home,
May watch and pray together
   Until Thou, Lord, shalt come;
In Thee for aye united
   Our song of hope we raise,
Till that blest shore is sighted
   Where all shall turn to praise.

431   7.7.7.7.

O OUR Saviour, crucified!
   Near Thy Cross would we abide,
There to look with steadfast eye
   On Thy dying agony.

2 Jesus bruised and put to shame
   Tells us all Jehovah's Name;
God is love, we surely know
   By the Saviour's depths of woe.

3 In His spotless soul's distress
   We perceive our guiltiness;
O how vile our low estate!
   Since our ransom was so great.

4 Dwelling on Mount Calvary,
   Contrite shall our spirits be;
Rest and holiness shall find,
   Fashioned like our Saviour's mind.

432   S.M.

O PATIENT, spotless One!
   Our hearts in meekness train,
To bear Thy yoke, and learn of Thee,
   That we may rest obtain.

2 Saviour, Thou art enough
   The mind and heart to fill;
Thy patient life - to calm the soul;
   Thy love - its fear dispel.

3 O fix our earnest gaze
   So wholly, Lord, on Thee,
That, with Thy beauty occupied,
   We elsewhere none may see.

433   C.M.

O PRECIOUS blood, O glorious
      death,
By which the sinner lives!
   When stung by sin, this blood we
      view,
And all our joy revives.

2 The blood that purchased our release,
   And purged our crimson stains,
We challenge earth and hell to show
   A sin it cannot cleanse.

3 Our scarlet crimes are made as wool,
    And we brought nigh to God;
  Thanks to that wrath-appeasing death,
    That heaven-procuring blood.

4 The blood that makes His glorious
    Church
  From every blemish free;
    And Oh the riches of His love!
  He poured it out for me.

5 The Father's everlasting love,
    And Jesus' precious blood,
  Shall be our endless themes of praise
    In yonder blest abode.

6 In patience let us then possess
    Our souls till He appear;
  Our Head already is in heaven,
    And we shall soon be there.

434   S.M.

O PRECIOUS exercise
    To strike the priestly chord,
To view with clear, anointed eyes
  The beauty of the Lord!

2 O precious theme for praise,
    The moral wealth so vast
  That meets the meditative gaze
    In all the way He passed!

3 O precious privilege!
    The watching cherubim
  Cannot, in priesthood, thus engage
    Converted hearts with Him.

4 O precious hour to us,
    Led by our Lord, to raise
  To Thee, His God and Father, thus
    Our sacrifice of praise!

435   7.6.7.6.D.

O PRECIOUS heavenly Bridegroom,
    Our hearts run after Thee,
Drawn by Thy love unmeasured
    Displayed at Calvary.
Thy name like precious ointment,
    Is fragrant to us now,
Whilst with adoring wonder,
    Low at Thy feet we bow.

2 Within the hallowed circle,
    Where Thou art Lord and Head,
  We join in deep thanksgiving
    To Thee whose blood was shed.
  We praise Thee and adore Thee,
    For all Thy love and grace,
  Whilst with amazing wonder,
    Thy worth and work we trace.

3 O let my soul remember
    That night of deepest woe,
  The bitter dews of sorrow,
    Which clung around Thy brow;
  Jehovah's face was hidden,
    The sun refused to shine,
  Whilst Thou didst bear for sinners,
    The storm of wrath divine.

4 Enraptured with Thy beauty,
    My heart would ever gaze,
  Upon Thy precious Person
    And ponder all Thy ways,
  What fragrance, strength and glory,
    What gaze and truth I see,
  How "altogether lovely",
    My Lord art Thou to me.

5 Then in those many mansions,
    Without a veil between,
  Our Lord in all His beauty
    Shall face to face be seen.
  O how our hearts shall praise Him,
    O how our tongues will bless,
  Throughout eternal ages,
    His love and faithfulness.

436   P.M.

OH safe to the Rock that is higher
    than I
My soul in its conflicts and sorrows
    would fly;
So sinful, so weary, Thine, Thine
    would I be;
Thou blest Rock of Ages I'm hiding
    in Thee.

  Hiding in Thee, hiding in Thee,
    Thou blest Rock of Ages,
      I'm hiding in Thee.

2 In the calm of the noontide, in
    sorrow's lone hour,
  In times when temptation casts o'er
    me its power;
  In the tempests of life, on its wide,
    heaving sea,
  Thou blest Rock of Ages, I'm hiding
    in Thee.

3 How oft in the conflict, when
    pressed by the foe,
  I have fled to my refuge, and
    breathed out my woe;
  How often, when trials like sea-
    billows roll,
  Have I hidden in Thee, O Thou rock
    of my soul.

437   8.6.8.8.6.8.8.
O SOLEMN hour! O hour alone,
    In solitary night,
When God the Father's only Son,
  As Man, for sinners lost, undone,
Expires - amazing sight!
  The Lord of glory crucified!
  The Lord of Life has bled and died!

2 O mystery of mysteries!
    Of life and death the tree!
  Centre of two eternities,
    Which look with rapt, adoring eyes,
  Onward, and back to Thee!
    O Cross of Christ, where all His pain
  And death is our eternal gain.

3 Oh how our inmost hearts do move,
    While gazing on that Cross!
  The death of the incarnate Love!
    What shame, what grief, what joy
    we prove,
  That He should die for us!
    Our hearts were broken by that cry,
  "Eli, lama sabachthani!"

4 Worthy of death, O Lord, we were;
    That vengeance was our due;
  In grace Thou, spotless Lamb, didst
    bear
  Thyself our sins, and guilt, and fear;
    Justice our Surety slew.
  With Thee, our Surety, we have died;
    With Thee, we there were crucified.

5 Quickened with Thee with life divine,
    Raised with Thee from the dead;
  Thine Own, now human and divine,
    Shall with Thee in Thy glories shine,
  The Church's living Head!
    We, who were worthy but to die,
  Now with Thee, "Abba Father", cry.

438   P.M.
O SOUL, are you weary and
    troubled?
No light in the darkness you see?
  There's light for a look at the
    Saviour
And life more abundant and free!

  Turn your eyes upon Jesus,
    Look full in His wonderful face,
  And the things of earth will grow
    strangely dim,
  In the light of His glory and grace.

2 Through death into life everlasting
    He passed, and we follow Him there;
  O'er us sin no more hath dominion -
    For more than conquerors we are!

3 His Word shall not fail you - He
    promised;
  Believe Him, and all will be well:
    Then go to a world that is dying,
    His perfect salvation to tell!

439   L.M.
O SPOTLESS Lamb of God, in
    Thee
The Father's holiness we see;
  And with delight Thy children trace,
In Thee, His wondrous love and grace.

2 For Thou didst leave Thy throne
    above
  To teach us that our "God is Love";
    And now we see His glory shine
  In every word and deed of Thine.

3 When we behold Thee, Lamb of God,
    Beneath our sins' tremendous load;
  Bearing our curse upon the tree,
    How great our guilt with grief we
    see.

4 There we with joy Thy grace behold;
    Its height and depth can ne'er be
        told!
  It bursts our chains and sets us free,
    And sweetly draws our souls to
        Thee.

5 The Cross reveals Thy love below;
    But better soon our hearts shall
        know,
  When we behold Thy face above,
    The fulness of our Father's love.

440
7.6.7.6.D.

OH, teach me what it meaneth -
    That Cross uplifted high,
With Thee, the Man of Sorrows,
    Condemned to bleed and die!
Oh, teach me what it cost Thee
    To make a sinner whole;
And teach me, Saviour, teach me -
    The value of a soul!

2 Oh, teach me what it meaneth -
    That sacred crimson tide,
The blood and water flowing
    From Thine own wounded side:
Teach me that if none other
    Had sinned, but I alone,
Yet still Thy blood, Lord Jesus,
    Thine only, must atone.

3 Oh, teach me what it meaneth -
    Thy love beyond compare,
The love that reacheth deeper
    Than depths of self-despair!
Yes, teach me, till there gloweth
    In this cold heart of mine
Some faint, yet true reflection,
    Of that pure love of Thine!

4 O infinite Redeemer!
    I bring no other plea;
Because Thou dost invite me,
    I cast myself on Thee!
Because Thou dost accept me,
    I love and I adore;
Because Thy love constraineth,
    I'll praise Thee evermore!

441
10.4.10.4.10.10.

OH, teach us, Lord, Thy
    searchless love to know,
Thou, who hast died.
    Before our feeble faith, Lord Jesus,
        show
Thy hands and side;
    That our glad hearts, responsive
        unto Thine,
May wake with all the power of love
    divine.

2 Thy death has brought to light the
    Father's heart,
And ours has won;
    And now we contemplate Thee as
        Thou art,
God's glorious Son!
    And know that we are loved with
        that great love,
That rests on Thee in those bright
    courts above.

3 Thy flesh is meat, Thy blood, blest
    Saviour, shed,
Is drink indeed;
    On Thee, the true, the heavenly,
        living Bread,
Our souls would feed,
    And live with Thee in life's eternal
        home,
Where sin, nor want, nor woe, nor
    death can come.

442
C.M.

OH, teach us more of Thy blest
    ways,
Thou holy Lamb of God!
    And fix and root us in Thy grace,
As those redeemed by blood.

2 Oh, tell us often of Thy love,
    Of all Thy grief and pain!
And let our hearts with joy confess
    From thence comes all our gain.

3 For this, Oh, may we freely count
    Whate'er we have but loss!
The dearest object of our love
    Compared with Thee but dross!

4 Engrave this deeply on our hearts,
    With an eternal pen,
That we may, in some small degree,
    Return Thy love again.

443   8.7.8.8.7.
O H, the bitter shame and sorrow,
    That a time could ever be,
When I let the Saviour's pity
    Plead in vain; and proudly answered,
All of self, and none of Thee!

2 Yet He found me: I beheld Him
    Bleeding on the accursèd tree,
Heard Him pray, Forgive them, Father!
    And my wistful heart said faintly,
Some of self, and some of Thee!

3 Day by day His tender mercy,
    Healing, helping, full and free:
Sweet and strong, and ah! so patient,
    Brought me lower, while I whispered,
Less of self, and more of Thee!

4 Higher than the highest heaven,
    Deeper than the deepest sea,
Lord, Thy love at last hath conquered;
    Grant me now my spirit's longing,
None of self, and all of Thee!

444   8.7.8.7.D.
O H, the brightness of the glory
    Shining in the Saviour's face!
Telling all the blessèd story
    Of the ways of God in grace:
Lowly, hated, and rejected
    In the world He came to save,
By the glory of the Father
    Raised triumphant from the grave.

2 Centre of the Father's counsels,
    He for whom all things were made;
Object of the Father's pleasure,
    Who the Father's name displayed;
All the Father's will accomplished,
    Unto death the path He trod;
Now in highest glory seated,
    Centre of the throne of God.

3 There we see Him crowned with glory,
    Glory in His unveiled face,
And in peace and rest before Him,
    In that glory learn of grace:
For it shineth in the visage
    Of the One who for us died,
Bore our sins and all their judgment,
    Jesus Christ the crucified.

4 Called to share the Father's pleasure
    In His well-belovèd Son,
Seated on His throne in heaven
    For the work on earth well done,
We adore Him, and are waiting
    To behold Him face to face;
In His presence praise the glory,
    Learn the riches of His grace.

445   8.7.8.7.D.
O THE deep, deep love of Jesus!
    Vast, unmeasured,
boundless, free;
    Rolling as a mighty ocean
In its fulness over me:
    Underneath me, all around me,
Is the current of Thy love,
    Leading onward, leading homeward,
To my glorious rest above.

2 O the deep, deep love of Jesus!
    Spread His praise from shore to
        shore;
How He loveth, ever loveth,
    Changeth never, nevermore:
How He watches o'er His loved ones,
    Died to call them all His own;
How for them He intercedeth,
    Watcheth o'er them from the throne.

3 O the deep, deep love of Jesus!
    Love of every love the best;
'Tis an ocean vast of blessing,
    'Tis a haven sweet of rest:
O such love! the love of Jesus;
    'Tis a heaven of heavens to me;
And it lifts me up to glory,
    For it lifts me up to Thee.

4 O the deep, deep love of Jesus!
    'Twould take ages to explore
But a drop of all this ocean
    Or a grain from off its shore:

Yet our hearts are beating highly,
If our faith is sometimes dim,
For the glory and the rapture
We shall have when we have Him.

446
C.M.

O THOU, my soul, bless God
the Lord;
And all that in me is
Be stirrèd up His holy name
To magnify and bless.

2 Bless, O my soul, the Lord thy God,
And not forgetful be
Of all His gracious benefits
He hath bestowed on thee:

3 All thine iniquities who doth
Most graciously forgive;
Who thy diseases all and pains
Doth heal, and thee relieve;

4 Who doth redeem thy life, that thou
To death may'st not go down;
Who thee with loving kindness doth
And tender mercies crown.

5 As far as east is distant from
The west, so far hath He
From us removèd, in His love,
All our iniquity.

6 Such pity as a father hath
Unto his children dear;
Like pity shews the Lord to such
As worship Him in fear.

7 O bless the Lord, all ye His works,
Wherewith the world is stored
In His dominions everywhere:
My soul, bless thou the Lord!

447
8.7.8.7.D.

O THOU tender, gracious Shepherd,
Shedding for us Thy life's blood,
Unto shame and death delivered,
All to bring us nigh to God!
Now our willing hearts adore Thee;
Now we praise Thy changeless love,
While by faith we come before Thee,
Faith which lifts our souls above.

2 As our Surety we behold Thee,
Ransoming our souls from death;
As the willing Victim view Thee,
Yielding up to God Thy breath.
In the broken bread we own Thee,
Bruised for us and put to shame;
And this cup, O Lord, we thank Thee,
Speaks our pardon through Thy
name.

3 Blessèd supper of thanksgiving,
Feast of more than angels' food!
Bread of life and cup of blessing -
This is fellowship with God!
Feeble praise we now are bringing;
But when, Lord, we see Thy face,
Better songs of triumph singing,
We shall own Thy matchless grace.

448
C.M.

OH, what a lonely path were ours,
Could we, O Father, see
No home of rest beyond it all,
No guide or help in Thee!

2 But Thou art near and with us still
To keep us on the way
That leads along the vale of tears
To the bright world of day.

3 There shall Thy glory, O our God!
Break fully on our view;
And we, Thy saints, rejoice to find
That all Thy Word was true.

4 There Jesus, on His heavenly throne,
Our wondering eyes shall see;
While we the blest associates there
Of all His joy shall be.

5 Sweet hope! we leave without a sigh
A blighted world like this;
To bear the cross, despise the shame,
For all that weight of bliss.

6 Yet little do Thy saints at best,
Endure, O Lord, for Thee;
Whose suffering soul bore all our sins
And sorrows on the tree:

7 Who faced our fierce, our ruthless foe,
Unaided and alone;
To win us for Thy crown of joy,
To raise us to Thy throne.

449

P.M.

OH what a wonderful, wonderful
day -
Day I will never forget;
    After I'd wandered in darkness away,
Jesus my Saviour I met.
    Oh what a tender, compassionate
    friend -
He met the need of my heart;
    Shadows dispelling, with joy I am
    telling,
He made all the darkness depart!

*Heaven came down and glory filled
my soul,
When at the Cross the Saviour
made me whole;
My sins were washed away
And my night was turned to day -
Heaven came down and glory filled
my soul!*

2 Born of the Spirit with life from above
    Into God's family divine,
    Justified fully through Calvary's love,
    Oh what a standing is mine!
    And the transaction so quickly was
    made
    When as a sinner I came,
        Took of the offer of grace He did
        proffer -
    He saved me, oh praise His dear name!

3 Now I've a hope that will surely endure
    After the passing of time;
    I have a future in heaven for sure,
        There in those mansions sublime.
    And it's because of that wonderful day
        When at the Cross I believed;
    Riches eternal and blessings supernal
        From His precious hand I received.

450

11.11.11.11.

OH, what shall we feel in Thy
presence when first
The visions of glory upon us shall
burst!
Our souls now are longing and
thirsting for Thee;
Oh, when, blessèd Saviour, Thy face
shall we see?

2 That face, once so marred, we shall
    gaze on at length,
    And fearless behold, as the sun in
    its strength;
    Those eyes, flames of fire, that so
    searching we prove,
    Shall beam on us then inexpressible
    love.

3 Thy voice, like great waters, how
    calmly our soul
    Shall hear in the glory its deep
    waters roll;
    Though now it rebukes us, and
    humbles our pride,
    It shall speak only love to Thy
    glorified Bride.

4 O Thou who this world as a lone
    pilgrim trod,
    Thy Father's our Father, Thy God is
    our God;
    To Thee we behold the bright
    seraphim bow:
    Lord Jesus, what glory doth rest on
    Thee now!

5 Thy Spirit has shown God's deep
    purpose to be
    To empty, then fill us with glory like
    Thee;
    And now Thou dost wait - Thy full joy
    to impart,
    For that day of espousals - the joy
    of Thy heart.

6 Now moment by moment, to answer
    our needs,
    Thy blood, holy Saviour, in
    righteousness pleads;
    And sheltered by that, how serene
    and how calm,
    Our souls on Thy bosom are
    shielded from harm.

7 We see Thee, Lord Jesus, with
    great glory crowned,
    And waiting Thy coming, in peace
    would be found;
    The visions of glory have turned all
    to dross;
    For Thee give us grace to count all
    things but loss.

451   P.M.

O WONDERFUL, wonderful
   Word of the Lord!
True wisdom its pages unfold;
   And though we may read them a
      thousand times o'er,
They never, no never, grow old!
   Each line hath a treasure, each
      promise a pearl,
That all if they will may secure;
   And we know that when time and
      the world pass away,
God's Word shall for ever endure.

2 O wonderful, wonderful Word of the
   Lord!
   The lamp that our Father above
      So kindly has lighted to teach us
      the way
   That leads to the arms of His love!
      Its warnings, its counsels, are
      faithful and just;
   Its judgments are perfect and pure;
      And we know that when time and
      the world pass away,
   God's Word shall for ever endure.

3 O wonderful, wonderful Word of the
   Lord!
   Our only salvation is there;
      It carries conviction down deep in
      the heart,
   And shows us ourselves as we are.
      It tells of a Saviour, and points to
      the Cross,
   Where pardon we now may secure;
      For we know that when time and
      the world pass away,
   God's Word shall for ever endure.

4 O wonderful, wonderful Word of the
   Lord!
   The hope of our friends in the past;
      Its truth, where so firmly they
      anchored their trust,
   Through ages eternal shall last.
      O wonderful, wonderful Word of
      the Lord!
   Unchanging, abiding and sure;
      For we know that when time and
      the world pass away,
   God's Word shall for ever endure.

452   L.M.

O H, wondrous hour, when
   Jesus, Thou,
Co-equal with the eternal God,
   Beneath our sin didst deign to bow,
And in our stead didst bear the rod!

2 On Thee, the Father's blessèd Son,
   Jehovah's utmost anger fell:
   That all was borne, that all is done,
      Thine agony, Thy Cross can tell.

3 When most in Satan's awful power,
   Dear Lord, Thy suffering spirit seemed,
   Then, in that dark and fearful hour,
      Our souls were by Thy blood
      redeemed.

4 'Tis in Thy Cross, Lord, that we learn
      What Thou in all Thy fulness art;
   There, through the darkening cloud,
      discern
   The love of Thy devoted heart.

5 'Twas mighty love's constraining
   power
   That made Thee, blessèd Saviour,
      die;
   'Twas love, in that tremendous hour,
      That triumphed in Thy mighty cry.

6 'Twas all for us - our life we owe,
      Our hope, our crown of joy, to Thee;
   Thy sufferings in that hour of woe,
      Thy victory, Lord, have made us
      free.

453   8.8.4.8.8.4.

O WONDROUS Saviour! Jesus,
   Lord,
Worthy alone to be adored,
   We worship Thee!
Thou holy, spotless Son of God,
   To Thee the incarnate living Word,
All glory be.

2 In Thee all human graces blend,
      And to Thy Father e'er ascend,
   As incense rare;
      Fragrant to Him Thou ever art,
   Source of rejoicing to His heart,
      Most sweet and fair.

3 Fairer than all the sons of men,
    Beyond all praise of tongue or pen,
  Thou peerless One!
    In grace, in patient tenderness,
  In truth, in holy faithfulness,
    Thine equal - none!

4 Matchless, incomparable, divine! -
    In Jesus all perfections shine -
  Oh, blessèd Name!
    How shall we tell its worth abroad,
  How tell the praises of our Lord,
    Or spread His fame?

5 This, this shall be our endless theme,
    When glorified we share with Him
  The Father's home.
    And see in blessèd wondrous grace
  Our God revealed in Jesus' face,
    Lord Jesus, come!

454
10.10.11.11.

OH worship the King all-
    glorious above,
  Oh gratefully sing His power and His
    love;
  Our shield and defender, the
    Ancient of Days,
  Pavilioned in splendour and girded
    with praise.

2 Oh tell of His might, oh sing of His grace,
    Whose robe is the light, whose
      canopy space;
  His chariots of wrath the deep
    thunderclouds form,
  And dark is His path on the wings of
    the storm.

3 The earth, with its store of wonders
    untold,
  Almighty, Thy power hath founded
    of old;
  Hath stablished it fast by a
    changeless decree,
  And round it hath cast, like a mantle,
    the sea.

4 Thy bountiful care what tongue can
    recite?
  It breathes in the air, it shines in the
    light;

It streams from the hills, it descends
    to the plain,
  And sweetly distils in the dew and
    the rain.

5 Frail children of dust, and feeble as
    frail,
  In Thee do we trust, nor find Thee
    to fail;
  Thy mercies how tender, how firm
    to the end,
  Our Maker, Defender, Redeemer, and
    Friend.

6 O measureless Might! Ineffable Love!
    While angels delight to hymn
      Thee above,
  The humbler creation, though feeble
    their lays,
  With true adoration shall lisp to Thy
    praise.

455
C.M.

OF Thee, Lord, we would never tire;
    This new and living food
  Can satisfy our hearts' desire,
    For life is in Thy blood.

2 If through the night a happy song
    Our wearied spirits raise,
  What greater joys shall cause ere long
    Eternal bursts of praise!

3 To look within and see no stain,
    Abroad no curse to trace;
  To shed no tears, to feel no pain,
    To see Thee face to face.

4 To find each hope of glory gained,
    Fulfilled each precious word,
  And fully all to have attained
    The image of our Lord.

5 For this we're pressing onward still,
    And in this hope would be
  More subject to the Father's will,
    Lord Jesus, more like Thee.

456 P.M.

ON a hill far away stood an old
rugged Cross,
The emblem of suff'ring and shame;
And I love that old Cross where
the dearest and best
For a world of lost sinners was slain.

*So I'll cherish the old rugged Cross,
Till my trophies at last I lay down;
I will cling to the old rugged Cross,
And exchange it some day for a
crown.*

2 Oh, that old rugged Cross, so
despised by the world,
Has a wondrous attraction for me,
For the dear Lamb of God left His
glory above,
To bear it to dark Calvary.

3 In that old rugged Cross, stained
with blood so divine,
A wondrous beauty I see;
For 'twas on that old Cross Jesus
suffered and died,
To pardon and sanctify me.

4 To that old rugged Cross I will ever
be true,
Its shame and reproach gladly bear;
Then He'll call me some day to
my home far away,
Where His glory forever I'll share.

457 L.M.

ON Christ salvation rests secure;
The Rock of Ages must endure;
Nor can that faith be overthrown
Which rests upon the "Living Stone".

2 No other hope shall intervene;
To Him we look, on Him we lean;
Other foundations we disown,
And build on Christ, the "Living
Stone".

3 In Him it is ordained to raise
A temple to Jehovah's praise,
Composed of all His saints, who own
No Saviour but the "Living Stone".

4 View the vast building, see it rise;
The work, how great! the plan,
how wise!
O wondrous fabric! power unknown,
That rests it on the "Living Stone".

5 But most adore His precious Name;
His glory and His grace proclaim;
For us, the lost, condemned, undone,
He gave Himself, the "Living Stone".

458 8.7.8.7.4.7.

ON His Father's throne is seated
Christ the Lord, the Living One;
All His toil on earth completed,
All His work for sinners done:
In the glory
See Him, God's eternal Son!

2 Every knee shall bow before Him,
Every tongue confess His name;
Ransomed myriads now adore Him,
Who endured the sinner's shame:
From the glory
God doth now His worth proclaim!

3 Man the Cross to Him awarded;
Man the Saviour crucified;
Sin's full judgment stands recorded -
Thus was Justice satisfied:
To the glory
God exalted Him who died.

4 Son of Man, His incarnation
Opened first the tale of grace;
Son of Man, in new creation
Leader of a chosen race!
Well may glory,
Give to Him the honoured place!

459 S.M.

ON Jordan's bank He stands;
Impressive, lovely sight,
Obedient to the law's demands,
The Father's chief delight!

2 The wilderness, with each
Deep testing, doth but show
No evil shaft His soul could reach,
No tempter Him o'erthrow.

3 He serves in harmony
   With all God's holy will,
Integrity of heart has He;
   His hand is full of skill.

4 The Father loves the Son
   Who ever pleased Him well;
Each movement of that Holy One
   Some beauty forth doth tell.

5 And here, O God, we bow;
   In Him do we rejoice;
We worship by the Spirit now,
   Praising with heart and voice.

6 While we remember Him,
   Our thanks to Thee would flow
For beauties that shall ne'er grow dim
   Seen in His path below.

460   L.M.
O N merit not my own I stand,
   On doings which I have not done,
Merit beyond what I can claim,
   Doings more perfect than my own.

2 Upon a life I have not lived,
   Upon a death I did not die,
Another's life, Another's death,
   I stake my whole eternity.

3 Not on the tears which I have shed,
   Not on the sorrows I have known,
Another's tears, Another's griefs,
   On them I rest, on them alone.

4 Jesus, O Son of God, I build
   On what Thy Cross has done for me;
There both my death and life I read,
   My guilt, my pardon there I see.

5 Lord, I believe; oh, deal with me,
   As one who has Thy Word believed!
I take the gift, Lord, look on me
   As one who has Thy gift received.

6 I taste the love the gift contains,
   I clasp the pardon which it brings,
And pass up to the living source
   Above, whence all this fulness
      springs.

7 Here at Thy feast, I grasp the pledge
   Which life eternal to me seals,
Here in the bread and wine I read
   The grace and peace Thy death
      reveals.

8 O fulness of the eternal grace,
   O wonders past all wondering!
Here in the hall of love and song,
   We sing the praises of our King.

461   P.M.
O N that bright and golden
   morning when the Son of Man
shall come,
   And the radiance of His glory we
      shall see;
When from every clime and nation
   He shall call His people home -
What a gathering of the ransomed
   that will be!

   What a gathering! what a gathering!
      What a gathering of the ransomed
         in the summer land of love!
   What a gathering! what a gathering,
      Of the ransomed in that happy
         home above!

2 When the blest who sleep in Jesus
   at His bidding shall arise
From the silence of the grave, and
   from the sea;
And with bodies all celestial they
   shall meet Him in the skies -
What a gathering and rejoicing there
   will be!

3 When our eyes behold the City, with
   its "many mansions" bright,
And its river, calm and restful,
   flowing free -
When the friends that death has
   parted shall in bliss again unite -
What a gathering and a greeting
   there will be!

4 Oh, the King is surely coming, and
   the time is drawing nigh
When the blessèd day of promise
   we shall see;
Then the changing "in a moment, in
   the twinkling of an eye",
And for ever in His presence we
   shall be.

462   6.4.6.4.6.6.6.4.

ON that most holy morn
    At Bethlehem,
When Christ the Lord was born
    At Bethlehem,
He came, O wondrous sight!
Forth from the realms of light
Into a scene of night,
    At Bethlehem.

2 That quiet time He knew
    At Nazareth
Saw one with purpose true,
    At Nazareth,
Grow up in all His ways
To God His Father's praise.
Precious indeed those days
    At Nazareth!

3 Compassing plain and hill,
    In Galilee,
Serving with subject will,
    In Galilee,
He Whom the Father sent
Journeyed with fixed intent
In all the way He went
    In Galilee.

4 Having the end in view -
    Jerusalem,
Onward He moved unto
    Jerusalem,
Gethsemane to face,
To die in wondrous grace
At the appointed place -
    Jerusalem.

463   7.6.7.6.D.

ON that same night, Lord Jesus,
    In which Thou wast betrayed,
When without cause man's hatred
    Against Thee was displayed,
We hear Thy gracious accents -
    "This do; remember Me";
With joyful hearts responding
    We would remember Thee.

2 We think of all the darkness
    Which round Thy spirit pressed;
Of all those waves and billows
    Which rolled across Thy breast;

'Tis there Thy grace unbounded,
    And perfect love we see;
With joy and yet with sorrow
    We do remember Thee.

3 We know Thee now as risen,
    "The First-born from the dead";
We see Thee now ascended,
    The Church's glorious Head:
In Thee by grace accepted,
    With heart and mind set free,
We think of all Thy sorrow,
    And thus remember Thee.

4 Till Thou shalt come in glory
    And call us hence away,
To share with Thee the brightness
    Of that unclouded day,
We show Thy death, Lord Jesus,
    And here would seek to be
More to that death conformèd
    Whilst we remember Thee.

464   8.7.8.7.D.

ON Thy broken body feeding,
    Lord, our hearts in one unite;
Here our souls behold Thee bleeding,
    Put to grief in sinners' sight.
O that Jesus thus should love us,
    Love us unto death and shame!
Let the dear remembrance move us,
    While we meet in His blest Name.

2 Here the pledge of Thy returning
    Tells of all the joys of home,
And our hearts within us burning,
    Cry "Amen, Lord Jesus, come!"
Soon, full soon, we thus together
    In the Father's house shall meet;
And the heavenly courts for ever
    Tread with undefilèd feet.

465   6.6.6.6.D.

ONCE more before we part,
    Bless the Redeemer's Name;
Let every tongue and heart
    Praise and adore the Lamb!

    Jesus, the sinner's Friend,
      Him whom our souls adore,
    His praises have no end;
      Praise Him for evermore.

2 Lord, in Thy grace we came;
    That blessing still impart;
We met in Jesus' Name;
    In Jesus' Name we part.

3 Still on Thy holy Word
    We'd live, and feed, and grow;
Go on to know the Lord,
    And practise what we know.

466
11.10.11.10. with Chorus

ONE day when heaven was filled
    with His praises,
One day when sin was as black as
    could be,
Jesus came forth to be born of a virgin,
    Dwelt among men, my example
    is He!

Living, He loved me;
Dying, He saved me;
Buried, He carried my sins far away;
Rising, He justified freely forever,
    One day He's coming,
    O glorious day!

2 One day they led Him up Calvary's
    mountain,
One day they nailed Him to die on
    the tree
Suffering anguish, despised and
    rejected
Bearing our sins, my Redeemer is He!

3 One day they left Him alone in the
    garden,
One day He rested, from suffering
    free;
Angels came down o'er His tomb to
    keep vigil
Hope of the hopeless, my Saviour
    is He!

4 One day the grave could contain
    Him no longer,
One day the stone rolled away from
    the door;
Then He arose, over death He had
    conquered,
Now is ascended, my Lord evermore!

5 One day the trumpet will sound for
    His coming
One day the skies with His glories
    will shine;
Wonderful day, my belovèd ones
    bringing;
Glorious Saviour, this Jesus is mine!

467
8.4.8.4.8.8.8.4.

ONE there is above all others;
    Oh, how He loves!
His is love beyond a brother's;
    Oh, how He loves!
Earthly friends may fail or leave us,
    One day soothe, the next day
    grieve us,
But this Friend will ne'er deceive us;
    Oh, how He loves!

2 'Tis eternal life to know Him;
    Oh, how He loves!
Think, Oh think, how much we owe Him;
    Oh, how He loves!
With His precious blood He bought us,
    In the wilderness He sought us,
To His fold He safely brought us;
    Oh, how He loves!

3 Blessèd Jesus! would you know Him?
    Oh, how He loves!
Give yourselves entirely to Him;
    Oh, how He loves!
Leave the past for bright tomorrow,
    From His Word now courage borrow,
Jesus carries all your sorrow;
    Oh, how He loves!

4 We have found a friend in Jesus;
    Oh, how He loves!
'Tis His great delight to bless us;
    Oh, how He loves!
How our hearts delight to hear Him -
    Bid us dwell in safety near Him:
Why should we distrust or fear Him?
    Oh, how He loves!

5 Through His Name we are forgiven;
    Oh, how He loves!
Backward shall our foes be driven
    Oh, how He loves!
Best of blessings He'll provide us,
    Naught but good shall e'er betide us,
Safe to glory He will guide us;
    Oh, how He loves!

468 L.M.

"OUR Father!" Oh, what gracious
ways
And thoughts of love that Name
conveys!
It tells us of the tender care
Belovèd children ever share.

2 Our Father! by Thy mercies past,
We learn on Thee our cares to cast;
And while our wants are known to
Thee,
We need not fear whate'er they be.

3 How oft when wand'ring far away,
Thy care has hedged up all our way;
So bidding us return and live,
And learn how much Thou canst
forgive.

4 And though we came with tardy feet,
It was our Father ran to meet;
It was upon our Father's breast
We found again a place of rest.

5 How precious are Thy thoughts to us!
How dear Thy Name revealèd thus!
Oh, make us followers of Thee,
As Thy dear children ought to be!

469 10.10.10.10.

OUR God and Father, we draw
near to Thee
In all the worth of Thy belovèd Son;
All Thou hast e'er desired from
man we see
In Him, Thy Christ, Thine own
anointed One.

2 No thought of His e'er moved apart
from Thine;
Each holy footstep gave Thee fresh
delight;
Perfect expression of Thy will divine
Thou hadst in Him - come forth
from glory bright.

3 Thou ever lovedst Him - ere time
began
He was beside Thee, object of Thy
heart;
One with Thyself in Thine eternal plan,
In Godhead glory one in all Thou art.

4 And now Thou lov'st Him, for
Himself He gave;
Theme of our song when time shall
cease to be;
Laid down His life that Thou, O God,
shouldst have
Fruit of Thy love, in sons who
worship Thee.

470 L.M.

OUR God, whose justice did awake,
The sword against Thy Well-
beloved,
Thou didst Thine own dear Son
forsake,
To mercy by His cries unmoved!

2 Thy perfect image, Thy delight,
He ever had beheld Thy face;
Thy bosom was, of native right,
His proper, secret dwelling-place.

3 Yet was the Lord made flesh, and
nailed,
By men, His creatures, to the tree;
By all the powers of hell assailed,
And bruised, and pierced, and slain
by Thee!

4 In His own majesty arrayed,
He spake and built the universe;
Yet to redeem us He was made
A dying outcast and a curse!

5 His depths unsearchable of woe
Alone our utmost guilt proclaim;
Through Jesus' Cross make us to
know
The utmost glories of Thy name!

471 6.4.6.4.6.6.6.4.

OUR grateful hearts would raise,
Father to Thee,
Their overflowing praise,
Father to Thee.
Brought from the shades of night,
From Satan's power and might,
Into Thy glorious light,
Father to Thee.

2 What boundless grace has flowed,
  Saviour through Thee.
On rebels now bestowed,
  Saviour in Thee;
Peace through Thy precious blood,
  Blest now with every good,
And reconciled to God,
  Saviour in Thee.

3 Here in Thy blessèd name,
  Gathered to Thee.
Thy death we now proclaim,
  Gathered to Thee.
Here in Thy presence sweet,
  With saints in light made meet,
Now through Thy work complete,
  Gathered to Thee.

4 Hark how the chorus swells,
  Lord unto thee,
All fulness in Thee dwells,
  Yea, Lord in Thee;
Head of the church art Thou,
  In resurrection now,
Low at Thy feet we bow,
  Lord unto Thee.

472   11.10.11.10.

OUR great Redeemer liveth! this
  assurance
Calms anxious fears and satisfies
  the heart;
Yes, Jesus lives! at God's right hand
  He reigneth,
And in His great salvation we have
  part.

2 A living Christ, so strong, so pure,
  so tender,
Bears every ransomed soul before
  the throne;
Complete in Him we stand, saved
  by His merit -
It was His blood which did for sin
  atone.

3 And now we live in Him, our great
  Redeemer,
Who, living, intercedes for us above,
  Yet by His Spirit dwells with us,
  and keeps us
Enfolded in His mighty arms of love.

4 Redeemer, Lord! with gratitude
  unfeignèd,
We bless Thy holy name that Thou
  has taught
Our hearts to know Thee, loving,
  caring, pleading:
Now grant us grace to love Thee as
  we ought.

473   7.6.7.6.

OUR hearts are full, O Father,
  Whilst here we meet as one,
We bring the deep perfection
  Of Thy belovèd Son.

2 What rest, what joy and fragrance,
  Ascending up to God,
Rose from His life so holy,
  And His most precious blood.

3 Yea, Thou hast found Thy portion,
  Thy joy, Thy deep delight,
In Him whose every action
  Was pleasing in Thy sight.

4 We too with joy behold Him,
  His wondrous worth we trace,
And know ourselves accepted
  In Him through sovereign grace.

5 So with full hearts we gather,
  Though many yet as one,
To give Thee thanks, O Father,
  For Thy belovèd Son.

474   10.10.10.10.

OUR hearts are glad, for we have
  seen the Lord;
The living Lord, victorious from the
  grave.
O joy to see Him, joy to hear His word,
  Our Lord and Master, strong to
  bless and save!

2 His hands, His feet He showed us,
  and the place
Where deeply pierced at last the
  cruel spear.
O precious scars! O deathless love
  and grace
That still in those redeeming wounds
  appear!

3 Most wondrous sight! All else is
    poor and dim
  To eyes that thus have viewed the
    risen One.
  All power is His, all glories meet in
    Him,
  The sinner's Saviour, God's Belovèd
    Son.

4 So we are glad, our spirits all aglow,
    Filled with a new and strangely
      thrilling joy.
  Power from Himself inbreathing,
    forth we go -
  O may His service all our days
    employ!

475   P.M.

OUR Lord is now rejected
    And by the world disowned,
By the *many* still neglected,
    And by the *few* enthroned;
But soon He'll come in glory!
    The hour is drawing nigh,
For the crowning day is coming
    By and by.

Oh, the crowning day is coming!
  Is coming by and by!
When our Lord shall come in power
  And glory from on high!
Oh, the glorious sight will gladden
  Each waiting, watchful eye,
In the crowning day that's coming
  By and by.

2 The heavens shall glow with splendour;
    But brighter far than they
  The saints shall shine in glory,
    As Christ shall them array:
  The beauty of the Saviour
    Shall dazzle every eye,
  In the crowning day that's coming
    By and by.

3 Our pain shall then be over,
    We'll sin and sigh no more;
  Behind us all our sorrow,
    And nought but joy before.
  A joy in our Redeemer,
    As we to Him are nigh,
  In the crowning day that's coming
    By and by.

4 Let all who look for "hasten"
    The coming joyful day
  By earnest consecration
    To walk the narrow way;
  By gathering in the lost ones
    For whom our Lord did die,
  For the crowning day that's coming
    By and by.

476   C.M.D.

OUR souls are in God's mighty hand,
    We're precious in His sight;
And you and I shall surely stand
    With Him in glory bright.

    We'll stem the storm, it won't be long,
      We'll anchor by and by
    In the haven of eternal rest,
      With Jesus ever nigh.

2 Him eye to eye we then shall see,
    Our face like His shall shine;
  Oh, what a glorious company,
    Where saints and angels join!

3 Oh, what a joyful meeting there!
    In robes of white arrayed;
  We all shall join in praising Him
    Whose glories never fade.

4 Then let us hasten to that day,
    When all shall be brought home;
  Come, O Redeemer, come, we pray,
    Lord Jesus, quickly come!

477   S.M.D.

OUR voice, with one accord,
    To Thee, His God we raise,
While in the midst is He, the Lord,
    The Leader of the praise,
The Subject of our song,
    Our Centre as we sing,
Our Lord His gathered ones among,
    Through Whom our praise we bring.

2 With every heart as one,
    As by the Spirit moved,
  We muse on Thy Belovèd Son,
    The Man by Thee approved.
  As to the past we turn,
    And each His path surveys,
  Our raptured hearts within us burn,
    Our lips are filled with praise.

3 A holy priesthood, near,
  Through Jesus' blood, we draw
To Thee, His God and Father here
  With reverence and awe.
As if with feet unshod,
  By Him through Whom we live,
A sacrifice of praise, O God,
  The fruit of lips we give.

4 Remembering Thy Son,
  Our praise to Thee ascends,
'Tis heaven's song on earth begun,
  The song that never ends.
Our hearts are tuned anew
  As thus, with one accord,
That wealth of grace and truth we view,
  Remembering our Lord.

478
P.M.

OURS are peace and joy divine,
  Who are one with Christ,
When, like branches in the vine,
  We abide in Christ.
As a living grafted shoot,
  Nourished from a hidden root,
We may bear all holy fruit
  Through "the love of Christ".

  Love of Christ, love of Christ,
  Clusters grow on every branch
  Through "the love of Christ".

2 Christian pity moves our heart
  Through "the love of Christ";
Others' woes pierce like a dart
  When there's love to Christ.
Gospel tidings we must tell,
  Sinners warn to flee from hell,
Lure and win, alarm, compel,
  By "the love of Christ".

  Love of Christ, love of Christ,
  Heaven's ranks we'll seek to swell
  For "the love of Christ".

3 We will love with tender care,
  Knowing love to Christ,
Brethren who His image bear,
  For "the love of Christ".
Jesus only shall we know,
  And our love to all shall flow
In His blood-bought Church below,
  For "the love of Christ".

  Love of Christ, love of Christ,
  We now love all ransomed ones
  For "the love of Christ".

4 Now we live and walk by faith
  Through "the love of Christ":
We can triumph over death,
  One in life with Christ.
Rooted, settled, knowing more,
  Depths and heights of love explore,
Till we gain the heavenly shore
  Through "the love of Christ".

  Love of Christ, love of Christ,
  When He comes we then shall know
  All "the love of Christ".

479
11.10.11.10.

PEACE, peace is mine! 'Tis peace
  of Jesus' making,
The purchase of His own most
  precious blood;
He bore my sins, and suffered
  God's forsaking,
While judgment poured on Him its
  whelming flood.

2 Peace, peace is mine, for He who
  once descended
Has passed in triumph through
  death's dark domain;
As Victor He to God's right hand
  ascended,
And now is seen, the Lamb who
  once was slain.

3 Peace, peace is mine! On high is
  Christ appearing,
Within the veil my great High Priest
  is He;
Honour and glory as a crown He's
  wearing,
Who wore on earth the crown of
  thorns for me.

4 Peace, settled peace - a foretaste
  here of glory!
May mine e'er as an even river flow!
  His love constrains me now to tell
  the story -
The story old, whose fulness none
  can know.

5 Thus too may others come and
   share the blessing -
   Peace, peace divine - then raise the
   anthem high,
   The name of Jesus "Lord of all"
   confessing,
   And live for Him whose coming
   draweth nigh!

480   L.M.

POOR, weak, and worthless
   though I am,
I have a rich, almighty Friend;
   Jesus, the Saviour, is His name;
He freely loves, and without end.

2 He ransomed me from hell with blood,
   And by His power my foes controlled;
He found me wand'ring far from God,
   And brought me to His chosen fold.

3 He cheers my heart, my want supplies,
   And says that I shall shortly be
Enthroned with Him above the skies;
   Oh, what a friend is Christ to me!

4 But ah! my inmost spirit mourns,
   And well my eyes with tears may
      swim,
To think of my perverse returns;
   I've been a faithless friend to Him.

5 Sure, were not I most vile and base,
   I could not thus my Friend requite!
And were not He the God of grace,
   He'd frown and spurn me from
      His sight.

481   11.12.12.10.

PRAISE appreciative, worship
   adoring,
Offer we unitedly to Thee, O God,
   while here
As a holy priesthood, by the Spirit
   pouring
Thanks for Thy Son into Thine open
   ear.

2 His the condescension outwith our
   measure;
Mighty God essentially, He stooped
   to lowly birth,
Taking up in manhood, for Thy
   perfect pleasure,
That servant form, that subject place
   on earth.

3 To Thyself attentive, morning by
   morning,
As the learner Thee He heard with
   opened ear each day,
In a scene rebellious, facing hate
   and scorning,
Holy, and true, and steadfast in His
   way.

4 Measureless the glory to Thee
   accruing,
Thy delight was centred in Thy well-
   belovèd Son.
Manifest perfections in Him thus
   reviewing,
We voice our praise to Thee for
   such an One.

482   12.10.12.10.D.

PRAISE Him! praise Him! Jesus,
   our blessèd Redeemer!
Sing, ye saints! His wonderful love
   proclaim;
Hail Him! hail Him! mightiest angels
   in glory,
Strength and honour give to His
   holy Name.
Like a shepherd, Jesus will feed His
   people,
In His arms He carries them all day
   long;
O ye saints that dwell in the light of
   His presence
Praise Him! praise Him! ever in
   joyful song.

2 Praise Him! praise Him! Jesus, our
   blessèd Redeemer!
For our sins He suffered, and bled,
   and died;
He's our Rock, our hope of eternal
   salvation,
Hail Him! hail Him! Jesus, the Crucified.

Loving Saviour, meekly enduring
    sorrow,
Crowned with thorns that cruelly
    pierced His brow;
Once for us rejected, despised, and
    forsaken,
Prince of Glory! He is triumphant now.

3 Praise Him! praise Him! Jesus, our
    blessèd Redeemer!
Heavenly portals loud with
    hosannahs ring!
Jesus, Saviour, reigneth for ever
    and ever;
Crown Him! crown Him! prophet,
    and priest, and king.
Death is vanquished! tell it with joy,
    ye faithful,
Where is now thy victory, boasting
    grave?
Jesus lives! no longer thy portals
    are cheerless;
Jesus lives! the mighty and strong
    to save.

483   8.7.8.7.8.7.

PRAISE, my soul, the King of
    heaven;
To His feet thy tribute bring;
    Ransomed, healed, restored,
    forgiven,
Who like thee His praise shall sing?
        Praise Him! praise Him!
Praise the everlasting King.

2 Praise Him for His grace and favour
    To our fathers in distress;
Praise Him, still the same as ever,
    Slow to chide and swift to bless:
        Praise Him! praise Him!
Glorious in His faithfulness.

3 Father-like He tends and spares us,
    Well our feeble frame He knows;
In His hands He gently bears us,
    Rescues us from all our foes:
        Praise Him! praise Him!
Widely as His mercy flows.

4 Frail as summer flower we flourish;
    Blows the wind and it is gone;
But, while mortals rise and perish,

God endures unchanging on:
        Praise Him! praise Him!
Praise the high eternal One.

5 Angels in the height adore Him!
    Ye behold Him face to face;
Saints triumphant bow before Him!
    Gathered in from every race:
        Praise Him! praise Him!
Praise with us the God of grace.

484   P.M.

PRAISE, praise ye the Name of
    Jehovah, our God;
Declare, O declare ye His glories
    abroad;
Proclaim ye His mercy from nation
    to nation,
Till the uttermost islands have heard
    His salvation.

*For His love floweth on free and full
    as a river,
And His mercy endureth for ever
    and ever.*

2 Praise, praise ye the Lamb who for
    sinners was slain,
Who went down to the grave and
    ascended again;
And who soon shall return, when
    these dark days are o'er,
To set up His kingdom in glory and
    power.

3 Then the heavens, the earth, and
    the sea shall rejoice;
The fields and the forests shall lift
    the glad voice;
The sands of the desert shall
    flourish in green,
And Lebanon's glory be shed o'er
    the scene.

4 Her bridal attire and her festal array
    All Nature shall wear on that
    glorious day;
For her King cometh down with His
    people to reign,
And His presence shall bless her
    with Eden again.

485 8.7.8.7.4.7.

PRAISE the Lord, and leave
tomorrow
In Thy loving Father's hands;
Burden not thyself with sorrow,
For secure the promise stands.
    He is faithful!
Leave thy troubles in His hands.

2 Trust today, and leave tomorrow,
    Each day has enough of care;
Therefore, whatsoe'er thy burden,
    God will give thee strength to bear.
    He is faithful!
Cast on Him thine every care.

3 Pray today, and let tomorrow
    Bring with it whate'er it may;
Hear thy loving Father promise
    Strength according to thy day.
    He is faithful!
Trust Him, therefore, come what may.

4 Watch today, and leave tomorrow,
    For tomorrow may not come;
For today thy loving Saviour
    May appear to take thee home.
    He is faithful!
Look for Him, the coming One.

5 Work today, and leave tomorrow;
    All around there's urgent need;
All around there's sin and sorrow;
    Broadcast, daily sow thy seed.
    God is faithful!
He shall bless thy work indeed.

6 Thus by trusting, watching, praying,
    Each day, as our time rolls on,
We shall find the promised blessing,
    Daily strength till Jesus come.
    He is faithful!
He will come to take us home.

486 8.7.8.7.4.7.

PRAISE the Lord, who died to
save us,
Praise His ever gracious Name;
    Praise Him that He lives to bless us,
Now and evermore the same:
    Blessèd Saviour!
We would all Thy love proclaim.

2 Grace it was, yea, grace abounding,
    Brought Thee down to save the lost;
Ye above, His throne surrounding,
    Praise Him, praise Him all His host:
    Saints! Adore Him!
Ye are they who owe Him most.

3 We, of all His hand created,
    Objects of such grace alone,
By eternal love elected,
    Destined now to share His throne,
    Sing with wonder,
Sing of what our Lord hath done.

4 Praise His Name, who died to save us;
    'Tis by Him His people live;
And in Him the Father gave us
    All that boundless love could give:
    Life eternal
In our Saviour we receive.

487 P.M.

PRAISE the peerless name of Jesus,
    Sing of Him for evermore;
Praise the precious name of Jesus,
    Tell its value o'er and o'er.
Jesus Christ is God's salvation;
    All who live through Jesus' name,
Were in death and condemnation,
    Heirs of Adam's sin and shame.
'Tis through Thy death, Lord Jesus,
    Faith can wondrous blessings claim.

2 Precious blood, the blood of Jesus,
    Did for all my sins atone;
Sprinkled blood, the blood of Jesus,
    Speaks for ever from the throne.
Telling how His life was given,
    And that He who once was dead -
Son of Man, God's Son from heaven -
    Is the Saviour, as He said.
O, precious blood of Jesus!
    For a world of sinners shed.

3 At this name supreme of Jesus
    Every knee, God saith, shall bow;
Lord of all, 'tis this same Jesus
    Whom the world refuses now.
Every eye shall gaze upon Him,
    Every tongue confess His name;
Every glory centres in Him,
    Wronged of men, and put to shame.
O, blessèd name of Jesus!
    Now His matchless worth proclaim.

4 Praise the peerless name of Jesus,
  Tell of Him for evermore;
See Him in God's glory - Jesus,
  Who the weight of judgment bore.
In the Cross, Thy death, Lord Jesus,
  God requirèd what is past;
Thou art Alpha and Omega,
  Thou art First and Thou art Last;
Now in Thy name, Lord Jesus,
  All God's counsel standeth fast.

488   8.8.8.5.

PRAISE the Saviour, ye who
  know Him!
Who can tell how much we owe Him?
  Gladly let us render to Him
    All we are and have.

2 Jesus is the Name that charms us,
    He for conflict fits and arms us;
Nothing moves, and nothing harms us,
    When we trust in Him.

3 Trust in Him, ye saints, for ever;
    He is faithful, changing never;
Neither force nor guile can sever
    Those He loves from Him.

4 Keep us, Lord, oh keep us cleaving
    To Thyself, and still believing,
Till the hour of our receiving
    Promised joys in heaven.

5 Then we shall be where we would be,
    Then we shall be what we should be,
That which is not now, nor could be,
    Then shall be our own.

489   7.7.7.7.

PRAISE thy Saviour, O my soul!
  He has drunk the bitter gall,
Paid thy ransom, set thee free;
  Praise Him, praise Him cheerfully.

2 O the wonders of His love!
    See Him coming from above
To atone and die for thee;
    Praise Him, praise Him cheerfully.

3 See the waves and billows roll
    O'er His sinless, spotless soul;
O my soul, it was for thee!
    Praise Him, praise Him cheerfully.

4 Yes, with joy we'll praise Him now,
    Till with saints above we bow,
And to all eternity
    Praise Him, praise Him cheerfully.

490   14.14.4.7.8.

PRAISE to the Lord, the
  Almighty, the King of creation;
O my soul, praise Him, for He is
  thy health and salvation;
All ye who hear,
  Brethren and sisters draw near,
Praise Him in glad adoration.

2 Praise to the Lord, who o'er all
    things so wondrously reigneth,
Shelters thee under His wings, yea,
  so gently sustaineth!
Hast thou not seen
  How thy desires e'er have been
Granted in what He ordaineth?

3 Praise to the Lord, who doth
    prosper thy work and defend thee;
Surely His goodness and mercy
    here daily attend thee:
Ponder anew
    What the Almighty can do
If with His love He befriend thee.

4 Praise to the Lord, who, when
    darkness and sin is abounding,
Who, when the godless do triumph,
    all virtue confounding,
Sheddeth His light,
    Chaseth the horrors of night,
Saints with His mercy surrounding.

5 Praise to the Lord, O let all that is
    in me adore Him;
All that hath life and breath come
    now with praises before Him;
Let the Amen
    Sound from His people again:
Gladly for aye we adore Him.

491   11.10.11.10.

PRAISE ye Jehovah! Praise the
  Lord most holy,
Who cheers the contrite, girds with
  strength the weak;
Praise Him who will with glory crown
  the lowly,
And with salvation beautify the meek.

2 Praise ye the Lord for all His loving-
   kindness,
   And all the tender mercies He has
   shewn;
   Praise Him who pardons all our sin
   and blindness,
   And calls us sons, and seals us for
   His own.

3 Praise ye Jehovah - Source of all
   our blessing
   Before His gifts earth's richest
   boons wax dim;
   Resting in Him, His peace and joy
   possessing,
   All things are ours, for we have all
   in Him.

4 Praise ye the Father, God the Lord,
   who gave us,
   With full and perfect love, His only
   Son!
   Praise ye the Son, who died Himself
   to save us!
   Praise ye the Spirit! Praise the
   Three in One!

492 C.M.

"PRAISE ye the Lord!" again, again,
   The Spirit strikes the chord;
Nor toucheth He our hearts in vain;
   We praise, we praise the Lord.

2 "Rejoice in Him!" again, again,
   The Spirit speaks the word;
And faith takes up the happy strain
   Our joy is in the Lord.

3 "Stand fast in Christ!" ah! yet again
   He teaches all the band;
Our best endeavours are in vain,
   In Christ alone we stand.

4 "Clean every whit!" Thou saidst it, Lord;
   Shall one suspicion lurk?
Thine, surely, is a faithful word,
   And Thine a finished work.

5 For ever be the glory given
   To Thee, O Lamb of God!
No joy for us, in earth or heaven,
   We owe not to Thy blood.

493 C.M.

PRAYER is the soul's sincere desire,
   Uttered or unexpressed,
The motion of a hidden fire
   That trembles in the breast.

2 Prayer is the burden of a sigh,
   The falling of a tear,
The upward glancing of an eye
   When none but God is near.

3 Prayer is the simplest form of speech
   That infant lips can try;
Prayer, the sublimest strains that reach
   The Majesty on high.

4 Prayer is the Christian's vital breath,
   The Christian's native air;
His watchword at the gates of death:
   He enters heaven with prayer.

5 The saints, in prayer, appear as one
   In word, and deed, and mind,
While with the Father and the Son
   Sweet fellowship they find.

6 O Thou by whom we come to God,
   The Life, the Truth, the Way!
The path of prayer Thyself hast trod:
   Lord, teach us how to pray!

494 8.7.8.7.4.7.

PRECIOUS is the blood of Jesus
   Unto sinners who believe;
From the wrath of God it frees us,
   And salvation we receive:
      It is finished!
Sounds with joy through earth and
   heaven.

2 Jesus now in heaven is seated,
   And by faith on Him we rest;
Soon the Church will be completed,
   And the saints with Him be blest:
      Grace and glory
In our Saviour we receive.

3 Soon will pass the night of sorrow,
   And the Lord in glory come;
We shall see Him on the morrow,
   And the Bride be welcomed home:
      Hallelujah!
Glory, glory to the Lamb!

495 8.5.8.5.D.

PRECIOUS thought - my Father
  knoweth!
In His love I rest:
    For whate'er my Father doeth
Must be always best;
    Well I know the heart that planneth
Naught but good for me;
    Joy and sorrow interwoven,
Love in all I see.

2 Precious thought - my Father knoweth!
    Careth for His child;
Bids me nestle closer to Him,
    When the storms beat wild;
Though my earthly hopes are
    shattered,
And the tear-drops fall,
    Yet He is Himself my solace,
Yea, my "all in all".

3 Sweet to tell Him all He knoweth!
    Roll on Him the care;
Cast upon Himself the burden,
    That I cannot bear,
Then, without a care oppressing,
    Simply to lie still,
Giving thanks to Him for all things,
    Since it is His will

4 Oh, to trust Him then more fully!
    Just to simply move
In the conscious calm enjoyment
    Of the Father's love;
Knowing that life's chequered pathway
    Leadeth to His rest;
Satisfied the way He taketh
    Must be always best.

496 11.11.11.11.

PRESS forward and fear not!
    Though billows may roll,
The word of Jehovah
    Their rage can control;
Though waves rise in anger,
    Their tumult shall cease;
One word of His bidding
    Shall hush them to peace.

2 Press forward and fear not!
    Though trial be near;
The Lord is our refuge,
    Whom, then, shall we fear?

His staff is our comfort,
    Our safeguard His rod;
Then let us be steadfast,
    And trust in our God.

3 Press forward and fear not!
    Be strong in the Lord,
In the power of His promise,
    The truth of His word;
Through the sea and the desert
    Our pathway may tend,
But He who hath saved us
    Will save to the end.

4 Press forward and fear not!
    Though rough be our way;
Why should we e'er shrink
    From our path in dismay?
We tread but the road
    Which our Leader has trod;
Then let us press forward,
    And trust in our God.

497 S.M.

PUT thou thy trust in God,
    In duty's path go on;
Walk in His strength with faith and
    hope,
So shall thy work be done.

2 Give to the winds thy fears;
    Hope, and be undismayed;
God hears thy sighs and counts
    thy tears,
God shall lift up thy head.

3 He everywhere hath sway,
    And all things serve His might;
His every act pure blessing is,
    His path unsullied light.

4 Commit thou all thy griefs
    And ways into His hands,
To His sure truth and tender care
    Who earth and heaven commands.

5 Through waves, and clouds, and
    storms
He gently clears the way;
    Wait thou His time; so shall this night
Soon end in joyous day.

6 When He makes bare His arm
    Who shall His work withstand?
  When He His people's cause
    defends,
  Who then shall stay His hand?

7 Leave to His sovereign sway
    To choose and to command;
  So shalt thou, wondering, own His
    way
   How wise, how strong His hand.

8 We comprehend Him not
    Yet earth and heaven tell
  God sits as Sovereign on the throne
    And ruleth all things well!

498   P.M.

R EDEEMED! how I love to
    proclaim it,
  Redeemed by the blood of the Lamb;
    Redeemed through His infinite
      mercy,
  His child and for ever I am.

    Redeemed! Redeeemed!
    Redeemed by the blood of the Lamb,
    Redeemed! Redeemed!
    His child and forever I am.

2 Redeemed, and so happy in Jesus,
    No language my rapture can tell,
  I know that the light of His presence
    With me doth continually dwell.

3 I think of my blessèd Redeemer,
    I think of Him all the day long;
  I sing, for I cannot be silent,
    His love is the theme of my song.

4 I know I shall see in His beauty
    The King in whose law I delight,
  Who lovingly guardeth my footsteps,
    And giveth me songs in the night.

5 I know there's a crown that is waiting
    In yonder bright mansions for me,
  And soon, with the spirits made
    perfect,
  At home with the Lord I shall be.

499   S.M.

R EJECTED and despised,
    As with averted face,
  He moved 'mong men unrecognised,
    And in the outside place.

2 Through this sad scene of sin,
    All pitiful, He passed,
  The love that lived His heart within
    To manifest at last.

3 No form or comeliness
    To please a fallen race,
  Yet lovely in His lowly dress,
    And wondrous in His grace!

4 Thus undesired was He
    Whom all in heaven adored;
  No unanointed eye can see
    The beauty of the Lord.

5 But One has touched our eyes
    And lips, to see and sing,
  Our hearts, this priestly sacrifice
    To Thee, O God, to bring.

500   6.6.6.6.8.8.

R EJOICE! the Lord is King;
    Your Lord and King adore;
  Mortals, give thanks and sing,
    And triumph evermore:
  Lift up your heart, lift up your voice;
    Rejoice, again I say, rejoice.

2 Jesus, the Saviour, reigns,
    The God of truth and love;
  When He had purged our stains
    He took His seat above:
  Lift up your heart, lift up your voice;
    Rejoice, again I say, rejoice.

3 His kingdom cannot fail;
    He rules o'er earth and heaven;
  The keys of death and hell
    Are to our Jesus given:
  Lift up your heart, lift up your voice;
    Rejoice, again I say, rejoice.

4 He sits at God's right hand
    Till all His foes submit,
  And bow to His command,

And fall beneath His feet:
Lift up your heart, lift up your voice;
  Rejoice, again I say, rejoice.

5 Rejoice in glorious hope;
    Jesus, our Lord, shall come
  And take His servants up
    To their eternal home;
  We soon shall hear th' archangel's
    voice;
  The trump of God shall sound, rejoice!

501
S.M.

REST of the saints above,
  Jerusalem of God!
Who, in thy palaces of love,
  Thy golden streets have trod?

2 Who shall to me that joy
    Of saint-thronged courts declare,
  Tell of that constant, sweet employ
    My spirit longs to share?

3 That rest secure from ill,
    No cloud of grief e'er stains;
  Unfailing praise each heart doth fill,
    And love eternal reigns.

4 The Lamb is there, my soul!
    There God Himself doth rest
  In love divine, diffused through all -
    With Him supremely blest.

5 God and the Lamb! 'tis well;
    I know that source divine,
  Of joy and love no tongue can tell,
    And know that all is mine.

6 There on the hidden bread,
    Of Christ - once humbled here -
  God's treasured store - for ever fed,
    His love my soul shall cheer.

7 There in effulgence bright,
    Saviour and Guide, with Thee
  I'll walk, and In Thy heavenly light
    Whiter my robe shall be!

8 God and the Lamb shall there
    The light and temple be,
  And radiant hosts for ever share
    The unveiled mystery.

502
S.M.D.

"REVIVE Thy work, O Lord!"
  Thy mighty arm make bare;
Speak with the voice which wakes
    the dead,
And make Thy people hear.

"Revive Thy work, O Lord!"
  And give refreshing showers;
The glory shall be all Thine own,
  The blessing, Lord, be ours!

2 "Revive Thy work, O Lord!"
    Disturb this sleep of death;
  Quicken the smould'ring embers, Lord,
    By Thine almighty breath.

3 "Revive Thy work, O Lord!"
    Create soul-thirst for Thee;
  And hung'ring for the Bread of Life
    O may our spirits be!

4 "Revive Thy work, O Lord!"
    Give power unto Thy Word;
  Grant that Thy blessèd Gospel may
    In living faith be heard.

5 Revive Thy work, O Lord!
    And make Thy servants bold;
  Convict of sin and work once more
    As in the days of old.

6 Revive Thy work, O Lord,
    Exalt Thy precious Name;
  And, by the Holy Ghost, our love
    For Thee and Thine inflame.

503
8.7.8.7.

RISE, my soul! behold 'tis Jesus,
  Jesus fills Thy wond'ring eyes;
See Him now in glory seated,
  Where thy sins no more can rise.

2 There, in righteousness transcendent,
    Lo! He doth in heaven appear,
  Shows the blood of His atonement
    As thy title to be there.

3 All thy sins were laid upon Him,
    Jesus bore them on the tree;
  God, who knew them, laid them on Him,
    And, believing, thou art free.

4　God now brings thee to His dwelling,
　　　Spreads for thee His feast divine,
　　Bids thee welcome, ever telling
　　　What a portion there is thine.

5　In that circle of God's favour,
　　　Circle of the Father's love,
　　All is rest, and rest for ever,
　　　All is perfectness above.

6　Blessèd, glorious word "forever"!
　　　Yea, "forever!" is the word;
　　Nothing can the ransomed sever,
　　　Nought divide them from the Lord.

504   8.7.8.7.

R ISE, my soul! thy God directs thee;
　　Stranger hands no more impede;
Pass thou on; His hand protects thee,
　　Strength that has the captive freed.

2　Is the wilderness before thee?
　　　Desert lands where drought abides?
　　Heavenly springs shall there restore
　　　thee,
　　Fresh from God's exhaustless tides.

3　Light divine surrounds thy going;
　　　God Himself shall mark thy way;
　　Secret blessings, richly flowing,
　　　Lead to everlasting day.

4　Art thou weaned from Egypt's
　　　pleasures?
　　God in secret shall thee keep;
　　　There unfold His hidden treasures,
　　There His love's exhaustless deep.

5　In the desert God will teach thee
　　　What the God that thou hast found;
　　Patient, gracious, powerful, holy,
　　　All His grace shall there abound.

6　Though thy way be long and dreary,
　　　Eagle strength He'll still renew;
　　Garments fresh and foot unweary
　　　Tell how God hath brought thee
　　　　through.

7　When to Canaan's long-loved dwelling
　　　Love divine thy foot shall bring,
　　There, with shouts of triumph swelling,
　　　Zion's songs in rest to sing.

8　There no stranger God shall meet
　　　thee;
　　Stranger thou in courts above!
　　　He who to His rest shall greet thee
　　Greets thee with a well-known love.

505   8.7.8.7.4.7.

R ISE, my soul, with joy and gladness,
　　And the praise of Jesus sing;
He removes all cause of sadness -
　　Only Jesus life could bring;
　　　He redeemed me -
Glory to the eternal King!

2　Well He knew my lost condition -
　　　Sinless offering God must have;
　　Vain my tears and deep contrition,
　　　Nought that I could do would save:
　　　　He redeemed me,
　　For His precious life He gave.

3　Now He lives, He lives for ever,
　　　And for all His people pleads;
　　One with Him, now nought can sever
　　　Those for whom He intercedes:
　　　　He redeemed me,
　　And to glory safely leads.

4　Bright the prospect of that glory,
　　　Seen by faith at God's right hand;
　　There we shall recount the story,
　　　In that happy, happy land:
　　　　He redeemed me -
　　Wondrous all His love has planned!

506   7.7.7.7.7.7.

R OCK of Ages, cleft for me,
　　Let me hide myself in Thee!
Let the water and the blood,
　　From Thy riven side which flowed,
Be of sin the double cure;
　　Cleanse me from its guilt and
　　　power.

2　Not the labour of my hands
　　　Can fulfil Thy law's demands;
　　Could my zeal no respite know,
　　　Could my tears for ever flow,
　　All for sin could not atone;
　　　Thou must save, and Thou alone.

3　Nothing in my hand I bring,
　　　Simply to Thy Cross I cling;
　　Naked, come to Thee for dress;

Helpless, look to Thee for grace;
Foul, I to the fountain fly;
Wash me, Saviour, or I die.

4 While I draw this fleeting breath,
When mine eyelids close in death,
When I soar to worlds unknown,
See Thee on Thy judgment throne,
Rock of Ages, cleft for me,
Let me hide myself in Thee.

507   8.5.8.3.

R OUND Himself we come so
  gladly
In this simple way;
    Into His blest Name we gather
    Here today.

2 Glories all-excelling centre
    In that Holy One;
Infinite effulgence gleaming
    Through the Son!

3 He Who knows the Father's bosom
    As His dwelling-place
Now the Father's heart revealeth
    In His grace;

4 And a wealth of heav'nly features
    In His ways express,
Day by day, His own inherent
    Preciousness.

5 Thus before Thyself, His Father,
    Sweetest hymns of praise,
Reminiscent of His pathway
    Do we raise.

508   8.4.8 4.8.8.8.4.

R OUND His steps the sweetest
  fragrance
    Ever shall cling;
With Himself in blest remembrance,
    Gladly we sing;
    Now in holy convocation,
All our true appreciation
    Of the Son, in presentation
      To God we bring.

2 Excellence surpassing shining
    Through every day,
Grace and glory intertwining
    His perfect way,
As a tender plant inviting,
    Meekness with His might uniting,
Virtues rare His pathway lighting
    In rich array!

3 In Him all the Father's pleasure
    Centred we see;
Preciousness in boundless measure,
    True dignity!
His the path of grace excelling,
    Works and words beyond all telling,
All the fulness in Him dwelling
    In majesty.

509   7.6.7.6.D.

S AFE in the arms of Jesus,
  Safe on His gentle breast,
There by His love o'ershaded,
  Sweetly my soul shall rest.
Hark! 'tis the voice of angels,
  Borne in a song to me,
Over the fields of glory,
  Over the jasper sea.

Safe in the arms of Jesus,
  Safe on His gentle breast
There by His love o'ershaded,
  Sweetly my soul shall rest.

2 Safe in the arms of Jesus,
  Safe from corroding care,
Safe from the world's temptations,
  Sin cannot harm me there.
Free from the blight of sorrow,
  Free from my doubts and fears;
Only a few more trials,
  Only a few more tears!

3 Jesus, my heart's dear refuge,
  Jesus has died for me;
Firm on the Rock of Ages
  Ever my trust shall be.
Here let me wait with patience,
  Wait till the night is over;
Wait till I see the morning
  Break on the golden shore.

510

6.6.8.4.D.

SALVATION to our God!
  Salvation to the Lamb!
The shedding of His precious blood
  Our only claim.
Our God salvation gives,
  And through the Lamb it flows;
Once slain for us - for us He lives,
  Our sole repose.

2 The Lamb once slain is seen
    On God's eternal throne;
  And His redeemed are white and clean
    Through Him alone.
  Salvation's joyful sound
    Bursts from the blood-bought throng,
  And holy angels all around
    Take up the song.

3 Our hearts are tuned for this,
    Their songs our tongues employ;
  The Lamb, the spring of all our bliss,
    And God our joy.
  Salvation to our God,
    Thanksgiving, power, and might!
  And to the Lamb who shed His blood,
    Our life and light.

511

P.M.

SATISFIED with Thee, Lord Jesus,
  I am blest;
Peace which passeth understanding,
  On Thy breast;
No more doubting,
  No more trembling,
No more trembling,
  Oh, what rest!

2 Occupied with Thee, Lord Jesus,
    In Thy grace;
  All Thy ways and thoughts about me,
    Only trace
  Deeper stories
    Of the glories,
  Of the glories
    Of Thy grace.

3 Taken up with Thee, Lord Jesus,
    I would be;
  Finding joy and satisfaction
    All in Thee;
  Thou the nearest
    And the dearest,
  And the dearest
    Unto me.

4 Listening for Thy shout, Lord Jesus,
    In the air;
  When Thy saints shall rise with joy to
    Meet Thee there.
  Oh, what gladness!
    No more sadness,
  No more sadness,
    Sin nor care.

5 Longing for the bride, Lord Jesus,
    Of Thy heart;
  To be with Thee in the glory,
    Where Thou art.
  Love so groundless,
    Grace so boundless,
  Grace so boundless
    Wins my heart.

6 When Thy blood-bought church,
    Lord Jesus,
  Is complete;
    When each soul is safely landed
  At Thy feet;
    What a story
  In the glory,
    In the glory
  She'll repeat!

7 Oh, to praise Thee there, Lord Jesus,
    Evermore!
  Oh, to grieve and wander from Thee
    Nevermore!
  Earth's sad story
    Closed in glory,
  Closed in glory
    On yon shore!

8 Then Thy church will be, Lord Jesus,
    The display
  Of Thy richest grace and kindness
    In that day;
  Marking pages,
    Wondrous stages,
  Wondrous stages,
    O'er earth's way.

512

8.7.8.7.D.

SAVIOUR, lead us by Thy power
  Safe into the promised rest;
Choose the path, the way whatever
  Seems to Thee, O Lord, the best:
Be our guide in every peril,
  Watch and keep us night and day,
Else our foolish hearts will wander
  From the straight and narrow way.

2 Since in Thee is our redemption,
   And salvation full and free,
Nothing need our souls dishearten
   But forgetfulness of Thee:
Naught can stay our steady progress,
   More than conquerors are we,
If our eyes, whate'er the danger,
   Look to Thee, and none but Thee.

3 In Thy presence we are happy;
   In Thy presence we're secure;
In Thy presence all afflictions
   We can steadfastly endure;
In Thy presence we can conquer,
   We can suffer, we can die;
Wandering from Thee we are feeble;
   Let Thy love then keep us nigh.

513   P.M.

S AVIOUR, more than life to me,
   I am clinging, clinging close to
Thee;
   Let Thy precious blood applied,
Keep me ever, ever near Thy side.

Every day, every hour,
   Let me feel Thy cleansing power;
May Thy tender love to me
   Bind me closer, closer, Lord, to
      Thee.

2 Through this changing world below,
   Lead me gently, gently as I go;
Trusting Thee I cannot stray,
   I can never, never lose my way.

3 Let me love Thee more and more,
   Till this fleeting, fleeting life is o'er;
Till my soul is lost in love,
   In a brighter, brighter world above.

514   8.7.8.7.

S AVIOUR, round these emblems
   blessèd,
Here we gather to Thy name;
   We remember Thy blest Person,
All Thy suffering, death and shame.

2 We recall Thy grace in coming,
   From Thy Father's side above,
To this scene of sin and darkness,
   To make known His perfect love.

3 In Thy blessèd Holy Person,
   God and man in one unite;
All the fulness of the Godhead
   Manifested to our sight.

4 We remember all Thy pathway
   Of delight and joy to God;
Bringing glory ever to Him,
   Perfect was Thy way, O Lord.

5 With these emblems thus before us,
   We recall Thy death of shame;
Yet remember all the glory
   That it brought to Thy blest name.

515   8.7.8.5.D.

S AVIOUR, Thou art waiting, waiting,
   Waiting for Thy blood-bought Bride,
Waiting for Thy heart's deep longing
   To be satisfied;
Waiting for the joyous moment,
   Watching us with tender care,
Till at Thy command upspringing,
   We Thy glory share.

2 Saviour, we are waiting, waiting,
   Waiting, blessèd Lord, for Thee,
Waiting for the calling upward,
   With our Lord to be:
Long and lone hath been the pathway,
   Oft our hearts have failed with fear;
But the guiding star of morning
   Heralds Thee as near.

3 They are waiting, waiting, waiting,
   Loved ones who have gone before -
Waiting for the sweet home-bringing,
   Parting nevermore,
Oh, the joy, the bliss, the rapture -
   All our tears and sorrows past,
Singing, with triumphant praises,
   "Safely home at last!"

4 Keep us, blessèd Jesus, waiting,
   Clinging to Thy precious word;
Every footstep of the journey,
   Waiting for our Lord;
Waiting till within the mansions
   We behold Thy glorious face,
Singing all the wondrous story
   Of Thy matchless grace.

516   8.7.8.7.4.7.

SAVIOUR, through the desert
   lead us!
Without Thee we cannot go;
   Thou from cruel chains hast freed us,
Thou hast laid the tyrant low;
   Let Thy presence
Cheer us all our journey through.

2 With a price Thy love has bought us;
   Saviour, what a love is Thine!
Hitherto Thy power has brought us,
   Power and love in Thee combine:
Lord of Glory,
   Ever on Thy people shine.

3 Through a desert, waste and cheerless,
   Though our destined journey lie,
Rendered by Thy presence fearless,
   We may every foe defy:
Nought shall move us
   While we see Thee, Saviour, nigh.

4 When we halt, no track discovering,
   Fearful lest we go astray,
O'er our path Thy pillar hovering,
   Fire by night, and cloud by day,
Shall direct us
   That we may not miss our way.

5 When we hunger Thou wilt feed us;
   Manna shall our camp surround;
Faint and thirsty, Thou wilt heed us,
   Streams shall from the rock abound:
Happy people!
   What a Saviour we have found!

517   6.4.6.4.6.6.6.4.

SAVIOUR, Thy dying love
   Thou gavest me,
Nor should I aught withhold,
   My Lord, from Thee;
In love my soul would bow,
   My heart fulfil its vow,
Some offering bring Thee now,
   Something for Thee.

2 At the blest mercy-seat
   Pleading for me,
My feeble faith looks up,
   Jesus, to Thee;

Help me the cross to bear,
   Thy wondrous love declare,
Some song to raise, or prayer,
   Something for Thee.

3 Give me a faithful heart,
   Likeness to Thee;
That each departing day
   Henceforth may see
Some work of love begun,
   Some deed of kindness done,
Some wanderer sought and won,
   Something for Thee.

4 All that I am and have,
   Thy gifts so free;
In joy, in grief, through life,
   O Lord, for Thee!
And when Thy face I see
   My ransomed soul shall be,
Through all eternity,
   Something for Thee.

518   7.7.7.6.

SAVIOUR, we remember Thee!
   Thy deep woe and agony,
All Thy suffering on the tree:
   Saviour, we adore Thee.

2 Calvary! O Calvary!
   Mercy's vast unfathomed sea,
Love, eternal love to me:
   Saviour, we adore Thee.

3 Darkness hung around Thy head,
   When for sin Thy blood was shed,
Victim in the sinner's stead:
   Saviour, we adore Thee.

4 Jesus, Lord, Thou now art risen!
   Thou hast all our sins forgiven;
Haste we to our home in heaven:
   Saviour, we adore Thee.

5 Soon, with joyful, glad surprise,
   We shall hear Thy word - Arise!
Mounting upward to the skies:
   Glory, glory, glory!

6 Saviour, we Thy love adore;
   We will praise Thee more and more;
Spread Thy Name from shore to shore:
   Saviour, we adore Thee.

519
C.M.D.

SHOW me Thy face - one
  transient gleam
Of loveliness divine,
  And I shall never think or dream
Of other love save Thine;
  All lesser lights will darken quite,
All lower glories wane,
  The beautiful of earth will scarce
Seem beautiful again.

2 Show me Thy face - my faith and love
    Shall henceforth fixèd be,
  And nothing here have power to move
    My soul's serenity.
  My life shall seem a trance, a dream,
    And all I feel and see,
  Illusive, visionary -Thou
    The one reality.

3 Show me Thy face - I shall forget
    The weary days of yore;
  The fretting ghosts of vain regret
    Shall haunt my soul no more.
  All doubts and fears for future years
    In quiet trust subside;
  And naught but blest content and calm
    Within my breast abide.

4 Show me Thy face - the heaviest cross
    Will then seem light to bear;
  There will be gain in every loss,
    And peace with every care.
  With such light feet the years will fleet,
    Life will seem brief as blest,
  Till I have laid my burden down
    And entered into rest.

5 Show me Thy face - and I shall be
    In heart and mind renewed,
  With wisdom, grace, and energy
    To work Thy work, endued.
  Shine clear, though pale, behind
    the veil,
  Until, the veil removed,
    In perfect glory I behold
  The face that I have loved!

520
L.M.

SHOW me Thy wounds, exalted
  Lord!
Thou hast the power and skill divine,

Since Justice smote Thee with the
    sword,
  To make my heart resemble Thine.

2 Oh, grant me ever to behold,
    With heavenly wisdom's piercing eye,
  Thy pains of death, for they unfold
    Thy name, Thou Son of God,
      Most High!

3 Show me Thy wounds, and by Thy skill
    May I, my Saviour, be refined,
  To do, like Thee, the Father's will,
    And serve Him with a perfect mind.

521
7.7.7.7.D.

SIMPLY trusting every day,
  Trusting through a stormy way;
Even when my faith is small,
  Trusting Jesus, that is all.

Trusting Him while life shall last,
  Trusting Him till earth is past,
Till within the jasper wall;
  Trusting Jesus, that is all.

2 Brightly doth His Spirit shine
    Into this poor heart of mine;
  While He leads I cannot fall,
    Trusting Jesus, that is all.

3 Singing, if my way is clear,
    Praying, if the path is drear;
  If in danger, for Him call;
    Trusting Jesus, that is all.

4 Trusting as the moments fly,
    Trusting as the days go by;
  Trusting Him whate'er befall,
    Trusting Jesus, that is all.

522
8.7.8.7. with Chorus

SING the wondrous love of Jesus,
  Sing His mercy and His grace;
In the mansions, bright and blessèd,
  He'll prepare for us a place.

When we all get to heaven,
  What a day of rejoicing that will be!
When we all see Jesus,
  We'll sing and shout the victory!

2 While we walk the pilgrim pathway,
    Clouds will overspread the sky;
But when trav'lling days are over,
    Not a shadow, not a sigh.

3 Let us, then, be true and faithful,
    Trusting, serving every day;
Just one glimpse of Him in glory
    Will the toils of life repay.

4 Onward to the prize before us!
    Soon His beauty we'll behold;
Soon the pearly gates will open;
    We shall tread the streets of gold.

523   7.7.7.6.

SING to God my spirit sing,
    Joyful praise and worship bring!
He whom sinners mocked as King -
    He shall bear the glory!

2 He in lowly guise who came
    Bore the spitting and the shame,
His the highest place and name -
    He shall bear the glory.

3 He who wept above the grave,
    He who stilled the raging wave,
Meek to suffer, strong to save -
    He shall bear the glory.

4 He who sorrow's pathway trod,
    He that every good bestowed,
Son of Man and Son of God -
    He shall bear the glory.

5 He who bled with scourging sore,
    Thorns and scarlet meekly wore,
He who every sorrow bore -
    He shall bear the glory.

6 Monarch of the smitten cheek,
    Scorn of Jew and scorn of Greek,
Priest and King, divinely meek -
    He shall bear the glory.

7 On the rainbow-circled throne
    Mid the myriads of His own,
Nevermore to weep alone -
    He shall bear the glory.

8 Man of slighted Nazareth -
    King who wore the thorny wreath -
Son obedient unto death -
    He shall bear the glory.

9 His the grand eternal weight,
    His the priestly-regal state;
Him the Father maketh great -
    He shall bear the glory.

10 He who died to set us free,
    He who lives and loves e'en me,
He who comes, whom I shall see -
    He shall bear the glory.

524   11.10.11.10.

SO send I you to labour
    unrewarded,
To serve unpaid, unloved, unsought,
    unknown,
To bear rebuke, to suffer scorn and
    scoffing -
So send I you to toil for Me alone.

2 So send I you - by grace made
        strong to triumph
    O'er hosts of hell, o'er darkness,
        death and sin,
    My name to bear and in that name
        to conquer -
    So send I you, My victory to win.

3 So send I you to bind the bruised
        and broken,
    O'er wand'ring souls to work, to
        weep, to wake,
    To bear the burdens of a world
        a-weary -
    So send I you to suffer for My sake.

4 So send I you - to take to souls in
        bondage
    The Word of Truth that sets the
        captive free,
    To break the bonds of sin, to loose
        death's fetters -
    So send I you, to bring the lost to Me.

5 So send I you to loneliness and
        longing,
    With heart a-hung'ring for the loved
        and known,
    Forsaking home and kindred, friend
        and dear one -
    So send I you to know My love alone.

6 So send I you - My strength to know
        in weakness,
    My joy in grief, My perfect peace in
        pain,

To prove My pow'r, My grace, My
promised presence -
So send I you, eternal fruit to gain.

7 So send I you to leave your life's
ambition,
To die to dear desire, self-will resign,
To labour long, and love where
men revile you -
So send I you to lose your life in Mine.

8 So send I you - to bear My cross
with patience,
And then one day with joy to lay it
down,
To hear My voice, "Well done, My
faithful servant -
Come share My throne, My kingdom
and My crown!"

525   L.M.D.
S OME day the silver cord will break,
  And I no more as now shall sing;
But, Oh, the joy when I shall wake
Within the palace of the King!

And I shall see Him face to face,
And tell the story - Saved by grace;
And I shall see Him face to face,
And tell the story - Saved by grace.

2 Some day my earthly house will fall,
I cannot tell how soon 'twill be,
But this I know - my All in All
Has now a place in heav'n for me.

3 Some day, when fades the golden sun
Beneath the rosy-tinted west,
My blessèd Lord shall say, "Well done!"
And I shall enter into rest.

4 Some day; till then I'll watch and wait,
My lamp all trimmed and burning
bright,
That when my Saviour ope's the gate,
My soul to Him may take its flight.

526   9.9.9.9. with Chorus
S OME glorious morning, sorrow
  will cease,
Some glorious morning, all will be
peace;
Heartaches all ended, labour all done,
Heaven will open - Jesus will come.

Some golden daybreak, Jesus will
come;
Some golden daybreak, battles all
won,
He'll shout the vict'ry, break through
the blue,
Some golden day-break, for me, for
you.

2 Sad hearts will gladden, all shall be
bright,
Goodbye forever to earth's dark night;
Changed in a moment, like Him
to be,
Oh, glorious daybreak, Jesus I'll see!

3 Oh, what a meeting, there in the skies,
No tears nor crying shall dim our
eyes;
Loved ones united, eternally,
Oh, what a daybreak, that morn
will be!

527   7.6.7.6.D.
S OMETIMES a light surprises
  The Christian while he sings;
It is the Lord who rises
With healing in His wings;
When comforts are declining,
He grants the soul again
A season of clear shining,
To cheer it after rain.

2 In holy contemplation
We sweetly then pursue
The theme of God's salvation,
And find it ever new;
Set free from present sorrow,
We cheerfully can say -
E'en let the unknown morrow
Bring with it what it may.

3 It can bring with it nothing,
But He will bear us through;
Who gives the lilies clothing,
Will clothe His people too:
Beneath the spreading heavens
No creature but is fed;
And He who feeds the ravens,
Will give His children bread.

4 Though vine nor fig tree neither
    Their wonted fruit shall bear;
Though all the fields should wither
    Nor flocks nor herds be there;
Yet God the same abiding,
    His praise shall tune my voice,
For, while in Him confiding,
    I cannot but rejoice.

528   7.7.7.7.

S ON of God, exalted now,
  Highest honours crown Thy brow;
On the Father's throne divine,
    All the Conqueror's triumphs Thine.

2 Here Thy cup was grief and shame,
    Here, despised Thy lowly name;
Hour of darkness, power of hell,
    On Thy spotless soul then fell.

3 Now Thy travail all is o'er,
    Thou shalt humbled be no more;
Joy to Thee shall ever flow
    From Thy toil and shame below.

4 Son of God, exalted now,
    Thee we worship, bending low;
This the Father claims for Thee -
    Reverent lip and bowèd knee.

5 Gather now full many a gem,
    Saviour, for Thy diadem -
Trophies of Thy toil and love,
    Meet to shine in courts above.

6 Speed the bright, millennial day,
    Call Thy Bride to come away;
Through the earth let joy and song
    Thy glad triumph roll along!

529   8.7.8.7.D.

S ON of God, 'twas love that made
  Thee
Die, our ruined souls to save;
    'Twas our sins' vast load that laid
    Thee,
Lord of Life, within the grave;
    But Thy glorious resurrection
Showed Thee conqueror o'er the tomb;
    So the saints by Thy protection
Through Thy work shall overcome.

2 Thou to heaven hast now ascended,
    Ent'ring there by Thine own blood;
All Thy work of suff'ring ended,
    Fully wrought the will of God.
For Thy Church Thou still art caring,
    For us pleading in Thy love;
And our place of rest preparing
    In the Father's house above.

3 Now the Holy Ghost doth gather
    Unto God Thy people here;
We, as sons, cry, "Abba, Father!"
    His great love excluding fear:
What a debt of love we owe Thee,
    Love that we can ne'er express,
Since we, through the Spirit, know Thee,
    Christ the Lord, our righteousness.

530   8.7.8.7.D.

S ON of God! with joy we praise Thee,
  On the Father's throne above;
All Thy wondrous work display Thee,
    Full of grace, and full of love:
Lord, accept our adoration -
    For our sins Thou once wast slain;
Through Thy blood we have salvation,
    And with Thee we soon shall reign.

2 God, in Thee His love unfolding,
    Shows how rich has been His grace;
We are blest, with joy beholding
    All His glory in Thy face;
In His counsel, ere creation,
    All the Church He chose in Thee;
And our Surety for salvation
    Thou wast then ordained to be.

3 When it seemed that sin must sever
    All the chosen heirs from God,
Thou, with love which faileth never,
    Didst redeem us by Thy blood:
Oh, the mercy which hath blest us,
    Purposed thus ere time began -
Mercy which in Thee hath kept us,
    Mercy vast, like heaven's span!

531   S.M.

S OON shall our Master come,
  Our toil and sorrow cease;
He'll call His waiting servants home
    To endless joy and peace.

2 *Now* may we do His will,
   In all His footsteps tread;
And, in a world of evil, still
   To grieve Him only dread.

3 May we His name confess
   'Midst suffering, shame, and loss;
Stand forth His faithful witnesses,
   And glory in the Cross.

4 Watchful may we be found,
   Our loins well girded be;
In works of faith and love abound,
   Till we our Master see.

5 Then shall we soar above,
   Nor cease our sweet employ,
And hear Him say, with tenderest love,
   "Enter thy Master's joy".

532   10.10.10.10.10.10.
S OON will the Master come -
   soon pass away
Our times of conflict, grief and
   suffering here;
Our night of weeping end in
   cloudless day,
And sorrow's moment like a dream
   appear:
Eternity with Jesus, in the skies -
   How soon that Sun of
      righteousness may rise!

2 We shall behold Him whom unseen
   we love,
   We shall be with Him whom we long
   to see;
   We shall be like Him, fit for realms
   above -
   With Him, and like Him, for eternity:
   If now to sit at Jesus' feet our
      choice,
   How will fruition then our souls rejoice!

533   P.M.
S ORROWS abounding,
   Beyond human sounding,
Darkness surrounding,
   Low He prayed and wept;
Deep were they sleeping
   Who watch should have kept,
While He, with weeping,
   Prayed the while they slept.

2 Sorrows exceeding,
   Beyond human heeding,
Burdened His pleading
   In that gloomy glade;
Prayer with strong crying
   And tears there He made
On the ground, lying
   Prostrate as He prayed.

3 Sorrows unsparing,
   Beyond human bearing,
Too deep for sharing,
   Bowed His holy head;
Darkness besetting,
   Of prospects so dread,
With blood-like sweating
   Tearfully He pled.

4 Sorrows o'erflowing,
   Beyond human knowing,
Too deep for showing,
   Unto agony!
There, the cup taking,
   He rose to obey
Unto forsaking,
   In humility.

534   8.7.8.7.4.7.
S OVEREIGN grace! o'er sin
   abounding,
Ransomed souls, the tidings swell;
   'Tis a deep that knows no sounding;
Who its breadth or length can tell?
      On its glories
Let my soul for ever dwell!

2 What from Christ the soul can sever,
   Bound by everlasting bands?
Once in Him, in Him for ever,
   Thus the eternal covenant stands:
      None shall pluck thee
From the Strength of Israel's hands.

3 Heirs of God, joint-heirs with Jesus
   Long ere time its race began;
To His Name eternal praises,
   O what wonders love hath done!
      One with Jesus;
By eternal union one.

4 On such love, my soul, still ponder,
   Love so great, so rich, so free!
Say, while lost in holy wonder,
   Why, O Lord, such love to me?
      Hallelujah!
Grace shall reign eternally.

535 P.M.

SOWING the seed by the daylight
fair,
Sowing the seed by the noonday glare,
  Sowing the seed by the fading light,
Sowing the seed in the solemn night;
  Oh, what shall the harvest be?

Sown in the darkness or sown in
* the light,*
Sown in our weakness or sown in
* our might;*
Gathered in time or eternity,
* Sure, ah, sure will the harvest be!*

2 Sowing the seed by the wayside high,
  Sowing the seed on the rocks to die,
Sowing the seed where the thorns
  will spoil,
Sowing the seed in the fertile soil;
  Oh, what shall the harvest be?

3 Sowing the seed with an aching heart,
  Sowing the seed while the
    teardrops start,
Sowing in hope till the reapers come
  Gladly to gather the harvest home;
Oh, what shall the harvest be?

536 6.5.6.5.

SPEAK, Lord, in the stillness,
  While I wait on Thee;
Hush my heart to listen
  In expectancy.

2 Speak, O blessèd Master,
  In this quiet hour;
Let me see Thy face, Lord,
  Feel Thy touch of power.

3 For the words Thou speakest,
  They are life indeed;
Living Bread from heaven
  Now my spirit feed.

4 All to Thee is yielded,
  I am not my own;
Blissful, glad surrender,
  I am Thine alone.

5 Speak, Thy servant heareth,
  Be not silent, Lord;

Waits my soul upon Thee
  For the quickening word.

6 Fill me with the knowledge
  Of Thy glorious will;
All Thine own good pleasure
  In Thy child fulfil.

7 Like a watered garden,
  Full of fragrance rare,
Lingering in Thy presence
  Let my life appear.

537 8.7.8.7.

"STRICKEN, smitten and afflicted",
  See Him dying on the tree!
'Tis the Christ, by man rejected;
  Yes, my soul, 'tis He! 'tis He!

2 Many hands were raised to wound Him,
  None would interpose to save;
But the awful stroke that bowed Him
  Was the stroke that Justice gave.

3 Mark the Sacrifice appointed!
  See *Who* bears the awful load!
'Tis the Word, the Lord's Anointed,
  Son of man and Son of God!

4 Here we have a firm foundation;
  Here the refuge of the lost:
Christ, the rock of our salvation:
  His the name in which we boast.

5 Lamb of God, for sinners wounded!
  Sacrifice to cancel guilt!
None shall ever be confounded
  Who on Thee their hopes have built.

538 L.M.

SWEET are the seasons when
  we wait
To hear what God our Lord will say,
  For they who watch at Wisdom's
    gate
Are never empty sent away.

2 Behold us, Lord, a few of Thine,
  Who hither come to seek Thy face;
In mercy on Thy people shine
  And let Thy presence fill the place.

3 How sweet, how blessèd is the thought
   That Thou dost hear Thy people's
      cries!
   And whether Thou dost give, or not,
      'Tis love that grants, and love denies.

4 O teach us, Lord, to wait Thy will,
   To be content with all Thou dost;
   For us, Thy grace sufficient still,
      With most supplied when needing
      most.

5 Till life shall end, thus let it be,
      And, O sustain us in that hour;
   That conflict past, we hope to see
      The Saviour whom we here adore.

6 We hope at length to take our part
      With yonder host, through trouble
      brought;
   We hope to see Thee as Thou art
      And then to praise Thee as we
      ought.

539   S.M.

S WEET feast of love divine!
      'Tis grace that makes us free
To feed upon this bread and wine,
   In memory, Lord, of Thee.

2 Here every welcome guest
      Waits, Lord, from Thee to learn
   The secrets of Thy Father's breast,
      And all Thy grace discern.

3 Here conscience ends its strife,
      And faith delights to prove
   The sweetness of the Bread of Life,
      The fulness of Thy love.

4 That blood that flowed for sin
      In symbol here we see,
   And feel the blessèd pledge within
      That we are loved of Thee.

5 Oh! If this glimpse of love
      Is so divinely sweet,
   What will it be, O Lord, above,
      Thy gladdening smile to meet!

6 To see Thee face to face,
      Thy perfect likeness wear,
   And all Thy ways of wondrous grace
      Through endless years declare.

540   L.M.D.

S WEET hour of prayer! sweet
      hour of prayer!
That calls me from a world of care,
   And bids me at my Father's throne
Make all my wants and wishes known.
   In seasons of distress and grief,
My soul has often found relief,
   And oft escaped the tempter's snare,
By thy return, sweet hour of prayer!

2 Sweet hour of prayer! sweet hour
   of prayer!
The joy I feel, the bliss I share,
   Of those whose anxious spirits burn
With strong desires for thy return!
   With such I hasten to the place
Where God, my Saviour, shows His
   face,
And gladly take my station there,
   And wait for thee, sweet hour of
   prayer!

3 Sweet hour of prayer! sweet hour
   of prayer!
Thy wings shall my petition bear
   To Him whose truth and faithfulness
Engage the waiting soul to bless;
   And since He bids me seek His face,
Believe His Word and trust His grace,
   I'll cast on Him my every care,
And wait for thee, sweet hour of
   prayer!

4 Sweet hour of prayer! sweet hour
   of prayer!
May I thy consolation share,
   Till, from Mount Pisgah's lofty height,
I view my home and take my flight.
   This robe of flesh I'll drop, and rise
To seize the everlasting prize,
   And shout, while passing through
   the air,
"Farewell, farewell, sweet hour of
   prayer!"

541   L.M.

S WEET is the savour of His Name
      Who suffered in His people's
stead;
   His portion here, reproach and
   shame:
He liveth now; He once was dead.

2 He once was dead; the very same
  Who sits on yonder throne above;
Who bears in heaven the greatest
  Name,
Whom angels serve, whom angels
  love.

3 He once was dead; the very same
  Who made the worlds - a work of
    power,
Who now upholds the mighty frame,
  And keeps it till the final hour.

4 He once was dead; but now He lives,
  His glory fills all heaven above;
Its blessèdness to heaven He gives,
  The fountain He of joy and love.

5 His people shall His triumph share,
  With Him shall live, and with Him
    reign;
In heaven their joy is full, for there
  They see the Lamb for sinners slain.

542   8.7.8.7.

S WEET the moments, rich in
  blessing,
Which before the Cross we spend,
  Life, and health, and peace
    possessing
From the sinner's dying Friend.

2 Here we rest, in wonder viewing
  All our sins on Jesus laid,
And a full redemption flowing
  From the sacrifice He made.

3 Here we find the dawn of heaven,
  While upon the Cross we gaze,
See our trespasses forgiven,
  And our songs of triumph raise.

4 Oh that near the Cross abiding,
  We may to the Saviour cleave!
Nought with Him our hearts dividing,
  All for Him content to leave.

5 May we still, the Cross discerning,
  There for peace and comfort go;
There new wonders daily learning,
  All the depths of mercy know.

543   7.7.7.7.

S WEET the theme of Jesus' love!
  Sweet the theme, all themes above;
Love, unmerited and free,
  Our triumphant song shall be.

2 Love so vast that nought can bound;
  Love too deep for thought to sound;
Love which made the Lord of all
  Drink the wormwood and the gall.

3 Love which led Him to the Cross,
  Bearing there unuttered loss;
Love which brought Him to the gloom
  Of the cold and darksome tomb.

4 Love which made Him thence arise
  Far above the starry skies;
There, with tender, loving care,
  All His people's griefs to share.

5 Love which will not let Him rest
  Till His chosen all are blest;
Till they all for whom He died
  Live rejoicing at His side.

544   7.7.7.7.

S WEETER sounds than music knows
  Charm me in Immanuel's Name;
All her hopes my spirit owes
  To His birth, His Cross, His shame.

2 When He came, the angels sang,
  "Glory be to God on high!"
Lord, unloose my stammering tongue;
  Who should louder sing than I?

3 Did the Lord a man become
  That He might the law fulfil,
Bleed and suffer in my room;
  And canst thou, my tongue, be still?

4 No! I must my praises bring,
  Though they worthless are and weak,
For should I refuse to sing,
  Sure the very stones would speak.

5 O my Saviour, Shield, and Sun,
  Shepherd, Counsellor, and Friend!
Every precious name in one;
  I will love Thee without end.

545

7.7.7.7.

TAKE my life, and let it be
Consecrated, Lord, to Thee;
Take my moments and my days,
Let them flow in ceaseless praise.

2 Take my hands, and let them move
At the impulse of Thy love;
Take my feet, and let them be
Swift and *beautiful* for Thee.

3 Take my voice, and let me sing
Always, only, for my King;
Take my lips, and let them be
Filled with messages from Thee.

4 Take my silver and my gold,
Not a mite would I withhold;
Take my intellect, and use
Every power as Thou shalt choose.

5 Take my will, and make it Thine,
It shall be no longer mine;
Take my heart - it is Thine own,
It shall be Thy royal throne.

6 Take my love; my Lord, I pour
At Thy feet its treasure-store:
Take myself, and I will be
Ever, only, ALL for Thee.

546

8.7.8.7. with Chorus

TAKE the name of Jesus with you,
Child of sorrow and of woe;
It will joy and comfort give you -
Take it, then, where'er you go.

Precious name, Oh, how sweet!
Hope of earth and joy of heaven;
Precious name, Oh, how sweet!
Hope of earth and joy of heaven.

2 Take the name of Jesus ever,
As a shield from every snare;
If temptations round you gather,
Breathe that holy name in prayer.

3 Oh, the precious name of Jesus!
How it thrills our souls with joy,
When His loving arms receive us,
And His songs our tongues employ!

4 At the name of Jesus bowing,
Falling prostrate at His feet;
King of kings in heaven we'll crown Him
When our journey is complete.

547

8.7.8.7.D.

TAKE the world, but give me Jesus,
All its joys are but a name;
But His love abideth ever,
Through eternal years the same.

Oh, the height and depth of mercy!
Oh, the length and breadth of love!
Oh, the fulness of redemption,
Pledge of endless life above.

2 Take the world, but give me Jesus,
Sweetest comfort of my soul;
With my Saviour watching o'er me
I can sing, though billows roll.

3 Take the world, but give me Jesus,
Let me see His constant smile;
Then throughout my pilgrim journey
Light will cheer me all the while.

4 Take the world, but give me Jesus,
In His Cross my trust shall be,
Till, with clearer, brighter vision,
Face to face my Lord I see.

548

11.11.11.11.

TAKE time to be holy, speak oft
with thy Lord;
Abide in Him always, and feed on
His Word.
Make friends of God's children, help
those who are weak;
Forgetting in nothing His blessing
to seek.

2 Take time to be holy, the world
rushes on;
Spend much time in secret, with
Jesus alone.
By looking to Jesus, like Him thou
shalt be;
Thy friends in thy conduct His
likeness shall see.

3 Take time to be holy, let Him be thy
Guide;
And run not before Him, whatever
betide.

In joy or in sorrow, still follow thy Lord,
   And, looking to Jesus, still trust in
      His Word.

4 Take time to be holy, be calm in thy
      soul;
   Each thought and each motive
      beneath His control.
   Thus led by His Spirit to fountains
      of love,
   Thou soon shalt be fitted for service
      above.

549
6.4.6.4.6.6.6.4.

TEACH me Thy way, O Lord,
   Teach me Thy way!
Thy gracious aid afford,
   Teach me Thy way!
Help me to walk aright,
   More by faith, less by sight;
Lead me with heavenly light,
   Teach me Thy way!

2 When I am sad at heart,
   Teach me Thy way!
When earthly joys depart,
   Teach me Thy way!
In hours of loneliness,
   In times of dire distress,
In failure or success,
   Teach me Thy way!

3 When doubts and fears arise,
   Teach me Thy way!
When storms o'erspread the skies
   Teach me Thy way!
Shine through the cloud and rain,
   Through sorrow, toil and pain;
Make Thou my pathway plain,
   Teach me Thy way!

4 Long as my life shall last,
   Teach me Thy way!
Where'er my lot is cast,
   Teach me Thy way!
Until the race is run,
   Until the journey's done,
Until the crown is won,
   Teach me Thy way!

550
C.M.

THAT night in which He was
   betrayed,
In love's attention sweet,
   And with the lowly towel arrayed,
He washed His followers' feet.

2 That night in love the loaf He took,
   He blessed, He brake, He gave,
And mem'ry gives the backward look
   That parting love would crave.

3 That night the cup He took, anew
   Gave thanks, and lovingly,
He poured it out and said, "This do
   In memory of Me".

4 That night His thoughtful love was
      shown,
   When He provision made,
   Not for Himself, but for His own,
And to His Father prayed.

5 That night the last few steps He took
   Of all that wondrous way,
And passed o'er Kidron's wintry brook
   Into Gethsemane.

6 That night, that sad and solemn night,
   Alone, He wept and prayed;
That night, that memorable night
   In which He was betrayed.

551
S.M.

"THAT sight" of love unveiled
   Our vision fills anew -
Upon a Cross, by foes assailed,
   The Son of God we view.

2 In such a scene of hate,
   With scorn upon Him cast,
His grace appears, His meekness
      great,
   His condescension vast.

3 Deep calleth unto deep,
   While sorrows that appal
Like raging floods around Him sweep;
   Unmoved, He bears it all.

4 We see His purpose true,
    The Scriptures to fulfil,
In absolute obedience to
    His Father's holy will.

5 The gathered fragrance sweet
    From all the path He trod,
Now at His death, ascends complete
    As incense unto God.

6 Our sacrifice of praise
    To Thee, O God, we bring;
We worship as on Him we gaze,
    And as of Him we sing.

552
6.6.6.6.8.8.

THE atoning work is done,
    The Victim's blood is shed;
And Jesus now has gone
    His people's cause to plead.
He stands in heaven, their great
    High Priest,
And bears their names upon His
    breast.

2 He sprinkled with His blood
    The mercy-seat above;
For justice had withstood
    The purposes of love:
But justice now withstands no more,
    And mercy yields its boundless
        store.

3 No temple made with hands
    His place of service is;
In heaven itself He stands,
    A heavenly priesthood His:
In Him the shadows of the law
    Are all fulfilled, and now withdraw.

4 And though awhile He be
    Hid from the eyes of men,
His people look to see
    Their great High Priest again:
In brightest glory He will come
    And take His waiting people home.

553
10.10.10.10.

THE bread and wine are spread
    upon the board,
The guests are here, invited by the
    Lord;
Why come they thus? Why tarry for
    a space?
But for Thy presence, O Thou King
    of grace.

2 Hush, O our hearts, as in the sacred
    name
We bow in worship and the promise
    claim -
Where two or three are gathered
    there am I,
Unseen, yet present to faith's
    opened eye.

3 Here in our midst art Thou, O risen
    Lord;
Worthy, O Lamb once slain, to be
    adored;
Here in our midst to lead Thy
    people's praise,
And incense sweet unto the Father
    raise.

4 We do remember Thee, as Thou
    hast said,
And think upon Thee as we break
    the bread,
Recall Thy dying love, Thy Cross
    and shame,
Drinking the cup of blessing in Thy
    name.

5 Thus do we show the death of our
    dear Lord,
While in our hearts His love is shed
    abroad;
So is faith quickened for the conflict
    here,
Till in a little while He shall appear.

6 Only a little while we pilgrims stay
    To spread the table on our desert
        way;
Soon will He come, and coming take
    us home,
Amen, e'en so, Lord Jesus quickly
    come!

554
7.6.7.6.D.

THE Church's one foundation
    Is Jesus Christ her Lord:
She is His new creation
    By water and the Word;
From heaven He came and sought her
    To be His holy bride;
With His own blood He bought her,
    And for her life He died.

2 Elect from every nation,
   Yet one o'er all the earth,
Her charter of salvation
   One Lord, one faith, one birth:
One holy name she blesses,
   Partakes one holy food,
And to one hope she presses,
   With every grace endued.

3 Though with a scornful wonder
   Men see her sore oppressed,
By schisms rent asunder,
   By heresies distressed,
Yet saints their watch are keeping,
   Their cry goes up, "How long?"
And soon the night of weeping
   Shall be the morn of song.

4 'Mid toil and tribulation,
   And tumult of her war,
She waits the consummation
   Of peace for evermore,
Till, with the vision glorious,
   Her longing eyes are blest,
And the great Church victorious
   Shall be the Church at rest.

5 Yet she on earth hath union
   With God the Three in One,
And mystic sweet communion
   With those whose rest is won;
Oh, happy ones and holy!
   Lord, give us grace that we,
Like them, the meek and lowly,
   On high may dwell with Thee!

555   7.6.7.6.D.

THE cloudless day is nearing,
   When Thou, O Lord, wilt come,
Thy radiant beauty wearing,
   To take Thy people home!
Bright hosts on hosts around Thee
   Shall catch Thy living rays,
And all who once have found Thee
   Breathe out new songs of praise.

2 But how shall I then know Thee
   Amid those hosts above?
What tokens true will show me
   The object of my love?
Thy glories, all excelling,
   In pure effulgence shine;
But glory in Thee dwelling
   Will ne'er proclaim Thee mine.

3 Thy wounds, Thy wounds, Lord Jesus,
   Those deep, deep wounds will tell
The sacrifice that frees us
   From self, and death, and hell!
These link Thee once for ever
   With all who own Thy grace;
No hand these bonds can sever,
   No hand these scars efface.

4 O Jesus! Lord most blessèd,
   Thou Lamb of God divine,
Thou standest forth confessèd,
   I wondering, claim Thee mine.
I worship and adore Thee,
   Transported with Thy love;
Prostrate myself before Thee,
   And dwell in light above.

556   L.M.

THE countless multitude on high,
   Who tune their songs to Jesus'
name,
All merit of their own deny,
And Jesus' worth alone proclaim.

2 Firm on the ground of sovereign grace
   They stand before Jehovah's throne;
The only song in that blest place
   Is - "Thou art worthy, Thou alone!"

3 "Salvation's glory all be paid
   To Him who sits upon the throne,
And to the Lamb whose blood was
shed;
Thou! Thou art worthy, Thou alone."

4 "For Thou wast slain, and in Thy blood
   These robes were washed so
      spotless pure!
Thou mad'st us kings and priests
   to God:
For ever let Thy praise endure!"

5 Let us with joy adopt the strain
   We soon shall sing for ever there -
"Worthy's the Lamb for sinners slain
   Worthy alone the crown to wear!"

6 Without one thought that's good to
      plead,
   Oh, what could shield us from
      despair,
But this, though we are vile indeed,
   The Lord our righteousness is there!

557
C.M.

THE Cross! the Cross! the blood-
    stained Cross!
The Cross of Christ I see,
    It tells me of that precious blood
That once was shed for me.

2 The wrath! the wrath! the awful wrath
    That Jesus felt for me!
When bearing my sin's heavy load
    He died on Calvary.

3 But Jesus lives! the Saviour lives!
    In heaven He pleads for me;
And boldly I approach to God,
    His blood my only plea.

4 The crown! the crown! the glorious
    crown!
The crown of victory!
    The crown of life! it shall be mine
When I the Saviour see.

5 He comes! He comes! the Saviour
    comes!
Who bled and died for me;
    Then will I sing, with rapture sing,
When gazing, Lord, on Thee.

558
7.6.7.6.D.

THE day of glory bearing
    Its brightness far and near
The day of Christ's appearing,
    We now no longer fear;
For we shall rise to meet Him
    Triumphant in the sky,
And every heart shall greet Him
    With songs of victory.

2 He once, a spotless Victim,
    For us, on Calvary bled;
Jehovah did afflict Him,
    And bruise Him in our stead;
To Him by grace united,
    We joy in Him alone;
And now, by faith, delighted,
    Behold Him on the throne.

3 There He is interceding
    For all who on Him rest;
And grace from Him proceeding
    Tells how in Him we're blest:
Soon, to His place in glory,
    His waiting saints He'll raise,
To chant their joyful story
    In songs of loudest praise!

559
C.M.

THE day returns, into His Name,
    O God, we gather thus
To give to Thee through Him Who
    came
To make Thee known to us.

2 His glories great, His matchless worth,
    In all His path we trace,
His life recall, His death tell forth
    And praise His love and grace.

3 Sweet are the accents to Thine ear
    That praise that Worthy One
Whom we remember, gathered here,
    Thy well-belovèd Son.

4 The loaf and cup before us spread
    The precious truths declare,
His body giv'n, His blood thus shed,
    His grace beyond compare.

5 With such sweet symbols of His love
    Laid thus before our gaze,
Our hearts we lift to Thee above
    In sacrifice of praise.

560
9.8.9.8.

THE day Thou gavest, Lord, is
    ended;
The darkness falls at Thy behest;
    To Thee our morning hymns
    ascended,
Thy praise shall sanctify our rest.

2 We thank Thee that Thy Church
    unsleeping,
While earth rolls onward into light,
    Through all the world her watch is
    keeping,
And rests not now by day or night.

3 As o'er each continent and island
    The dawn leads on another day,
The voice of prayer is never silent,
    Nor dies the strain of praise away.

4 The sun that bids us rest is waking
    Our brethren 'neath the western sky;
And hour by hour fresh lips are
    making
Thy wondrous doings heard on high.

5 So be it, Lord! Thy throne shall never,
    Like earth's proud empires, pass
        away;
    Thy kingdom stands, and grows for
        ever,
    Till all Thy creatures own Thy sway.

561   L.M.

T HE gloom of dark Gethsemane,
    The sore amaze, the mystery,
The blood-like sweat, the agony,
        Remembering! Remembering!

2 The holy calm, the clam'rous cry,
    Of "crucify!" yea, "crucify!"
The silent Man led forth to die,
        Remembering! Remembering!

3 The shame, the pain, the darkness
        dread,
    The lonely cry, the bowèd head,
        The Prince of Life becoming dead,
        Remembering! Remembering!

4 Rememb'ring Him, Whom we adore,
    Whose griefs, O God, we ponder o'er,
The loaf we break, the cup we pour,
        Remembering! Remembering!

562   7.6.7.6.D.

T HE glory shines before me,
    I cannot linger here;
Though clouds may darken o'er me,
    My Father's house is near:
If through this barren desert
    A little while I roam,
The glory shines before me,
    I am not far from home.

2 Beyond the storms I'm going,
    Beyond this vale of tears,
Beyond the floods o'erflowing,
    Beyond the changing years:
I'm going to the better land,
    By faith long since possessed:
The glory shines before me,
    For this is not my rest.

3 The Lamb is there the glory!
    The Lamb is there the light!
Affliction's grasp but tears me
    From phantoms of the night:

The voice of Jesus calleth me,
    My race will soon be run;
The glory shines before me,
    The prize will soon be won

4 The glory shines before me,
    I know that all is well;
My Father's care is o'er me,
    His praises I would tell:
The love of Christ constraineth me,
    His blood hath washed me white;
Where Jesus is in glory,
    'Tis home, and love, and light.

563   6.6.8.4.D.

T HE God of Abraham praise,
    Who reigns enthroned above,
Ancient of everlasting days,
    And God of love.
Jehovah, great I AM!
    By earth and heaven confessed,
I bow and bless the sacred Name,
    For ever blessed.

2 The God of Abraham praise,
    At whose supreme command
From earth I rise, and seek my joys
    At His right hand.
He calls me to forsake
    Earth's wisdom, fame, and power,
And Him my only portion make,
    My shield and tower.

3 The God of Abraham praise,
    Whose all-sufficient grace
Shall guide me all my pilgrim days,
    In all my ways.
He calls a worm His friend,
    He calls Himself my God;
And He shall save me to the end
    Through Jesus' blood.

4 He by Himself hath sworn,
    I on His oath depend,
I shall, on eagle-wings upborne,
    To heaven ascend:
I shall behold His face,
    I shall His power adore,
And sing the wonders of His grace
    For evermore.

5 The whole triumphant host
　　Give thanks to God on high;
　"Hail, Father, Son, and Holy Ghost!"
　　They ever cry.
　Hail, Abraham's God, and mine!
　　I join the heavenly lays;
　All might and majesty are Thine,
　　And endless praise!

564
C.M. with Chorus

THE head that once was crowned
　　with thorns
Is crowned with glory now!
　A royal diadem adorns
The mighty Victor's brow!

He lives!
　I know He lives!
He lives!
　I know He lives!
I know that my Redeemer lives!

2 The highest place that heaven affords
　　Is His by sovereign right;
　The King of kings and Lord of lords,
　　And heaven's eternal Light.

3 Delight of all who dwell above,
　　The joy of saints below;
　To us still manifest Thy love
　　That we its depths may know.

4 To us Thy Cross with all its shame,
　　With all its grace be given!
　Though earth disowns Thy lowly name
　　All worship it in heaven.

5 Who suffer with Thee, Lord, below,
　　Shall reign with Thee above;
　Then let it be our joy to know
　　Thy way of peace and love.

6 To us Thy Cross is life and health
　　Though shame and death to Thee -
　Our glory, peace and boundless wealth
　　Throughout eternity.

565
7.6.7.6.D.

THE holiest now we enter
　　In perfect peace with God;
Regaining our lost centre
　　Through Christ's atoning blood:
Though great may be our dulness
　　In thought, and word, and deed,
We glory in the fulness
　　Of Him who meets our need.

2 Much incense is ascending
　　Before the eternal throne;
　God graciously is bending
　　To hear each feeble groan.
　To all our prayers and praises
　　Christ adds His sweet perfume,
　And love the censer raises
　　Their odours to consume.

3 O God, we come with singing,
　　Because the great High Priest
　Our names to Thee is bringing,
　　Nor e'er forgets the least:
　For us He wears the mitre
　　Where holiness shines bright;
　For us His robes are whiter
　　Than heaven's unsullied light.

566
8.6.8.4.

"THE hour" arrives; they reach "the
　　place",
The Cross they raise on high,
　The Lord of glory and of grace
　　They leave to die.

2 With holy awe we call to mind
　　That solemn scene of woe,
　The depth to which, in love so kind,
　　He there would go.

3 Surrounding Him, the wicked throng
　　Relentless rage disclose:
　Against the One Who did no wrong
　　Their wrath arose.

4 And His the pain, the bitter smart,
　　The ignominious place,
　The parchèd lips, the melted heart,
　　The marrèd face.

5 There His perfection would we view,
　　Displayed in such a death -
　Devoted, meek, submissive, true
　　To His last breath!

6 So for Himself we offer now
　　Our thanks, O God, to Thee;
　In glad response our hearts we bow
　　Adoringly.

567 8.7.8.7.

THE King of love my Shepherd is,
  Whose goodness faileth never;
I nothing lack if I am His
  And He is mine for ever.

2 Where streams of living water flow
    My ransomed soul He leadeth,
  And where the verdant pastures grow
    With food celestial feedeth.

3 Perverse and foolish oft I strayed,
    But yet in love He sought me,
  And on His shoulder gently laid,
    And home, rejoicing, brought me.

4 In death's dark vale I fear no ill
    With Thee, dear Lord, beside me;
  Thy rod and staff my comfort still,
    Thy Cross before to guide me.

5 Thou spread'st a table in my sight;
    Thy unction grace bestoweth;
  And O what transport of delight
    From Thy pure chalice floweth.

6 And so through all the length of days
    Thy goodness faileth never;
  Good Shepherd, may I sing Thy praise
    Within Thy house for ever!

568 C.M.

THE Lamb of God to slaughter led,
  The King of Glory see!
The crown of thorns upon His head,
  They nail Him to the tree!

2 The Father gives His only Son;
    The Lord of Glory dies
  For us, the guilty and undone,
    A spotless Sacrifice!

3 Thy Name is holy, O our God!
    Before Thy throne we bow;
  Thy bosom is Thy saints' abode,
    We call Thee Father now!

4 Enthroned with Thee, now sits the Lord,
    And in Thy bosom dwells;
  Justice, that smote Him with the sword,
    Our perfect pardon seals.

5 Eternal death was once our doom;
    Now death has lost its sting;
  We rose with Jesus from the tomb,
    Jehovah's love to sing.

569 S.M.

THE Lord Himself shall come,
  And shout a quickening word;
Thousands shall answer from the
  tomb -
"For ever with the Lord".

2 Then, as we upward fly,
    That resurrection word
  Shall be our shout of victory -
    "For ever with the Lord".

3 How shall I meet those eyes?
    Mine on Himself I cast,
  And own myself the Saviour's prize -
    Mercy from first to last.

4 Knowing as I am known!
    How shall I love that word!
  How oft repeat before the throne -
    "For ever with the Lord!"

5 That resurrection word,
    That shout of victory -
  Once more - "For ever with the Lord",
    Amen, so let it be!

570 10.10.10.10.

THE Lord is risen: the Red Sea's
  judgment flood
Is passed in Him who bought us
  with His blood.
The Lord is risen: we stand beyond
  the doom
Of all our sin, through Jesus' empty
  tomb.

2 The Lord is risen: with Him we also
    rose,
  And in His grave see all our
    vanquished foes.
  The Lord is risen: beyond the
    judgment land
  In Him, in resurrection-life, we stand.

3 The Lord is risen: we're now
redeemed to God,
And tread the desert which His feet
have trod.
The Lord is risen: the sanctuary's
our place,
Where now we dwell before the
Father's face.

4 The Lord is risen: the Lord is gone
before;
We long to see Him and to sin no
more!
The Lord is risen: our trumpet shout
shall be,
"Thou hast prevailed! Thy people,
Lord, are free!"

571
C.M.

THE Lord of Glory, being found
In fashion as a Man,
With moral glory fitly crowned,
His path on earth began.

2 The form of God to Him pertained;
Complete equality
Was not an object to be gained,
For very God was He.

3 Not to His own things did He look,
But, in amazing grace,
Emptied Himself, and stooping, took
The servant's form and place.

4 And faithfulness, and tender grace
Adorned the words He spoke;
He needed not e'er to retrace
One step, or word revoke.

5 In Him the Father found delight,
All inexpressible,
Radiance of moral glory bright,
Fragrance ineffable.

6 Self-humbled One Whose
preciousness
Was told in every breath,
He served in full devotedness,
Obedient unto death.

572
8.7.8.7.8.8.7.

THE Lord of Glory! Who is He?
Who is the King of Glory?
Only the Son of God can be
The Christ, the King of Glory:
Consider all His wounds, and see
How Jesus' death upon the tree
Proclaims Him King of Glory.

2 Above all heavens, at God's right hand,
Now sits the King of Glory;
The angels, by His favour, stand
Before the throne of Glory;
Swiftly they fly at His command
To guard His own of every land,
To keep the heirs of glory.

3 Death and the grave confess the Lamb
To be the King of Glory;
The powers of darkness dread His
Name,
Creation shows His glory.
He said: "E'er Abram was, I am";
Jesus is evermore the same,
The Almighty King of Glory.

4 Thrice happy who in Him believe,
They soon will share His glory;
Born of His Spirit, they receive
His sacred pledge of glory;
Taught by His Cross, for sin they grieve,
He calls them brethren, and they
cleave
To Him, their hope of glory.

573
11.10.11.10.

THE Lord will perfect that which
doth concern me,
His way is perfect, so His goal must be;
All life's events in harmony are
working
For those clear issues which I yet
shall see.

2 The Lord will perfect that which doth
concern me,
And will complete each half-formed
thing He sends:
His rich designs most carefully are
woven,
There are with Him no loose or
broken ends.

3 The Lord will perfect that which doth
      concern me,
   And finish what His grace has here
      begun;
   He gathers up life's fragments,
      losing nothing,
   And turns to good account each
      single one.

4 The Lord will perfect that which doth
      concern me,
   Will do it in so many different ways;
      By loss or gain, by high success
         or failure,
   By steady course or unexpected
      phase.

5 The Lord will perfect that which doth
      concern me,
   Expecting me to show Him on my part
      A trust intelligent and full of interest
   In all these purposes of His great
      heart.

574   C.M.

THE Lord's my Shepherd, I'll not
      want:
He makes me down to lie
   In pastures green; He leadeth me
The quiet waters by.

2 My soul He doth restore again;
      And me to walk doth make
   Within the paths of righteousness,
      E'en for His own name's sake.

3 Yea, though I walk in death's dark vale,
      Yet will I fear none ill;
   For Thou art with me; and Thy rod
      And staff me comfort still.

4 My table Thou hast furnishèd
      In presence of my foes;
   My head Thou dost with oil anoint,
      And my cup overflows.

5 Goodness and mercy all my life
      Shall surely follow me;
   And in God's house for evermore
      My dwelling-place shall be.

575   P.M.

THE love of God is greater far
      Than tongue or pen can ever tell;
It goes beyond the highest star,
      And reaches to the lowest hell;
The guilty pair, bowed down with care,
      God gave His Son to win;
His erring child He reconciled,
      And pardoned from his sin.

Oh, love of God, how rich and pure!
   How measureless and strong!
It shall forevermore endure -
   The saints' and angels' song.

2 When hoary time shall pass away,
      And earthly thrones and kingdoms
         fall,
   When men who here refuse to pray,
      On rocks and hills and mountains
         call,
   God's love, so sure, shall still endure,
      All measureless and strong;
   Redeeming grace to Adam's race -
      The saints' and angels' song.

3 Could we with ink the ocean fill,
      And were the skies of parchment
         made,
   Were every stalk on earth a quill,
      And every man a scribe by trade;
   To write the love of God above
      Would drain the ocean dry;
   Nor could the scroll contain the whole,
      Though stretched from sky to sky.

576   8.8.8.6. with Chorus

THE love that Jesus had for me,
      To suffer on the cruel tree
That I a ransomed soul might be,
      Is more than tongue can tell!

His love is more than tongue can tell!
His love is more than tongue can tell!
   The love that Jesus had for me
Is more than tongue can tell!

2 The many sorrows that He bore,
      And oh, that crown of thorns He wore,
   That I might live for evermore,
      Is more than tongue can tell!

3 The peace I have in Him, my Lord,
  Who pleads before the throne of
    God,
  The merits of His precious blood,
    Is more than tongue can tell!

4 The joy that comes when He is near,
  The rest He gives, so free from fear,
  The Hope in Him, so bright and clear,
    Is more than tongue can tell!

577 P.M.

THE Name of Jesus is so sweet,
  I love its music to repeat;
It makes my joys full and complete,
  The precious Name of Jesus!

"Jesus", oh, how sweet the name!
  "Jesus", every day the same;
"Jesus", let all saints proclaim
  Its worthy praise forever!

2 I love the Name of Him whose heart
  Knows all my griefs and bears a part;
Who bids all anxious fears depart -
  I love the Name of Jesus!

3 That Name I fondly love to hear,
  It never fails my heart to cheer;
Its music dries the falling tear,
  Exalt the Name of Jesus!

4 No word of man can ever tell
  How sweet the Name I love so well;
Oh, let its praises ever swell!
  Oh, praise the Name of Jesus!

578 8.7.8.7.D.

THE night is wearing fast away,
  The glorious day is dawning,
When Christ shall all His grace display,
  The fair millennial morning.
Gloomy and dark the night hath been,
  And long the way, and dreary;
And sad the weeping saints are seen,
  And faint, and worn, and weary.

2 Ye mourning pilgrims, dry your tears,
  And hush each sigh of sorrow;
The light of that bright morn appears,
  The long Sabbatic morrow.
Lift up your heads! behold from far
  A flood of splendour streaming!
It is the bright and Morning Star
  In living lustre beaming.

3 And see that star-like host around
  Of angel bands attending;
Hark! hark! the trumpet's gladdening
    sound,
  'Mid shouts triumphant blending.
  He comes! the Bridegroom
    promised long;
Go forth with joy to meet Him,
  And raise the new and nuptial song,
In cheering strains to greet Him.

579 L.M.

THE perfect righteousness of God
  Is witnessed in the Saviour's
blood;
  'Tis in the Cross of Christ we trace
His righteousness, yet wondrous
  grace.

2 God could not pass the sinner by;
  Justice demands that he must die;
But in the Cross of Christ we see
  How God can save, yet righteous be.

3 The judgment fell on Jesus' head;
  'Twas in His blood sin's debt was paid;
Stern justice can demand no more,
  And mercy can dispense her store.

4 The sinner who believes is free,
  Can say, "The Saviour died for me";
Can point to the atoning blood
  And say, "This made my peace
    with God".

580 7.6.7.6.D.

THE sands of time are sinking,
  The dawn of heaven breaks;
The summer morn I've sighed for -
  The fair, sweet morn awakes:
Dark, dark hath been the midnight,
  But dayspring is at hand,
And glory, glory dwelleth
  In Immanuel's land.

2 O Christ! He is the fountain,
  The deep, sweet well of love;
The streams on earth I've tasted,
  More deep I'll drink above;
There, to an ocean's fulness,
  His mercy doth expand,
And glory, glory dwelleth
  In Immanuel's land.

3 I've wrestled on towards heaven,
    'Gainst storm, and wind, and tide,
Now, like a weary traveller
    That leaneth on his guide,
Amid the shades of evening,
    While sinks life's lingering sand,
I hail the glory dawning
    From Immanuel's land.

4 With mercy and with judgment
    My web of time He wove,
And aye the dews of sorrow
    Were lustred with His love.
I'll bless the hand that guided,
    I'll bless the heart that planned,
When throned where glory dwelleth
    In Immanuel's land.

5 Oh, I am my Beloved's
    And my Belov'd is mine;
He brings a poor vile sinner
    Into His "house of wine".
I stand upon His merit;
    I know no other stand,
Not e'en where glory dwelleth
    In Immanuel's land.

6 The Bride eyes not her garment,
    But her dear Bridegroom's face;
I will not gaze at glory,
    But on the King of grace.
Not at the crown He giveth,
    But on His piercèd hand;
The Lamb is all the glory
    Of Immanuel's land.

581
P.M.

THE Saviour comes! No outward
    pomp
Bespeaks His presence nigh;
    No earthly beauty shines in Him
To draw the carnal eye.

All beauty may we ever see,
    In God's belovèd Son,
The chiefest of ten thousand He,
    The only lovely One!

2 Rejected and despised of men,
    Behold a Man of woe!
Grief was His close companion here
    Through all His life below.

3 Yet all the griefs He felt were ours,
    Ours were the woes He bore;
Pangs, not His own, His spotless soul
    With bitter anguish tore.

4 His sacred blood hath washed our souls
    From sin's polluting stain;
His stripes have healed us, and His
    death
Revived our souls again.

5 We all, like sheep, have gone astray,
    In ruin's fatal road;
On Him were our transgressions laid;
    He bore the mighty load.

6 He died to bear the guilt of men,
    That sin might be forgiven;
He lives to bless them and defend,
    And plead their cause in heaven.

582
L.M.

THE Saviour lives, no more to die;
    He lives our Head, enthroned
on high;
    He lives triumphant o'er the grave;
He lives eternally to save.

2 He lives to still His people's fears;
    He lives to wipe away their tears;
He lives their mansions to prepare;
    He lives to bring them safely there.

3 The chief of sinners He receives;
    His saints He loves, and never
    leaves;
He'll guard us safe from every ill,
    And all His promises fulfil.

4 Abundant grace will He afford,
    Till we are present with the Lord;
And prove what we have sung before,
    That Jesus lives for evermore.

5 Then let our souls in Him rejoice,
    And sing His praise with cheerful
    voice;
Our doubts and fears for ever gone,
    For Christ is on the Father's throne.

583

P.M.

THE Saviour's blood, on Calvary shed,
  Has full atonement made;
Captivity He captive led,
  My ransom price He paid;
The crown has found a worthy brow;
As "Lord of all" behold Him now!

Ever, my heart, keep cling…ing …
  Cling to the Lord alone …
His work is done, His victory won;
  Well may my heart keep singing,
  Well may my heart keep singing!

2 In Him "accepted" and "complete",
    As He is, so am I;
  The judgment storm on Him did beat
    He lives, no more to die!
  Atoning blood - I hear its voice!
    It speaketh peace! my heart, rejoice!

3 The great High Priest within the veil,
    Both Priest and Sacrifice,
  To keep His own will never fail,
    Made His at such a price!
  They soon will see Him coming out;
    With rapture greet His welcome
      shout!

584

L.M.

THE sorrows of the daily life,
  The shadows o'er my path
which fall,
  Too oft obscure the glory's light
Until I rise above them all.

2 Until upon the mountain height
    I stand, my God, with Thee alone,
  Bathed in the fullest, clearest light,
    The glory that surrounds the throne.

3 Calm in Thy secret presence, Lord,
    I rest this weary soul of mine;
  Feed on the fulness of Thy word,
    And die to all the things of time.

4 Oh! take my fevered hands in Thine,
    And keep me, Master, nearer Thee,
  Walking above the things of time,
    In closest fellowship with Thee.

5 The child of God must walk alone,
    If he would live and walk with Thee;
  And only to such hearts are known
    The joys of Thy blest company.

6 Alone with Thee, O Master, where
    The light of earthly glory dies,
  Misunderstood by all, I dare
    To do what Thine own heart will
      prize.

7 Such be my path through life down
    here,
  One long, close, lonely walk with Thee,
    Until past every doubt and fear,
  Thy face in light above I see.

585

C.M.

THE veil is rent: Lo! Jesus stands
  Before the throne of grace;
And clouds of incense from His hands
  Fill all that glorious place.

2 His precious blood is sprinkled there,
    Before and on the throne;
  And His own wounds in heaven
      declare
  His work on earth is done.

3 "'Tis finished!" on the Cross He said,
    In agonies and blood;
  'Tis finished! now He lives to plead
    Before the face of God.

4 'Tis finished! here our souls can rest,
    His work can never fail;
  By Him, our Sacrifice and Priest,
    We enter through the veil.

5 Within the holiest of all,
    Cleansed by His precious blood,
  Before Thy throne Thy children fall,
    And worship Thee, our God.

6 Boldly our heart and voice we raise,
    His Name, His blood, our plea;
  Assured our prayers and songs of
      praise
  Ascend by Him to Thee.

586   8.8.8.6.

THE wanderer no more will roam,
   The lost one to the fold hath
come,
      The prodigal is welcomed home,
         O Lamb of God, in Thee!

2 Though clad in rags, by sin defiled,
   The Father hath embraced His child;
And I am pardoned, reconciled,
         O Lamb of God, in Thee!

3 It is the Father's joy to bless,
   His love provides for me a dress,
A robe of spotless righteousness,
         O Lamb of God, in Thee!

4 Now shall my famished soul be fed,
   A feast of love for me is spread,
I feed upon the children's bread,
         O Lamb of God, in Thee!

5 Yea, in the fulness of His grace,
   He puts me in the children's place,
Where I may gaze upon His face,
         O Lamb of God, in Thee.!

6 I cannot half His love express,
   Yet, Lord, with joy my lips confess,
This blessèd portion I possess,
         O Lamb of God, in Thee!

7 Thy precious name it is I bear,
   In Thee I am to God brought near,
And all the Father's love I share,
         O Lamb of God, in Thee!

8 And when I in Thy likeness shine,
   The glory and the praise be Thine,
That everlasting joy is mine,
         O Lamb of God, in Thee!

587   8.5.8.3.

THEE we praise, our God and Father,
   Thou Thy love hast shown;
Ere the world was, Thou didst
   choose us
      For Thine own.

2 Thou Thine only Son hast given,
   Thou art glorified,
For, in love to bring us near Thee,
   He has died.

3 By the Spirit now indwelling
   We with Christ have part;
Father! we Thy sons now call Thee,
   From our heart.

4 Love divine, our present portion,
   Heaven's choicest store;
Thee we worship, God and Father,
   Thee adore!

5 Soon in Thine own house around Thee
   Still our praise shall swell;
Sons before Thee ever joying
   We shall dwell.

6 For His praise who glorified Thee
   We like Him shall be;
Firstborn He of many brethren
   Praising Thee.

588   P.M.

THERE have been names that I
   have loved to hear,
But never has there been a name
   so dear
To this heart of mine, as the name
   divine,
The precious, precious name of Jesus.

*Jesus is the sweetest name I know,
   And He's just the same as His
      lovely name,
And that's the reason why I love
   Him so;
Oh, Jesus is the sweetest name I
   know.*

2 There is no name in earth or heaven
   above,
That we should give such honour
   and such love
As the blessèd name, let us all
   acclaim,
That wondrous, glorious name of
   Jesus.

3 And some day I shall see Him face
   to face
To thank and praise Him for His
   wondrous grace,
Which He gave to me, when He
   made me free,
The blessèd Son of God called Jesus.

589
C.M.

THERE is a fold whence none
can stray,
And pastures ever green,
  Where sultry sun, or stormy day,
Or night is never seen.

2 There is a Shepherd living there,
  The Firstborn from the dead,
Who tends with sweet, unwearied care
  The flock for which He bled.

3 There congregate the sons of light,
  Fair as the morning sky,
And taste of infinite delight
  Beneath their Saviour's eye.

4 Their joy bursts forth in strains of love,
  In one harmonious song,
And through the heavenly courts above
  The echoes roll along.

5 O may our faith take up that sound
  Though toiling here below!
'Midst trials may our joys abound,
  And songs amidst our woe.

6 Until we reach that happy shore,
  And join to swell their strain,
And from our God go out no more,
  And never weep again.

590
C.M.

THERE is a fountain filled with
blood,
Drawn from Emmanuel's veins;
  And sinners plunged beneath that
  flood,
Lose all their guilty stains.

2 The dying thief rejoiced to see
  That fountain in his day;
And there have I, as vile as he,
  Washed all my sins away!

3 Dear dying Lamb, Thy precious blood
  Shall never lose its power,
Till all the ransomed church of God
  Be saved to sin no more.

4 E'er since, by faith, I saw the stream
  Thy flowing wounds supply,
Redeeming love has been my theme,
  And shall be till I die.

5 Then in a nobler, sweeter song,
  I'll sing Thy power to save;
When this poor lisping, stammering
  tongue
Lies silent in the grave.

6 Lord, I believe Thou hast prepar'd
  (Unworthy though I be)
For me a blood-bought free reward,
  A golden harp for me!

7 'Tis strung, and tun'd, for endless
  years,
And form'd by power divine;
  To sound in God the Father's ears
No other name but Thine.

591
C.M.

THERE is a green hill far away,
  Without a city wall,
Where the dear Lord was crucified,
  Who died to save us all.

2 We may not know, we cannot tell
  What pains He had to bear;
But we believe it was for us
  He hung and suffered there.

3 He died that we might be forgiven,
  He died to make us good,
That we might go at last to heaven,
  Saved by His precious blood.

4 There was no other good enough
  To pay the price of sin;
He only could unlock the gate
  Of heaven, and let us in.

5 O dearly, dearly has He loved,
  And we must love Him too,
And trust in His redeeming blood,
  And try His works to do.

592
C.M.

THERE is a Name I love to hear,
  I love to speak its worth;
It sounds like music in mine ear,
  The sweetest Name on earth.

2 It tells me of a Saviour's love,
  Who died to set me free;
It tells me of His precious blood,
  The sinner's perfect plea.

3 It tells me of a Father's smile
   Beaming upon His child;
   It cheers me through this "little while",
   Through desert, waste, and wild.

4 It bids my trembling soul rejoice,
   It dries each rising tear;
   It tells me in a "still, small voice"
   To trust and never fear.

5 Jesus! the Name I love so well,
   The Name I love to hear;
   No saint on earth its worth can tell,
   No heart conceive how dear.

6 This Name shall shed its fragrance still
   Along life's thorny road,
   Shall sweetly smooth the rugged hill
   That leads me up to God.

7 And there, with all the blood-bought
      throng,
   From sin and sorrow free,
   I'll sing the new, eternal song
   Of Jesus' love to me.

593 C.M.

THERE is an eye that never sleeps
   Beneath the wing of night;
There is an ear that never shuts
   When sink the beams of light.

2 There is an arm that never tires
   When human strength gives way;
There is a love that never fails
   When earthly loves decay.

3 That eye is fixed on seraph throngs,
   That arm upholds the sky,
That ear is filled with heavenly songs,
   That love is throned on high.

4 But there's a power which faith can
      wield,
   When mortal aid is vain,
That eye, that arm, that love to reach,
   That listening ear to gain.

5 That power is prayer, which soars
      on high,
   Through Jesus to the throne,
      And moves the hand which moves
         the world,
   To bring deliverance down.

594 P.M.

THERE is coming a day
   When no heartaches shall come;
No more clouds in the sky,
   No more tears to dim the eye;
All is peace for evermore
   On that happy, golden shore,
What a day, glorious day, that will be!

What a day that will be
   When my Jesus I shall see!
And I look upon His face,
   The One who saved me by His
      grace;
When He takes me by the hand,
   And leads me through the
      Promised Land,
What a day, glorious day, that will be!

2 There'll be no sorrow there,
   No more burdens to bear;
No more sickness, no pain,
   No more parting over there;
And forever I will be
   With the One who died for me,
What a day, glorious day, that will be!

3 There will be reunion there
   In that upper garden fair,
Loved ones gathered round His feet,
   What a joy again to meet!
There where faith gives way to sight,
   In that city of delight,
What a day, glorious day, that will be!

595 P.M.

THERE will never be a sweeter story,
   Story of the Saviour's love divine,
Love that brought Him from the
   realms of glory
Just to save a sinful soul like mine.

Isn't the love of Jesus
   Something wonderful,
Wonderful, wonderful!
   Oh, isn't the love of Jesus
Something wonderful,
   Wonderful it is to me!

2 Boundless as the universe around me,
   Reaching to the farthest soul away,
Saving, keeping love it was that
   found me
That is why my heart can truly say -

3 Love beyond our human comprehending,
  Love of God in Christ, how can
    it be!
  This will be my theme and never
    ending -
  Great redeeming love of Calvary

596
P.M.

THERE'S a call comes ringing
  o'er the restless wave,
Send the light! … Send the light!
  There are souls to rescue, there are
    souls to save,
Send the light! … Send the light!

Send the light … the blessèd
  Gospel light;
Let it shine … from shore to shore!
  Send the light … and let its
    radiant beams
Light the world for evermore!

2 We have heard the Macedonian call
    today,
  Send the light! … Send the light!
    And our grateful off'ring at the
      Cross we lay,
  Send the light! … Send the light!

3 May the grace of Jesus ev'rywhere
    abound,
  Send the light! … Send the light!
    And a Christ-like spirit ev'rywhere
      be found,
  Send the light! … Send the light!

4 Let us not grow weary in the work
    of love,
  Send the light! … Send the light!
    Let us gather jewels for a crown
      above,
  Send the light! … Send the light!

597
P.M.

THERE'S a land that is fairer than
  day,
And by faith we can see it afar;
  For the Father waits over the way,
To prepare us a dwelling-place there.

In the sweet … by-and-by
  We shall meet on that beautiful
    shore;
In the sweet … by-and-by
  We shall meet on that beautiful
    shore.

2 We shall sing on that beautiful shore
    The melodious songs of the blest;
  And our spirits shall sorrow no more -
    Not a sigh for the blessing of rest.

3 To our bountiful Father above,
    We will offer our tribute of praise,
  For the glorious gift of His love,
    And the blessings that hallow our
      days.

4 We shall rest on that beautiful shore -
    In the joys of the saved we shall
      share:
  All our pilgrimage-toil will be o'er,
    And the conqueror's crown we
      shall wear.

598
P.M.

THEY nailed my Lord upon the tree
  And left Him, dying, there:
Through love He suffered there for me;
  'Twas love beyond compare.

Crucified! Crucified!
  And nailed upon the tree!
With piercéd hands and feet and side!
  For you! … For me!

2 Upon His head a crown of thorns,
    Upon His heart my shame;
  For me He prayed, for me He died,
    And, dying, spoke my name.

3 "Forgive them, O forgive!" He cried,
    Then bowed His sacred head;
  "O Lamb of God! my sacrifice!
    For me Thy blood was shed".

4 His voice I hear, His love I know;
    I worship at His feet;
  And kneeling there, at Calvary's Cross,
    Redemption is complete.

599
P.M.

THINE be the glory,
  Risen, conquering Son;
Endless is the victory
  Thou o'er death hast won.
Angels in bright raiment
  Rolled the stone away,
Kept the folded grave-clothes
  Where Thy body lay.

Thine be the glory,
*   Risen, conquering Son;*
Endless is the victory
*   Thou o'er death hast won!*

2 Lo! Jesus meets us,
      Risen from the tomb;
   Lovingly He greets us,
      Scatters fear and gloom;
   Let the church with gladness
      Hymns of triumph sing,
   For her Lord now liveth;
      Death hath lost its sting.

3 No more we doubt Thee,
      Glorious Prince of life!
   Life is nought without Thee;
      Aid us in our strife;
   Make us more than conquerors,
      Through Thy deathless love;
   Bring us safe through Jordan
      To Thy home above.

600   7.6.7.6.D.

THINE ever - loved and chosen
      In Thy deep thoughts of grace,
Before the world's foundation,
      Or dayspring knew its place;
Thine only - sought and followed,
      When in the far-off land;
Then kept, and fed, and guided,
      By Thine unwearied hand.

2 Thine, only Thine, Lord Jesus!
      Whom need we now beside?
   For ever in Thy presence
      Our weary souls we hide:
   All other refuge faileth,
      All other springs run dry,
   Thou, Lord, alone art changeless,
      And Thou art ever nigh.

3 Thine ever, Lord, Thine only,
      E'en in the glory-light,
   When bursts the dawn of heaven
      Upon our raptured sight,
   One deep joy shall enfold us,
      Shall swell our highest song -
   That we are Thine, Thine only,
      'Mid all the gathered throng!

4 Thine only, Lord; oh, keep us
      More closely at Thy side!
   While here we wait and worship,
      Our hearts would there abide:

We crave no other gladness,
   We seek no other rest,
Till raisèd in Thy likeness,
   We shall with Thee be blest!

601   11.10.11.10.

THINE is the love, Lord, that
      draws us together,
Guiding our steps from the
   wilderness ways;
Soon face to face we'll adore Thee
   for ever,
Now our glad hearts would be filled
   with Thy praise.

2 Faithful Thy grace o'er our pathway
      has waited,
   Deep the delight we have found,
      Lord, in Thee;
   Now with this treasure our spirits are
      freighted,
   Bowed at Thy feet, and the
      fragrance set free.

3 For us, Lord Jesus, Thyself Thou
      hast given;
   Suff'rings unfathomed for us hast
      Thou known;
   Now, in accord with the homage of
      heaven,
   Rises a song from the hearts of
      Thine own.

4 Jesus, Lord Jesus, we love and
      adore Thee;
   Glorious Thy Name, all our praises
      above;
   Peerless Thy beauty, we worship
      before Thee;
   Hushed are our spirits, at rest in Thy
      love.

602   8.8.8.8.

THIS world is a wilderness wide;
      I have nothing to seek nor to
choose;
      I've no thought in the waste to
         abide;
   I have nought to regret nor to lose.

2 The Lord is Himself gone before;
      He has marked out the path that
         I tread;
   It's as sure as the love I adore;
      I have nothing to fear nor to dread.

3 The path where my Saviour is gone
    Has led up to His Father and God,
To the place where He's now on the
    throne;
And His strength shall be mine on
    the road.

4 And with Him shall my rest be on high,
    When in holiness bright I sit down,
In the joy of His love ever nigh,
    In the peace that His presence
       shall crown.

5 'Tis the treasure I've found in His love
    That has made me a pilgrim below;
And 'tis there, when I reach Him above,
    As I'm known, all His fulness I'll
       know.

6 And, Saviour! 'tis Thee from on high
    I await till the time Thou shalt come,
To take him Thou hast led by Thine
    eye
To Thyself in Thy heavenly home.

7 Till then, 'tis the path Thou hast trod
    My delight and my comfort shall be;
I'm content with Thy staff and Thy rod,
    Till with Thee all Thy glory I see.

603
8.7.8.7.D.

T HOU art coming, O our Saviour!
    Coming, God's anointed King!
Every tongue Thy Name confessing,
    Well may we rejoice and sing.
Thou art coming! Rays of glory,
    Through the veil Thy death has rent,
Gladden now our pilgrim pathway,
    Glory from Thy presence sent.

Thou art coming! Thou art coming!
    We shall meet Thee on Thy way;
Thou art coming! We shall see Thee,
    And be like Thee on that day:
Thou art coming! Thou art coming!
    Jesus, our belovèd Lord!
O the joy to see Thee reigning,
    Worshipped, glorified, adored!

2 Thou art coming! Not a shadow,
    Not a mist, and not a tear,
Not a sin, and not a sorrow
    On that sunrise grand and clear:

Thou art coming: Blessèd Saviour,
    Nothing else seems worth a
       thought;
O how marvellous the glory,
    And the bliss Thy pain hath bought!

3 Thou art coming! We are waiting
    With a "hope" that cannot fail,
Asking not the day or hour,
    Anchored safe within the veil:
Thou art coming! At Thy table
    We are witnesses for this,
As we meet Thee in communion,
    Earnest of our coming bliss.

604
8.6.8.6.8.8.

T HOU art the Everlasting Word,
    The Father's only Son,
God manifestly seen and heard,
    And heaven's belovèd One.

Worthy, O Lamb, of God, art Thou!
    That every knee to Thee should
       bow.

2 In Thee, most perfectly expressed,
    The Father's glories shine,
Of the full Deity possessed,
    Eternally divine!

3 True image of the Infinite,
    Whose essence is concealed;
Brightness of uncreated light,
    The heart of God revealed.

4 But the high myst'ries of Thy name
    An angel's grasp transcend;
The Father only (glorious claim!)
    The Son can comprehend.

5 Yet loving Thee, on whom His love
    Ineffable doth rest,
Thy members all, in Thee, above,
    As one with Thee are blest.

6 Throughout the universe of bliss,
    The centre Thou, and Sun,
Th' eternal theme of praise is this,
    To heaven's belovèd One.

605 8.8.8.8.8.8.

THOU hidden love of God, whose
  height,
Whose depth unfathomed no man
  knows,
I see from far Thy beauteous light,
  And inly sigh for Thy repose:
My heart is pained, nor can it be
  At rest till it finds rest in Thee.

2 Is there a thing beneath the sun
    That strives with Thee my heart
     to share?
  O tear it thence, and reign alone
    The Lord of every motion there!
  Then shall my heart from earth be
    free,
  When it has found repose in Thee.

3 O hide this self from me that I
    No more, but Christ in me shall live!
  My vile affections mortify,
    Nor let one darling sin survive:
  In all things nothing may I see,
    Nothing desire, or seek, but Thee.

4 Each moment calls from earth away
    My heart which lowly waits Thy call;
  Speak to my inmost soul and say,
    "I am thy Life, thy God, thy All!"
  To know Thy power, to hear Thy voice,
    To feel Thy love, be all my choice.

606 9.8.9.8.9.8. with Chorus

THOU life of my life, blessèd
  Saviour
Thy death was the death that was
  mine,
For me was Thy Cross and Thine
  anguish,
  Thy love and Thy sorrow divine;
    Thou hast suffered the Cross and
    the judgment,
That I might forever go free -

A thousand, a thousand
  thanksgivings,
I bring, my Lord Jesus, to Thee!

2 For me hast Thou borne the
  reproaches,
  The mockery, hate, and disdain,
    The blows and the spittings of
    sinners,

The scourging, the shame and the
  pain;
To save me from bondage and
  judgment,
Thou gladly hast suffered for me -

3 O Lord, from my heart do I thank
  Thee
For all Thou hast borne in my room,
  Thine agony, dying unsolaced,
Alone in the darkness and gloom,
  That I, in the glory of heaven,
For ever and ever might be -

607 P.M.

THOU, my everlasting portion!
  More than friend or life to me,
All along my pilgrim journey,
  Saviour, let me walk with Thee!
Close to Thee, close to Thee,
  Close to Thee, close to Thee,
All along my pilgrim journey,
  Saviour, I would walk with Thee!

2 Not for ease or worldly pleasure,
    Nor for fame my prayer shall be,
  Gladly will I toil and suffer,
    Only let me walk with Thee.
  Close to Thee, close to Thee,
    Close to Thee, close to Thee,
  Gladly will I toil and suffer,
    So that I may walk with Thee.

3 Lead me through the vale of shadows,
    Bear me o'er life's fitful sea;
  Then the gate of life eternal
    I shall enter, Lord, with Thee.
  Close to Thee, close to Thee,
    Close to Thee, close to Thee,
  Then the gate of life eternal
    I shall enter, Lord, with Thee.

608 6.6.4.6.6.6.4.

THOU who did'st come to die
  From the bright realms on high,
    Thou art our peace:
Peace Thou dost now impart
To each believing heart,
Peace that shall ne'er depart;
    Thou art our peace.

2 Thou who did'st rise again,
Thy tomb was sealed in vain,
    Thou art our life:

All power to Thee is given,
Exalted Lord in heaven,
And we with Thee are risen,
    Thou art our life.

3 Thou who wilt surely come
To take Thy loved ones home,
    Thou art our hope:
What joys and bliss untold
Will to our gaze unfold
When we Thy face behold!
    Thou art our hope.

4 Peace, life and hope, O Lord,
Thou giv'st us in Thy Word,
    Blest be Thy name:
We would our praise outpour,
Would worship and adore
Now and for evermore;
    Blest be Thy name.

609   6.6.4.6.6.6.4.

T HOU whose almighty word
    Chaos and darkness heard,
        And took their flight,
Hear us, we humbly pray,
And, where the gospel day
Sheds not its glorious ray,
        Let there be light.

2 Thou who didst come to bring,
On Thy redeeming wing,
        Healing and sight,
Health to the sick in mind,
Sight to the inly blind,
Oh now to all mankind
        Let there be light.

3 Spirit of truth and love,
Life-giving, holy Dove,
        Speed forth Thy flight;
Move on the water's face,
Bearing the lamp of grace,
And in earth's darkest place
        Let there be light.

4 Blessèd and holy Three,
Glorious Trinity,
        Wisdom, Love, Might,
Boundless as ocean's tide
Rolling in fullest pride,
Through the world, far and wide,
        Let there be light.

610   11.11.11.11.

T HOUGH faint, yet pursuing, we
    go on our way;
The Lord is our leader, His strength
    is our stay;
Though suff'ring, and sorrow, and
    trial be near,
The Lord is our refuge - why then
    should we fear?

2 He raiseth the fallen, He cheereth
    the faint;
If the weak are opprest, He hears
    their complaint;
The way may be dreary, and thorny
    the road,
But let us not falter; our help is in God.

3 And to His green pastures our
    footsteps He leads;
His flock in the desert how kindly He
    feeds!
The lambs in His bosom He tenderly
    bears,
And brings back the wanderer safe
    from the snares.

4 Though clouds may surround us,
    our God is our light;
Though foes are around us, our God
    is our might;
So faint, yet pursuing, whatever may
    come;
The Lord is our Leader, and heaven
    our home!

5 And there shall His people eternally
    dwell,
With Him who has led them so
    safely and well;
The toilsome way over, the
    wilderness passed,
And Canaan the blessèd is theirs at
    the last.

611   6.6.6.6.8.8.

T HOUGHT-VIEWS that ne'er
    grow dim
Stir in our hearts, O God,
    As we remember Him
In all the path He trod:
    Thy Holy Son, in manhood grace,
Whose holy steps again we trace.

2 Thoughts of those holy feet,
   Steadfast from day to day,
Most beautiful and sweet,
   Treading that lowly way,
On for the glory of Thy Name,
   And down toward a Cross of shame!

3 Thoughts of His human tears,
   His sympathy of heart,
'Mid human griefs and fears
   His perfect human part;
Ready to weep with them that weep,
   In human pity, kind and deep!

4 Thoughts of His wondrous grace;
   The Lord of Glory He,
Yet, in the lowest place,
   Veiling His Majesty!
As one that serveth moving through
   Thy heart to show, Thy will to do!

612   10.10.10.10.
THRICE blessèd hope that
   cheers the weary soul,
As through this scene of sin we
   sadly roam,
That "this same Jesus" Who has
   made us whole
Is coming back again to take us
   home!

2 "This same" the men in white
   apparel said
To those who upward gazed where
   He had gone;
Thus hope within their troubled
   hearts was shed,
And holy joy upon their faces shone.

3 We muse upon the measure of His
   love,
The manner of His words, His
   works, His ways,
Until we yearn to be with Him above,
   And on the fulness of His glory
   gaze.

4 What joy it gives to dwell upon the
   thought
That soon He'll come and take His
   own away,
And we shall upward to Himself be
   caught,
To be with Him for all eternity!

5 Meanwhile we'll turn us to the daily
   task,
And try to do it as He'd have it done,
   And answer for our hope to all
   who ask;
We're working, waiting for the
   Coming One.

613   S.M.D.
THROUGH Him to Thee, His God,
   Adoring thanks we raise:
The grace of Aaron's budded rod
   Has touched our lips with praise,
And taught us thus to be
   Through Him, this holy hour,
A holy priesthood unto Thee
   In resurrection power.

2 Rememb'ring Him, we each,
   In praise to Thee, express
The most our feeble thoughts can
   reach
Of all His preciousness.
   And thus, through Him, we seek
To rise, with hearts as one,
   To this, the privilege to speak
To Thee about Thy Son.

3 We seek Thy pleasure here,
   We know Thy heart's delight,
We would be pleasing to Thine ear
   And pleasing in Thy sight,
And move in this, the mind
   That marked the perfect One:
For Thou art pleased with them that
   find
Their pleasure in Thy Son.

4 Our hearts are drawn to Him
   Whose life was all for Thee:
The light that nought on earth could
   dim,
Veiled in humanity,
   Revealed in perfect grace
Through all that lowly way,
   A glory nought shall e'er efface,
Fresh for eternity!

614   8.4.8.4.8.8.8.4.
THROUGH the love of God our
   Saviour
      All will be well.
Free and changeless is His favour;
      All, all is well.

Precious is the blood that healed us,
Perfect is the grace that sealed us,
Strong the hand stretched forth to
shield us,
    All must be well.

2 Though we pass through tribulation,
    All will be well.
Ours is such a full salvation;
    All, all is well.
Happy, still in God confiding,
Fruitful, if in Christ abiding,
Holy, through the Spirit's guiding,
    All must be well.

3 We expect a bright tomorrow;
    All will be well.
Faith can sing through days of sorrow,
    All, all is well.
On our Father's love relying,
Christ our every need supplying,
Whether living now, or dying,
    All must be well.

615   8.4.8.4.8.8.8.4.

THROUGH Thy precious body
   broken
    Inside the veil;
O what words to sinners spoken
    Inside the veil!
Precious as the blood that bought us,
Perfect as the love that sought us,
Holy as the Lamb that brought us
    Inside the veil.

2 When we see Thy love unshaken
    Outside the camp;
Scorned by man, by God forsaken,
    Outside the camp;
Thine own love alone can charm us,
Shame need now no more alarm us,
Glad we follow, nought can harm us
    Outside the camp.

3 Lamb of God, through Thee we enter
    Inside the veil;
Cleansed by Thee, we boldly venture
    Inside the veil:
Not a stain; a new creation;
Ours is such a full salvation;
Low we bow in adoration
    Inside the veil.

4 Unto Thee, the homeless stranger
    Outside the camp,
Forth we hasten, fear no danger
    Outside the camp.
Thy reproach, far richer treasure
Than all Egypt's boasted pleasure;
Drawn by love that knows no measure,
    Outside the camp.

5 Soon Thy saints shall all be gathered
    Inside the veil:
All at home, no more be scattered,
    Inside the veil.
Nought from Thee our hearts shall
   sever;
We shall see Thee, grieve Thee never;
"Praise the Lamb!" shall sound for ever
    Inside the veil.

616   L.M.

THY broken body, gracious Lord,
   Is shadowed by this broken
bread:
    The wine, which in this cup is poured,
    Points to the blood which Thou hast
    shed.

2 And while we meet together thus,
    We show that we are one in Thee;
Thy precious blood was shed for us,
    Thy death, O Lord, has set us free.

3 Brethren! in Thee, in union sweet,
    For ever be Thy grace adored!
'Tis in Thy Name that now we meet,
    And know Thee with us, gracious
    Lord

4 We have one hope that Thou wilt come;
    Thee in the air, we wait to see,
When Thou wilt take Thy people home,
    And we shall ever reign with Thee.

617   10.10.10.10.

THY grace, O Lord, that
   measured once the deep
Of Calv'ry's woe, to seek and save
   Thy sheep,
Has touched our hearts and made
   them long for Thee,
Thyself our treasure and our all to be.

2 Thy glory, Lord, at God's right hand
  above,
  Supreme of all in that blest scene
  of love,
  In sonship tells our hearts their
  wondrous place,
  In Thee accepted by the Father's
  grace.

3 Thy fulness, Lord, of light and love
  divine,
  No thought can grasp, nor human
  mind define.
  The whole vast scene of glory will
  display
  That fulness in a quickly-coming day.

4 When all things filled by Thee are
  wholly blest,
  And God's deep love eternally shall
  rest
  In that which ever speaks to Him of
  Thee,
  Thy greatness, Lord, the universe
  shall see.

5 Thy beauties, Lord, Thy holy
  precious worth,
  Surpassing far the deepest joys of
  earth,
  Attract our hearts - our joy Thy
  constant love,
  Thyself our object in those scenes
  above.

618   6.6.6.6.6.6.

THY life was given for me,
  Thy blood, O Lord, was shed
That I might ransomed be,
  And quickened from the dead;
Thy life was given for me;
  What have I given for Thee?

2 Long years were spent for me
  In weariness and woe,
That through eternity
  Thy glory I might know;
Long years were spent for me:
  Have I spent one for Thee?

3 Thy Father's home of light,
  Thy rainbow-circled throne,
Were left for earthly night,
  For wanderings sad and lone.
Yea, all was left for me:
  Have I left aught for Thee?

4 Thou, Lord, hast borne for me
  More than my tongue can tell
Of bitterest agony,
  To rescue me from hell;
Thou sufferedst all for me:
  What have I borne for Thee?

5 And Thou hast brought to me,
  Down from Thy home above,
Salvation full and free,
  Thy pardon and Thy love;
Great gifts Thou broughtest me;
  What have I brought to Thee?

6 O let my life be given,
  My years for Thee be spent;
World-fetters all be riven,
  And joy with suffering blent;
Thou gavest Thyself for me;
  I give myself to Thee.

619   7.7.8.7.D.

THY love we own, Lord Jesus;
  In service unremitting,
Within the veil Thou dost prevail,
  Each soul for worship fitting.
Encompassed here with failure,
  Each earthly refuge fails us;
Without, within, beset with sin,
  Thy Name alone avails us.

2 Thy love we own, Lord Jesus!
  For though Thy toils are ended,
Thy tender heart doth take its part
  With those Thy grace befriended.
Thy sympathy, most precious!
  Thou succourest in sorrow,
And bidst us cheer while pilgrims here,
  And haste the hopeful morrow.

3 Thy love we own, Lord Jesus!
  Thy way is traced before Thee;
Thou wilt descend, and we ascend,
  To meet in heavenly glory.
Soon shall the blissful morning
  Call forth Thy saints to meet Thee,
Our only Lord, alone adored,
  With gladness then we'll greet Thee.

4 Thy love we own, Lord Jesus!
  And wait to see Thy glory,
To know as known, and fully own
  Thy perfect grace before Thee:

We plead Thy parting promise,
Come, Savour, to release us;
Then endless praise our lips shall raise
For love like Thine, Lord Jesus.

620   7.7.8.7.D.

THY Name we bless, Lord Jesus!
That Name all names excelling:
How great Thy love, all praise above,
Should every tongue be telling.
The Father's loving-kindness
In giving Thee was shown us;
Now by Thy blood redeemed to God,
As children He doth own us.

2 From that eternal glory
Thou hadst with God the Father,
He gave His Son, that He in one
His children all might gather.
Our sins were all laid on Thee,
God's wrath Thou hast endurèd;
It was for us Thou suffer'dst thus,
And hast our peace securèd.

3 Thou from the dead wast raisèd,
And from all condemnation
Thy saints are free, as risen in Thee,
Head of the new creation!
On high Thou hast ascended
To God's right hand in heaven;
The Lamb once slain, alive again,
To Thee all power is given.

4 Thou hast bestowed the earnest
Of that we shall inherit;
Till Thou shalt come to take us home,
We're sealed by God the Spirit.
We wait for Thine appearing,
When we shall know more fully
The grace divine that made us Thine,
Thou Lamb of God most holy!

621   7.7.7.7.7.7.

"TILL He come!" Oh let the words
Linger on the trembling chords;
Let the "little while" between
In their golden light be seen;
Let us think how heaven and home
Lie beyond that "Till He come!"

2 When the weary ones we love
Enter on their rest above,
When their words of love and cheer
Fall no longer on our ear,
Hush! be every murmur dumb,
It is only "Till He come!"

3 Clouds and darkness round us press;
Would we have one sorrow less?
All the sharpness of the Cross,
All that tells the world is loss,
Death, and darkness, and the tomb,
Pain us only "Till He come!"

4 Sweet the feast of love divine,
Broken bread and outpoured wine;
Sweet memorials, till the Lord
Call us round His heavenly board,
Some from earth, from glory some,
Severed only "Till He come!"

622   L.M.

'TIS finished all: our souls to win
His life the blessèd Jesus gave,
Then rising, left His people's sin
Behind Him in His opening grave.

2 Past suff'ring now, the tender heart
Of Jesus, on His Father's throne,
Still in our sorrow bears a part,
And feels it as He felt His own.

3 Sweet thought! we have a Friend
above,
Our weary, faltering steps to guide,
Who follows with the eye of love
The little flock for which He died.

4 O Jesus, teach us more and more
On Thee alone to cast our care;
And, gazing on Thy Cross, adore
The wondrous grace that brought
Thee there.

623   C.M.

'TIS past, the dark and dreary night:
And, Lord, we hail Thee now,
Our Morning Star, without a cloud
Of sadness on Thy brow.

2 Thy path on earth, the Cross, the grave,
    Thy sorrows all are o'er;
  And, oh, sweet thought! Thine eye
    shall weep,
  Thy heart shall break no more.

3 Deep were those sorrows, deeper still
    The love that brought Thee low,
  That bade the streams of life from
    Thee,
  A lifeless Victim, flow.

4 The soldier, as he pierced Thee,
    proved,
  Man's hatred, Lord, to Thee;
    While in the blood that stained the
      spear,
  Love, only love, we see.

5 Drawn from Thy pierced and
    bleeding side,
  That pure and cleansing flood
    Speaks peace to every heart that
      knows
  The virtues of Thy blood.

6 Yet 'tis not that we know the joy
    Of cancelled sin alone,
  But, happier far, Thy saints are called
  To share Thy glorious throne.

7 So closely are we linked in love,
    So wholly one with Thee,
  That all Thy bliss and glory then
  Our bright reward shall be.

8 Yes, when the storm of life is calmed,
    The dreary desert past,
  Our way-worn hearts shall find in Thee
  Their full repose at last.

624   P.M.
'TIS the blessèd hour of prayer,
    when our hearts lowly bend,
  And we gather to Jesus, our Saviour
    and Friend;
  If we come to Him in faith, His
    protection to share,
  What a balm for the weary! O how
    sweet to be there!

Blessèd hour of prayer,
Blessèd hour of prayer,
  What a balm for the weary!
O how sweet to be there!

2 'Tis the blessèd hour of prayer,
    when the Saviour draws near
  With tender compassion His people
    to hear;
  When He tells us we may cast at
    His feet every care:
  What a balm for the weary! O how
    sweet to be there!

3 'Tis the blessèd hour of prayer,
    when the tempted and tried,
  To the Saviour who loves them, their
    sorrows confide;
  With a sympathising heart He
    removes every care:
  What a balm for the weary! O how
    sweet to be there!

4 At the blessèd hour of prayer,
    trusting Him we believe
  That the blessing we're needing
    we'll surely receive;
  In the fulness of delight we shall
    lose every care;
  What a balm for the weary! O how
    sweet to be there!

625   L.M.
'TIS we, O Lord, whom Thou hast
    shown
  The deadly bitterness of sin;
    We, who forgiving love have known,
  May fitly bring thank-offerings in.

2 Thy presence called for Israel's praise,
    Encompassed by their mortal foes;
  And when in death they met their gaze,
    What songs of glorious triumph rose.

3 And we have known redemption, Lord,
    From bondage worse than theirs
      by far;
  Sin held us by a stronger cord,
    Yet by Thy mercy free we are.

4 O blessèd Lord! Thy groans and tears,
    Thy death the power of darkness
      broke;
  Bursting the chains we wore for years
    It freed us from the iron yoke.

5 Divine Deliverer! Thou alone
   Thy people from the deep couldst
      bring;
   The glorious triumph all Thine own:
   Thy Name, Thy might, Thy grace,
      we sing.

626
C.M.

To Calvary, Lord, in spirit now,
   Our weary souls repair,
To dwell upon Thy dying love,
   And taste its sweetness there.

2 Sweet resting-place of every heart,
   That feels the plague of sin,
   Yet knows that deep mysterious joy,
   The peace with God, within.

3 There, through Thine hour of
      deepest woe,
   Thy suffering spirit passed;
      Grace there its wondrous victory
         gained,
   And love endured its last.

4 Dear suffering Lamb! Thy bleeding
      wounds,
   With cords of love divine,
      Have drawn our willing hearts to
         Thee,
   And linked our life with Thine.

5 Our longing eyes would fain behold
   That bright and blessèd brow,
   Once wrung with bitterest anguish,
      wear
   Its crown of glory now.

6 Thy sympathies and hopes are ours:
   We long, O Lord, to see
   Creation, all below, above,
      Redeemed and blest by Thee.

627
11.11.11.11. with Chorus

To God be the glory, great things
   He hath done,
So loved He the world that He gave
   us His Son,
Who yielded His life an atonement
   for sin,
And opened the Life Gate that all
   may go in.

Praise the Lord, praise the Lord,
   Let the earth hear His voice!
Praise the Lord, praise the Lord,
   Let the people rejoice!
Oh, come to the Father, through
   Jesus the Son,
And give Him the glory, great things
   He hath done.

2 Oh, perfect redemption, the
      purchase of blood,
   To every believer the promise of God;
      The vilest offender who truly
         believes,
   That moment from Jesus a pardon
      receives.

3 Great things He hath taught us,
      great things He hath done,
   And great our rejoicing through
      Jesus the Son;
   But purer, and higher, and greater
      will be
   Our wonder, our transport, when
      Jesus we see.

628
6.4.6.4.6.6.6.4.

To Thee, His God, we bring,
   Remembering,
This our thank-offering,
   Remembering,
Rememb'ring Him as He
   Never again shall be:
His journey to the tree
   Remembering!

2 Those nights on Olivet
   Remembering,
Locks with the night dews wet
   Remembering,
Remembering those days
   Calling for constant praise,
Ours unto Thee we raise,
   Remembering!

3 His path of grace most sweet
   Remembering,
The fragrance of His feet
   Remembering,
Remembering His face
   Set like a flint in grace
To reach at last that place,
   Remembering!

4 That prospect to His soul
  Remembering,
That road to such a goal
  Remembering,
Remembering Thy Son,
  And all His work well done
That worthy, worthy One
  Remembering!

629   7.6.7.6.D.
TO Thee, O gracious Saviour!
  My spirit turns for rest,
My peace is in Thy favour,
  My pillow on Thy breast:
Though all the world deceive me,
  I know that I am Thine,
And Thou wilt never leave me,
  O blessèd Saviour mine!

2 In Thee my trust abideth,
  On Thee my hope relies,
O Thou whose love provideth
  For all beneath the skies:
O Thou whose mercy found me,
  From bondage set me free,
And then for ever bound me
  With threefold cords to Thee.

3 My grief is in the dullness
  With which this sluggish heart
Doth open to the fulness
  Of all Thou dost impart:
My joy is in Thy merit,
  And holiness divine,
My comfort in Thy Spirit
  That binds my life to Thine.

4 Alas, that I should ever
  Have failed in love to Thee,
The only One who never
  Forgot or slighted me!
Oh for a heart to love Thee
  More truly as I ought,
And nothing place above Thee
  In deed, or word, or thought!

5 Oh for that choicest blessing
  Of living in Thy love!
And thus on earth possessing
  The peace of heaven above:
Oh for the bliss that by it
  The soul securely knows,
The holy calm and quiet
  Of faith's serene repose!

630   S.M.
TOGETHER at the feast,
  A sacrifice we raise
To Thee, O God, through our Great
  Priest
Who leads our hymn of praise.

2 Our hearts are occupied
  With Thy Belovèd Son,
In Whom Thou hast been glorified,
  By Whom Thy will was done.

3 Our eyes afresh survey
  That path of purest grace,
And mark the beauties of His way,
  That time shall ne'er efface.

4 Our minds recall again
  Those words of grace so free,
Those mighty deeds of power, as when
  He quelled the storm at sea.

5 Our hands we thus would fill
  With gathered incense sweet -
The fragrance inexpressible
  That lingered round His feet.

6 Through Him, O God, we raise
  In worship rev'rently,
United sacrifice of praise,
  Acceptable to Thee.

631   7.7.8.7.
'TWAS love that sought Gethsemane,
  Or Judas ne'er had found Thee;
'Twas love that nailed Thee to the tree,
  Or iron ne'er had bound Thee.

2 'Twas love that lived, 'twas love that
  died,
With endless life to bless us;
  Well hast Thou won Thy blood-
  bought Bride,
Worthy art Thou, Lord Jesus!

632   L.M.
'TWAS on that night, when
  doomed to know
The eager rage of every foe,
  That night in which He was
  betrayed,
The Saviour of the world took bread.

2 And after thanks and glory given
   To Him that rules in earth and
     heaven,
  That symbol of His flesh He broke,
   And thus to all His followers spoke.

3 My broken body thus I give
   For you, for all; take, eat, and live:
  And oft the sacred rite renew
   That brings My wondrous love to
     view.

4 Then in His hands the cup He raised,
   And God anew He thanked and
     praised,
  While kindness in His bosom glowed,
   And from His lips salvation flowed.

5 My blood I thus pour forth, He cries,
   To cleanse the soul in sin that lies;
  In this the covenant is sealed,
   And heaven's eternal grace revealed.

6 With love to man this cup is fraught,
   Let all partake the sacred draught;
  Through latest ages let it pour
   In memory of My dying hour.

633
4.6.8.8.4.

UNTIL He come,
   And we shall be at home,
The feast we keep, His death proclaim,
And spread abroad His precious
     Name,
     Until He come.

2 As sons of light,
   We look beyond the night,
  With eagerness to hail the dawn,
  When bursts the Morning Star upon
     Our waiting sight!

3 Our hearts would be
   From every hindrance free,
  And centred on the Coming One,
   Whose every glory as the Son
     We long to see.

4 For Him we wait,
   And watch at wisdom's gate,
  In readiness to do His will,
   For Him, each day with service fill
     While thus we wait.

634
8.7.8.7.8.7.

UNTO Him who loved us, gave us
   Every pledge that love could give;
Freely shed His blood to save us;
   Gave His life that we might live;
Be the kingdom, and dominion,
   And the glory evermore!

635
C.M.

UNTO the end with even pace,
   Through such a scene as this,
With not one thing done out of place,
   And not one word amiss!

2 Unto the end His kindness such
   As never need ignored:
  Malchus received that healing touch,
   And Peter sheathed his sword.

3 Unto the end He loved His own
   With an unchanging love,
  True as the everlasting throne,
   All other loves above.

4 Unto the end, calm and serene,
   That lowly path He trod:
  There moral Majesty was seen
   Marking the Son of God.

5 O Blessèd God those steps we trace
   Through such a scene as this;
  Sing of that priceless wealth of grace
   With priestly emphasis.

636
C.M.

WALK in the light, so shalt thou
   know
That fellowship of love
   His Spirit only can bestow,
Who reigns in light above.

2 Walk in the light, o'er sin abhorred
   Thou shalt the victory gain;
  The blood of Jesus Christ Thy Lord
   Cleanseth from every stain.

3 Walk in the light, and thou shalt find
   Thy heart made truly His,
  Who dwells in cloudless light
    enshrined,
   In whom no darkness is.

4 Walk in the light, and e'en the tomb
  No fearful shade shall wear;
Glory shall chase away the gloom,
  For Christ hath conquered there.

5 Walk in the light, and thine shall be
  A path, though thorny, bright;
For God, by grace, shall dwell in thee,
  And God Himself is light!

637   L.M.D.
WAS it for me, for me alone,
    The Saviour left His glorious
throne;
  The dazzling splendours of the sky?
Was it for me He came to die?

  It was for me, …
    Yes, all for me, …
  O love of God, …
    So great, so free …
  O wondrous love, …
    I'll shout and sing, …
  He died for me, …
    My Lord and King!

2 Was it for me sweet angel strains
    Came floating o'er Judea's plains,
That starlight night so long ago?
    Was it for me God planned it so?

3 Was it for me the Saviour said,
    "Pillow thy weary, aching head,
Trustingly on thy Saviour's breast"?
    Was it for me? Can I thus rest?

4 Was it for me He wept and prayed,
    My load of sin before Him laid;
That night within Gethsemane?
    Was it for me, that agony?

5 Was it for me He bowed His head
    Upon the Cross, and freely shed
His precious blood - that crimson tide?
    Was it for me the Saviour died?

638   6.4.6.4.6.6.6.4.
WE are but strangers here;
    Heaven is our home!
Earth is a desert drear;
    Heaven is our home!
Danger and sorrow stand
    Round us on ev'ry hand;
Heaven is our father-land,
    Heaven is our home!

2 What though the tempest rage?
    Heaven is our home!
Short is our pilgrimage;
    Heaven is our home!
And time's wild wintry blast
    Soon will be overpast;
We shall reach home at last;
    Heaven is our home!

3 There at our Saviour's side;
    Heaven is our home!
We shall be glorified;
    Heaven is our home!
There with the good and blest,
    Those we've loved most and best,
We shall for ever rest;
    Heaven is our home.

4 Therefore we'll murmur not;
    Heaven is our home!
Whate'er our earthly lot;
    Heaven is our home!
For we shall surely stand
    There at our Lord's right hand;
Heaven is our father-land:
    Heaven is our home!

639   8.7.8.7.D.
WE are waiting for the moment
    That is ever drawing nigh,
To be caught up all together,
    And to meet our Lord on high.

  Blessèd moment, drawing nearer
    While the days are passing by!
  Blessèd prospect, shining clearer,
    Drawing nigh, drawing nigh!

2 Not a single pang of parting,
    Not a sigh and not a tear!
When He calls us, in an instant
    We'll be there instead of here.

3 We shall see Him, and be like Him,
    Nevermore to fail and die,
For He'll change these feeble bodies
    In the twinkling of an eye.

4 We are waiting, we are watching,
    Cleaving to His precious Word,
Pleased to bear the world's
    reproaching
Till the coming of our Lord.

640   S.M.

WE bless our Saviour's Name,
　　Our sins are all forgiven;
To suffer once, to earth He came,
　　And now He's crowned in heaven.

2　His precious blood was shed,
　　　His body bruised for sin;
　Rememb'ring this, we break the bread,
　　　And, joyful, drink the wine.

3　While we remember Thee,
　　　Lord, in our midst appear!
　Let each by faith Thy body see
　　　While we assemble here.

4　We never would forget
　　　Thy rich, Thy precious love;
　Our theme of joy and wonder here,
　　　Our endless song above!

5　Oh let Thy love constrain
　　　Our souls to cleave to Thee!
　And ever in our hearts remain
　　　That word, "Remember Me!"

641   7.6.7.6.D.

WE bless Thee, God and Father,
　　We joy before Thy face;
Beyond dark death for ever
　　We share Thy Son's blest place:
He lives a Man before Thee
　　In cloudless light above,
In Thine unbounded favour,
　　Thine everlasting love.

2　His Father and our Father,
　　　His God and ours Thou art;
　And He is Thy Belovèd,
　　　The gladness of Thy heart:
　We're His, in joy He brings us
　　　To share His part and place,
　To know Thy love and favour,
　　　The shining of Thy face.

3　Thy love that now enfolds us
　　　Can ne'er wax cold or dim;
　In Him that love doth centre,
　　　And we are loved in Him:
　In Him Thy love and glory
　　　Find their eternal rest;
　The many sons - His brethren -
　　　In Him how near, how blest!

642   7.6.7.6.D.

WE come, our gracious Father,
　　With many hearts as one,
And here we only gather
　　In memory of Thy Son:
We prize each happy token
　　Of peace with Thee, our God;
The bread, His body broken;
　　The wine, His precious blood.

2　Whilst breaking bread, we ponder,
　　　Lord Jesus, on Thy love,
　And see, with silent wonder,
　　　What drew Thee from above.
　Complete in Thy completeness,
　　　The Church, Thy favoured Bride,
　Possesses all the meetness
　　　Thy perfect love supplied.

643   8.8.8.8.

WE feast on the fruit that He
　　bears,
And oh, it is sweet to our taste -
　　The virtues and glories He wears,
　The beauties wherewith He is graced.

2　But still as we study Him more,
　　　And ponder His words and His
　　　　ways,
　New beauties unnoticed before
　　　Are blossoming out to our gaze.

3　And humbly, yet gladly, we own,
　　　Though daily new glimpses we get,
　There's many a glory unknown
　　　That's still in the bud to us yet.

4　Yes, such is His fulness, and such
　　　The freshness and dew of His
　　　　youth,
　Time's withering hand cannot touch
　　　His treasures of goodness and
　　　　truth.

5　He's th' Rod and the Branch and
　　　the Root,
　And still, to the wondering soul,
　　　Will bud and will bloom and bear
　　　　fruit
　While years of eternity roll.

644 C.M.

WE look upon the loaf and cup,
    And thus, with one accord,
Our praise, O God, we offer up,
    Remembering our Lord.

2 We linger o'er the lowly place,
    The veiled infinitude,
The unseen splendour of the grace,
    'Mid man's ingratitude.

3 We meditate on matchless worth
    That marked His outward ways,
And told the inner glories forth -
    Too much for mortal gaze.

4 We muse on more than heart can hold,
    On more than tongue can tell,
And simply say, like those of old,
    "He hath done all things well".

5 We ponder o'er the path He trod,
    The way His work was done,
And raise our hymn of praise, O God,
    For Thy Belovèd Son.

645 C.M.

WE love to sing with one accord
    The riches of Thy grace;
We love to come before Thee, Lord,
    On earth no happier place.

2 We love to lean upon Thy breast
    In the repose of faith,
And find our soul's enduring rest
    In what Thy Spirit saith.

3 He witnessed to the constant guilt
    That marked the path we trod;
He witnessed that Thy blood was spilt
    To bring us nigh to God.

4 He made us look to Thee alone,
    And showed us our release;
He brings the message from the throne,
    Of mercy, grace, and peace.

5 In songs of praise we would record
    Thy mercy while we live,
And standing in Thy presence, Lord,
    Far sweeter praises give.

646 10.10.10.10.

WE praise Thee, Lord, in strains
    of deepest joy,
Responsive to Thy voice of holy love;
    We hail Thee, source of bliss
    without alloy,
Bright inlet to the light of heaven
    above.

2 Thou hast made known the Father
    whom we've seen
In Thy blest Person - infinite delight!
    It more than satisfies, as here we
    glean
The foretaste of His love, till all be
    light.

3 Father, Thou lovest! favour all divine,
    A cloudless favour rests upon us
    here;
Thy face shines on us as it still doth
    shine
On Thy blest Son, whose image we
    shall bear

4 We praise Thee, Lord, for in Thy
    blessèd face
God's glory shines for us without a
    veil;
And now Thou leadest us in
    righteous grace
To that blest place where praises
    never fail.

5 We live of Thee, we've heard Thy
    quickening voice
Speaking of love beyond all human
    thought,
Thy Father's love, in which we now
    rejoice,
As those in spirit to Thy Father
    brought.

647 P.M.

WE praise Thy great love,
    Our Father and God;
Rejoicing in Jesus,
    Whom Thou hast bestowed.

Hallelujah! Thine the glory!
    Hallelujah! Amen!
Hallelujah! Thine the glory!
    Revive us again.

2 We praise Thee, O God,
   For the joy Thou hast given
To Thy saints in communion,
   These foretastes of heaven.

3 We praise Thee, O God,
   For the Word of Thy love,
Which unfolds Thy rich grace
   And Thy glory above.

4 Accepted in Christ,
   Who has stood in our place,
We shall show in the glory
   Thy riches of grace.

5 We work for Him now,
   Till, God's purpose complete,
The Bride and the Bridegroom
   In glory shall meet.

   Hallelujah! Thine the glory!
   Hallelujah! Amen!
   Hallelujah! Thine the glory!
   Come quickly again.

6 Lord Jesus, we wait
   For the day Thou shalt come;
We long for Thy presence,
   Our heavenly home.

648   8.5.8.3.

WE remember glory shining
   'Midst the moral night;
Grace and Truth in One combining
   Love and Light.

2 We remember fragrance flowing
   From His holy feet,
Rose to God in all His going,
   Pure and sweet.

3 We remember moral glory
   Marking all His way;
Telling Love's eternal story
   Day by day.

4 We remember all the beauty
   Of the path He trod.
Pleasurable path of duty,
   All for God!

5 We remember every movement
   Faultless was and true;
Every touch beyond improvement
   Through and through.

6 We remember, we remember,
   And, with one accord,
Thanks, O God, through Him we
   render
For our Lord!

649   11.10.11.10.

WE rest on Thee, our Shield and
   our Defender!
We go not forth alone against the foe;
   Strong in Thy strength, safe in
      Thy keeping tender,
We rest on Thee, and in Thy Name
   we go.

2 Yes, in Thy Name, O Captain of
   salvation!
In Thy dear Name, all other names
   above;
Jesus our Righteousness, our sure
   Foundation,
Our Prince of glory and our King of
   love.

3 We go in faith, our own great
   weakness feeling,
And needing more each day Thy
   grace to know;
Yet from our hearts a song of
   triumph pealing,
"We rest on Thee, and in Thy Name
   we go".

4 We rest on Thee, our Shield and our
   Defender!
Thine is the battle, Thine shall be
   the praise;
When passing through the gates of
   pearly splendour,
Victors, we rest with Thee, through
   endless days.

650   8.8.8.8.8.8.

WE saw Thee not when Thou
   didst come
To this poor world of sin and death,
   Nor e'er beheld Thy cottage home
In that despisèd Nazareth;
   But we believe Thy footsteps trod
Its streets and plains, Thou Son of
   God.

2 We did not see Thee lifted high
  Amid that wild and savage crew,
Nor heard Thy meek, imploring cry,
  Forgive, they know not what they do;
Yet we believe the deed was done
  Which shook the earth, and veiled
    the sun.

3 We stood not by the empty tomb
  Where late Thy sacred body lay,
Nor sat within that upper room,
  Nor met Thee in the open way;
But we believe the angel said,
  Why seek the living with the dead?

4 We did not mark the chosen few
  When Thou didst through the
    clouds ascend,
First lift to heaven their wondering view,
  Then to the earth all prostrate bend;
Yet we believe that mortal eyes
  Beheld that journey to the skies.

5 And now that Thou dost reign on high,
  And thence Thy waiting people bless,
No ray of glory from the sky
  Doth shine upon our wilderness;
But we believe Thy faithful word,
  And trust in our redeeming Lord.

651 — L.M.

WE sing the praise of Him who
  died,
Of Him who died upon the Cross,
  The sinner's Hope - though men
    deride,
For Him we count the world but loss.

2 Inscribed upon the Cross we see,
  In shining letters, "God is love";
The Lamb who died upon the tree
  Has brought us mercy from above.

3 The Cross! it takes our guilt away;
  It holds the fainting spirit up;
It cheers with hope the gloomy day,
  And sweetens every bitter cup.

4 It makes the coward spirit brave,
  And nerves the feeble arm for fight;
It takes its terror from the grave,
  And gilds the bed of death with light.

5 The balm of life, the cure of woe,
  The measure and the pledge of love,
The sinner's refuge here below,
  The theme of praise in heaven
    above.

6 To Christ, who won for sinners grace
  By bitter grief and anguish sore,
Be praise from all the ransomed race
  Forever and forevermore.

652 — C.M.

WE thank Thee, O His Father,
  God,
For Thy Belovèd Son,
  For all the way His feet have trod,
And all His hands have done.

2 We thank Thee for His path pursued
  In freshest dew of youth,
With every virtue fair endued,
  And full of grace and truth.

3 We thank Thee for the *Light* He brought,
  The *Love* in Him bestowed;
We thank Thee for the *Truth* He
  taught,
And for the *Grace* He showed.

4 We thank Thee for the healing touch,
  The heart to sympathise,
The gentle word that meant so much,
  So good, so kind, so wise.

5 We thank Thee for His steadfast
    strength
That failed not in the way,
  That brought Him to the Cross at
    length
Thy glory to display.

6 We thank Thee, O His Father, God:
  With movèd hearts as one,
Remembering the path He trod,
  We thank Thee for Thy Son.

653 — 10.10.10.10.

WE would prepared, O God,
  this lordly day,
Surround Thy Son in sweet simplicity,
  Gathered into His holy Name alone,
As living stones to Him the Living
  Stone,

2 We know Him in our midst, the risen Lord,
The Leader of our praise, as in accord
    With Him, and through Him, thus we offer Thee
Thanksgiving now and praise befittingly.

3 While we through priestly eyes His path review,
His preciousness throughout appears anew;
From meditating hearts to Thee arise
    Worship and praise in priestly exercise.

4 And thus we come with joy, O God to Thee,
Our hearts engaged, in holy liberty,
    With Him on earth, the holy, spotless One,
The perfect Man, Thy well-belovèd Son.

654   C.M.

WE would remember, Lord, Thy Cross,
The tempest and the flood,
    Thy soul for sin an offering,
Thy precious, out-poured blood.

2 Thine opened side, Thy piercèd hands,
    Are tokens of Thy woe,
Unfolding that deep shoreless love
    Our hearts so feebly know.

3 O God, we worship, we adore!
    Thy love our theme must be;
And ever, as the ages roll,
    Shall praise ascend to Thee!

655   P.M.

WE'LL all gather home in the morning,
On the banks of the bright jasper sea,
We'll meet the redeemed and the faithful;
What a gathering that will be!

What a gathering, gathering,
    Gathering that will be!
What a gathering, gathering,
    What a gathering that will be!

2 We'll all gather home in the morning,
    At the sound of the great Jubilee;
We'll all gather home in the morning,
    What a gathering that will be!

3 We'll all gather home in the morning,
    Our blessèd Redeemer to see!
We'll meet with the friends gone before us;
What a gathering that will be!

4 We'll all gather home in the morning,
    To sing of redemption so free;
We'll praise Him for grace so abounding;
What a gathering that will be!

656   8.8.8.8.

WE'LL sing of the Shepherd that died,
That died for the sake of the flock;
    His love to the utmost was tried,
But firmly endured as a rock.

2 When blood from a victim must flow,
    This Shepherd, by pity, was led
To stand between us and the foe,
    And willingly die in our stead.

3 Our song then for ever should be
    Of the Shepherd who gave Himself thus;
No subject's so glorious as He,
    No theme's so affecting to us.

4 We'll sing of such subjects alone,
    None other our tongues shall employ,
Till fully His love becomes known
    In yonder bright regions of joy.

657   L.M.

WE'VE no abiding city here -
    This may distress the worldly mInd,
    But should not cost the saint a tear,
Who hopes a better rest to find.

2 We've no abiding city here -
    Sad truth were this to be our home!
But let this thought our spirits cheer,
    We seek a city yet to come.

3 We've no abiding city here -
   Then let us live as pilgrims do;
   Let not the world our rest appear,
   But let us haste from all below.

4 We've no abiding city here -
   We seek a city out of sight:
   It needs no sun - "The Lord is there";
   It shines with everlasting light.

5 Jehovah is her joy and strength;
   Secure, she smiles at all her foes,
   And weary travellers at length
   Within her sacred walls repose.

6 O sweet abode of peace and love,
   Where pilgrims freed from toil are
      blest,
   Soon shall we, with our Lord above,
   In thy blest mansions find our rest!

658   P.M.

WHAT a fellowship, what a joy
   divine,
Leaning on the everlasting arms;
   What a blessèdness, what a
      peace is mine,
Leaning on the everlasting arms.

Lean…ing, lean…ing,
   Safe and secure from all alarms;
Lean…ing, lean…ing,
   Leaning on the everlasting arms.

2 Oh, how sweet to walk in this pilgrim
      way,
   Leaning on the everlasting arms;
   Oh, how bright the path grows
      from day to day,
   Leaning on the everlasting arms.

3 What have I to dread, what have I
      to fear,
   Leaning on the everlasting arms?
   I have blessèd peace with my
      Lord so near,
   Leaning on the everlasting arms.

659   8.7.8.7.D.

WHAT a Friend we have in Jesus,
   All our sins and griefs to bear!
What a privilege to carry
   Everything to God in prayer!

Oh, what peace we often forfeit,
   Oh, what needless pain we bear!
All because we do not carry
   Everything to God in prayer.

2 Have we trials and temptations?
   Is there trouble anywhere?
We should never be discouraged:
   Take it to the Lord in prayer!
Can we find a friend so faithful,
   Who will all our sorrows share?
Jesus knows our every weakness:
   Take it to the Lord in prayer.

3 Are we weak and heavy-laden,
   Cumbered with a load of care?
Blessèd Saviour, still our refuge:
   Take it to the Lord in prayer!
Do thy friends despise, forsake thee?
   Take it to the Lord in prayer!
In His arms He'll take and shield thee,
   Thou shalt find a solace there.

4 Blessèd Saviour, Thou hast promised
   Thou wilt all our burdens bear;
May we ever, Lord, be bringing
   All to Thee in earnest prayer!
Soon in glory, bright, unclouded,
   There will be no need for prayer -
Rapture, praise, and endless worship
   Shall be our sweet portion there.

660   C.M.

WHAT grace, O Lord, and
   beauty shone
Around Thy steps below!
   What patient love was seen in all
Thy life and death of woe!

2 For ever on Thy burdened heart
   A weight of sorrow hung;
Yet no ungentle, murmuring word
   Escaped Thy silent tongue.

3 Thy foes might hate, despise, revile,
   Thy friends unfaithful prove;
Unwearied in forgiveness still,
   Thy heart could only love.

4 Oh, give us hearts to love like Thee!
   Like Thee, O Lord, to grieve
Far more for others' sins, than all
   The wrongs that we receive.

5 One with Thyself, may every eye,
   In us, Thy brethren, see
That gentleness and grace that spring
   From union, Lord, with Thee.

661
6.6.6.6.8.8.

W HAT holy mem'ries fill
      Our hearts today, O God,
As, in Thy blessèd will,
   Hands filled and feet unshod,
Before Thyself with joyful lays,
We offer up adoring praise!

2 Memories of Thy Son,
   In loveliness unique,
Whose purpose was but one,
   Thy pleasure here to seek,
With opened ear and single eye,
In lowliness to live and die!

3 Memories of the way
   Traced by those holy feet,
While fragrance rose each day,
   Unutterably sweet;
His motives and His perfect ways,
Alike conducive to Thy praise!

4 With mem'ries such as these
   Filling our hearts, we bow,
And seek, O God, to please
   Thyself in worship now.
Through Him to Thee our thanks we
   bring,
While of His worthiness we sing.

662
S.M.

W HAT raised the wondrous
      thought,
Or who did it suggest,
   That blood-bought saints to glory
      brought
Should with the Son be blest?

2 Father, the thought was Thine,
   And only Thine could be -
Fruit of the wisdom, love divine,
   Peculiar unto Thee.

3 And Jesus joys to own
   His chosen Bride as His -
Flesh of His flesh, bone of His bone -
   To share His weight of bliss.

4 The Father and the Son,
   And Holy Spirit too,
In counsel deep, and power have
   shewn,
What wonders love can do.

5 Now, Saviour, Thy delight
   Is to prepare Thy Bride,
Till in the glory, clothed in white,
   She's seated at Thy side.

5 Sealed with the Holy Ghost,
   We triumph in that love,
Thy wondrous thought has made
   our boast
Glory with Christ above.

663
P.M.

W HAT though the way be lonely,
      And dark the shadows fall;
I know where'er it leadeth,
   My Father planned it all.

I sing thro' the shade and the
   sunshine,
I'll trust Him whatever befall;
   I sing for I cannot be silent,
My Father planned it all.

2 There may be sunshine tomorrow,
   Shadows may break and flee;
'Twill be the way He chooses,
   My Father's plan for me.

3 He guides my falt'ring footsteps
   Along the weary way,
For well He knows the pathway
   Will lead to endless day.

4 A day of light and gladness,
   On which no shade will fall,
'Tis this at last awaits me -
   My Father planned it all.

664
6.6.6.6.8.8.

W HAT was it, O our God,
      Led Thee to give Thy Son,
To yield Thy well-beloved
   For us by sin undone?
'Twas love unbounded led Thee thus
To give Thy well-beloved for us.

2 What led the Son of God
   To leave His throne on high,
To shed His precious blood,
   To suffer and to die?
'Twas love, unbounded love for us,
Led Him to die and suffer thus.

3 What moved Thee to impart
   Thy Spirit from above?
Therewith to fill our heart
   With heavenly peace and love!
'Twas love, unbounded love to us,
   Moved Thee to give Thy Spirit thus.

4 What love to Thee we owe,
   Our God, for all Thy grace,
Our hearts should overflow
   In everlasting praise:
Help us, O Lord, to praise Thee thus
For all Thy boundless love to us.

665   8.8.8.8.8.8.
WHAT will it be to dwell above,
   And with the Lord of glory reign,
Since the blest knowledge of His love
   So brightens all this dreary plain?
No heart can think, no tongue can tell
   What joy 'twill be with Christ to
      dwell!

2 When sin no more obstructs the sight,
   When sorrow pains the heart no more,
When we shall see the Prince of light,
   And all His works of grace explore -
What heights and depths of love divine
   Will there through endless ages
      shine!

3 And God has fixed the happy day
   When the last tear shall dim our eyes,
When He will wipe these tears away,
   And fill our hearts with glad surprise
To hear His voice, and see His face,
   And know the fulness of His grace.

4 This is the joy we seek to know,
   For this with patience we would wait
Till, called from earth and all below,
   We rise our glorious Lord to meet,
Our harps to strike, our crowns to wear,
   And praise the love that brought us
      there!

666   11.10.11.10.
WHAT will it be when all life's toil
   is finished,
And we have entered our eternal rest;
   When past for ever is the night of
      weeping,
And with Thee, Lord, we are for
   ever blest!

2 What will it be when all the strife is
      over,
   And all Thy saints, now scattered far
      and wide,
Shall be without one shade of variation,
   All like Thee, Lord, united by Thy
      side!

3 What will it be when sorrow's day is
      ended,
   And pain and grief for ever passed
      away;
When with Thee, Lord, we share the
      bright forever,
   In perfect peace throughout the
      perfect day!

4 What will it be? - In blest anticipation
   E'en now our hearts outpour in
      praise to Thee;
But when we see Thee face to face
   in glory,
Then purer, sweeter, shall our
   praises be.

667   P.M.
WHEN all my labours and trials
   are o'er,
And I am safe on that beautiful shore,
   Just to be near the dear Lord I adore,
Will through the ages be glory for me.

Oh, that will be … glory for me,…
   Glory for me, …glory for me, ...
When by His grace I shall look on
   His face,
That will be glory, be glory for me!

2 When by the gift of His infinite grace
   I am accorded in heaven a place,
Just to be there, and to look on His face,
   Will through the ages be glory for me.

3 Friends will be there I have loved
    long ago;
  Joy like a river around me will flow;
      Yet, just a smile from my Saviour,
      I know,
  Will through the ages be glory for me.

668   8.8.8.8.8.8.

W HEN first to Jesus' Cross I came,
    My heart o'erwhelmed with
sin and shame,
    Conscious of guilt, and full of fear,
  Yet, drawn by love, I ventured near;
    And pardon found, and peace
      with God,
  In Jesus' rich *atoning blood.*

2 My sin is gone, my fears are o'er;
    I shun God's presence now no more:
  With child-like faith I seek His face,
    The God of all abounding grace:
  Sprinkled before the throne of God,
    I see that rich *atoning blood.*

3 Before my God my Priest appears -
    My Advocate the Father hears;
  That blood is e'er before His eyes,
    And day and night for mercy cries;
  It speaks, it ever speaks to God,
    The voice of that *atoning blood.*

4 By faith that voice I also hear;
      It answers doubt, it stills each fear:
  Th' accuser strives in vain to move
      The wrath of Him whose name is
      love:
  Each charge against th' elect of God
    Is silenced by th' *atoning blood.*

5 Here I can rest without a fear;
    By this, to God I now draw near,
  By this, I triumph over sin,
      For this has made and keeps me
      clean;
  And when I reach the throne of God,
    I still will sing the atoning blood

669   L.M.

W HEN I survey the wondrous
    Cross
On which the Prince of Glory died,
  My richest gain I count but loss,
And pour contempt on all my pride.

2 Forbid it, Lord, that I should boast,
    Save in the Cross of Christ, my
    God;
  All the vain things that charm me most,
    I sacrifice them to His blood.

3 See from His head, His hands, His
    feet,
  Sorrow and love flow mingled down;
      Did e'er such love and sorrow meet,
  Or thorns compose so rich a crown?

4 His dying crimson, like a robe,
    Spreads o'er His body on the tree;
  Then I am dead to all the globe,
    And all the globe is dead to me.

5 Were the whole realm of nature mine
    That were an offering far too small;
  Love so amazing, so divine,
    Demands my heart, my life, my all!

670   P.M.

W HEN my life-work is ended,
    and I cross the swelling tide,
  When the bright and glorious
    morning I shall see;
  I shall know my Redeemer when I
    reach the other side,
  And His smile will be the first to
    welcome me.

  I shall know … Him,
    I shall know Him,
  As redeemed by His side I shall stand;
    I shall know … Him,
  I shall know Him
      By the print of the nails in His hand.

2 Oh, the soul-thrilling rapture when I
    view His blessèd face,
  And the lustre of His kindly beaming
    eye;
  How my full heart will praise Him for
    the mercy, love and grace,
  That prepare for me a mansion in
    the sky.

3 Oh, the dear ones in glory, how they
    beckon me to come,
  And our parting at the river I recall;
      To the sweet vales of Eden they
      will sing my welcome home,
  But I long to meet my Saviour first
    of all.

4 Thro' the gates to the city in a robe
    of spotless white,
  He will lead me where no tears will
    ever fall;
  In the glad song of ages I shall
    mingle with delight,
  But I long to meet my Saviour first
    of all.

671 P.M.

WHEN peace, like a river,
    attendeth my way,
When sorrows, like sea-billows, roll;
  Whatever my lot, Thou hast
    taught me to say,
"It is well, it is well with my soul!"

  It is well with my soul,
    It is well, it is well with my soul!

2 Though Satan should buffet, though
    trials should come,
  Let this blest assurance control,
    That Christ hath regarded my
      helpless estate,
  And hath shed His own blood for
    my soul.

3 My sin - oh, the bliss of this glorious
    thought!
  My sin - not in part but the whole,
    Is nailed to His Cross, and I bear
      it no more;
  Praise the Lord, praise the Lord, O
    my soul!

4 For me, be it Christ, be it Christ
    hence to live!
  If Jordan above me shall roll,
    No pang shall be mine, for in
      death as in life,
  Thou wilt whisper Thy peace to my
    soul.

5 But, Lord, 'tis for Thee, for Thy
    coming we wait;
  The sky, not the grave, is our goal:
    Oh, trump of the angel! oh, voice
      of the Lord!
  Blessèd hope! blessèd rest of my
    soul!

672 7.7.7.7.7.7.

WHEN this passing world is done,
    When has sunk yon glaring sun,
When we stand with Christ in glory,
  Looking o'er life's finished story,
Then, Lord, shall I fully know -
  Not till then - how much I owe.

2 When I stand before the throne,
    Dressed in beauty not my own;
  When I see Thee as Thou art,
    Love Thee with unsinning heart:
  Then, Lord, shall I fully know -
    Not till then - how much I owe.

3 When the praise of heaven I hear,
    Loud as thunders to the ear,
  Loud as many waters' noise,
    Sweet as harp's melodious voice:
  Then, Lord, shall I fully know -
    Not till then - how much I owe.

4 Chosen, not for good in me;
    Wakened up from wrath to flee;
  Hidden in the Saviour's side;
    By the Spirit sanctified;
  Teach me, Lord, on earth to show
    By my love, how much I owe.

5 Oft I walk beneath the cloud,
    Dark, as midnight's gloomy shroud;
  But, when fear is at the height,
    Jesus comes, and all is light;
  Blessèd Jesus! bid me show
    Doubting saints how much I owe.

6 Oft the nights of sorrow reign -
    Weeping, sickness, sighing, pain;
  But a night Thine anger burns -
    Morning comes and joy returns;
  God of comforts! bid me show
    To Thy poor, how much I owe.

673 P.M.

WHEN upon life's billows you
    are tempest tossed,
When you are discouraged, thinking
  all is lost,
Count your many blessings, name
  them one by one,
And it will surprise you what the
  Lord hath done.

Count your blessings,
  Name them one by one,
Count your blessings,
  See what God hath done!
Count your blessings,
  Name them one by one,
And it will surprise you what the
  Lord hath done.

2 Are you ever burdened with a load
    of care?
  Does the cross seem heavy you are
    called to bear?
  Count your many blessings, every
    doubt will fly,
  And you will keep singing as the
    days go by.

3 When you look at others with their
    lands and gold,
  Think that Christ has promised you
    His wealth untold;
  Count your many blessings, wealth
    can never buy,
  Your reward in heaven, nor your
    home on high.

4 So, amid the conflict, whether great
    or small,
  Do not be disheartened, God is over
    all;
  Count your many blessings, angels
    will attend,
  Help and comfort give you to your
    journey's end.

674　　8.7.8.7.D. with Chorus

W HEN we reach our peaceful
      dwelling
On the strong, eternal hills,
  And our praise to Him is swelling,
Who the vast creation fills;
  When the path of prayer, and duty,
And affliction, all are trod,
  And we wake and see the beauty
Of our Saviour and our God:

Oh 'twill be a glorious morrow
  To a dark and stormy day,
When we smile upon our sorrow,
  And the storms have passed away.

2 With the light of resurrection,
    When our changèd bodies glow,
  And we gain the full perfection
    Of the bliss begun below;
  When the life the flesh obscureth
    In each radiant form shall shine,
  And the joy that aye endureth
    Flashes forth in beams divine.

3 Shall the memory be banished
    Of His kindness and His care,
  When the wants and woes are vanished,
    Which He loved to soothe and share?
  All the way by which He led us,
    All the grievings which He bore,
  All the patient love He taught us,
    Shall we think of them no more?

4 We shall read the tender meaning
    Of the sorrows and alarms,
  As we trod the desert, leaning
    On His everlasting arms;
  And His rest will be the dearer
    When we think of weary ways,
  And His light will shine the clearer
    As we muse on cloudy days.

675　　　　　　　P.M.

W HEN we walk with the Lord,
      In the light of His Word,
What a glory He sheds on our way!
  While we do His good will,
He abides with us still,
  And with all who will trust and obey.

Trust and obey,
  For there's no other way
To be happy in Jesus,
  But to trust and obey.

2 Not a shadow can rise,
    Not a cloud in the skies,
  But His smile quickly drives it away;
    Not a doubt nor a fear,
  Not a sigh nor a tear,
    Can abide while we trust and obey.

3 Not a burden we bear,
    Not a sorrow we share,
  But our toil He doth richly repay;
    Not a grief nor a loss,
  Not a frown nor a cross,
    But is blest if we trust and obey.

4 But we never can prove
    The delights of His love
Until all on the altar we lay;
    For the favour He shows,
    And the joy He bestows,
    Are for them who will trust and obey.

5 Then in fellowship sweet
    We will sit at His feet,
Or we'll walk by His side in the way;
    What He says we will do,
    Where He sends we will go;
    Never fear, only trust and obey.

676
L.M.

WHERE high the heavenly
    temple stands,
The house of God not made with hands,
    A great High Priest for us appears,
And lives to silence all our fears.

2 He who for us as Surety stood,
    And poured on earth His precious
        blood,
Pursues in heaven His gracious plan -
    The Saviour and the Friend of man.

3 Partaker of the human name,
    He knows the frailty of our frame,
And still remembers, in the skies
    His tears, and griefs, and agonies.

4 In every pang that rends the heart,
    The "Man of sorrows" bears a part;
He knows and feels our every grief,
    And gives the suffering saint relief.

5 With boldness, therefore, at the throne,
    Let us make all our sorrows known;
And seek His grace and heavenly
        power,
To help us in each trying hour.

677
8.4.8.4.8.8.8.4.

WHERE the few together gather
    Into His Name,
Pleasing Thee, His God and Father,
    Each mind the same,
In the midst His place He taketh,
    Holy thus the gath'ring maketh;
Every thought of Him awaketh
    Praise in His Name.

2 And Himself the praise is leading
    Here at the feast,
By the Spirit now proceeding
    Through our Great Priest;
As the purest incense blending,
    Hearts in full accord attending,
Fragrance this for Thee ascending
    Here at the feast!

3 Musing on His path, beholding
    One from above,
Every precious grace unfolding
    In perfect love,
Thanks to Thee His Father rend'ring,
    Thus we break the loaf while
        pond'ring,
Thus we pour the cup, rememb'ring
    Him Whom we love.

678
8.7.8.7.D.

WHO can cheer the heart like
    Jesus,
By His presence all divine?
    True and tender, pure and precious,
O how blest to call Him mine!

All that thrills my soul is Jesus;
    He is more than life to me;
And the fairest of ten thousand,
    In my blessèd Lord I see.

2 Love of Christ so freely given,
    Grace of God beyond degree,
Mercy higher than the heaven,
    Deeper then the deepest sea.

3 What a wonderful redemption!
    Never can a mortal know
How my sin, though red like crimson,
    Can be whiter than the snow.

4 Every need His hand supplying,
    Every good in Him I see;
On His strength divine relying,
    He is all in all to me.

5 By the crystal flowing river
    With the ransomed I will sing,
And forever and forever,
    Praise and glorify the King.

679 P.M.

WHO is He in yonder stall,
At whose feet the shepherds fall?

'Tis the Lord! oh, wondrous story!
'Tis the Lord! the King of glory!
At His feet now let us fall,
Own Him Saviour, Lord of all!

2 Who is He in deep distress,
Fasting in the wilderness?

3 Who is He the people bless
For His words of gentleness?

4 Who is He to whom they bring
All the sick and sorrowing?

5 Who is He who stands and weeps
At the grave where Lazarus sleeps?

6 Who is He the gathering throng
Greet with loud, triumphant song?

7 Lo! at midnight, who is He
Prays in dark Gethsemane?

8 Who is He on yonder tree,
Dies in grief and agony?

9 Who is He who from the grave
Comes to succour, help and save?

10 Who is He who from His throne
Rules through all the world alone?

680 10.10.10.10.

WITH conscience purged, through
Jesus' blood made meet,
We would draw near, with rinsèd
hands and feet,
To Thee, His God and Father, to
express
Appreciation of His preciousness.

2 Brighter than gold, the Lord amidst
His own,
In sovereign glory, makes His
presence known;
Into His Name thus gathered, are
we found
Assembled round Himself on holy
ground.

3 Frankincense pure, abiding, redolent,
The fragrance of His steps do we
present;
That lovely life again with joy we trace,
Replete for Thee with every
beauteous grace.

4 Myrrh, with its mem'ries of His
anguish sore,
Speaketh, through loaf and cup, as
oft before,
Of that great climax to the path He
trod,
The death so precious in Thy sight,
O God.

5 Thoughts of His Person, path, and
passion deep
Well up within us as the feast we keep;
Rememb'ring Him, our praises
here redound
To Thee, O God, for all His worth
profound.

681 L.M.

WITH fitting reverence and awe,
To Thee His Father near we draw,
His Word, His will, His wish our law,
Remembering! Remembering!

2 The perfect path, the patient grace,
The stately step, the steadfast face,
The servant form, the lowly place,
Remembering! Remembering!

3 The sympathy in man's distress,
The heart to feel, the hand to bless,
The tear, the touch, the tenderness,
Remembering! Remembering!

4 His fragrance thus to Thee we raise,
Hands filled, and hearts attune
with praise,
His walk, His works, His words, His
ways
Remembering! Remembering!

682 P.M.

WITH harps and with vials there
stand a great throng,
In the presence of Jesus, and sing
this new song:

Unto Him who hath loved us and
washed us from sin,
Unto Him be the glory for ever! Amen!

2 All these once were sinners, defiled
   in His sight,
  Now arrayed in pure garments in
   praise they unite:

3 He maketh the rebel a priest and a
   king,
  He hath bought us and taught us
   this new song to sing:

4 How helpless and hopeless we
   sinners had been,
  If He never had loved us till
   cleansed from our sin!

5 Aloud in His praises our voices shall
   ring,
  So that others, believing, this new
   song shall sing:

683   8.7.8.4.8.4.

W ITH His lowly condescension
     We, O God, engaged would be;
And of Thy Beloved make mention
   In praise to Thee,
Though with meagre comprehension
   His worth we see.

2 Fragrance sweet to Thee ascended
   From His thoughts and words and
    ways,
  As He to Thy will attended
   Through all those days;
  Grace and truth so fully blended
   Thyself portrays.

3 He, on earth Thy dearest treasure,
   Ever precious in Thy sight,
  Finding in Thy perfect pleasure
   His own delight,
  Moral wealth surpassing measure
   Brought thus to light.

4 Thus upon Him meditating,
   Moral glories fill our gaze;
  Radiant beauties emanating
   From all His ways
  Move our hearts, appreciating,
   Worship to raise.

684   S.M.

W ITH Jesus in our midst,
    We gather round the board;
Though many, we are one in Christ,
  One body in the Lord.

2 Our sins were laid on Him
   When bruised on Calvary;
  With Christ we died and rose again,
   And sit with Him on high.

3 Faith eats the bread of life,
   And drinks the living wine;
  Thus we, in love together knit,
   On Jesus' breast recline.

4 Soon shall the night be gone,
   And we with Jesus reign;
  The marriage supper of the Lamb
   Shall banish all our pain.

685   C.M.

W ITH joy we meditate the grace
    Of our High Priest above;
His heart o'erflows with tenderness,
  His very name is Love

2 Touched with a sympathy within,
   He knows our feeble frame;
  He knows what sore temptations mean,
   For He endured the same.

3 But spotless, undefiled, and pure,
   Our great Redeemer stood,
  No stain of sin did e'er defile
   The holy Lamb of God.

4 He, when He sojourned here below,
   Poured forth His cries and tears,
  And, though exalted, feels afresh,
   What every member bears.

5 Then boldly let our faith address
   His mercy and His power;
  We shall obtain delivering grace
   In each distressing hour.

686   9.8.9.8.

W ITH overflowing hearts we
    gather
Around Thy Son with one accord;
   Before Thyself, His God and Father,
With joy we magnify the Lord.

2 Again we call to mind His moving,
   A sinless Man 'mid sinful men;
   While Thou wert watching and
      approving
   By mighty signs beyond their ken.

3 Thy Holy Spirit actuating
   His every movement day by day,
   While precious fragrance emanating,
   Arose for Thee in all His way!

4 The grace and truth throughout
      prevailing
   In righteousness His worth proclaim,
   Those deep perfections all unveiling
   The matchless honour of His Name.

5 In holy-priesthood exercises
   A sacrifice to Thee we raise;
   Through Him the incense sweet arises,
   Who, in the midst, thus leads the
      praise.

687   8.8.6.8.8.6.
WITH praise, O God, our hearts
      abound
As for Thy pleasure we are found
   A holy priesthood now,
As for Thy Son we offer Thee
   Our thanks appreciatively
While we in worship bow.

2 Each beauteous grace was found
      in Him,
   And moral glories nought could dim
      Shone with effulgence rare;
   In love and truth and faithfulness,
      In every virtue measureless,
   In all beyond compare.

3 Himself alone Thy heart could fill,
      Obedient ever to Thy will,
   And ever Thy delight;
      No heart could know, no tongue
         express
   How fragrant in His preciousness,
      How pleasing in Thy sight.

4 As we recall His path below,
      To Thee, O God, our hearts o'erflow
   In praise befittingly
      For Him Who ever pleased Thee well,
   Whose perfect movements freshly
      dwell
   Before our minds today.

688   L.M.
WITH purposed heart He goes
      to meet
Exceeding sorrows that await:
   His path, unblemished and complete,
Upon a Cross must culminate.

2 By hatred moved, men spurn His grace;
      In Him no beauty do they see,
   But, in their scorn, avert the face
      And speak of Him despitefully.

3 The favoured ones who walk with Him,
      To whom the Father He would show,
   Their hearts so slow, their eyes so
      dim,
   Still miss the truth He'd have them
      know.

4 The Father only comprehends
      The Son, or rightly can appraise
   The moral glory that attends,
      From first to last, His perfect ways.

5 What matters else? Since God
      approves,
   Nought can distract, none can deter;
      Obediently He onward moves,
   The Cross to reach, and triumph there.

689   L.M.
WITH rev'rence we remember
      Him,
In all the heavenly path He trod;
   And view those glories nought
      could dim
Revealed in Thy Beloved, O God.

2 From highest heaven, His rightful
      place
   As Father of eternity,
      In servant form He came, in grace
   Unfolding love's infinity.

3 When He from Jordan came that day,
      His earthly ministry begun,
   Thy voice from heaven was heard
      to say,
   "This is My well-belovèd Son".

4 To Thee, O God, in heaven above,
      Arose as fragrance sweet each day
   The savour of the way, in love,
      He walked before Thee perfectly.

5 We muse upon that Heavenly One
    In all His holy, heavenly ways;
And thus, remembering Thy Son,
    Pour forth to Thee adoring praise.

690 C.M.

WITH steady pace the pilgrim
    moves
Towards the blissful shore,
    And sings with cheerful heart and
        voice,
"'Tis better on before".

2 His passage through a desert lies
    Where furious lions roar;
He takes his staff, and, smiling, says,
    "'Tis better on before".

3 When tempted to forsake his God
    And give the contest o'er,
He hears a voice which says, "Look up!
    'Tis better on before".

4 When stern affliction clouds his cheek,
    And want stands at the door,
Hope cheers him with her sunniest note,
    "'Tis better on before".

5 And if on Jordan's bank he stands,
    And sees the radiant shore,
Bright angels whisper, "Come away!
    'Tis better on before".

6 And so it is, for high in heaven
    They never suffer more;
Eternal calm succeeds the storm;
    "'Tis better on before!"

691 8.7.8.7.

WITH Thy Son our occupation,
    As we trace the path He trod,
Holy is our meditation,
    And our praise to Thee, O God.

2 Perfect walk and true devotion,
    Might and meekness intertwined,
Heavenly grace in every motion,
    Lowliness of heart and mind!

3 Works of might and deeds of healing,
    All the wonders of His hand,
Each in turn afresh revealing
    Boundless power at His command!

4 Ways of holiness and duty,
    Righteousness and matchless love,
Dignity and moral beauty,
    Mark Him out as from above.

5 Words of grace, and truth abiding,
    Flowing from His lips each day,
Tell of wisdom vast residing
    In Himself inherently.

6 Walk, and works, and ways
    transcending!
Words so precious and so pure!
    From the whole sweet fragrance
        blending
Ever shall for Thee endure.

692 S.M.

WITHOUT a cloud between;
    To see Him face to face;
Not struck with dire amazement dumb,
    But triumphing in grace.

2 Without a cloud between;
    To see Him as He is;
Oh, who can tell the height of joy,
    The full transporting bliss?

3 Without a cloud between;
    My longing spirit waits
For that sweet hour, from which my soul
    Its highest glory dates.

4 Without a cloud between;
    How changed will all appear!
How different from the earthly path -
    Our soul's experience here!

5 Without a cloud between;
    Lord Jesus, haste the day,
The morning bright without a cloud,
    And chase our tears away.

693 8.8.8.4.

WITHOUT a trace of Adam's sin,
    As Man unique in origin,
All fair without, all pure within,
    Our Blessèd Lord!

2 Without a waver in His ways,
    Steadfast and true through all
        those days,
Subject of everlasting praise,
    Our Blessèd Lord!

3 Without a flaw from first to last,
Through all His perfect path He
passed,
Till by an evil world outcast,
Our Blessèd Lord!

4 Without a fault among His foes,
As round Him clouds of darkness
close,
Still fragrance to His Father flows,
Our Blessèd Lord!

5 Without a murmur, suff'ring so
The righteous wrath of God to know,
The righteous love of God to show,
Our Blessèd Lord!

6 Without the law, O God, we raise
Our voice in voluntary praise
Of Him Who fills our heart, our gaze,
Our Blessèd Lord!

694 P.M.

WONDERFUL birth, to a
manger He came,
Made in the likeness of man, to
proclaim
God's boundless love for a world
sick with sin,
Pleading with sinners to let Him
come in.

Wonderful name He bears,
Wonderful crown He wears,
Wonderful blessings His triumphs
afford;
Wonderful Calvary,
Wonderful grace so free.
Wonderful love of my wonderful Lord!

2 Wonderful life, full of service so free,
Friend to the poor and the needy
was He;
Unfailing goodness on all He
bestowed,
Undying love to the vilest He showed.

3 Wonderful death, for it meant not
defeat,
Calvary made our salvation complete.
Wrought our redemption, and
when He arose,
Banished forever the last of His foes.

4 Wonderful hope, He is coming again,
Coming as King o'er the nations
to reign;
Glorious promise, His word cannot
fail,
His righteous kingdom at last must
prevail!

695 P.M.

WONDERFUL grace of Jesus,
Greater than all my sin;
How shall my tongue describe it,
Where shall its praise begin?
Taking away my burden,
Setting my spirit free,
For the wonderful grace of Jesus
reaches me.

Wonderful the matchless grace of
Jesus,
Deeper than the mighty rolling sea;
Higher than the mountain,
Sparkling like a fountain,
All-sufficient grace for even me;
Broader than the scope of my
transgressions,
Greater far than all my sin and shame;
Oh magnify the precious name of
Jesus,
Praise His name!

2 Wonderful grace of Jesus,
Reaching to all the lost,
By it I have been pardoned,
Saved to the uttermost;
Chains have been torn asunder,
Giving me liberty,
For the wonderful grace of Jesus
reaches me.

3 Wonderful grace of Jesus,
Reaching the most defiled.
By its transforming power
Making him God's dear child,
Purchasing peace and heaven
For all eternity -
And the wonderful grace of Jesus
reaches me.

696 L.M.

WORTHY of homage and of
praise;
Worthy by all to be adored;
Exhaustless theme of heavenly lays;
Thou, Thou art worthy, Jesus, Lord.

2 Now seated on Jehovah's throne,
    The Lamb once slain, in glory bright;
'Tis thence Thou watchest o'er
    Thine own,
Guarding us through the deadly fight.

3 To Thee, e'en now, our song we
    raise,
Though sure the tribute mean must
    prove,
No mortal tongue can tell Thy ways,
    So full of light and life and love.

4 Yet, Saviour, Thou shalt have full
    praise;
We soon shall meet Thee on the cloud,
    We soon shall see Thee face to
    face,
In glory praising as we would.

697   P.M.

WORTHY, worthy is the Lamb!
    Worthy, worthy is the Lamb!
Worthy, worthy is the Lamb
    That was slain!

Praise Him, hallelujah!
Bless Him, hallelujah!
Praise Him, hallelujah!
    Praise the Lamb!

2 Thou redeem'st our souls to God
    Thou redeem'st our souls to God
Thou redeem'st our souls to God
    By Thy blood.

3 Thou hast made us kings and priests
    Thou hast made us kings and priests
Thou hast made us kings and priests
    To our God.

4 We shall ever reign with Thee,
    We shall ever reign with Thee,
We shall ever reign with Thee,
    Lamb of God.

698   12.12.12.10.

WORTHY, worthy, worthy Thou
    of adoration!
Glory in the highest! glad praise we
    offer Thee!
Crowned with glory, honour - worthy
    coronation -

Thee on the throne, O Son of God,
    we see!

2 Worthy, worthy, worthy, Lamb of
    God most holy!
Blessèd all Thy footprints from
    Bethlehem to the tree;
Without spot or blemish, ever meek
    and lowly,
Perfect Thy life - God found repose
    in Thee!

3 Worthy, worthy, worthy! Perfect our
    salvation!
Costly was our ransom, once paid in
    blood by Thee;
We are with Thee risen - past our
    condemnation;
No longer bondmen - through Thy
    death we're free.

4 Worthy, worthy, worthy, Lord of life
    and glory!
Love divine our portion - ours to
    eternity!
Now we sing Thy praises, theme of
    sacred story!
Soon in the glory we shall reign with
    Thee.

5 Thou alone art worthy! Praise from
    every nation,
Praises loud and lasting, shall yet
    ascend to Thee;
"Blessing, honour, glory", sings the
    whole creation -
Heaven, earth and ocean, in full
    harmony.

699   P.M.

YE gates, lift up your heads on
    high;
Ye doors that last for aye,
    Be lifted up, that so the King
Of glory enter may:
    But who of glory is the King?
The mighty Lord is this;
    Ev'n that same Lord that great in
    might
And strong in battle is.

2 Ye gates, lift up your heads; ye doors,
    Doors that do last for aye,
Be lifted up, that so the King
    Of glory enter may:
But who is He that is the King,
    Of glory? who is this?
The Lord of hosts, and none but He,
    the King of glory is.
Hallelujah! Hallelujah! Hallelujah!
Hallelujah! Hallelujah!
    Amen, Amen, Amen

700   10.10.11.11.

YE servants of God,
    Your Master proclaim,
And publish abroad
    His wonderful name,
The name all-victorious
    Of Jesus extol;
His kingdom is glorious,
    He'll reign over all.

2 God ruleth on high,
    Almighty to save,
And still He is nigh,
    His presence we have;
The great congregation
    His triumphs shall sing,
Ascribing salvation
    To Jesus their King.

3 Salvation to God
    Who sits on the throne!
Let all cry aloud,
    And honour the Son!
The praises of Jesus
    The angels proclaim,
Fall down on their faces,
    And worship the Lamb.

4 Then let us adore,
    And give Him His right;
All glory, and power,
    And wisdom, and might;
All honour and blessing,
    With angels above,
And thanks never-ceasing,
    And infinite love.

Subjects Index

DIVINE LOVE

THE NAME OF JESUS

HIS BIRTH AND LIFE ON EARTH

HIS SUFFERINGS AND DEATH

HIS RESURRECTION

HIS ASCENSION AND GLORY

THE CROSS

REDEMPTION AND SALVATION

BAPTISM

OUR BLESSING IN CHRIST

OUR GREAT HIGH PRIEST

DIVINE INTERCESSION AND CARE

PRAYER

SCRIPTURE READING

ASPIRATION AND CONSECRATION

PILGRIMAGE AND REST

HEAVEN ANTICIPATED

CLOSING AND DOXOLOGIES

Index of First Lines

Index of Authors

Metrical Index of Hymns

S.M.

S.M.D.

C.M.

C.M.D.

L.M.

L.M.D.

4.6.8.8.4.

7.7.7.6.

7.7.7.7.

7.7.7.7.7.7.

7.7.7.7.D.

7.7.7.8.

7.7.8.7.D.

8.3.8.3.8.8.8.3.

8.4.8.4.8.8.8.4.

8.5.8.3.

8.8.6.8.8.6.

8.8.8.4.

8.8.8.6.

10.10.10.10.

10.10.10.10.10.10

10.10.11.11.

11.10.11.10

11.11.11.11

11.12.12.10.

12.11.12.11.